Politics in
the Twentieth
Century

Politics in the Twentieth Century

Abridged Edition

Hans J. Morgenthau

THE UNIVERSITY OF CHICAGO PRESS

CHICAGO AND LONDON

International Standard Book Number: 0-226-53825-7
Library of Congress Catalog Card Number: 70-148581

THE UNIVERSITY OF CHICAGO PRESS, CHICAGO 60637
The University of Chicago Press, Ltd., London

Originally published as 3 volumes, © 1962 by the University of Chicago.

Contents

Acknowledgments

The essays which comprise this volume have been reprinted without change. I gratefully acknowledge the permission of the following publications and publishers to use copyrighted material: American Academy of Political and Social Science, *American Political Science Review*, *Bulletin of the Atomic Scientists*, *Challenge*, *Chicago Sun-Times*, *China Quarterly*, *Commentary*, Committee for Economic Development, *Commonweal*, *Confluence*, Dartmouth College, *Encyclopaedia Britannica*, Harper and Row, *International Social Science Bulletin* (UNESCO), National War College, *New Republic*, *New York Times*, *Review of Politics*, Stevens and Sons Ltd., University of Chicago Press, University of Maryland Press, University of Notre Dame Press, and *Yearbook of World Affairs*.

Introduction
The Purpose of Political Thought

This volume contains a selection of essays which were originally published in 1962 in the three volumes of *Politics in the Twentieth Century*. They have been selected in view of their substance and of their more than passing interest. Looking back on the original collection of these essays from the distance of nearly a decade, one cannot help but be struck by the persistence of the intellectual and political problems with which the Western World in general and the United States in particular have been confronted in recent times. None of these problems has been "solved" once and for all. In spite of all the efforts to come to terms with them intellectually and to deal with them politically, they are still with us, either in their original manifestation or modified by new conditions. The best we have been able to do has been to live with them without being overwhelmed by them, to change their appearance, and to nibble at their edges. Thus, if there was any merit in what was said about them ten or twenty years ago, that merit has not been affected by the passage of time.

This resistance of all philosophic and political problems to definitive solutions is disheartening on two grounds. First of all, America has always lived in the inveterate expectation that problems exist to be solved and that if they are not, it must be on account of lack of effort, knowledge, or virtue. Supply what is missing, and there is no problem that will long resist massive intelligent efforts supported by good intentions. Thus the intractability of certain philosophic and political problems puts into question the conception of the world which Americans have taken for granted, in which they have felt at home, and in which they have been largely successful. It is more particularly the experience of unexpected and seemingly unwarranted failure which has shocked us into self-doubt and disorientation.

Second, this failure to come to terms intellectually and politically with the problems that face us, so damaging to the self-image of America, raises the general question of the relevance of theoretical thought to the solution of philosophic and political problems. Since Plato, political thinkers have flattered themselves by the conviction

that the welfare of the state depends upon their arguments and propositions; and that conviction has in modern times been supplemented by
the belief in the progressive amelioriation of political conditions by
dint of the accumulation of political knowledge and insight. The
retrogressive developments since World War I have been fatal to the
assumption of so simple a relationship between political thought and
political action.

In determining the ups and downs of political history, political
thought can indeed be crucially important in defining the interests at
stake and mapping out the power position of the parties concerned.
Thus political thought is a vital element in the struggle for power. But
this is not the same as saying that political thought necessarily contributes to the improvement of political conditions and to progress
understood as approximation to a political ideal, at the service of which
both political thought and political action are supposed to be. Improvement and progress are relative terms whose content is determined by the interests at stake and whose realization is contingent
upon the distribution of power in society. What one group hails as
improvement and progress in view of its interests, another group will
find irrelevant or detrimental to its interests, putting forward a conception of improvement and progress of its own. Such conflicts of
interest, reflected in intellectual controversies, cannot be solved by
political thought. Political thought can clarify them, and such clarification may indeed sometimes contribute to their solution either through
compromise or the victory of one group over the other.

What political thought cannot do is to save us from politics, that is,
the division of political society into masters and subjects, rulers and
ruled. As long as political society exists, it will be so divided. Some
rulers will be wiser, more benevolent, and more responsible than
others, and—most importantly—some political societies will impose
narrower limits upon the power, and stricter standards of accounta-
bility on the actions, of the rulers than others. Taking the inevitability
of this division for granted, political thought can define these limits and
standards, postulate them as being beyond the capacity of the powers-
that-be to change, rouse the citizens to their violations, admonish the
powers-that-be to observe them; that is, speak truth to power. Beyond
the concrete historic issues which occasioned many of these essays,
that may well be the permanent function they perform.

PART I

The Decline of Democratic Politics

1 *The Escape from Power*

The refusal of our civilization to recognize the facts of political life is nowhere more strikingly formulated than in the first sentence of the first chapter of Rousseau's *Social Contract:* "Man is born free, but everywhere he is in chains." This statement expresses a persistent conviction of Western political thought, and its correctness has not often been questioned. It is, however, one of the most erroneous and distorting statements one can make about the facts of political life. The historian Émile Faguet has very well pointed to the logical weakness of this statement by explaining through the same kind of argument the nature of cows. "All cows," he said, "are born carnivorous, and everywhere they live on herbs." The absurdity of the statement as applied to cows is obvious. The absurdity of the same type of reasoning as applied to humans is less obvious, but not less real; for it is impossible to distinguish empirically between the status in which a man is born and the status in which he lives.

Yet this erroneous statement has had very important consequences for the understanding of the realities of political life; for it has made it appear that the normal and natural state of man is freedom and that his living in chains, his living in political servitude, is only an accident, something that can be remedied and abolished by a political mechanism or a legislative device or a social reform or an economic artifact.

Any realistic conception of politics must start with an assumption which is the exact opposite of Rousseau's. It must assume that man is born and lives in chains. He is the object of political domination, and the fact that points to his freedom is not an empirical fact, is not a condition of his existence, but is a condition of his moral life. In other words, freedom is a condition not of his empirical existence but of his moral existence. Man lives in chains, but everywhere he wants to be free. He revolts against the empirical fact of political domination, and he wants to escape those chains which bind him in servitude.

This is, however, not the whole story; for man living in chains not

From Lyman Bryson *et al.* (eds.), *Conflicts of Power in Modern Culture* (New York: Harper and Row, 1947).

only wants to be free but also wants to be master. In other words, man's aspiration for power is not an accident of history; it is not a temporary deviation from a normal state of freedom; it is an all-permeating fact which is of the very essence of human existence. So we find, when we look at the facts of political life as they really are, that man lives in chains, but everywhere he wants to be a master.

This conception of man as a political being differs indeed fundamentally from the optimistic and superficial philosophy by which, in imitation of Rousseau and others, the nineteenth and twentieth centuries have conceived political life. They tried to escape the recognition of political domination and of the aspiration for power as ubiquitous facts by four fundamental devices: scientism, the dual moral standard, perfectionism, and totalitarianism. Most, if not all, of these devices are children of the nineteenth century. One of them, perfectionism, has an older history, but the other three have their roots, if not their flowering, in the intellectual movements of the nineteenth century.

What is scientism? It is the belief that the problems of social life are in essence similar to the problems of physical nature and that, in the same way in which one can understand the laws of nature and, by using this knowledge, dominate nature and harness it to one's own ends, one can understand the facts of society and, through this knowledge, create a gigantic social mechanism which is at the command of the scientific master.

However, three basic distinctions between the social and the physical world defeat this scientist conception of society. First of all, in the natural world we deal primarily with typical situations and typical phenomena as such. In the social world we deal primarily with individual events and individual phenomena as such. Furthermore, the social scientist is not a detached observer of social events as the natural scientist is a detached observer of the phenomena of nature. A physicist or chemist who investigates the qualities of uranium does so regardless of the religious, moral, political, social, or economic stake he may have in the result of his investigations. The political scientist or economist who investigates, say, a labor problem is of necessity determined in his outlook and in his methods and in the results at which he arrives by his personal involvement in the problem. Finally, the natural sciences deal with lifeless matter, and even where they deal with human beings or living matter they deal with them as some sort of mechanism. They do not deal with man as a rational being or a moral person. On the other hand, the social scientist deals with human beings as such, with the particularly human quality of human beings which is their rational and moral character. It is for these three reasons that the analogy between the natural and the social sciences falls to the ground.

Furthermore, scientism holds to the belief that political conflicts and political problems can be solved scientifically in the same way in which the problems of nature can be solved scientifically. The existence of political problems, of political conflict, of war, and of revolution, is assumed to be primarily the result of lack of knowledge, of lack of skill in the handling of social and political situations. Here, we are again in the presence of the idea, which we found underlying the first sentence of the first chapter of Rousseau's *Social Contract*, that the political phenomenon is a kind of accident, a kind of temporary deviation from the rule of reason which ought to dominate the life of man.

Actually, political problems grow out of certain conflicts of interests, certain basic antagonisms which no amount of knowledge can eliminate as such. Knowledge and political skill may solve these problems peacefully, but there is no scientific device that can solve the problems of war, of labor, of freedom, of authority in the same way in which the problem of, say, the air-cooled engine has been solved.

The problem of the air-cooled engine was solved when the scientists dealing with it found the formula by virtue of which the air-cooled engine could be constructed, and, once the formula was found, the natural scientists could, as it were, forget about the problem of the air-cooled engine and direct their attention to other problems. Political problems are not of this kind; they cannot be solved by the invention of a mechanical formula which will allow mankind to forget about them and turn its attention toward a not-yet-solved political problem. Being projections of human nature into society, they cannot be solved at all. They can only be restated, manipulated, and transformed, and each epoch has to come to terms with them anew.

The ideal of scientism as applied to politics is the disappearance of politics altogether. Scientism assumes that the abolition of politics can and will usher in an ideal state of society. The political philosophy of Marxism, for instance, is inspired by the belief, typical of scientism, that political domination and war are the outgrowth of a single cause, in this case of a particular economic system, and that with the disappearance of that system war and political domination will of themselves disappear. The main idea of scientism is clearly recognizable here: one needs only to use the right formula, to apply the right mechanical device, and the political domination of man by man and the violent clashes of human collectivities will disappear as temporary aberrations from the rule of co-operation and of reason.

The second attempt at escaping from the facts of political life we find in the idea of the dual standard of morality. This idea assumes that politics cannot perhaps be eliminated completely from human life but that it can be, as it were, quarantined. It can be relegated to a certain corner where certain bad principles of ethics apply, whereas the great majority of mankind will continue to live according to the good rules of ethics. In other words, there exists a dual standard of morality, one applicable to the political sphere and to the politicians, and another applicable to the rest of mankind. It is this dual standard of morality that was strikingly formulated by the greatest Italian statesman of modern times, Cavour, when he said: "If we had done for ourselves what we have done for Italy, what scoundrels we would have been."

But political domination and the lust for power cannot be limited to a particular segment of humanity which, because of its profession, is unable to comply with the generally applicable, respectable rules of ethics. This lust for power and this fact of political domination are universal experiences of mankind. In politics, it is true, they find their most extreme, violent, and brutal manifestations, but they are to be found wherever men live together in social groups, and that is everywhere. They are everywhere, hidden behind ideologies, disguised by the conventions of the good society. Hence, the idea of the dual standard of morality is another form of escapism from the brutal facts of political life and the ubiquitous lust for power.

The third type of escapism from these facts is perfectionism. Perfectionism recognizes the facts of political life as they exist. The perfectionist, however, believes that, by a sheer act of will on the part of the individual either through social reform or education or moral exhortation, man can be changed and can be made to abandon the evils of politics and the lust for power out of which those evils grow. The political philosophy of Woodrow Wilson provides the classical example of perfectionist escapism. Political domination and power politics with all the liabilities they impose on man, with all the evils they create, are the outgrowth of certain wicked political systems, such as autocracy or monarchy. Once democracy, brought to all countries of the earth either by force of arms or preferably by education and exhortation, has been universally accepted, the evils of politics will have been made an end to, and reason will rule over domestic and international society.

The contemporary advocacy of world government contains an element of perfectionist escapism. Actually, even if it were possible to establish world government tomorrow, the facts of political life would still be with us. The same problems growing out of the lust for power, the same conflicts resulting from the competition for power, the same mastery of one man over the other, and the revolt of the others against the mastery of one, the same basic fact that man is born in chains and everywhere wants to be master—these would still remain the elemental experiences of political life, even if world government were established.

The technological conditions and potentialities of the age have indeed made world government a rational necessity, but they have not made it a panacea for the evils and liabilities of politics. World government as such cannot resolve, for instance, the conflict between the Soviet Union and the United States by peaceful means. Regardless of constitutional changes on the international scene, this problem will continue to exist as it exists today, and, hence, the question of war or peace will continue to demand an answer. The answer to this question, under present world conditions, does not lie in world government but in facing squarely concrete problems which, if they are not solved peacefully, could lead to war—concrete problems such as American security as against Russian security, the unification of Germany, peace in the Middle East.

These problems are not to be solved by world government, any more than the problem of slavery was solved by the establishment of the government of the United States. A civil war, which after all is also a war, against the established government had to be fought in order to solve at least superficially the problem of slavery. Since the political problem was not solved when the government was established, it continued to pose itself, demanding a solution, and the lack of a solution led to the same disastrous results it would have led to if the government had not existed. The same would be true of world government. If the political problems separating the Soviet Union from the United States cannot be solved peacefully on their own terms, that is, by political means, world government would not save the world from the next war. The next war would, then, be a civil instead of a world war, and it would be only a matter of terminology whether Western civilization would perish in the course of the one instead of the other.

Western civilization has resorted during the past one hundred and fifty years to many other perfectionist devices in order to escape the facts of political life. For instance, men like Proudhon, Cobden, and Bright saw in free trade the one mechanism, the one political and economic reform, that would enable man to escape the fate that has been with him from the beginning of history. In its nature the escapism of free trade is not different from the escapism of world government or of the United Nations or of disarmament or of other mechanical devices whereby since the First World War men have tried to escape the combination of modern technology and the lust for power, which threatens to engulf and destroy them.

The fourth type of escapism we call totalitarianism, meaning by totalitarianism not merely the particular historic phenomenon which occurred in the twenties and thirties in Italy and in the thirties in Germany and after 1917 in Russia but a state of mind which is the exact opposite of perfectionism. Whereas perfectionism creates an abstract ideal to which it tries to elevate political life through force or exhortation or reform, totalitarianism, that is, the totalitarian state of mind, identifies the ideal with the facts of political life. What is, is good because it is, and power is to the totalitarian not only a fact of social life with which one must come to terms but also the ultimate standard for judging human affairs and the ideal source of all human values. He says "Yes" to his lust for power, and he recognizes no transcendent standard, no spiritual concept which might tame and restrain the lust for power by confronting it with an ideal alien and hostile to political domination.

So the gap between the political ideal and political reality, which perfectionism tries to resolve in favor of the ideal by elevating political reality to the level of the ideal, totalitarianism also tries to eliminate but by the opposite procedure, that is, by tearing the ideal down to the level of the brutal facts of political life. The excesses of power politics, the barbarities and evil propensities of the Bolshevist and Nazi regimes are foreordained in this identification of the realities of political life with the ideal of human life as such.

The totalitarian state of mind is a universal phenomenon. In its Fascist manifestation, it has lost its empires but won many souls. The Western democracies have widely accepted the Fascist standards without knowing it.

They, too, tend to equate and identify political success with moral superiority, thus seeking to eliminate the gap between the moral ideal and the facts of political life. They, too, try to resolve the tension between the two in favor of the political facts. This is perhaps the most dangerous manifestation of political escapism; for, while here the political facts as facts are recognized, their moral significance is obscured. Power is glorified as the source of all material and moral good, and those transcendent concepts by which power must be tamed, restrained, and transformed are denied an independent existence.

2 *The Moral Dilemma of Political Action*

On the plane of political action, the most common escape, especially in the United States, from the autonomy of politics has taken the form of moralism, that is, the substitution of what is popularly believed to be moral principles for the rules of politics. In the domestic sphere, the opportunities for the consistent substitution of moralism for politics are limited; for here failure, swift and obvious, is the punishment for violating the political rules. The situation is different in the international sphere; for success and failure in foreign policy are ambiguous terms, and the causal nexus between them and the actions seemingly leading up to them is often hard to establish. Since it is not always obvious what constitutes failure and what is responsible for it, false doctrines and practices have here a good chance to survive failure. Thus it is not by accident that foreign policy has provided the main opportunity for the moralistic attack upon the autonomy of the political sphere.

Dominant elements in Western culture, and American culture in particular, have consistently misunderstood the nature of foreign policy, and they have done so in the name of morality. In the process, our culture has deformed its understanding of morality and corrupted its moral judgment as well. It has imagined that the tension between foreign policy and morality, given in immediate experience, could easily be made to disappear in one of two ways. Either there could be a kind of reconciliation, a compromise by which foreign policy would be made moral, at least up to the point of non-violence and harmonious co-operation, and the moral law would be adapted to the exigencies of politics; perhaps there might even be two different kinds of moral law, one for man as such and as citizen of his nation and one for the relations among nations. Or else men would have a choice between power politics, morally bad, and another kind of foreign policy not tainted with the lust for power. In any event, there was presumed to be a way out of the dilemma with which the demands of foreign policy appear to confront the moral conscience.

From the *Year Book of World Affairs*, 1951; *American Perspective*, Winter, 1950; and the Introduction to Ernest Lefever's *Ethics and United States Foreign Policy* (1957).

The truth is that there is no way out. The moral dilemma of foreign policy is but a special and—it is true—particularly flagrant case of the moral dilemma which faces man on all levels of social action. Man cannot help sinning when he acts in relation to his fellow men; he may be able to minimize that sinfulness of social action, but he cannot escape it. For no social action can be completely free of the taint of egotism which, as selfishness, pride, or self-deception, seeks for the actor more than is his due. What is true of all social action is particularly true of political action and, within the latter, of foreign policy. For man's aspiration for power over other men, which is of the very essence of politics, implies the denial of what is the very core of Judeo-Christian morality—respect for man as an end in himself. The power relation is the very denial of that respect; for it seeks to use man as means to the end of another man. This denial is particularly flagrant in foreign policy; for the civilizing influences of law, morality, and mores are less effective here than they are on the domestic political scene.

How was it possible for our culture to misunderstand this moral dilemma of foreign policy and, turning its gaze from it, try to smooth and gloss over the conflict, thus doing justice neither to the responsibilities of foreign policy nor to the majesty of the moral law? This escape from both power politics and true morality stems in the main from three factors: man's ambivalent relationship to power and morality, the illusions of nineteenth-century liberalism, and the misunderstanding of the American experience.

The objective position of man on the political scene is always and of necessity ambivalent. While he seeks power over others, others seek power over him. His intellectual and moral attitudes toward power reflect this ambivalence of his objective position. While he takes the power drives of others for what they are or worse, he will close his eyes to his own aspirations for power, which appear to him as something different and nobler—justified by necessity and ethics —than they actually are. Thus ideological concealments, rationalizations, and justifications of necessity blind us both to the ubiquity and the moral deficiency of the aspiration for power. As John Adams put it:

Power always thinks it has a great soul and vast views beyond the comprehension of the weak and that it is doing God's service when it is violating all His laws. Our passions, ambitions, avarice, love and resentment, etc., possess so much metaphysical subtlety and so much overpowering eloquence that they insinuate themselves into the understanding and the conscience and convert both to their party.

Two historic experiences strengthened this ideological misunderstanding and depreciation of power. One was the experience of the Victorian age, as interpreted by liberal philosophy; the other, the experience of the first century of American history, as interpreted by a humanitarian, pacifist philosophy. To both, the struggle for power, especially on the international scene, appeared as the passing product of an ephemeral historic configuration. The liberals identified power politics with the rule of the aristocracy, a historic accident bound to disappear with the disappearance of autocratic government and its manifestations, such as trade barriers and colonialism.

The American experience seemed to provide experimental proof for the assumption that nations have a choice between power politics and a foreign policy not tainted by the lust for power. The Founding Fathers decided that the United States could not afford to get involved in the power politics of the European nations. Yet, to quote Washington, "The toils of European ambition, rivalship, interest, humor, or caprice," with which the United States should have nothing to do, were the only manifestations of power politics before the eyes of America. Abstention from European power politics could, therefore, be taken to mean abstention from power politics as such. This aloofness from European power politics remained a political fact at least until the end of the nineteenth century, if not until the intervention of the United States in the First World War in 1917. While in fact this isolation was the result of a complicated interplay of political and military forces, it was interpreted primarily, if not exclusively, as the result of a deliberate choice. The United States had turned her back on power politics and was applying to her foreign relations the same humanitarian principles of human betterment and peaceful competition which had worked so well at home and had made her both unique and great as a nation among nations.

The experiences of two world wars and of the aftermath of the Second have disabused many of us of these illusions. We have learned that we cannot escape the temptation and liabilities of power politics by an act of will. We must learn to live with them and still remain civilized; that is, we must make the best of them. Yet even at best, we cannot afford to forget that they are ever with us. These historic experiences have reawakened both our understanding of politics and our moral sensibilities. We have begun to resurrect from the rubble of false philosophies which did not stand the test of experience the great perennial truths about politics and morality of which Western civilization is the record. In this task political thinkers and theologians have joined. And it reveals as much about the nature of religious thought as about politics that many of the most important modern insights about politics have come from the pens of theologians.

Yet the illusions of the past are still with us. In *Speaking Frankly*, the account of his tenure as Secretary of State, Mr. James F. Byrnes reports an episode which occurred at the Paris Peace Conference in 1946:

> After a heated session in Paris one afternoon, Chip Bohlen [then adviser to the American delegation] remained behind talking to a member of the Soviet delegation. The Soviet representative said it was impossible for him to understand the Americans. They had a reputation for being good traders and yet Secretary Byrnes for two days had been making speeches about principles—talking, he said, like a professor.
> "Why doesn't he stop this talk about principles, and get down to business and start trading?" the Soviet representative asked Chip in all sincerity.
> Chip attempted most unsuccessfully to explain that there were some questions which, in the opinion of Americans, involved principle and could not be settled by bargaining.[1]

This episode is significant not only for the pathetically honest lack of understanding between East and West that it reveals but more particularly for the light it sheds upon two diametrically opposed conceptions of foreign policy. On the one side, there is the political realist, the Machiavellian bargainer, who conceives of foreign policy exclusively in terms of power and for whom the end of power justifies all—or almost all—means employed; on the other side, there is the moralist, "talking like a professor"—or should one rather say "like a preacher"?—whose ability to bargain is strictly circumscribed, both in width and in depth, by his insistence upon principles which must be reflected in the bargain but cannot be made its object.

[1] (New York: Harper & Bros., 1947), pp. 280–81.

It is as tempting as it would be false to conceive of the opposition between these two schools of foreign policy as yet another example of the struggle between good and evil, between a noble and benevolent philosophy and practice of politics and a base and nefarious one. Such juxtapositions are tempting, for they fit quite naturally into the black-white pattern in which the struggle between East and West presents itself to the popular mind. Yet they are false just the same. They are false not only because any black-white pattern, conceived in moral and intellectual terms, is by definition inadequate to do justice to a political situation in which on either side good and evil, wisdom and error, are inextricably blended and intertwined. They are false also, and primarily, because what in Mr. Byrnes's episode is presented by implication as a typical expression of Russian realism, or Bolshevist lack of principle, or Soviet amoralism, can in fact look back on a respectable ancestry in the Western practice of foreign policy.

That member of the Soviet delegation, if he had known it and if he had dared to, might well have reminded Mr. Bohlen of Richelieu and Mazarin, of Cromwell and the two Pitts, of Hamilton and Jefferson the statesman, of Castlereagh and Canning, of Cavour, Disraeli, and Bismarck. And Mr. Bohlen, in turn, might have summoned to Mr. Byrnes's defense the shades of Fox and Burke, of Madison and Jefferson the philosopher, of Gladstone and Wilson. If they had felt in need of living witnesses, the Russian might have cited Winston Churchill; the American, Cordell Hull. In one word, then, what stood between the United States and the Soviet representatives in Paris in 1946 was the issue of moral principles versus the reason of state—the issue which Machiavelli had raised into the full consciousness of the Western world and which since then has never ceased to trouble its conscience and to transform into problems those acts of politics which in pre-Machiavellian times had been performed as a matter of course.

It is one of the glories of the political tradition of the English-speaking peoples, unrivaled in any other civilization, that their political theory, as their law, has in the main been developed not in comprehensive systematic efforts but in a series of debates concerned with the practical merits of limited, concrete issues. Three factors have fortuitously co-operated in making the political theory of the

English tongue a succession of "cases" debated in the forum of public opinion: an empirical bent of mind, aiming at immediate practical results rather than theoretical consistency; the ability to see in the concrete issue the particular instance of a general proposition rather than empirical proof for a priori abstractions; and, finally, the institution of public debate which is supposed to determine the decision in view of the rational merits of the case. Thus it has come about that while the issue of reason of state versus moral principles has on the Continent been fought out in the philosophic polemics of the Machiavellians and the anti-Machiavellians, leaving the issue in the end where they found it, in the English-speaking world the issue was always settled, at least for the moment; for, rising as it did from a concrete situation which demanded a decision, it had to be decided one way or the other. That decision, it is true, was, like the decision of the judge, only provisional and decided the issue only within the narrow confines of the situation within which it had arisen. It never purported to offer an abstract proposition settling the issue once and for all. It lacked in generality what it possessed in definiteness.

Thus it follows from the way the English-speaking peoples think in political matters that their political thought must be distilled from the debates through which the political issues of the day were settled. The problem that confronts us here has troubled the thought and life of the Anglo-American world before. To understand its nature and to assess its bearing upon the political issues of our day, the debates on great issues of the past can give us guidance. The problem has perhaps nowhere been stated with greater elemental simplicity, undiluted by side issues and undisguised by ideological rationalizations, than in the debate between Disraeli and Gladstone on the occasion of the "Bulgarian Atrocities." Disraeli made the case for the national interest in his speech in the House of Lords of July 18, 1878, on his return from the Congress of Berlin:

But I must make this observation to your lordships. We have a substantial interest in the East; it is a commanding interest, and its behest must be obeyed. But the interest of France in Egypt, and her interest in Syria, are, as she acknowledges, sentimental and traditionary interests; and, although I respect them, and although I wish to see in Lebanon and Egypt the influence of France fairly and justly maintained, and although her officers and ours in that part of the world—and especially in Egypt—are acting together with confidence and trust, we must remember that our connection with the East is not merely an affair of sentiment and tradition, but that we have urgent and substantial and enormous interests which we must guard and keep. Therefore, when we find that the progress of Russia is a progress which, whatever may be the intentions of Russia, necessarily in that part of the world produces such a state of disorganisation and want of confidence in the Porte, it comes to this—that if we do not interfere in vindication of our own interests, that part of Asia must become the victim of anarchy, and ultimately become part of the possessions of Russia.

. . . We do not, my lords, wish to enter into any unnecessary responsibility; but there is one responsibility from which we certainly shrink; we shrink from the responsibility of handing to our successors a weakened or a diminished Empire. Our opinion is, that the course we have taken will arrest the great evils which are destroying Asia Minor and the equally rich countries beyond. We see in the present state of affairs the Porte losing its influence over its subjects; we see a certainty, in our opinion, of increasing anarchy, of the dissolution of all those ties which, though feeble, yet still exist and which have kept society together in those countries. We see the inevitable result of such a state of things, and we cannot blame Russia for availing herself of it. But, yielding to Russia what she has obtained, we say to her—"Thus far, and no farther." Asia is large enough for both of us. There is no reason for these constant wars, or fears of wars, between Russia and England. Before the circumstances which led to the recent disastrous war, when none of those events which we have seen agitating the world had occurred, and when we were speaking in "another place" of the conduct of Russia in Central Asia, I vindicated that conduct, which I thought was unjustly attacked, and I said then—what I repeat now—there is room enough for Russia and England in Asia.

But the room that we require we must secure. We have, therefore, entered into an alliance—a defensive alliance—with Turkey, to guard her against any further attack from Russia.

The case for the other side was clearly stated in Gladstone's pamphlet, *Bulgarian Horrors and Russia in Turkestan*, which, in 1876, touched off the controversy:

My hope, therefore, is twofold. First, that, through the energetic attitude of the people of England, their Government may be led to declare distinctly, that it is for purposes of humanity alone that we have a fleet in Turkish waters. Secondly, that that fleet will be so distributed as to enable its force to be most promptly and efficiently applied, in case of need, on Turkish soil, in concert with the other Powers, for the defence of innocent lives, and to prevent the repetition of those recent scenes, at which hell itself might almost blush.

For it must not be forgotten that the last utterance on this subject was from the Prime Minister, and was to the effect that our fleet was in the

East for the support of British interests. I object to this constant system of appeal to our selfish leanings. It sets up false lights; it hides the true; it disturbs the world. Who has lifted a finger against British interests? Who has spoken a word? If the declaration be anything beyond mere idle brag it means that our fleet is waiting for the dissolution of the Turkish Empire, to have the first and the strongest hand in the seizure of the spoils. If this be the meaning, it is pure mischief: and if we want to form a just judgment upon it, we have only to put a parallel case. What should we say, if Russia had assembled an army on the Pruth, or Austria on the Danube, and Prince Gortschakoff or Count Andrassy were to announce that it was so gathered, and so posted for the defence of Russian, or of Austrian interests respectively?

Perhaps, in these unusual circumstances, before describing what it is that we should seek and should desire, it may be well to consider what we should carefully eschew. In the channel, which we have to navigate, with or without our Government, there are plenty of false lights set up for us, which lead to certain shipwreck. The matter has become too painfully real for us to be scared at present by the standing hobgoblin of Russia. Many a time has it done good service on the stage: it is at present out of repair, and unavailable. It is now too late to argue, as was argued some time back by a very clever and highly enlightened evening journal, that it might be quite proper that twelve or thirteen millions of Christians in Turkey should remain unhappy, rather than that (such was the alternative hardily presented) two hundred millions of men in India should be deprived of the benefits of British rule, and thirty millions more in the United Kingdom made uncomfortable by the apprehension of such a catastrophe.

This very juxtaposition of "power" politics and "moral" politics is fundamentally mistaken. It derives from the assumption that the principles of morality have the same substantive quality as, say, the principles of politics, economics, or law. This assumption leads logically to the conclusion that it is both possible and desirable to replace the principles of politics with those of morality. In truth, this substitution is possible only at the price of political failure and, hence, is neither possible nor desirable on rational grounds.

Morality is not just another branch of human activity, co-ordinate to the substantive branches, such as politics or economics. Quite to the contrary, it is superimposed upon them, limiting the choice of ends and means and delineating the legitimate sphere of a particular branch of action altogether. This latter function is particularly vital for the political sphere. For the political actor is peculiarly tempted to blind himself to the limits of his power and thereby to overstep the boundaries of both prudence and morality.

It is not ignorance or misjudgment, that is, intellectual errors, against which the Greek tragedians and biblical prophets warn the powerful of the world but *hubris* and pride. The self-esteem engendered by power, which equates power and virtue, in the process loses all sense of moral and political proportion. Indeed, it is from the moral delusions and corruptions, the poisonous fruits of power, that these intellectual errors receive the strength to lead nations to disaster as though it were truth and not error that led them. The moral corruption of power blinds nations to the distinction between truth and error. Dazzled by the pride of power, they take truth for error, and vice versa, and make ready with unsuspecting confidence to jump into the abyss as if it were the consummation of their dreams.

A nation emerges victorious from a war, and in the exaltation of its supreme power it rejects as unacceptable, if not as outright offensive, the idea that it won the victory because it had better trained and better fed troops, more and better arms, and superior leadership. Providence, either as a personal divinity or as the objective logic of the historic process, has given victory to the nation which deserved it by virtue of its moral superiority. That alleged moral superiority is then taken to be a permanent quality which not only explains past victories but also justifies the national claim to be the lawgiver and arbiter of mankind.

A nation, thus supernaturally endowed, not only has the ability but believes that it has a sacred duty to reform the world in the image of its own supposed superiority. It can and must promote or forestall revolution or reform, as the case may be. It must contain other nations, advance itself, and never retreat. There is nothing it cannot do. What is more, there is nothing it ought not to do. It must and can bring salvation to all the world. By the standards of this national moral delusion, humanity naturally divides into two groups: one all black and the other all white. By definition those who are for you are good, and those who are against you are wicked.

Only future generations will be able to understand fully to what extent in our atomic policy the self-destructive tendencies of power have been at work; how the use of the atomic bomb and our emphasis upon its monopolistic possession and decisive importance have called into existence the very forces that nullify that advantage and turn it against us; how that possession has tempted us from miscalculation to miscalculation, overrating our own and underrating the power of other nations; how the emphasis on secrecy, assuming the permanency of that monopolistic possession, has done more than anything else to destroy the advantage it was intended to preserve; and how, finally, the awareness of such tremendous power has nourished a sense of mission which assumes in its holder an exclusive moral worth and duty of a magnitude commensurate with so much power.

3   The Military Displacement of Politics

The autonomy of the political sphere is endangered not only by the misunderstanding of the nature and role of morality but also by the imperialism of other spheres of substantive action, of which in our culture the economic and military are the most important ones. The economic attack upon the political sphere dominated the nineteenth and the first decades of the twentieth centuries. Marxism and liberalism are its outstanding manifestations. When the experience of totalitarianism seemed to have proved conclusively that politics is not a derivation of economics but has an autonomous realm of its own, the Second World War and its aftermath raised the issue of the autonomy of politics again. This time, it was the military which infringed upon it.

The fundamental error behind all the individual blunders committed toward the end of the Second World War, and immediately afterward, was the neglect of Karl von Clausewitz' dictum that war is the continuation of policy by other means. The peaceful and warlike means by which a nation pursues its interests form a continuous process in which, though one means may replace the other, the ends remain the same. We also failed to recognize that foreign policy itself is a continuum beginning with the birth of a state and ending only with its death; isolationists and interventionists alike tended to believe that the "normal" thing for a state was to have no foreign policy at all. What separated the interventionists from the isolationists was the belief that certain crises might require, at least temporarily, an active foreign policy. But even the interventionists felt that after solving the given crisis one could try to return to a position of detachment, though developing and supporting in the meantime international institutions designed to meet the next crisis if and when it should arise. Foreign policy was thus regarded as something like a policeman's night stick, to be used only when it was necessary to bring a disturber of the peace to reason; war, in turn, was like the policeman's gun, to be used only *in extremis* to rid the world of a criminal. But here the analogy ends: the policeman always carries his

From *Commentary*, October, 1952; and *World Politics*, January, 1955.

gun with him, but we threw ours away twice after it had done the job.

War, we could see, did have a necessary connection with what preceded it—that is, with the criminal aggression that provoked it—but it had no organic relation with what followed it. Its purpose was only to eliminate a disturbance by eliminating the disturber; once that was done, the world would presumably settle back into normalcy and order. War, then, was a mere technical operation to be performed according to the rules of military art—a feat of military engineering like building a dam or flattening a mountain. To allow considerations of political expediency to interfere with military operations was unwise from the military point of view and might well be considered an immoral subversion of one self-sufficient department of human action for the sake of another. (It might be added in passing that economic specialists—for instance, administrators of foreign aid—have shown a very similar reluctance, for similar reasons, to let political considerations "violate" the autonomy of economic operations.)

This quality of American thinking emerges clearly from the contrast between the non-political American approach to war and the continuous and generally fruitless insistence of Churchill and his subordinates on the political significance of military action. The British and the Russians knew from long experience that wars are not fought just to bring about the unconditional surrender of the enemy; wars are means to political ends, and military victory, if it is to bear political fruits, must be shaped to those ends.

American military leaders were aware of this difference in outlook, both on the battlefield and afterward. In April, 1945, when the British wanted Patton's army to liberate as much of Czechoslovakia as possible, and Prague in particular, for the sake of the political advantages to be gained thereby, General Marshall passed the suggestion on to General Eisenhower with this comment: "Personally, and aside from all logistic, tactical, or strategical implications, I would be loath to hazard American lives for purely political reasons." Marshall had nothing to worry about in this respect, for Eisenhower replied the next day: "I shall not attempt any move I deem militarily unwise merely to gain a political advantage unless I receive specific order from the Combined Chiefs of Staff." The matter rested there despite repeated and urgent appeals from Churchill and the British chiefs of staff. Similar decisions were made on other occasions. General Bradley in his memoirs has this to say of the British insistence that the Americans take Berlin before the Russians: "As soldiers we looked naïvely on this British inclination to complicate the war with political foresight and non-military objectives."

This concentration on military objectives to the neglect of political considerations has one virtue: it is apt to win wars quickly, cheaply, and thoroughly. Yet such victories may be short-lived, and an enormous political and military price may have to be paid for them later. To win a war without regard for the political consequences of the victory may create political problems as serious as, or worse than, those that the victory was intended to settle; but such a victory leaves a country at least in a position to learn and to try to settle political problems by peaceful means.

Have we learned these lessons? On the face of it, it seems we have. Certainly we have been almost obsessed with the need to fashion our postwar policies so as to avoid the mistakes we and others made during the Second World War. We have learned that a power vacuum will exert a well-nigh irresistible attraction on a great dynamic nation in its vicinity. We have learned that in order to confine such a nation within the limits necessary to our own security it is not enough to show good will and reasonableness and to embody virtuous intentions in legal instruments. We have learned that the balance of power, far from being just an arbitrary device of reactionary diplomats and Machiavellian scholars, is the very law of life for independent units dealing with other independent units—domestic or international—that want to preserve their independence. Independent power, in order to be kept in check, must be met by independent power of approximately equal strength. In the effort to apply these lessons, we have embarked upon a long-range policy of "containment" and rearmament.

We have also learned that an imperialist power confronted with a coalition of powers of varying strength will attempt to eliminate the weaker members one after the other, until the most powerful member is left in the end outmaneuvered and alone. We have therefore developed an intricate system of alliances in the Western Hemisphere, Europe, and Asia, which, whatever the differences of legal language and institutional device, all amount to a declaration that we shall defend the territorial integrity of the members of these alliances as we would our own. We call this system of alliances "collective security" and have put it into operation by defending the Republic of South Korea against aggression by North Korea.

In these ways, we have obviously learned from history. Why, then, are we as uncertain as ever about the success of our policies and still beset by doubts about the course we have been taking in recent years? Have we still missed one of the important lessons of recent history, or have we misunderstood what it seemed to teach us? The answer is not completely reassuring. Though we have learned the lessons of recent history, chapter and verse, though we have memorized them and have never tired of reciting and applying them whenever faced with a problem which seemed to be similar to one of those that we failed to solve during the Second World War, yet we have failed to see that behind the specific lessons of history learned from specific blunders there stands *the* lesson of history, of *all* history, which alone gives meaning to the lessons to be derived from any particular period.

All political action is an attempt to influence human behavior; hence, all political action must be aware of the complexities and ambiguities of the human factor and must itself be ambiguous and complex—and in the right way. The political actor, conscious of history, must be aware of the malleability of the human will; yet he must also be aware of the limits of suasion and of the need for objective barriers to the human will. While he is making use of suasion, he must not be oblivious to the role of power, and vice versa, and of each he must have just the right quantity and quality, neither too much nor too little, neither too early nor too late, neither too strong nor too weak.

He must choose the right admixture, not only in terms of human nature, permanent as such but with the relations of its elements ever changing, but also in terms of the changing historical circumstances under which those elements of human nature confront each other in the form of collectivities called nations. How much suasion and power and what kind is available on my side at a particular moment in history, and how much of it and what kind is likely to be available tomorrow? How much and what kind of susceptibility to sua-

23

sion and power is present on the other side at a particular moment of history, and how much and what kind is likely to be present tomorrow? And how much and what kind of suasion and power is the other side able to bring to bear upon me and others today and tomorrow? Such are the questions posed by the ever changing social environment.

When, during the closing years of the past war, we thought that Stalin was a somewhat gruff old gentleman who could be charmed into co-operation, we relied on suasion to a greater extent than the teachings of history justified. We think we have learned our lesson from this failure of a policy of suasion pure and simple. Now we seem to have forsworn suasion altogether and seem to rely exclusively upon force as a deterrent to the ambitions of the Soviet Union. We seem to forget that force as the instrument of a foreign policy aiming at the peaceful settlement of international conflicts must be a means to the end of foreign policy, not an end in itself. Force supplements suasion but does not replace it. Mr. Acheson, as Secretary of State, recognized this relation between suasion and force in the abstract when he proclaimed repeatedly that the objective of our foreign policy was the creation of situations of strength from which to negotiate a peaceful settlement with the Soviet Union. In practice, however, our foreign policy, preoccupied as it is with rearmament, seems to have lost sight of this objective. Consequently, it has not faced up squarely to the all-important question of timing: when shall we consider ourselves strong enough in relation to the Soviet Union to be able to negotiate from strength? A positive answer is being postponed to an ever more indefinite future. Trying to learn from history, we have set out on an armament race that must lead to war if it is not subordinated to the professed objective of a negotiated settlement. Here again we have learned but half the lesson and have replaced one error with another.

Most often political blunders consist in this overemphasis of one element in a situation at the expense of others. The twenties and thirties saw the underestimation by the Western world of the uses of power toward moral and legal ends. The Second World War saw but a seeming interruption of that trend, for power was used then in an effort to restore conditions of harmony and "normalcy" under which we could again rely on law and morality and, as it were, forget about power. We seemed at the time to have learned a lesson from our prewar relations with the Axis Powers: we had neglected power; now we would use it without limit until those who had compelled us to do so were forced to surrender their own power unconditionally. With that task accomplished, we would be able to return to the other extreme and build a new world, without power politics, on the foundations of law and morality.

Consistent with this point of view, we treated our wartime allies, including the Soviet Union, with that same disregard of considerations of power which had characterized our behavior toward everybody in the interwar period. Yet the same experience that had forced us into power politics against Hitler was to be repeated in our dealings with the Soviet Union. And here, too, we seem to have learned our lesson now. Having shown good will, we now "get tough." Since one cannot deal with the Soviet Union by legal contract and without regard for the realities of power, we will now use in dealing with her the instruments of power alone, without concern for legal stipulations to be agreed upon through mutual suasion. Just as the only alternative to appeasement of Germany, Japan, or Italy without power had been war, so the alternative to appeasement of the Soviet Union is another kind of war.

We also learned from the experiences of the thirties what a blunder isolationism was, which would let one fight only in defense of one's own country but not in defense of allies. But in learning that lesson we are by way of falling into the opposite error: having realized the error of fighting for nobody but one's self, we are now willing to fight for anybody threatened by the common enemy. Collective security, after all, is as abstract and non-political a principle of action as isolationism, equally impervious to the complexity of all political issues which must be decided not according to abstract principles but by the calculation of opposing interests and powers.

We intervened in Korea because the principle of collective security required it, thus seemingly avoiding the mistake Great Britain and France had made when they refused to defend Ethiopia in 1935–36 and Czechoslovakia in 1938. Actually, as pointed out before,[1] we made exactly the same mistake, only in a different way. In 1950, as

---

[1] See below, pp. 226 ff.

in 1935 and 1938, the issue might better have been decided in terms of the interests involved and the power available as against the interests and power of other nations. Instead, it was resolved in all three instances, either positively or negatively, in the abstract terms of collective security, a principle which could be applied against a major power only at the risk of world war. By substituting an abstract principle of law for the calculation of the concrete conditions of interests and power, we involved ourselves in a war that, in view of these relations of interests and power, we could neither win nor lose. Such are the results of a foreign policy that tries to avoid the mistakes of the past without understanding the principles that should have governed the actions of the past.

We realized what had been wrong with our policies, but in supplying what had been lacking we threw overboard what was no less essential than what we were trying to supply. Thus the very correction of past blunders created new ones. We had seen that diplomacy without power was not enough, so we added power and forgot about diplomacy. We had seen that a nation must stop aggression before it reaches her own shores, and we concluded that we had now to stop all aggression regardless of how our own interests and power were affected. We learned the specific lessons of the last two decades, but in the process we came to neglect the broad lesson of history: that political success depends upon the simultaneous or alternative use of different means at different times and the moderate use of all of them at all times.

Man is never able to look at history with the same objectivity as at inanimate nature. The moral limitation upon his understanding of history is pride: pride in his intellect, pride in his goodness, pride in the collectivity with which he identifies himself as against other collectivities.

Pride in intellect shows itself in the persistence with which ideas once adopted are applied time and again, regardless of the fact that they have been discredited by experience. A general whose strategy brought victory in one war finds in success an additional reason for using the same methods in the next war. He did it once, and he is going to do it again. What General MacArthur was able to do to the Japanese in the Second World War he must be able to do to the Chinese in the Korean War.

Even if a certain strategy has been unsuccessful, there is a strong tendency to try it out again, especially if the general sluggishness of the human mind encourages it. The Maginot line was a disastrous failure in the Second World War. But man is almost irresistibly attracted by the image of a wall behind which he will be safe from the enemy. Since the Maginot line was a failure, as was the Chinese Great Wall before it, why not build a bigger and better Maginot line? Or perhaps a bigger and better general will do what General Gamelin was unable to do with the Maginot line in 1940. The most subtle perversion of the lessons of history is that which appears to heed the experiences of the past and discard its faulty methods, while continuing nonetheless to think in terms of the past. To build a line of static fortifications parallel to the Rhine was certainly a mistake that we shall not emulate. Instead, we shall create a western European army that will defend Europe at the Elbe, at the Rhine, or wherever else it may be. We seem to have learned a lesson from history; but, in view of the novel requirements of global strategy and the numerical superiority of the Russian land armies, have we really?

Pride in intellect is joined by pride in virtue. All individuals and collectivities like to see their conflicts with others not in terms of interest and power determined by circumstances but in terms of moral values determined by abstract principles. When our policies fail, as they did in relation to the Soviet Union after the Second World War, the explanation cannot lie in our having miscalculated our interests and power in relation to the interests and power of the other side. Our failure must be the result of the wickedness of the other side, which took advantage of our guileless trust. We trusted once and were deceived; from now on we shall be on our guard and see the enemy for what he is. Yalta then becomes a symbol, not of the legal ratification of errors of political and military judgment, but of a moral deception that the wicked perpetrated upon the good.

While such one-sidedness, which impairs historical judgment and thus our ability to learn from history, seems inevitable in even the greatest of historians, there are specific manifestations of it that, as great statesmen have shown, can be controlled by moral discipline. One such manifestation is the habit of overestimating one's own power and underestimatng the other side's. The history of the relations between the Western world and the Soviet Union since 1917 could be written in terms of the underestimation of Russian power. From the Allied intervention in the Russian civil war through the debates on the implementation of the Franco-Russian alliance of 1935, the Russian offer of support to Czechoslovakia in 1938, the Anglo-French military mission to Moscow in 1939, the German attack upon the Soviet Union in 1941, the first atomic explosion in Russia in 1949, up to the very present, we have always underestimated the power of the Soviet Union. We have done so because we are inflexibly opposed on moral grounds to both communism and Russian imperialism. Thus our moral sentiment stands in the way of a correct appraisal of the realities of power. To separate our pride in our own moral superiority from our historical judgment, which might lead us to recognize the political and military superiority of the Soviet Union in certain respects, requires an effort at moral detachment which few are willing to make. It is easier and more satisfactory to conclude that political and military superiority necessarily go hand in hand with moral superiority. Yet the monopoly of the atomic bomb may have been, but was not of necessity, concomitant with a monopoly in virtue. Here again moral pride stands between our judgment and historical experience.

The classic example of this kind of pride, and of its disastrous political and military consequences, is Hitler's. Since Bismarck, it had been the basic axiom of German strategy that Germany could not win a two-front war. However, it was exactly such a war that she deliberately embarked upon both in 1914 and 1941. Hitler himself was resolved not to make this blunder, but he could not help making it, for he believed firmly that it was Germany's "mission" to triumph over her enemies. Holding such a faith, he was led to assume that Germany had already won the war against the West when she had not yet done so, and could therefore safely invade the Soviet Union.

If we find it so difficult to learn from history, the fault is not with history but with the pride and the intellectual limitations of men. History, in the words of Thucydides, is philosophy learned from examples. Those who are morally and intellectually inferior to its teachings, history leads to disaster. Those who are philosophers in the moral and intellectual sense, it teaches.

Of this ability to learn from history that the autonomy of the political sphere must be protected against encroachments of the military, Sir Winston Churchill provides the greatest contemporary example. Its literary manifestation is *Triumph and Tragedy*.[2] The range of this book is narrow in every respect—in subject matter, in style, and in purpose. It covers the period from the invasion of Normandy in June, 1944, to the Potsdam Conference of July, 1945. Its theme is, in the words of the author, "How the Great Democracies Triumphed, and So Were Able To Resume the Follies Which Had So Nearly Cost Them Their Life." Its central problem is simple: military strategy and its relation to foreign policy.

The style is of the same classic simplicity as the problem. As the problem raises a perennial issue of statecraft, so the mode of thought which the author brings to bear upon the problem moves within the perennial categories of political thought. Sir Winston Churchill's mind is not that of an intellectual who loves to think and know for the sake of thinking and knowledge. His is the intellect of a man of action who relives in thought past action and what preceded and followed it. Sir Winston thinks with a purpose which transcends thought. His purpose as a thinker is that of the man of action and, hence, is intensely personal; it is so in three different respects.

Its most personal purpose is to enable the author to relive in reminiscence his part in the drama of history, enjoying its victories, mourning its defeats. Yet this process of recollecting and reflective reliving is also one of simplification, of seeing, and of making others see, perhaps for the first time, the essence of one's action and its purpose, aside from what is but pretense and byplay. The first purpose, then, is autobiographical in the strict, classic sense of the term.

The second purpose is autobiographical in what one might call the political sense. It is to justify the author as past actor on the political scene. It is to prove that the author was right when he did what he did and when he gave advice that was not heeded. When the author must admit that he was wrong in action or advice, he at least evokes the sympathetic companionship of the reader, who learns to his satisfaction that the great and the powerful share in the human fallibility of all. Thus the author assigns himself the place in history which he deems his due or, at the very least, helps future historians to assign it to him.

Finally, the book teaches a lesson. By contrasting the mistakes of

[2] Boston: Houghton Mifflin Co., 1953.

the past with the principles of right action, the author calls our attention, by implication, to opportunities in the more recent past and in the future of making the same mistakes by neglecting the same principles. It is this contribution to political wisdom which makes this book important, particularly for us and at this time. What, then, transforms this autobiographical account of history into a source of political wisdom? With this question we approach the secret of Sir Winston's greatness.

That secret cannot be explained in this space, if it can be explained at all; it can only be adumbrated. It seems to lie in the conjuncture of three qualities, one intellectual, one practical, and one moral. These qualities are the intellectual grasp of statesmanship, the ability to act according to the requirements of statesmanship, and the subordination of all other considerations to these requirements. Others are as wise as Sir Winston; others again are as effective in action; and others still have dedicated themselves as single-mindedly to a purpose. Yet nobody alive combines to such a degree intellectual excellence with ability in action and dedication to a cause.

What John Stuart Mill said of Bentham applies also to Churchill: "The field of [his] labours was like the space between two parallel lines; narrow to excess in one direction, in another it reached to infinity." The field of Sir Winston's labors, of his interests, and of his understanding is narrow. Yet one is also struck with the enormity of the purposeful intellectual and moral force that sweeps through the narrow confines of his cause: to remember the past in order to learn how to act aright in matters political and military.

The outstanding quality of that intellectual force is the ability to see a problem in its true proportions, by not allowing the involvement of will and emotion to interfere with understanding. What is required of the statesman is, first of all, to see clearly: himself, the enemy, and then himself again as the enemy sees him. To see clearly means to see without passions, without the passion of pride, of hatred, and of contempt. The statesman must master the paradox of wanting passionately to win over an enemy to whom he feels passionately superior, and of having to view his relations with the enemy with the detachment and objectivity of the scholar. This book provides proof of the extent to which Sir Winston has mastered this paradox. His most spectacular failures are his support of "unconditional surrender" and his inability to reconcile Great Britain's moral and legal commitment to the independence of Poland with the political and military realities which the Russian conquest of eastern Europe had created.

The moral counterpart of the intellectual ability of mastering this paradox of passion and understanding is humility toward one's self and generosity toward others. As such, this moral attitude is not only a moral virtue in itself but one of the conditions for political success as well. The extent to which this book reveals these qualities is another measure of Sir Winston's greatness as a statesman. He deplores President Truman's decision to withdraw the American troops, on the eve of the Potsdam Conference, to the zonal borders agreed upon at Quebec and Yalta, a step against which he had repeatedly warned; and there is no doubt in his mind now, as there was none then, that he was right and Truman wrong. Yet he enumerates all the mitigating circumstances which can be cited in explanation and support of Mr. Truman's decision and adds: "Those who are only wise after the event should hold their peace." And, while he bends every effort to forestall Stalin's designs, with what understanding does he speak of Russian interests, and with what respect does he pay tribute to Stalin's qualities!

If the cause to which Sir Winston brings these qualities were less challenging intellectually, less demanding morally, and less vital for all of us, we would think less of Sir Winston's greatness. As it is, upon our ability to learn Sir Winston's lessons the survival of the West may well depend. That, then, completes Sir Winston's greatness: that he brings a great intellectual and moral force successfully to bear upon the greatest of all contemporary causes.

What are the lessons we can learn from Sir Winston's book? The relationships between political and military policy being its main theme, this book is a study in contrasts, the contrast between British and American policies, between Churchill's and Roosevelt's strategy and statecraft. That contrast can be defined in two fundamental and interrelated propositions. For Sir Winston, the war was a military means to a political end, and the influence of the political end upon the military means was to increase with the speed with which the armies of the Allies were approaching military victory. For the United States, the war was essentially a self-sufficient technical operation to be performed as quickly, as cheaply, and as thoroughly as the technical rules of warfare would allow. The political issue with which Sir Winston's strategy and statecraft were primarily concerned during the last year of the Second World War was no longer German and Japanese imperialism but the imperialism of the Soviet Union. For the American government, the approaching defeat of German and Japanese imperialism signified the elimination of the major political problem that faced the Western world, and what remained could safely be left to mutual good will, especially toward the Soviet Union, and to the United Nations.

In one word, Sir Winston's was a historic concept of the war, while the American was apocalyptic. Sir Winston viewed the war as part of a historic continuum, as a product of historic forces not in essence different from those that had preceded it and were likely to follow it, subject to historic laws, which are of the timeless essence of politics itself and for whose disregard a nation must pay a heavy price. Our government looked at the war as the catastrophic interruption of a normalcy which the victorious conclusion of the war would almost automatically restore. For us the war was like a thunderstorm darkening a peaceful scene; its passing would by itself restore peace. For Sir Winston the war—in its causes, manifestations, and consequences—was, as it were, part of the natural environment of nations, and its consequences would be determined by the policies carried on during the war.

In Sir Winston's thought and argument, as revealed in this book, one concern took precedence over all others: to meet the Russians as much to the east as possible. Whenever a military decision had to be made, small or great, Sir Winston hammered on this concern to the point of obnoxiousness. During the Italian campaign, he was obsessed with the opportunity to occupy Vienna before the Russians and urged that the invasion of southern France be sacrificed to the exploitation of this opportunity. After the Allied armies had crossed the Rhine, he urged striking directly at Berlin rather than southward, in order not to leave Berlin to the Russians. It was for similar reasons that he advised occupying as much as possible of Czechoslovakia, and more particularly Prague, and keeping what had been occupied. And when the war in Europe had ended with the surrender of Germany, he continued to view military operations in the light of their political consequences: he urged an over-all settlement with the Soviet Union while the armies of the United States were still intact and in Europe.

Sir Winston was defeated on every major issue. The only important exception was Greece, where he was able to act on his own, subordinating military to political considerations. When Greece was about to be conquered by communism and, through it, by Russian imperialism, he sent British forces to Greece to defeat that very underground army which had just been successfully fighting the Axis. It was argued then, as it is being argued now, that his advice was militarily unsound. However, this is not the point which Sir Winston's book raises. Sir Winston's concern—and ours—is not with the military soundness of this particular action or that but with the political quality of thinking which led to military action, however sound or unsound it might have been in its own military terms. It is the contrast between his own thinking and that of his American counterparts, and the political superiority of his to theirs, which is the main revelation of the book.

It would be as comforting as it would be false if one were to conclude that the main lesson of Sir Winston's book has been learned. Looking at Asia, the Middle East, and Europe—let alone at Washington—one cannot escape the conclusion that it has not been learned. Everywhere the requisite primacy of foreign policy over military policy is at best tenuous or ineffectual, if it exists at all. This book, then, is not only a repository of perennial wisdom; it also carries a very timely warning.

4 *The Great Betrayal*

The Van Doren case is a great event in American history.[1] It is the Hiss case of the academicians and the Dreyfus case of America. As the Hiss case pointed to the possibility of treason where it could least be tolerated—that is, in the foreign office—so the Van Doren case confronts America with the fact of mendacity where it can least be tolerated—that is, among the academicians—the professional guardians of the truth. Both cases, by bringing American society face to face with intolerable evil, test the moral judgment and fiber of America. As the Hiss case raised the specter of defenseless exposure to a foreign peril, so the Van Doren case presents us with the actuality of moral disintegration from within. As the Dreyfus case confronted French society with an inescapable moral choice, so does the Van Doren case American society, and as it was France and not Captain Dreyfus which was really on trial, so it is now America and not Professor Van Doren. Here, however, the analogy ends. For while the French institutions condemned an innocent man to be acquitted belatedly by public opinion, the American institutions have condemned a guilty man whom the preponderance of public opinion appears to acquit without further ado.

Thus the Van Doren case is a great event in the history of America in a dual sense. It brings to the fore certain qualities of American society, known before but perhaps never revealed with such poignancy, and it poses a moral issue which goes to the very heart of American society. The confrontation of Van Doren with America illuminates with a sudden flash the social landscape: it makes the familiar intrude into the senses with a novel sharpness; it reveals the presence of things hidden and unsuspected; it proves the inescapable reality of things suspected but hopefully obscured. It poses a general moral problem in a peculiarly American context and, by doing so, confronts America with a fundamental moral choice and puts the moral sensitivity of the nation to a crucial test. The American reac-

From the *New York Times Magazine*, November 22, 1959.

[1] Professor Charles Van Doren was a star of a TV quiz show which turned out to be rigged. The discovery of what went on behind stage created something of a public scandal.

tion to the Van Doren case bears eloquent testimony to the moral values of America. In what America says about Van Doren, the moral fiber of America itself stands revealed. By judging Van Doren, America bears judgment upon itself.

This is not a case of political or commercial corruption, such as Tweed, Teapot Dome, or Insull. Pecuniary corruption in the political and commercial spheres must be expected. For since the ultimate values of these fields are power, and wealth is a source of power, the abuse of wealth in the form of corruption is, as it were, foreordained by the very structure of these spheres; the ever present possibility of pecuniary corruption is built into them, however great or small the incidence of actual corruption may be in a particular period of history. Many politicians and businessmen are uncorrupted and fewer are uncorruptible, but they are all, by the very nature of their occupations, on familiar terms with corruption, encountering and skirting it even if they do not touch it.

Public reaction to political and commercial corruption is as predictable as the incidence of corruption itself. The familiarity of the fact evokes complacency, especially since many an onlooker preserves his virtue only for lack of opportunity to sin. The public rises in indignation only when the magnitude of the outrage exceeds the customary, when corruptive practices run counter to the political and commercial mores which are indifferent to some, such as implicit bribery, and condemn others, such as open blackmail, or when a prominent member of the other party or of the competition has been caught. The moral issue which political and commercial corruption poses is but the general issue of human fallibility. That fallibility was brought into the world by Eve and will be with us to the end of time. The best we can hope and strive for is to restrict its manifestations and mitigate its evil. In one form or other, we must live with it.

The Van Doren case raises an issue different from and more profound than political or commercial corruption. It arose in a sphere whose ultimate value is neither power nor wealth but truth. The professor is a man who has devoted his life to "professing," and what he is pledged to profess is the truth as he sees it. Mendacity in a professor is a moral fault which denies the very core of the professor's calling. Power and corruption go together, as do wealth and corruption;

pecuniary corruption is, as it were, their illegitimate offspring, pre-formed in their nature. Yet mendacity is the very negation of truth, the enemy which seeks its death. A mendacious professor is not like a politician who subordinates the public good to private gain or like a businessman who cheats. Rather he is like the physician who, pledged to heal, maims and kills, or like the policeman who, pledged to uphold the law, assists the criminal in breaking it. He is not so much the corrupter of the code by which he is supposed to live as its destroyer. This is the peculiar enormity of his outrage, which sets his deed apart from the common corruption of power and wealth.

It is in view of the nature of the deed that the reaction of American society must be judged. There is nothing extraordinary in the deed itself. The truth is being betrayed every day by those who are supposed to uphold it. What is extraordinary in the Van Doren case is the spectacular and stark simplicity with which the issue has been presented to the moral forum of America. The issue, thus presented, must be met head on. The verdict must be "guilty" or "not guilty"; there is no room for a hung jury or for a Pontius Pilate washing his hands in skeptical abstention.

The two institutions concerned—Columbia University and NBC—have acted honorably, appropriately, and expeditiously. NBC put the finger on the crux of the matter when it cited as grounds for dismissal, aside from the original deception, the subsequent series of deceptions masking the original one. Yet the reactions of the public contrast strikingly with those of the institutions. Of the nine members of the House of Representatives who heard the testimony, five addressed Van Doren in laudatory terms, "commending" and "complimenting" him and expressing their "appreciation." Two Congressmen expressed the hope that he would not be dismissed from his positions at Columbia University and NBC, and the chairman of the committee delivered a peroration predicting "a great future" for him. Only one member of the committee openly disagreed with the commendation of his colleagues. But even he did not convey awareness of the real issue, the scholar's special commitment to the truth.

Nor did the comments of most of Van Doren's students as reported by the press. One expressed "faith in him as a man" and called him "a fine gentleman," another thought that "what he did was not wrong," a third called the acceptance of his resignation "very unfair." The two students who are quoted as having approved of the acceptance justified it with the embarrassment Van Doren's continued affiliation would have caused the University. As one of them put it: "If Mr. Van Doren had remained, the school would have become associated with everything he had done." And a petition bearing the signature of 650 students demanded that he be rehired. None of the students whose reactions were recorded showed the slightest inkling of the moral issue raised by the case. And but a small minority of editorial comment and letters to newspapers did so.

How is this perversion of moral judgment, praising what deserves to be condemned and even at best remaining indifferent to the real issue, to be explained? The explanation of Congressional reaction is simple. The five members of Congress who approved Van Doren applied the standards of political behavior to the academic sphere. What they would have found pardonable and even praiseworthy in the politician they were unable to condemn in the scholar. Theirs was the fault of parochialism, which elevates the standards applicable to a particular sphere into absolutes applicable to all men regardless of circumstances. They dealt with the Van Doren case as though it were just another case of political corruption to be dealt with tolerantly, understandingly, and even approvingly after the culprit had come clean and returned to the fold of fairly honest politicians.

However, the complacency of the politicians points to a more profound issue, a moral dilemma built in, as it were, to the very fabric of American democracy. This is the dilemma between objective standards of conduct and majority rule, between the compliance in thought and deed with standards which are true regardless of time and place, and accommodation to the standards prevailing in a particular society in a particular time and place. America was founded upon the recognition of certain self-evident truths which men do not create but find in the nature of things. Yet American society and, more particularly, American democracy have lived in good measure, and in even greater measure as time went on, by conformity to whatever values appeared to be accepted by the elite or the majority of the moment.

At the beginning of American history and in its great moments of heroic dedication, the moral relativism, if not agnosticism, of that conformist attitude was mediated and even at times overwhelmed by the intellectual awareness of those eternal verities and the compliance with them in deeds. Yet in our day-to-day collective life that tension between objective standards and the ever changing preferences of society tends to be resolved in favor of the latter. Mr. Justice Holmes's famous dictum, "I have no practical criticism [with regard to laws] except what the crowd wants," is the classic expression of that resolution. It is also expressed in one Congressman's hope that Columbia University would not act "prematurely" and would at least wait to judge public reaction to Van Doren's statement.

The objective standards which constitute, as it were, the moral backbone of a civilized society are here dissolved into the ever changing amorphousness of public opinion. What a man ought or ought not to do is here determined not by objective laws immutable as the stars, but by the results of the latest public opinion poll. What is expected of a man is not compliance with those laws, but conformity to the demands of society, whatever they may be. A man who has gotten into trouble because he is temporarily out of step with public opinion needs only to slow down or hurry up, as the case may be, in order to get back into line, and all will be all right again with him and the world. Moral judgment thus becomes the matter of a daily plebiscite, and what is morally good becomes identical with what the crowd wants and tolerates. The Congressional reaction to the Van Doren case, then, is easily understood in terms of the trend, deeply ingrained in American society, toward making conformity with prevailing opinion the final arbiter of moral worth.

The moral illiteracy of the student is less easily explained. For the students, so one would like to think, are apprentices in that noble endeavor of discovering and professing the truth, not yet compelled by the demands of society to compromise their convictions; they behold truth in all its purity; and they must look at a mendacious professor as a student of the priesthood looks at a priest who blasphemes God. How is it possible for a young man of presumably superior intelligence and breeding, predestined to be particularly sensitive to the moral issue of truth, to be so utterly insensitive to it? These men were not born morally blind; for, as I have said elsewhere, man "is a moralist because he is a man." These men were born with a moral sense as they were born with a sense of sight; they were no more morally blind at birth than they were physically blind. What made them lose that moral sense? Who blinded them to the moral standards by which they—at least as students—are supposed to live?

The answer must be in the same sphere which produced Van Doren himself: the academic world. There is profound meaning in the solidarity between Van Doren and his students, and that meaning is found in the academic sphere which made them both what they are as moral beings. While public opinion has pinned responsibility on television, advertising, business, or low teachers' salaries, nobody seems to have pointed to the academic system which taught both teacher and students.

A system of higher education, dedicated to the discovery and transmission of the truth, is not a thing apart from the society which has created, maintains, and uses it. This is especially true of a decentralized and largely private system such as ours. The academic world partakes of the values prevailing in society and is exposed to the social pressures to conform to them. Its very concept of what truth is bears the marks of the relativism and instrumentalism dominant in American society; and by teaching that kind of truth, it strengthens its dominance over the American mind.

Yet even its commitment to this kind of truth is bound to come into conflict with the values and demands of society. The stronger the trend toward conformity within society and the stronger the commitment of the scholar to values other than the truth, such as wealth and power, the stronger will be the temptation to sacrifice the moral commitment to the truth for social advantage. The tension between these contradictory commitments typically issues in a compromise which keeps the commitment to the truth within socially acceptable bounds—exempting, for instance, the taboos of society from investigation—and restrains social ambitions from seriously interfering with the search for a truth cautiously defined. In the measure that truth is thus limited and defined, the search for it is deflected from its proper goal and thereby corrupted. On either end of the spectrum, one finds a small group which either is subversive of the truth by telling society what it wants to hear or else is subversive of society by telling society what it does not want to hear.

Contemporary American society offers enormous temptations for the academic world to follow the former path—that is, not only to corrupt the truth, but to betray it. In the process, the academic world tends to transform itself into a duplicate of the business and political worlds, with the search for truth subordinated to the values of these worlds. To the temptations of wealth and power held out by government, business, and foundations, the scholar has nothing to oppose but his honor committed to a truth which for him, as for society, is but a doubtful and for most of them at best a relative thing. He has his feet on an island of sand surrounded by the waves of temptation. The step from corruption to betrayal is big in moral terms but small in execution. What difference is there between receiving $129,000 under false pretenses from government, business, or a foundation, which has become almost standard operating procedure, and receiving the same amount under false pretenses from Revlon? The difference lies not in moral relevance but in the technique, which in the former case is discreet and elegant and remains within the academic mores, while in the latter it is blatant, vulgar, and obvious. Van Doren and his students were formed by a world which makes it easier for some of its members to receive money than reject it and condones the betrayal of truth for the sake of wealth and power, provided the academic amenities are preserved. Van Doren is indeed a black sheep in the academic world, but there are many gray ones among the flock.

In the world of Van Doren, American society beholds its own world, the world of business and politics, of wealth and power. It cannot condemn him without condemning itself, and since it is unwilling to do the latter, it cannot bring itself to do the former. Instead, it tends to absolve him by confusing the virtues of compassion and charity for the actor with the vice of condoning the act. Yet by refusing to condemn Van Doren, it cannot but condemn itself. For it convicts itself of a moral obtuseness which signifies the beginning of the end of civilized society. The Van Doren case is indeed the Dreyfus case in reverse. As France, by acquitting Dreyfus, restored itself as a civilized society ordered by the moral law, so must America by condemning Van Doren. Otherwise it will have signed the death warrant of its soul.

5 *Epistle to the Columbians on the Meaning of Morality*

Some of you, students of Columbia University, have written me, commenting on an article on the Van Doren case which was published in the *New York Times Magazine* of November 22, 1959. Since your letters either raise identical points or express the same general philosophic position, I am addressing you collectively. By doing this in public, I am already establishing an important difference between your and my position. For all of you request that, if I should write on this topic again, I not reveal your names; and one of you asks that the content of his letter not be revealed either. You appear to shun the public debate of public issues and prefer to drop opinions into the confidential darkness of the mailbox. I believe that in a democracy which still possesses its vitality public issues must be debated in the public forum and that the citizens must be seen, heard, and counted in the interchange of ideas and the interplay of interests, out of which a new consensus will arise.

But what are you afraid of? Why do you feel you must hide your faces and muffle your voices? Your letters are courteous, decent, intelligent, literate, and moving in their concern about the moral problem and their anxiety to be on the right side of it. The opinions you express are eminently respectable and even conformist to a fault. You say what almost everybody says and you say it better and with greater erudition than most, but there is not a rebel among you. The only deviation which you allow yourselves is a criticism of the trustees of your university for having acted hastily in accepting Van Doren's resignation; but that indiscretion you had already committed when you signed the petition asking that Van Doren be rehired. If your letters were published and the identity of the writers revealed, it is inconceivable that you would suffer in even the slightest degree, for you have done nothing to be ashamed of, you have

From the *New Republic*, December 22, 1959.

violated none of the mores of society, and you have much to be proud of by way of intellectual accomplishment and moral aspiration. Why, then, are you afraid?

I will tell you what frightens you. You are afraid of your shadows in the sunlight. You are afraid of the sound of your voices in the silence of the crowd. You are afraid of yourself. You are afraid to speak what is on everybody's lips as long as it is only you who would speak. Only when your voices merge into the chorus of the mass do you cease to be afraid. It is the protective anonymity of the crowd which gives you courage. To sign a petition in the company of 650 of your fellows, then, is one thing; to speak without assurance that you are not alone is quite another.

But imagine for a moment where man would be if his most intelligent, best educated, and most secure children had throughout history hidden their faces and spoken only in whispers. The great men whose lives and works you study are remembered exactly because they were not anonymous, because they showed their faces above the crowd and spoke in a loud voice all by themselves. What they spoke was more often than not the opposite of what the crowd believed and wanted to hear, and many of them lived in prison or in exile and died in disgrace or on the cross. Have you ever heard of two German students by the name of Scholl, brother and sister, who openly defied Hitler in the University of Munich and were hanged? Do you not remember the Hungarian, East German, Polish, and even Russian students who risked everything for their convictions and many of whom paid for them with their freedom and their lives? And you, risking nothing at all, refuse to speak above an anonymous whisper! Why are you so frightened by your own faces and your own voices? The answer to that question will become clear at the end of this letter; for it is intimately connected with the moral problem, to which we are turning now.

You are stung by my assertion that you are unaware of the moral problem posed by the Van Doren case, and you assure me that you disapprove of his conduct. But my point is proven by the very arguments with which you try to reconcile your disapproval of Van Doren's conduct with your petition to rehire him. The issue is for you confined in a three-cornered relationship between Van Doren, yourself, and Columbia University. Your concern is primarily with the misfortune of an attractive teacher, your regret in losing him, and the rigor of the university's decision. You support your position by five main arguments: the confession has swept the slate clean, Van Doren will not do it again, his teaching was above reproach, academic teaching is not concerned with substantive truth, and the university acted with undue haste. These arguments, taken at face value and erected into general principles of conduct, lead of necessity to the complete destruction of morality.

If confession, especially one which, as some of you conveniently forget, was not rendered by free moral choice but extracted by sheer necessity, can undo the deed, no evil could ever be condemned and no evildoer ever be brought to justice. If wrong could be so simply righted and guilt so painlessly atoned, the very distinction between right and wrong, innocence and guilt would disappear; for no sooner would a wrong be committed than it would be blotted out by a confession. Confession, even if freely rendered as an act of contrition and moral conversion, can mitigate the guilt but cannot wipe it out.

The argument that the morally objectionable act is not likely to be repeated assumes that the purpose of moral condemnation is entirely pragmatic, seeking to prevent a repetition of the deed; if what has been done once is not likely to be done again, we might as well forget it. Yet while it is true that according to the common law a dog is entitled to his first bite, it is nowhere written that a man is entitled to his first murder, his first fraud, or his first lie. The moral law is not a utilitarian instrument aiming at the protection of society, even though its observance has this effect, but its commands are absolute and must be obeyed for their own sake. Oedipus did not think that it was all right to marry his mother once since he did not do it again. Or would you suggest that Leopold and Loeb should have gone free because it was most unlikely that they would repeat what they had done?

The arguments of the good teacher and of teaching not being concerned with substantive truth go together. You assume, and some of your academic experience may well support your assumption, that the teacher is a kind of intellectual mechanic who fills your head with conventionally approved and required knowledge, as a filling-station attendant fills a tank with gas. You don't care what the teacher does from 10:00 A.M. to 9:00 A.M. as long as he gives you from 9:00 to 10:00 A.M. the knowledge which he has been paid to transmit. You recognize no relation between a teacher's general attitude toward the truth and his way of transmitting knowledge because you do not recognize an organic relation between transmitted knowledge and an objective, immutable truth. Yet the view that knowledge is but conventional—one conception of truth to be superseded by another—while seemingly supported by the radical transformation of physics, finds no support in the fields of knowledge dealing with man. If it were otherwise, Plato and Aristotle, Sophocles and Shakespeare, Montesquieu and Locke could mean nothing to us, except as objects for antiquarian exploration.

There is, then, in these fields an accumulation of knowledge, old knowledge being refined and added to, but not necessarily superseded, by new insights. The teacher of such knowledge is not only the recorder and transmitter of what goes by the name of knowledge in a particular time and place, but he is also and foremost the guardian and augmenter of a permanent treasure. This is not a part-time job to be performed during certain hours without relation with what goes on before and after. Quite to the contrary, this is a profession which requires the dedication and ethos of the whole man. Of such a man, it must be expected that he be truthful not only between 9:00 and 10:00 A.M. when he teaches, but always.

The last argument that the trustees of the university acted with undue haste is the most curious of all, and it gives the show away. One of you says that the trustees could not have evaluated the evidence during the four hours of their deliberations. Another mentions that the trustees acted before all the evidence was in. Still another argues that they wanted to wash their hands quickly of the whole business for fear of public opinion. And one advances the ingenious proposition that the students would not have protested if the trustees had waited a month or so with the acceptance of the resignation, pretending "however untruthfully," that they were investigating the case!

In truth, you do not mean any of these things, which are either patently at odds with the obvious facts or else absurd on their face. You look for reasons which justify your unwillingness to transcend that three-cornered relationship between yourself, your teacher, and your university and to judge the obvious facts by the standards of morality rather than adjust them for your and your teacher's convenience. You are sorry about losing an attractive teacher and you hate to see that teacher suffer; nothing else counts. But there is something else that counts and that is the sanctity of the moral law. Your dean, in an admirable statement, which I have seen quoted only in your student paper, has formulated it thus:

The issue is the moral one of honesty and the integrity of teaching. Appearing as a teacher, Mr. Van Doren engaged in an act of deception in professing to know what he did not know, and of dishonesty in accepting answers in a test of knowledge against an opponent he believed to be honest. Thereafter, he continued to act out the deception and continued to lie about his actions, even under oath, until after he had been subpoenaed by a committee of Congress. This behavior seems to me to have been contrary to the principles that a teacher stands for and undertakes to instill in his students. If these principles are to continue to have meaning at Columbia, Mr. Van Doren's ultimate offer to resign had to be accepted.

Here is indeed the nub of the matter.

You must have smiled indulgently or shrugged with impatience when you saw me refer to the sanctity of the moral law. Is not morality, so you might ask, a relative thing, the ever changing result of environment and circumstances? If this were so, let me ask you, how do you explain that we cannot only understand the moral relevance of the Ten Commandments, originating in a social environment and circumstances quite different from ours, but also make them the foundation for our moral life? How do you explain that the moral ideas of Plato and Pascal, of Buddha and Thomas Aquinas are similarly acceptable to our intellectual understanding and moral sense? If the disparate historic systems of morality were not erected upon a common foundation of moral understanding and valuation, impervious to the changing conditions of time and place, we could not understand any other moral system but our own, nor could any other moral system but our own have any moral relevance for us. It is only because we as moral beings have something in common with all other men—past and present—that we are able to understand, and make our own, the core of the moral systems of others. What is it that all men have in common as moral beings?

All men—civilized and barbarian—in contrast to the animals, are born with a moral sense; that is to say, as man is by nature capable of making logical judgments, so is he capable by nature of making moral judgments. As I have said in the *New York Times Magazine* article and elsewhere, man "is a moralist because he is a man." You in your groping for a tenable moral position, in your anxiety to justify yourself in moral terms, bear eloquent testimony to the innate character of that moral faculty. Civilized man shares with the barbarian the faculty of making moral judgments, but excels him in that he is capable of making the right moral judgments, knowing why he makes them. He knows—as Socrates, the Greek tragedians (to whom one of you rather wistfully refers), the Biblical prophets, and the great moralists and tragedians of all the ages knew—what is meant by the sanctity of the moral law.

The moral law is not made for the convenience of man, rather it is an indispensable precondition for his civilized existence. It is one of the great paradoxes of civilized existence that—in contrast to the existence of the animals and barbarians—it is not self-contained but requires for its fulfillment transcendent orientations. The moral law provides one of them. That is to say, human existence, not in its animal but in its civilized qualities, cannot find its meaning within itself but must receive it from a transcendent source.

You are still in all likelihood closer to your birth than to your death; yet in the measure that your life approaches its natural limits, you will become aware of the truth of that observation. For when you look back on your life in judgment, you will remember it, and you will want it to be remembered, for its connection with the things that transcend it. And if you ask yourself why you remember and study the lives and deeds of great men, why you call them great in the first place, you will find that they were oriented in extraordinary ways and to an unusual degree toward the things that transcend their own existence. That is the meaning of the passage from the Scriptures, "He that findeth his life shall lose it; and he that loseth his life for my sake shall find it."

This connection between our civilized existence and the moral law explains the latter's sanctity. By tinkering with it, by sacrificing it for individual convenience, we are tinkering with ourselves as civilized beings, we are sacrificing our own civilized existence. As

Kant put it: "If justice should perish, man's existence on earth would have lost its meaning."

The issue before you, when you were asked to sign that petition, was not the happiness of a particular man or, for that matter, your own, but whether you and your university could afford to let a violation of the moral law pass as though it were nothing more than a traffic violation. Socrates had to come to terms with that issue, and he knew how to deal with it. You did not know how to deal with it. And this is why you hide your faces and muffle your voices. For since your lives have lost the vital contact with the transcendence of the moral law, you find no reliable standard within yourself by which to judge and act. You are frightened by the emptiness within yourself, the insufficiency stemming from a self-contained existence. And so you flee into the protective cover of the anonymous crowd and judge as it judges and act as it acts. But once you have restored that vital connection with the moral law from which life receives its meaning, you will no longer be afraid of your shadow and the sound of your voice. You will no longer be afraid of yourself. For you will carry within yourself the measure of yourself and of your fellows and the vital link with things past, future, and above.

6 *The Decline of the Democratic Process*

The crisis of American politics, domestic and international, and the prevailing unawareness of its gravity and of its very existence are rooted in two misunderstandings and misuses of American democracy. They affect the very essence of democratic government. One concerns the position and functions of the President; the other, the relationship between the requirements of sound policy and the will of the majority. The major weaknesses of American policies can be traced to one or the other or both of these misunderstandings and misuses.

Democratic government is government by popular choice—choice of men and, through it, choice of policy. A government that can keep itself in power regardless of the preferences of the people is not democratic at all; a government whose choice by the people does not also imply a choice of policy is but imperfectly so. It follows that a perfectly democratic system of government must be partisan government in the sense that those who have been elected to govern stand for one set of policies and those who have been rejected at the polls are committed to another set of policies. The candidates for office have been judged by the policies with which they are identified and by their ability to carry them through, and at the next elections they will again be judged by these criteria.

The government of the United States, as presently constituted on its highest level, is not perfectly democratic. The President was re-elected in 1956, not because he stood for specific policies which the electorate preferred to those of his opponent, but because he was committed only to general aspirations shared by all men of good will. It is exactly this lack of partisanship, this commitment to unexceptional generalities which imply no commitment to anything concrete in terms of policy, which made him into the incarnation of the nation's better self, the symbol of its nobler longings. Thus he was re-elected, not on the strength of particular foreign policies executed or proposed, but as a symbol of the nation's longing for

From the *New Republic*, December 17, 1956.

peace, as the man who had brought peace to Korea and would preserve it elsewhere.

This popular image of the President reflects Mr. Eisenhower's own conception of the Presidency in theory and practice. Supported by an optimistic philosophy, unaware of man's propensities for evil and the tragic dilemmas of human existence, he has limited himself, by and large, to the enunciation of general principles, leaving the political task of their implementation to subordinates or to nobody in particular. His interest in factual information and day-by-day administration has been sporadic, and his intervention in the formation of policy has generally been reserved for crisis situations. Thus the President, by divorcing his person and his office from the partisanship of politics, has transformed the character of politics itself. Politics has lost its fanatical partisanship and bitter animosities, and the warming benevolence of a President who appears to be above politics envelops the nation as in a *union sacrée*.

It is the fatal weakness of Mr. Eisenhower's contribution to the substance of American foreign policy that it is informed by the same philosophy of abstention, conciliation, and pacification as is his domestic one. Conciliation and pacification as ends in themselves can, under certain circumstances, be virtues at home; they are, except under the rarest of circumstances, vices abroad. And one may well speculate whether the price the nation will have to pay in the long run even for its present domestic tranquillity in terms of moral stagnation, intellectual sterility, issues unrecognized, and problems unsolved will not turn out to be vastly excessive.

The price we must pay for international tranquillity as an end in itself is not a matter of speculation but of historic experience. Optimistic assumptions about human nature may be able to support for a while domestic policies carried on in a civilized Western society. They are bound to be disappointed on the international scene. For here conciliation and peace can hardly ever be ends in themselves but must be sought as the by-product of a political settlement which actually reconciles antagonistic interests and thereby deprives the parties concerned of the incentive to seek redress by force. At home and abroad, the President's philosophy spells avoidance of problems, abstention from action, tranquillity as an end in itself. Yet what can be tolerated in the short run at home—for here the agencies for thought and action other than the President continuously operate on behalf of the United States—becomes a mortal danger abroad. For if the United States does not reflect on the problems that concern it and does not try to solve them on its own terms, the enemies of the United States do so reflect and act. International peace and tranquillity achieved at the price of abstention from thought and action, then, are tantamount to retreat and surrender.

The new conception of the Presidency not only impairs the freedom of choice at democracy's decisive moment—the presidential elections—and leads to impotence in its application to foreign policy but it also impairs the day-by-day democratic processes by destroying the functions of the opposition. Historically, that destruction has manifested itself as the corruption of bipartisanship in foreign policy. Bipartisanship, as originally conceived at the end of the Second World War, carried the negative implication that a foreign policy ought not to be opposed by one party for the sole reason that the President and Secretary of State belonging to the other party were carrying it out. In positive terms, bipartisanship implied that the opposition party should support sound foreign policies and oppose unsound ones, regardless of the party affiliation of those carrying them out. Conceived in these terms, bipartisanship recognized the elemental fact that the consequences of foreign policy are not limited, as are those of many domestic ones, to a particular segment of the population identified with one or the other party, but affect the whole nation for generations to come. Bipartisanship drew from this fact the sound and indispensable conclusion that party strife for its own sake must stop at the point where the whole nation meets other nations in defense of its interests and its very existence.

However, bipartisanship, as originally conceived, never did imply that the opposition should not oppose when opposition appeared justified by the demerits of the foreign policy pursued. Nor did it imply that the opposition should forego what is not only its privilege but also its mission, whose fulfilment is indispensable for the proper functioning of the democratic process: to submit alternative policies for the administration to adopt or else for the people to support by changing the administration. An opposition that does not perform these two functions deprives the people in yet another way of that choice of policies essential to democracy.

This is indeed what the opposition was doing during Mr. Eisenhower's first term. It abdicated its mission, confounding bipartisanship with conformity. What did its titular head and its leaders in Congress contribute to public enlightenment, to the clarification of the issues, to intellectual and political pressure upon the administration? What the policy of the British Labour party was in successive international crises we know. But what was the policy of the Democratic party of the United States? The answer is simple and disquieting: there was no such policy. Nor is the picture that the mass media of communication present much more reassuring. A very few notable exceptions notwithstanding, the abdication of judgment and will of the political opposition was duplicated here. Everybody seemed to emulate the President's example and rise above politics, sharing in the nobility of his sentiments and general objectives. The result is national unity, paid for with the lifeblood of the democratic process. For this is not the unity of a people who, after weighing the alternatives, have decided what they want and how to get what they want. It is rather like a fog that makes us all brothers in blindness.

Yet among those whose duty it is to lead by criticizing and proposing—the public officials, politicians, correspondents, columnists, commentators, academicians—the failure is one of will rather than of judgment. Of those who keep silent or speak only by indirection so great as to confuse the ignorant and to be intelligible only to the informed, the great majority know the awful truth. Why is it that during Mr. Eisenhower's first term none of the policy-makers who express their misgivings and forebodings freely in private raised his voice in anguish or resigned in protest? And what of all the others who have to risk much less? They have all become the victims of the official conception of the Presidency, which allows only of whispered hints as some isolated deficiency here and there and must regard political attack and even frank debate, the very dynamics of democracy, as a sacrilege against the spirit of the nation, incarnate as it is in the person of the President.

The debilitating effect which a new conception of the Presidency and the corruption of bipartisanship reflecting it has had upon the foreign policy of the United States is, in turn, reflected and aggravated by a new conception of the office of the Secretary of State and a new method of gaining public and, more particularly, congressional support in the conduct of foreign policy.

Mr. Dulles' conception of his office in one respect curiously duplicates Mr. Eisenhower's conception of the Presidency: both conceive of their offices as being divorced from the day-by-day operations of policy formation and execution. What Gettysburg and Augusta are for the President, all the capitals of the world are for the Secretary of State: respectable escapes from the daily responsibilities of government. Here, however, the analogy ends. For while Mr. Dulles has shut himself off from the regular departmental channels of information and advice, he has kept a monopoly on major policy decisions and has taken an unprecedentedly large part in certain phases of their execution, so large a part as to keep him from his desk for about one-third of his tenure of office. The results have been unfortunate in four different respects.

The Secretary of State has been unable to perform adequately the very functions of policy formation which he considers his exclusive prerogative. Not even the wisest and most experienced of secretaries of state can afford to dispense with the information and advice of his subordinates; and the most traveled of secretaries of state can afford it even less. The great abilities and greater self-confidence of Mr. Dulles have not compensated for this deficiency. In consequence, Mr. Dulles has not had the time or the incentive, in terms of new knowledge and new ideas, to deal constructively with the drastic changes that have occurred in recent years on the international scene. This is one of the reasons why his tenure of office has been outstanding not for bold initiative and innovation in policy but rather for the virtually mechanical continuation of established routines long after they had served their purpose.

Mr. Dulles' assumption of the role of roving ambassador and ubiquitous negotiator has impaired the performance of his functions in yet another way. There is great wisdom, reflecting the nature of things, in the tradition that requires the head of the foreign office to stay at home and reflect and decide, and the ambassadors to go abroad and negotiate. This division of labor not only frees the head of the foreign office from preoccupation with details obstructing his over-all view of foreign relations but also protects him from involvement in the intrigues, indiscretions, and commitments inseparable from the routine of diplomacy. Mr. Dulles, by doing what ambassadors are supposed to do, has not been able to do the job only he could have done. Furthermore, he has wasted the prestige of his office on a multitude of minutiae, magnifying them far beyond their intrinsic importance. He owes his unpopularity abroad and the foreign mistrust of his word in good measure to that assumption of functions which no Secretary of State ought to assume.

The Secretary of State has also been unable to exert effective control over his department on behalf of his own policies. Mr. Dulles has sought to carry the formation of policy in his own head and leave the implementation of the policy through day-by-day administration and execution to subordinates. Yet in actual performance policy formation cannot be so neatly separated from implementation, and those who control the day-by-day operations of the Department uncontrolled by the Secretary become, by the very logic of their functions, makers of policy on their own. The permanent functional and frequent physical separation of the Secretary from the Department has transformed the top echelon of his subordinates into a sort of collective leadership performing the institutional functions of the Secretary without his permanent control and without his authority. Thus the undersecretary of state, the counselor, the legal adviser, certain deputy undersecretaries and assistant secretaries, severally or collectively, have been carrying out functions which only the Secretary should perform and can perform successfully.

Such a state of affairs is fraught with danger under the best of circumstances, that is, when the Secretary and his immediate subordinates see eye to eye on policy; for it is bound to result in misunderstandings, misinterpretations, disorganization, and the incoherence of policies. However, the circumstances under which Mr. Dulles' system has operated were never of the best. For reasons that shall be discussed in a moment, Mr. Dulles frequently appointed to key positions in his department men who were out of sympathy with his own policies. This being so, it is but natural that in the process of execution the Secretary's policies were often infused with the spirit of their opponents. The Secretary's policies were sometimes so completely perverted by his subordinates that deliberate sabotage provides the only plausible explanation.

The effects of this situation were clear to see in the Suez crisis of

November, 1956. The Department of State ceased to function as the instrument of a viable American foreign policy. It split into two factions, committed to radically different and mutually exclusive policies. One faction looked at the trend of American foreign policy with alarm and despair. The other faction welcomed that trend, being in good measure of its own making, with enthusiastic expectations. One day, one faction seemed to prevail; another day, the other, and there was nobody above them to mold out of the welter of opinion a foreign policy capable of execution and promising success.

These weaknesses were compounded by the revival of a propensity, which has at times exerted a strong influence upon the conduct of American foreign policy, to look at foreign policy with a lawyer's eye and to manipulate it with a lawyer's tools. It would certainly be preposterous to suggest that lawyers cannot make great statesmen and diplomatists; the pages of history are full of them. But those lawyers were transformed by their political experience into something more than lawyers; they were able to transcend the limits of their craft. It is the strength and weakness of Mr. Dulles that he has brought to his office a first-rate legal mind which excels in negotiations and in deft maneuver but fails in the constructive tasks of statesmanship. For the lawyer's mind is uncongenial to these tasks.

The lawyer sees reality dissolved into a sequence of isolated "cases," each to be dealt with on its "merits." Thus Great Britain and France committed "aggression" against Egypt and must not be allowed to get away with it. Little does it matter that this "case" has a history which antedates the invasion of Egypt and that it will make history long after the last British and French soldiers have left Egyptian territory. Let us first close this "case" by restoring the pre-invasion status quo, and we shall then turn to the next "case" if and when it arises. The subject matter with which the lawyer thus endeavors to deal being a continuum of which the particular "case" is an organic and inseparable element, the lawyer's method is singularly inadequate to deal with it. Its political manifestations are the conception of policy as the reaction to the initiative of others; improvisation, since before a "case" arises there is nothing to be done; aversion to long-range planning, since the scope of action is limited by the dimensions of the "case" and when the "case" is settled action must await another "case."

The lawyer is particularly averse to long-range planning that entails risks and requires daring because he has been conditioned in dealing with his clients—and is not the government just another client?—to chart a course that avoids trouble, minimizes risks, and is plainly calculable. He plans foreign policy as he would plan an estate. Examining a plan for action, he sets himself the task of finding its faults in terms of these criteria, and he cannot help finding them in any plan for international action. For such is the nature of foreign policy that success must be paid for with troubles, risks, and the threat of the unknown. To be fearful of that price means to do nothing, and the lawyer's caution becomes the paralysis of the statesman.

These deficiencies which have sapped the strength of American foreign policy are overshadowed in lasting importance by a dilemma which is, as it were, built into the constitutional and political system of the United States: how to reconcile the requirements of sound foreign policy with the requirement of popular and, more particularly, congressional support. The problem of how to reconcile these two factors which in the nature of things cannot be fully reconciled has bedeviled the conduct of American foreign policy since Washington's day. For, if American statesmen go too far in complying with the requirements of sound foreign policy, they are likely to lose the support of opinion at home; if they go too far in accommodating that opinion at the expense of what sound foreign policy requires, they risk jeopardizing the interests of the country and thus in the long run the support of opinion as well.

The task of the statesman, then, is twofold: to impress upon the people the requirements of sound foreign policy by telling them the facts of political life and what they require of the nation, and then to strike a compromise which leaves the essence of a sound foreign policy intact. It must be said, and it is being said with deep regret by one who expected great things in this regard from the co-operation between an immensely popular President and an experienced and skilful Secretary of State, that the Eisenhower administration has failed in both tasks. It is this failure which is in good measure responsible for the sterility of American foreign policy, for the dis-

asters which have befallen and threaten it, and for the popular ignorance of the bearing of these disasters upon the future of America
and of the world.

That the administration has failed to educate the people hardly
needs to be argued. Official statements have been consistently at
odds with the facts and their import for the interests and policies of
the United States. Let anyone make a compilation of the official
statements about the Suez Canal crisis and compare them with the
facts as reported by the same newspapers! Let anyone undertake a
history of world affairs since 1953, using only official statements and
forgetting everything else he knows, and what a mélange of fiction
and caricature we would get! In one word, the public relations expert has taken over from the statesman.

In the task of fashioning a compromise between the requirements
of foreign policy and the preferences of public opinion, the administration has likewise failed. The Secretary of State has been haunted
by the memory of his able and high-minded predecessor who failed
in this task because he failed to marshal public opinion in support of
sound policies and compounded his failure when in the end he even
embraced unsound ones without gaining popular support. Mr. Dulles
resolved not to repeat that failure. Instead of heeding Sir William
Harcourt's advice that "political heads of departments are necessary
to tell the civil service what the public will not stand," thus approaching the public with a sound and settled policy, he would first get
popular and, more particularly, congressional support at whatever
cost in policy commitments and then, with the home front secure,
face the nations of the world with the right policies. The plan was
ingenious but doomed to failure on two counts. Its success was predicated upon the possibility of appeasing the opponents of American
foreign policy as it had developed since 1939, and that possibility
never existed. No concession could reconcile these men to the
active involvement of the United States in the affairs of the world,
to its risks, liabilities, opportunities, and rewards. They had to be
disarmed and neutralized, not appeased. Yet by trying to appease
them, Mr. Dulles destroyed the very instrument without which no
foreign policy could be successfully pursued, his own department,
and narrowed his freedom of action to such an extent as to foreclose
any fresh initiative, any creative response to novel situations.

The destruction of the Department of State proceeded in two stages: the elimination of most of the able and experienced members of its higher ranks and the appointment to key positions of men whose main qualification was sympathy with the philosophy and policies of the irrreconcilable opposition. Thus foreign aid was administered by a man who did not believe in foreign aid; the Refugee Act was administered by a man who did not believe in immigration; some key men in the Far Eastern Division do not believe in negotiations with Communist China; and the only visible qualification of one undersecretary of state for his eminent position was the Hoover name which evokes memories dear to the opposition. The purpose of these appointments was to commit the opposition to the support of the foreign policies of the administration. Actually they committed a powerful group within the Department to the support of opposition policies. The opposition, far from giving hostages to Mr. Dulles, imprisoned him in a cell of old ideas and old policies from which he could not move when momentous opportunities for fresh initiatives—the atomic stalemate, the new Soviet policies, the stirrings of Asia and Africa, the disintegration of the alliances, the rise of Germany and Japan—knocked at the door.

What of the remedy? What of the cure? The cure is as grand and simple as the disease is stark and simple.

It is for the President to reassert his historic role as both the initiator of policy and the awakener of public opinion. It is true that only a strong, wise, and shrewd President can marshal to the support of wise policies the strength and wisdom latent in that slumbering giant—American public opinion. Yet while it is true that great men have rarely been elected President of the United States, it is upon that greatness, which is the greatness of its people personified, that the United States, from Washington to Franklin D. Roosevelt, has had to rely in the conduct of its foreign affairs. It is upon that greatness that Western Civilization must rely for its survival.

Those words we addressed in 1949 to Mr. Eisenhower's predecessor. If they were true then they are true today. Will Mr. Eisenhower heed their truth? Will he ever know that it exists?

7 *The Corruption of Patriotism*

Of the surrender of sound principles of policy to the pressures of demagogic politics and the resulting corruption of the democratic processes, the security policies of the United States, culminating in the years 1953–55, provide an extreme example. It is possible to explain the security system of the President's Executive Order 10450 of April 27, 1953—which incidentally the Eisenhower administration inherited and perfected but did not create—psychologically as a reaction to the laxity preceding it; it is impossible to defend it on rational and empirical grounds. We are faced with the stark fact, which the scholar cannot evade, that well-meaning and otherwise intelligent men were joined by the great majority of the people in embracing a philosophy of security, which is in truth a mythology, and a policy of security, which is in truth a series of ritualistic performances requiring human sacrifices, both completely divorced from reality and reason.

A critical analysis of the security regulations, as applied to the Department of State, must answer four basic questions. What is to be secured? Against whom is it to be secured? By what means is it being secured? What is the cost of security in terms of other goals to which the nation is equally committed?

A security system, in so far as it concerns the Department of State, must protect the integrity and secrecy of foreign policy. It has to assure, first of all, that the foreign policy of the United States is not determined by persons who owe primary loyalty to a foreign power and, hence, put its interests above those of the United States. Or, to put it in positive terms, it has to assure that those who determine American foreign policy are loyal to the United States. If there had ever existed, as is widely but falsely believed, in the Department of State a pro-Communist clique who deliberately worked for the triumph of communism in China, a security system would have to prevent such a situation from repeating itself.

It must, however, be said that the very mechanics by which the

From the *Bulletin of the Atomic Scientists*, April, 1955; and the *New Republic*, April 18, 1955.

foreign policy of the United States is conducted make it extremely unlikely that such a situation could ever arise. The formation of American foreign policy is characterized by a diffusion so extreme as to border on chaos. The determination of American foreign policy is subject to a multitude of influences, not only from within the Department of State, but also from a great number of executive agencies which are directly or indirectly concerned with the conduct of foreign policy. To them must be added the—often decisive—influence that both houses of Congress exert upon the conduct of American foreign policy. A multitude of people, typically organized in committees, on all levels of the governmental hierarchy are continuously called upon to analyze a certain political situation and to propose a policy dealing with it. Out of that welter of divergent opinions, certain basic propositions are slowly distilled which are submitted to the President for final approval. It is only when the President has spoken with the ultimate authority of his office, not infrequently choosing among alternative policies, that the foreign policy of the United States has been determined.

Given this diffuse process of policy formation, no one foreign agent, however highly placed, could deflect the foreign policy of the United States from its national course. For his advice favoring a foreign power would be counteracted by the multitude of loyal officials who also participate in the process of policy formation. For a foreign power to subvert the foreign policy of the United States, a network of agents is needed strategically located not only in the Department of State but also in the other governmental establishments, such as the White House and the National Security Council, which are directly concerned with the determination of American foreign policy. No foreign power was able to establish such a network when American public opinion was hardly aware of the problem of security and when security regulations were extremely lax. It is important in this context to remind ourselves that there is no evidence to suggest that any of the officials who were concerned with the conduct of American foreign policy and whose pro-Communist sympathies have been proven have been able, or have even attempted, to influence American foreign policy in favor of a foreign nation.

The classic activity of the foreign agent, at least in popular imagination, is indeed not the determination of policy but the transmission of secrets. The prototype of the foreign agent is the spy. Not only public opinion but all governments assume that espionage is an enterprise worthwhile for all. Hence, they embark upon espionage for themselves and endeavor to protect themselves against the espionage of others. However, this assumption, at least as it concerns foreign policy in contrast to military dispositions and planning, is open to radical doubt.

It stands, of course, to reason that genuine military secrets must be protected. The quality and quantity of weapons, the disposition of the armed forces, war plans, and codes fall into that category. In so far as the operations of the Department of State deal with such military secrets, they require protection on military grounds. Secret-service operations with which the Department of State concerns itself must be protected on similar grounds. The considerations of the problem of secrecy in the Department of State that follow, then, apply exclusively to foreign policy proper.

I was once told by an official of the Department of State that from his long experience he could remember only two documents the transmission of which would have been advantageous to a foreign power. From my own much more limited experience, I do not remember a single top-secret document, let alone any document of a lower security classification, the knowledge of which would have been advantageous to a foreign power. I would go so far as to say that if a foreign power would gain knowledge of all the classified documents I have seen or written, such knowledge might be advantageous to the United States rather than to that power, provided it would be advantageous to the United States to confound a foreign power as to the nature of our foreign policy and its future course. As concerns espionage with regard to foreign policy in general, it is hardly more than a racket, engaged in by shady characters frequently working both sides of the street. The typical information thus obtained is either phony, irrelevant, or public property.

That this cannot be otherwise, a consideration of foreign policy, especially as it must be practiced under present world conditions, will make obvious. The great lines of action which the foreign policies of the great powers are likely to take are predetermined by their respective national interests as they are rationally defined by the small group which ultimately decides upon the course of action. This has always been so and is so today. The Cold War has, however, imposed a peculiar rigidity upon the foreign policies of the great powers, which leaves very little room for maneuver in the implementation of their respective national interests. Given this situation, there can be hardly any secrets which rational analysis could not detect but which espionage would be able to uncover. In order to know what Chinese policy with regard to Korea or Formosa is likely to be, it is not necessary, and probably not even expedient, to pilfer the secret files of the foreign office in Peiping; it is only necessary to ask one's self what the national interest of China has been with regard to these two regions and what it is likely to be as interpreted by the present rulers of China. In order to know what the Soviet Union is up to with regard to Germany, and vice versa, it is not necessary, and will avail little, to have secret agents in the foreign offices of Bonn and Moscow. If rational analysis cannot answer our quest, nothing else will.

The security regulations, as applied to the Department of State, completely misunderstood the nature of foreign policy and the problem of security with regard to it. Executive Order 10450 distinguishes among different positions in view of their different relevance for security but leaves the actual determination of that relevance to the officers charged with the enforcement of the executive order [Sec. 3 (A) par. 2, (B) par. 1; Sec. 8 (A) 1]. In its application to the Department of State that distinction between different degrees of sensitivity disappeared. The security policy of the Department of State conceived of foreign policy as one vast operation, all elements of which, from the determination of policy to the washing of windows, are equally important in view of their bearing upon integrity and secrecy.

In truth, what needs protection from foreign subversion is not the whole process of foreign policy in all its ramifications but only those elements of it that, in the nature of things, are capable of being subverted, that is, that small area where decisions are actually made and which has access to military secrets and secret-service operations. Secrecy in foreign policy serves not so much the security of the United States in terms of concealment of its plans and operations as it protects its officials who must be free to express their opinions without concern for the favorable or unfavorable reaction of outsiders. If the officials who are engaged in the conduct of foreign policy could not rely upon their official actions and expressions of opinion being made in confidence, they would at the very least be tempted to surrender their own professional judgment of the merits of the case to outside pressures, domestic and foreign. In the absence of secrecy, an official could not be expected to express his opinions about the personnel and policies of a foreign government without anticipating the reactions of that government. Nor could he be expected to express his opinions about the policies of his own government without regard for domestic political reactions.

The main purpose of secrecy, then, is the protection of the professional integrity of the Foreign Service and affiliated agencies. Security regulations which seek to protect that professional integrity must obviously be different from those which seek to protect the United States against the betrayal of official secrets. Security regulations which are completely unaware of the former function but animated by an unrealistic assessment of the need for the performance of the latter are likely to fail in both. More will have to be said on this point later on.

Against whom are the integrity and secrecy of American foreign policy to be secured? How can we determine beforehand who is likely to be disloyal if participation in the conduct of American foreign policy should be intrusted to him? How does, in one word, the mark of Cain look, which is supposed to set the prospective traitor apart from the mass of loyal citizens? Section 8 of Executive Order 10450 undertakes to answer that question. It enumerates close to one hundred characteristics, any one of which excludes a man from government employment as a security risk, his employment being not "clearly consistent with the national security." Yet that list of characteristics, according to the preamble of Section 8, is not intended to be exhaustive but rather to establish general categories to which the security officials may add other related ones.

These characteristics fall into three different categories:

1. Those which make a person unfit for government service on obvious security grounds, such as "commission of any act of sabotage, espionage, treason or sedition . . ." [Sec. 8 (A) 2].

2. Characteristics which make a person unfit for government

service in general, without any special reference to security, such as "An adjudication of insanity, or treatment for serious mental or neurological disorder without satisfactory evidence of cure" [Sec. 8 (A) 1. IV].

3. Characteristics the absence of which in the composite reveal a picture of the "normal" good American, who alone is worthy of government employment, such as "any criminal, infamous, dishonest, immoral, or notoriously disgraceful conduct, habitual use of intoxicants to excess, drug addiction, or sex perversion" [Sec. 8 (A) 1. III].[1]

Here is indeed the crux of the matter. What the security regulations are trying to do in the third category is to localize treason as an outstanding but surreptitious evil by making it a function of other outstanding but patent evils. In this philosophy a man who has deviated drastically in other respects from the moral standards of society is more likely to deviate from those moral standards by committing treason than one who has not so deviated. This assumption is illogical to begin with, and there is not a shred of empirical evidence to support it. Its illogical character stems from the very nature of treason which is an act of disloyalty committed by a person who, in view of his revealed qualities, appears to be deserving of trust. If it were possible to identify the prospective traitor by some outward quality, the commission of treason would by definition become impossible. That the assumption of a necessary relationship between general immorality and the particular immorality of treason also is untenable on empirical grounds can be shown by putting the following two questions to the empirical test: Are people who deviate in a particular respect from the moral standards of society more likely to commit treason than others, and are traitors as a type likely to be immoral in other respects as well?

In order to answer the first of these two questions, let us take the type of immorality which not only constitutes a particularly radical and repulsive violation of "normal" moral standards but by general consensus is also most obviously conducive to treason: sexual perversion. That the homosexual is peculiarly prone to commit crimes

---

[1] Some of these characteristics taken in isolation, such as drug addiction, disqualify a person for government service in general and, hence, belong to the second category.

under the threat of blackmail is hardly doubted by anyone who faces the problem for the first time. Yet neither the histories of diplomacy and of treason nor the recollections of practitioners of diplomacy, in so far as I could ascertain, contain an instance of a homosexual having committed an act of treason under the threat of blackmail.

Nor is there any such evidence with regard to a very mild "deviation," completely devoid in itself of any negative moral connotation: that of having relatives behind the Iron Curtain. That an official who has relatives living behind the Iron Curtain is particularly susceptible to committing treason under blackmail sounds on the face of it so plausible that it is virtually accepted as self-evident. But who knows of an official who has violated security regulations under such circumstances? Here again, what on the face of it looks like common sense reveals itself on closer examination as superstition which unchallenged repetition has vested with the plausibility of truth.

Executive Order 10450 assumes the existence of two easily discernible types of men, one likely to commit treason, the other not. The composite picture of the latter, which emerges from Executive Order 10450 and its application to the personnel of the Department of State, is the ideal type of a Babbitt with strong pseudopuritanical connotations. He is a person who is "normal" in every respect, that is, who conforms to certain requirements which a "good" American is supposed to possess. In their application to the Department of State, these requirements run the whole gamut of actions, associations, attitudes, and opinions with which a person might identify himself. It is significant for the concern with conformity rather than with security that much emphasis has been put upon conformity with a conservative ideal in the field of political opinion and attitudes and with a pseudopuritanical ideal in the sphere of sexual behavior. In the course of security investigations, officials of the State Department have been asked about their attitude toward Franklin D. Roosevelt, the New Deal, and the recognition of the Communist government of China. Investigators have also shown an almost obsessive curiosity about the pre- and extramarital sexual activities of public officials.

It stands to reason that this ideal of the "good" American is at odds in one or the other respect with the actual behavior of most men who have ever lived and are now living. Hardly an American statesman from Franklin and Washington to Dulles and Eisenhower has, and could have, lived up to it, and most of them would fail the test on multiple grounds. And it is not by accident that men of undoubted loyalty and merit have been dismissed from the Foreign Service as security risks under Executive Order 10450. For that executive order makes virtually everybody a security risk and for two reasons. First of all, as already pointed out, few men will correspond in every respect to the ideal picture of the "good" American which is implicit in Executive Order 10450 and its application (and it may be doubted that those who do make desirable public servants). More importantly, few men will be so transparently good, approaching saintliness, that it can be said of them that their employment is "clearly consistent with the interests of the national security," which is the general standard repeated again and again by the executive order.

I am myself indifferent honest; but yet I could accuse me of such things, that it were better my mother had not borne me: I am very proud, revengeful, ambitious; with more offenses at my beck than I have thoughts to put them in, imagination to give them shape, or time to act them in. What should such fellows as I do crawling between earth and heaven? We are arrant knaves all; believe none of us.

These words of Hamlet all men can say of themselves and of each other. Even the best man's goodness is darkened at least by the shadow of a doubt, and thus he is a security risk within the meaning of Executive Order 10450.

The security regulations, as applied to the Department of State, operated essentially through three instrumentalities: security investigations, police supervision, and political pressure.

That a person be subjected to a security check before he is employed in a sensitive position by the Department of State is an obvious necessity. Yet in the eyes of the Department of State a man's loyalty is never settled once and for all (as actually it cannot be, in view of what we have said above). Since no man can ever be fully trusted, all men are forever suspect on grounds of security and, hence, are at all times subject to renewed security investigations. The case of Mr. John Paton Davies, Jr., who underwent nine security investigations, has gained nationwide attention; yet his case is but an extreme example of a fairly typical situation. Hundreds of officials of the Department of State have been subjected to multiple security investigations by different agencies, for different purposes, and on different grounds. A patently scurrilous denunciation can call forth a new security investigation, proceeding as though nothing at all were known of the individual's record as a private citizen and public official.

This multiplication of security investigations is institutionalized by the requirement that the personnel file of every official of the Department of State in whose personnel status a change, such as a new assignment or promotion, is contemplated be checked for security. In the course of such a check any old incident which has been satisfactorily explained in preceding security investigations can jeopardize the official's career and destroy his reputation. An official who has been suggested for a promotion by virtue of his professional competence (of which compliance with security regulations is obviously a part) may be suspended for months as a security risk because ten years ago, on the instigation of the government, he joined an organization infiltrated by Communists in order to combat their influence. Never mind that this incident was a matter of record from the very beginning, that it has been explained to the satisfaction of all concerned time and again; now it must be explained again and with it the whole life of the official, private and public, from the day of his birth to this, and it is he who must prove that the continuation of his employment is "clearly consistent with the interests of the national security," by collecting affidavits from public and private acquaintances testifying that they found nothing wrong with him. By requiring the official to disprove the suspicion of being a security risk, it eliminates for all practical purposes from the evidence to be weighed the positive record of his accomplishments. A man may have given outstanding service over a long period of time in the most sensitive positions. Let him have had dinner with somebody who is suspected of having once been a Communist, and he will be unable to prove that he is not a security risk.

The assumption that all men are really security risks and that this defect, shared by all men, can somehow be neutralized, if not eliminated, through the proper social arrangements cannot but give rise to a psychology which is indistinguishable from that of the police state. For given these two assumptions, eternal vigilance becomes the price of security. Treat everybody as though he were a traitor, and you will be safe from treason.

The Department of State acted upon these assumptions and established a system of supervision which in good part is supposed to operate covertly but of which everybody within the Department is—jokingly or indignantly—aware. The Bureau of Security of the Department of State employs, of course, a staff whose personnel and functions are officially known. Aside from this official staff, it employs a network of agents (both categories estimated to total more than a thousand) whose identity and functions are not supposed to be known. Individuals have been placed in the different functional and geographic units of the Department of State for the ostensible purpose of performing the substantive functions of these units, yet for the actual purpose of supervising and reporting on their colleagues. Delegations to international conferences are accompanied by individuals who perform similar functions, traditionally associated with a GPU or Gestapo. The Secretary of State himself has invested this system with the authority of his office by imposing, through Department Circular 95 of April 15, 1954, upon all officials of his Department the duty to be informers.

I am aware that no agency of the government can improve, or even maintain, its level of effectiveness unless it is receiving a stream of new ideas and constructive criticisms. I hope that the inspection operation will be the focal reception point of that stream. I have told Mr. McLeod that in his capacity as administrator of the inspection operation he should be available at any time to receive personally from any of our people the benefit of their thinking on improving operations and procedures or on other problems, official and personal.

In brief, I regard the internal inspection operation of the Department as one of its most important concerns. Its success will depend upon the cooperation and aid received generally from employees of the Department.

There have been persistent rumors, in the nature of things hard to verify, of tapped telephones, hidden microphones, steamed-open letters, and special rooms and devices for the grilling of suspects. But regardless of whether or not there is any evidence to support these rumors, the very fact that they could be spread and widely believed reveals a spirit vastly different from that which is supposed to prevail in an agency of a democratic government.

This emphasis upon the vital importance of investigation and supervision for purposes of security, institutionalized in a special bureau within the Department of State, inevitably led to a shift—lasting through most of Mr. Eisenhower's first term—of effective control over the operations of the Department from the Secretary and Undersecretary of State and the heads of the functional and geographic units to the Bureau of Security. This shift has occurred in all modern totalitarian states and has given rise to a phenomenon which has been aptly called the "dual state." It is characteristic of the "dual state" that in it, as a matter of law, the power of making decisions remains with the authorities charged by law with making them while, as a matter of fact, by virtue of their power over life and death, the agents of the secret police—co-ordinated to, but independent from, the official makers of decision—at the very least exert an effective veto over the decisions. Once the secret police has established itself firmly in an agency of the government, it will have less and less need for intervening drastically in day-by-day operations; for its omnipresence and reputed omnipotence will generally be sufficient for the constituted authorities to avoid any action which might displease the secret police.

The Bureau of Security in the Department of State, as originally constituted, was combined with, and hence had direct control over, four areas of operation: security, consular affairs, personnel, and inspection of United States missions abroad. While the administrator of the Bureau of Security has been deprived of direct responsibility for the two latter functions, it is generally believed that the first incumbent of the office retained effective control over personnel because the office of personnel continued to be administered in the spirit of, and in close co-operation with, the Bureau of Security. For the powers of the Bureau of Security by themselves are all-pervading in so far as the hiring, assignment, promotion, and firing of personnel are concerned.

The powers which the Bureau of Security assumed over the operations of the Department of State flowed only in part from its police functions as such. As in fully developed totalitarian systems the power of the secret police is in good measure the reflection of the political power of its head, a Himmler or a Beria, so did the power of the Bureau of Security over the Department of State reflect in good measure the political power of those whose political philosophy its leading officials represented, to whom they owed their positions and their primary loyalties as well. Those were not the President of the United States or the Secretary of State but certain members of Congress and, more particularly, of the Senate. The police system which was established in the Department of State was their secret police in a more profound sense than it was the secret police of the executive branch. It was through it that these members of Congress were kept informed about the—presumably secret—operations of the Department of State, and it was through it that they exerted a direct or indirect influence upon its operations. To an extent which changes with the ebbs and tides of political fortune, it was these members of Congress, and not the President or the Secretary of State, who determined the operations of the Department of State and its affiliated agencies.

The most spectacular instance of this extra-constitutional influence to have come to light thus far is provided by the International Information Administration. The report which the chief consultant to its director has published[2] leaves no doubt but that, at least from February through July, 1953, Senator McCarthy and his friends in Congress had taken over the functions which, according to the Constitution, the President and the Secretary of State are supposed to perform. These members of Congress determined the policies of the International Information Administration as concerns both personnel and substance. It was to them that the top officials of the agency reported; it was their approval which they had to seek; and it was their orders which they were supposed to execute. And when they finally incurred the displeasure of their congressional masters, they had to resign.

For these members of Congress, all men were suspect as traitors, but diplomats in particular were so. For they deviate in certain obvious respects from the ideal type of the "normal" good American: they know foreign languages, spend much of their lives abroad, have many contacts with foreigners, concern themselves professionally

---

[2] Martin Merson, *The Private Diary of a Public Servant* (New York: Macmillan Co., 1955).

with foreign countries—and they tend to be intellectuals, committing their brains rather than their passions to the conduct of foreign policy. Thus it is not by accident that an enterprise which started out to protect the integrity and secrecy of American foreign policy transformed itself, as we have seen, in an undertaking to assure conformity and ended in an attempt to make the United States safe from foreign policy as such. What began as a technical operation to improve the protection of the United States against subversion and espionage matured into an onslaught—"know-nothing" in its philosophy and isolationist in its implicit purpose—against the very existence of an active American foreign policy.

Obviously, to preserve the integrity and secrecy of foreign policy is only one among many objectives to which the United States is committed. A policy, however sound and successful in its own terms, must be evaluated in terms of the impact it has upon other national objectives, as important or even more important than its own. Such scrutiny is particularly required for a policy which is so unsound and unsuccessful as we believe the security policy of the Department of State to have been. What, then, has been the price in terms of equally or more important objectives we have had to pay for the security policy of the Department of State? That price is being paid primarily in three areas: the effectiveness of American foreign policy, the prestige of the United States abroad, and the security of the United States.

In the *New York Times* of January 17, 1954, five of the most distinguished older diplomatists of the United States, four of whom have been ambassadors and an equal number under or assistant secretaries of state, summarized the "sinister results" of the security policy of the Department of State in these words:

The conclusion has become inescapable, for instance, that a Foreign Service officer who reports on persons and events to the very best of his ability and who makes recommendations which at the time he conscientiously believes to be in the interest of the United States may subsequently find his loyalty and integrity challenged and may even be forced out of the service and discredited forever as a private citizen. A premium therefore has been put upon reporting and upon recommendations which are ambiguously stated or so cautiously set forth as to be deceiving.

When any such tendency begins its insidious work it is not long before accuracy and initiative have been sacrificed to acceptability and conformity. The ultimate result is a threat to national security. In this connection the history of the Nazi and Fascist foreign services before the Second World War is pertinent.

The forces which are working for conformity from the outside are being reinforced by the present administrative set-up within the Department of State which subordinates normal personnel administration to considerations of security.

It is obvious, of course, that candidates for the Foreign Service should be carefully investigated before appointment and that their work should at all times be under the exacting scrutiny of their professional superiors. But when initial investigation attaches undue importance to such factors as even a temporary departure from conservative political and economic views, casual association with persons holding views not currently in fashion or subscription to a periodical labeled as "liberal"; when subsequent investigation is carried to the point of delaying a promotion list for a year and routine transfers from one post to another; when investigations of individual officers must be kept up-to-date to within ninety days; when an easy path has been opened to even the anonymous informer; and when the results of these investigations are evaluated not by persons experienced in the Foreign Service or even acquainted at firsthand with conditions abroad, but by persons of quite different experience, it is relevant to inquire whether we are not laying the foundations of a Foreign Service competent to serve a totalitarian government rather than the government of the United States as we have heretofore known it.

Fear is playing an important part in American life at the present time. As a result the self-confidence, the confidence in others, the sense of fair play and the instinct to protect the rights of the nonconformist are—temporarily, it is to be hoped—in abeyance. But it would be tragic if this fear, expressing itself in an exaggerated emphasis on security, should lead us to cripple the Foreign Service, our first line of national defense, at the very time when its effectiveness is essential to our filling the place which history has assigned to us.

For an impartial professional observer, the conclusion is inevitable that more than a year after this letter was written the Department of State was hardly competent to serve any government, totalitarian or otherwise. Not only the morale but also the professional competence and capacity for teamwork of its members had drastically declined. The Department of State which the Eisenhower administration inherited was, to say the least, a useful instrument of foreign policy. Its obvious administrative weaknesses were compensated for by the intellectual ability, technical competence, and devotion of most of its top and middle layer officials. Many of these officials have either been dismissed or have voluntarily resigned. Of the officials of this type with whom the American High Commission in Germany was staffed in 1953, not a single one was left two years later. They could not have been replaced even under the best possible circumstances with a new team of equal competence and experience. For no nation is rich enough in diplomatic talent, demanding a rare combination of extraordinary qualities of mind and character, to be able to afford taking one team out of the game and replacing it with another one equally good. What is possible in football cannot be done in diplomacy.

The United States could not have afforded the loss of its ablest diplomatists even under the best of circumstances. Yet the circumstances under which the United States had to make good this loss were far from being the best. A system that makes security the overriding consideration gives a golden opportunity for advancement to the incompetent, the time server, and the informer, who has never uttered a wrong thought and who has never associated with the wrong person. A system that not only does not require professional competence but actually suspects it cannot help using standards of selection congenial to that point of view. But it goes without saying that those standards are incompatible with the standards by which diplomatists ought to be selected.

Not only has there been deterioration at the top and in the middle layers of the departmental hierarchy, but there has also been starvation at the bottom. A system characterized by repeated security investigations, police supervision, and political pressure has depleted the lower ranks of the Foreign Service. Many younger officials have been dismissed as security risks, and many more have resigned of their own volition. What is worse is that such a system must act as a deterrent upon both application for employment and employment itself. The number of graduates of our institutions of higher learning who in 1954 or 1955 chose to make the Foreign Service their career was small as compared with that of three or four years earlier. The few who applied then may have been the bravest and the most desperate, but they could hardly have been the best; and those who were able to pass the security test and were actually hired were not necessarily the best of them, and even many of them resigned soon in disgust.

This decline in the quality and quantity of the personnel of the Department of State was matched by the decline in the quality of its operations. The premonitions of the five diplomatists which we have quoted above were fully borne out by events. Objective analytical reporting, the prime function of diplomacy, fell to a low ebb in the Foreign Service. Diplomatic reports were no longer as regularly read by the officials at the respective geographic desks in Washington as they were in times past; for they contained frequently nothing more than digests of the newspapers of the countries concerned, which the official in Washington can and does read himself. Heads of missions refused to allow the transmission to Washington of reports painting a picture of the local situation at variance either with reports of other agencies or with the estimate of the situation prevailing in Washington.

This abdication of independent judgment is, of course, the result of the fear that deviation from the "official line" might jeopardize one's chances for advancement, if not one's very livelihood and reputation. Yet this fear is more than the subjective anticipation of an evil which is largely imaginary, as is much of the fear of being "controversial," so prevalent in academic life. That fear is, indeed, the fruit of bitter experience. Officials were dismissed for having reported facts that they were not supposed to report and for having advocated policies that they were not supposed to advocate; and officials were subjected to still another security investigation on the complaint of a foreign government which did not approve of the policies they advocated.

Under the impact of all these influences, the Department of State probably did not become more immune to subversion and treason than it was before. A case could even be made for the proposition that an official whom the "dual state" constantly subjects to the moral stress of having to reconcile his own professional judgments and moral principles with those of the organization in which he works may become particularly prone to laxity and failure of judgment in matters of security. In any event, the Department of State ceased to be the eyes, ears, and brains of the foreign policy of the United States. Its eyes became blind; its ears, deaf; and its brains, dull. Yet a foreign policy that makes itself incapable of knowing the facts with which it must deal and of understanding the problems it must solve can rely for success upon nothing but the vagaries of luck.

It must, however, be said that this dark picture is brightened by a few light spots. Through luck, personal connections, or the inefficiency of the security system, there remained in the Department of State a few officials who did not yield to the pressures which incessantly bore upon them. Forsaken from above, spied upon from below, surrounded by all manner of opportunists and worse, they risked their careers, their positions, and their honor in maintaining for themselves and in defending in their subordinates the traditional standards of intellectual integrity, professional competence, and devotion to duty. If and when out of the ruins of today a new foreign service will be built, worthy of the traditions and the mission of America, the nation will owe a great debt to these brave, able, and devoted men who defended in obscurity and against great odds the pitiful remnants of a fine tradition.

This disintegration of the Foreign Service of the United States is better known abroad than it is at home. The governments and the public of foreign countries have seen with amazement officials, of whose competence and loyalty they have had tangible evidence, investigated, dismissed, or forced to resign as security risks. Continuous contacts with our representatives abroad provide them with unmistakable evidence of the diminution of their professional competence. In consequence, the influence the United States should be able to exert by virtue of its material strength and of the mission it has assumed for the free world has drastically declined. The word of the United States is no longer listened to with respect. What is worse, the very image of the United States as the champion of justice and freedom against totalitarian oppression has been obscured. If the United States owed its position in the world to nothing but its material power, such foreign reactions would be of little consequence. In truth, however, the United States has been able to command the sympathies of millions of people abroad, not because it has more atomic bombs than the Soviet Union, but because it was founded upon, and has tried to live up to, certain principles of government to which those millions of people are also committed. Seeing the last best hope of the free world forsake these principles and even seemingly be proud of a security system that the London *Economist* has called a "vicious stupidity,"[3] many of our friends abroad began to doubt whether there is much to choose between East and West.

This loosening of the bonds of sympathy that unite America to its friends abroad raises a specter more ominous still: the loosening of the bonds of loyalty which tie the citizens of the United States to their own government. The United States was founded upon loyalty, not to a king or piece of territory, but to an ideal of political justice. We pledge allegiance to a flag which is a symbol of "liberty and justice for all." Loyalty which attaches to a man or a territory may not be affected by injustice perpetrated by that man or within that territory. A nation which was built on a common belief in certain principles of justice, whose citizens have voluntarily come together from all over the world to share in the practice of those principles, which owes its very existence to a revolt against injustice—such a nation stands and falls, as a nation, with its loyalty to those principles.

The loyalty of its citizens presupposes the loyalty of its government, not as a matter of verbalization but of policy, to those principles of justice. The government of such a nation cannot help committing injustices by sacrificing some of the freedom and interests of individuals to a higher good. The government of such a nation will be forgiven sporadic injustices not justified by the achievement of such a higher good. The government of such a nation will embark upon a deliberate policy of injustice only at the risk of weakening the very foundation of loyalty which supports its voluntary acceptance by its citizens.

A citizen, unjustly accused of disloyalty, condemned and ostracized, may well be tempted to conclude that if he is to be treated as disloyal he may as well act the part.[4] To the government's severance of the ties which unite government and citizen, he might want to respond in kind. The man whom his government has cast into the

---

[3] Jan. 8, 1955, p. 110.

[4] This psychological process is strikingly revealed in this statement by the leader of a juvenile gang, reported in the *New York Times* of March 25, 1958, p. 26: " 'That's the way it starts,' Vincent says, 'I've seen it happen many times. The police blame you for something you didn't do. You get a record. They send you away. So, then, the kid comes back and he says, "Well, I'm going to do something and get a record of my own. At least then if I'm sent up it will be for something I did myself." ' "

outer darkness may make common cause with the forces of darkness. The alienation of the government from the principles upon which it was founded and, in consequence, from some of its citizens may well have brought in its wake the alienation of some citizens from the government. Thus a policy which sought to protect the government from disloyalty may well have corrupted, by dint of its own corruption, if not the actions so at least the minds of some of the citizens upon whose loyal services the government could otherwise have counted. A policy intended to protect the country from treason is likely to have actually increased if not the actuality so at least the risk of treason.

Such, then, is the price we were paying for Executive Order 10450, as applied to the Department of State. It is a high price to pay. Paid for what? For nothing.

8 *The Subversion of Foreign Policy*

The destruction of the Foreign Service of the United States, in order to take the wind out of the sails of the domestic opposition, is paralleled by the paralysis and the distortion of the foreign policy of the United States. The first two years of Mr. Eisenhower's foreign policy provide a case study of the corrupting effects that considerations of domestic politics can exert upon the conduct of foreign policy. An attempt to assess this period of American foreign policy must overcome three formidable obstacles. One, the nature of the standards of evaluation, is inherent in the nature of all foreign policy; the second, the conduct of foreign policy in view of popular preferences, is peculiar to democratic foreign policy; the third, the utter contrast between the presentation and the substance of foreign policy, seems to be inherent in the nature of Mr. Eisenhower's foreign policy.

What is the standard by which we judge the quality of foreign policy? Is it success? If so, then inevitably the incompetent heir will reap the fruits of his wise predecessor's labors and take credit for the results of what was actually somebody else's achievement. Conversely, the great statesman to whom it has fallen to dispose of the bankrupt estate of the preceding government must take the blame for a failure which is not his own. The verdicts of popular history are indeed permeated with misjudgments of this kind.

Yet, how do we determine success and failure in foreign policy? Surveying the centuries, history is able to assess the contribution of a particular move at a particular time to the ultimate success or failure of a nation's foreign policy. The contemporary observer is handicapped by his ignorance of the consequences of contemporary policies. Judged by success alone, Hitler's foreign policy, if viewed in the perspective of 1938–40, made Bismarck's look like a mere preparation for greater things to come. But how did it look but five years later? Who did not think in 1929 that the Kellogg-Briand Pact was a great success, and who did not think so of the Teheran, Yalta,

From the *Year Book of World Affairs,* 1955.

and Potsdam agreements at the time of their conclusion? But who would think so now?

However, we do not object to the Kellogg-Briand Pact and the wartime agreements with the Soviet Union solely or even primarily for their lack of success. What we are critical of is the cause of their failure, that is, the wrong way of thinking about foreign policy which made the framers of these agreements expect success when failure could have been avoided only by fortuitous circumstances lying beyond the ken of their intentions and control. What makes foreign policy deserving of praise or blame is, then, not success or failure per se but a way of thinking about foreign policy which by virtue of its inherent qualities is likely to lead to success or failure. A foreign policy based upon correct thinking deserves to be called "good" even though it fails for reasons that have nothing to do with the quality of thought that went into it, and a foreign policy derived from wrong thinking must be called "bad" even though it succeeds in spite of the deficiences of the reasoning from which it stems.

What do we mean when we speak of correct thinking and the quality of reasoning on matters of foreign policy? We assume, as pointed out elsewhere in greater detail,[1] that there exists an objective rational standard by which the quality of political action can be judged. This assumption derives from the rational nature of man which the actor on the political scene cannot help bringing to bear upon his action to a greater or lesser degree. It is the degree of conformity between political action and rational requirements which determines the quality of the action. The active participant in politics as well as the detached observer of the political scene cannot but proceed on this assumption. For they would not be able to judge political action at all, beyond the crudest statements about success or failure, if they did not carry in their minds a picture of what a certain political action ought to have been. Actors and observers alike cannot help sharing in the assumption of the rationality of this picture; for otherwise they would have no common ground for correlating each other's thoughts and actions.

It is no argument to say that the rational requirements of foreign policy are difficult to ascertain and ambiguous in nature and that

[1] *Politics among Nations* (2d ed.; New York: Alfred A. Knopf, 1954), pp. 7–8.

their application to concrete problems is even more so. The fact remains that the assumption of the possibility of judging foreign policy rationally, in terms of the quality of reasoning underlying it, is the precondition for both the intellectual comprehension of foreign policy and for its objective evaluation.

This task of evaluation is even more complicated when foreign policy is carried on under the conditions of democratic control. Two factors make it so. First of all, a democratically conducted foreign policy, as pointed out in chapter 17, is of necessity a compromise between the rational requirements of good foreign policy and the emotional preferences of public opinion. If one wanted to overstate the case, one might say that a democratically conducted foreign policy is of necessity bad foreign policy. In any case, a foreign policy carried on under democratic control must fall short of the rational requirements of good foreign policy; for it must satisfy emotional preferences whose satisfaction is incompatible with meeting those requirements. It would, therefore, be unjust to judge a democratic foreign policy exclusively by its compliance with these requirements; such judgment must be qualified by the need, greater or lesser as the case may be but always present, to compromise with the emotional preferences of public opinion.

The ultimate judgment on a democratic foreign policy will then be composed of two specific judgments: one establishing the degree to which a foreign policy meets the rational requirements of good foreign policy, and the other assessing the need for compromise with public opinion and the degree to which foreign policy has met that need. Did it yield not enough and thus destroy the foundation of public opinion on which democratic foreign policy must operate? Or did it yield too much, deviating from rational requirements to such an extent as to condemn foreign policy to failure? It is answers to questions such as these which will determine the ultimate verdict. It is with them that we are here concerned.

The other factor complicating the evaluation of democratic foreign policy results from the one just discussed. Not only must democratic foreign policy make concessions to public opinion, but it must also present its foreign policy in terms acceptable to public opinion. That is to say, it must make it appear as though it responds to the emotional preferences of public opinion to a greater extent than it actually does. It must cover those of its rational elements that are least likely to find favor with public opinion with a veil of emotional pronouncements which are intended to conceal its true nature from the public eye. It is for the objective observer to distinguish between public pronouncements on foreign policy that reveal and those that conceal the true nature of the foreign policy actually pursued, by correlating pronouncement with action.

This is a very difficult task at best. It has been made even more difficult by the way United States foreign policy has been traditionally conducted and the particular way the Eisenhower administration has been conducting its foreign policy. The processes by which decisions on foreign policy are arrived at in the United States are chaotic in the extreme. The writer has endeavored elsewhere to analyze the constitutional and political factors that make them so.[2] It is a further peculiarity of the American system that this business of institutionalized chaos is carried on on the public stage. Given the importance of public opinion for the determination of foreign policy, this can hardly be otherwise; for that course of action which can mobilize public opinion in its support has gained a great advantage in the struggle for the ultimate determination of United States foreign policy. Thus it is possible, and has almost become customary, that on any pending question of foreign policy any member of the executive or legislative branches of the government, be it the Vice-President, the Secretary of State, the Chairman of the Joint Chiefs of Staff, the party leaders in Congress, or a ranking member of the foreign affairs committee of either house formulates his own foreign policy in public speech. Thus on United States over-all relations with the Soviet bloc as well as on more specific questions, such as American policies toward Communist China and the problems raised for American policy by the Indochina War, prominent members of the Eisenhower administration and of the Republican party in Congress have publicly advocated policies that did not become the policies of the United States. It was only from subsequent action, taken upon the responsibility of the President, that it was possible to determine in retrospect what the policy of the United States actually had been.

[2] "The Conduct of Foreign Policy," in S. D. Bailey (ed.), *Aspects of American Government* (London: Hansard Society, 1950), pp. 99 ff.

To complicate matters still further, action taken on the responsibility of the President has sometimes belied the President's own words. For it is a peculiarity of the Eisenhower administration that it is the first democratic government whose relations with the public imitate on a large and institutionalized scale the techniques of public relations experts and commercial advertising. This is so with regard to form and content. Mr. Robert Montgomery, a movie actor, has the official title of White House adviser on radio and television. The President on television conveys the impression that he smiles and raises his voice or hand not an impulse of his own but rather on somebody else's cue. The first cabinet meeting ever televised, in which the Secretary of State reported on the London Conference of 1954, conveyed the impression of a performance staged by experts and executed by amateurs. In the words of Mr. Alistair Cooke:

> The whole show had a relaxed, closed-door air, almost like a Cabinet meeting. In the lead part . . . Mr. Dulles gave a naturalistic performance of great ease and articulateness. Mr. Henry Cabot Lodge made the most of a single-sentence tribute to the President for his peaceful atomic energy proposals. Cast as the unsleeping watchdog of the people's purse, Mr. Secretary of the Treasury Humphrey expressed with moving verisimilitude his concern that the Paris Agreement should not cost the American taxpayer one extra nickel. Mrs. Hobby conveyed an intelligent anxiety over the Saar.
>
> Only Secretary of Agriculture Ezra Benson, an artless man from the West, had to be prodded into his line by Mr. Dulles, who suggested after an anxious pause that some of them might now be wondering "how the Soviet Union is taking this." Mr. Benson was indeed wondering just that, and made an alert retrieve. It was the only missed cue in an otherwise flawless performance, surely an enviable record for any amateur dramatic company.[3]

The ascendancy of the public relations expert over the responsible political leader has also been marked in the substance of what the leaders of the Eisenhower administration have told the people about the foreign policy they are pursuing. Here, too, the methods of salesmanship have largely replaced the principles of responsible democratic leadership, and, in consequence, it has become a principle of government to impress the public favorably at any price, even that of truth, rather than to inform it. Spectacular announcements have

[3] *Manchester Guardian Weekly,* Oct. 28, 1954, p. 2.

been made carrying the impression of momentous decisions in foreign policy which turned out to be meaningless in view of the actual policies pursued. Five major announcements of this kind, creating a great deal of public comment and controversy but no policies even faintly reflecting them, were made during the first two years of the Eisenhower administration: liberation, the unleashing of Chiang Kai-shek, agonizing reappraisal, the "new look," and intervention in Indochina.

During the election campaign of 1952 and during the first months of its tenure of office, the spokesmen for the Eisenhower administration announced that the old policy of containment was to be replaced by a policy of liberation. Yet as the London *Economist* put it as early as August 30, 1952, "Unhappily 'liberation' applied to Eastern Europe—and Asia—means either the risk of war or it means nothing . . . . 'Liberation' entails no risk of war only when it means nothing." Yet the Eisenhower administration has shied away from the risk of war at least as much as did its predecessor. And when the East German revolt in June, 1953, and the Hungarian revolution of October, 1956, coming closer to success than anybody had dared to expect, put the policy of liberation to the test of actual performance, it became obvious that in actuality the policy of liberation was indistinguishable from the policy of containment.

In his State of the Union message of February 2, 1953, President Eisenhower declared, "In June, 1950, following the aggressive attack on the Republic of Korea, the United States Seventh Fleet was instructed both to prevent attack upon Formosa and also to insure that Formosa should not be used as a base of operations against the Chinese Communist mainland." In view of the Chinese intervention in the Korean War, the President declared that he was "issuing instructions that the Seventh Fleet no longer be employed to shield Communist China." This announcement implied a fundamental change in the Far Eastern policies of the United States from the preservation of the status quo to the active attempt to restore Chiang Kai-shek's rule on the Asiatic mainland. In actuality, no such change occurred. Quite to the contrary, the Eisenhower administration seems to have been at least as anxious as its predecessor to limit the military activities of Chiang Kai-shek to strictly defensive measures. By making this limitation part of agreements with Chiang Kai-shek negotiated at the end of 1954, the Eisenhower administration went even beyond the unilateral declaration of policy contained in President Truman's instructions to the Seventh Fleet of June, 1950.

On December 14, 1953, Secretary of State Dulles declared at the meeting of the North Atlantic Council, "If, however, the European Defense Community should not become effective, if France and Germany remain apart, so that they would again be potential enemies, then indeed there would be grave doubt whether Continental Europe could be made a place of safety. That would compel an agonizing reappraisal of basic United States policy."[4] This statement implied the threat that in certain contingencies the United States might lose its interest in the military defense of Europe and leave it to its fate. This threat called forth much comment and little anxiety in Europe and elsewhere. As an incentive for France to ratify the European Defense Community, it was ineffective. For in order to take this threat seriously one would have had to assume that the United States had committed itself to the defense of western Europe, not because it deemed its own defense dependent upon it, but because it happened to approve of the policies of certain European nations. Few observers were, and no responsible statesman was, willing to make so fantastic an assumption.

However, the most far-reaching and most widely commented upon announcement of this kind was the Secretary of State's speech of January 12, 1954, proclaiming the "new look" in American foreign policy as the result of "some basic policy decisions" which the President and the National Security Council had taken. Mr. Lester Pearson, then Canadian secretary of state for external affairs, thought as late as March 15, 1954, that this speech "may turn out to be one of the most important of our times." The present writer, on March 29, 1954, published an article in the *New Republic* interpreting and evaluating this speech as if it meant what it said. Yet Mr. Walter Lippmann could say on March 18 that "The official explanations of the new look have become so voluminous that it is almost a career in itself to keep up with them" and characterize it as "a case of excessive salesmanship," concluding that "there is no doubt that the words of the text convey the impression that something momentous and novel has been decided. But everything that has been said since then

[4] *New York Times,* Dec. 15, 1953.

by the Chiefs of Staff, notably by Admiral Carney, and no less so by Mr. Dulles himself, make it plain that there has been no radical change in our strategic policy."

On the same day, the *Manchester Guardian* summed it all up by saying, "The 'new look' in American military strategy is mainly old merchandise in a new package. There is really nothing new in relying on 'massive mobile retaliatory power' as the principal safeguard of peace—nothing new, that is, except the sales campaign by which the Administration is trying to persuade the American people that some small changes make the strategy of 1954 fundamentally sounder than the strategy of 1953." On March 19, the Senate Committee on Foreign Relations was the scene of the following dialogue between Senator Mansfield and Mr. Dulles, who for all practical purposes buried the "new look" under the cover of military secrecy:

> SENATOR MANSFIELD: Do you consider this new policy a new policy?
> SECRETARY DULLES: It certainly has new aspects.
> SENATOR MANSFIELD: What are they?
> SECRETARY DULLES: Well, I am sorry I cannot go into that here. All I can say to you, and you will have to take it on faith, is that a series of new decisions have been taken by the National Security Council and many have been involved, close, and difficult decisions, but there is today on the record a series of decisions which are largely derived from this basic philosophy which were not there a year and a half ago.

While the "new look" was the most spectacular and far-reaching of these announcements, the official declarations concerning the Indochina War were politically the most harmful; for these dealt not with general principles of United States policy but with a concrete situation which required action here and now. On March 25, 1954, the President declared at his news conference that the defense of Indochina was of "transcendent importance." On March 29, the Secretary of State announced: "Under the conditions of today, the imposition on South-East Asia of the political system of Communist Russia and its Chinese Communist ally, by whatever means, would be a grave threat to the whole free community. The United States feels that that possibility should not be passively accepted, but should be met by united action. This might have serious risks, but these risks are far less than would face us a few years from now if we dare not be resolute today." The President and the Secretary of State referred to Indochina as the cork in the bottle of Southeast Asia and as the first in a row of dominoes whose fall would necessarily cause the downfall of the others. Yet no action of any kind reflected even faintly the conception of policy which these words seemed to convey. It was, in the words of the *Economist* of August 21, 1954, this "spectacle of vociferous inaction" which led to "the worst diplomatic disaster in recent American history."

This "foreign policy by hoax" has served to confuse the American people. It has raised doubts in the minds of many about the reliability of public pronouncements on anything and has thus led to the beginnings of a crisis of confidence which endangers democratic government itself. It has raised similar doubts in the minds of friends and enemies alike. The allies of the United States have been fearful lest political action might conform to official utterance. The enemies of the United States must similarly doubt the reliability of official announcements of policy, and they might even doubt it on the wrong occasion when the peace of the world may well depend upon whether or not a warning by the government of the United States is to be believed. The government of a great nation may, or even must, bluff from time to time; but it can afford to bluff only within the framework of a consistent policy understood by all. However, when it erects bluff into a principle of foreign policy, it risks that it would not be believed even if it should. While the spokesmen for the Eisenhower administration have benefited from this "foreign policy by hoax" in that they were able to pose for a fleeting moment as the initiators of new and bold policies, their prestige at home and abroad has suffered in the long run, as has the foreign policy of the United States.

This conduct of foreign policy for the apparent primary purpose of gaining popularity at home results from a misunderstanding of the fundamental relations which must exist between democratic government and public opinion. It also results from a misunderstanding of the conditions which the constitutional and political system of the United States imposes upon these relationships. This misunderstanding the Eisenhower administration has inherited from its predecessor, but it has immensely aggravated it. That aggravation has created a constitutional and political crisis of the first order, which is no less real for being in good measure hidden from the public view by the personal prestige of the President.

The Eisenhower administration assumes correctly that democratic government must be responsive to public opinion, but it errs grievously in the manner in which it tries to bring that response about. Regarding public opinion as the ultimate arbiter of foreign policy, it tries first to ascertain what the preferences of public opinion are and then to comply with them. In the process of bringing its foreign policy into harmony with public opinion, it assumes—and there lies its error—that public opinion with regard to a certain foreign policy pre-exists that foreign policy itself, somewhat in the manner in which a rule of law pre-exists the action to be judged by it. In truth, public opinion is not a static thing to be ascertained and quantified by polls as legal precedents are by the science of law and as the data of nature are by the natural sciences. Rather it is a dynamic thing to be created and continuously re-created by that selfsame political leadership which also creates the foreign policy to be supported by public opinion.

If the executive branch cannot obtain the support of public opinion for a certain policy it would like to pursue, it is not because public opinion—"naturally," as it were—is opposed to this particular foreign policy but because the political leadership of the executive branch has not been effective and has been replaced by political leadership hostile to this foreign policy. In other words, the contest is really not between the foreign policy of the executive branch and public opinion but between the former and other political forces propounding a different foreign policy. The executive branch, by surrendering passively its own initiative to the verdict of public opinion, in truth surrenders to the political opposition which has taken hold of public opinion. In consequence, the executive branch condemns itself to executing the foreign policy of its opponents, which it cannot help doing but half-heartedly and ineffectually; for, knowing better than the opposition and, furthermore, bearing responsibility for the consequences of its acts, whatever it does in order to satisfy the opposition always falls short of the standards which the opposition has erected and the executive branch has accepted as its own. In consequence, the foreign policy of the executive branch will always stand condemned in the eyes of public opinion as having sought and achieved less than public opinion had a right to expect in view of the standards which the executive branch professes as its own.

Of this vicious circle in which the executive branch is caught because it misunderstands the nature of public opinion and, in consequence, surrenders initiative in foreign policy to the opposition, the China policy of the Eisenhower administration is the classic example. There can be no doubt that a majority of the leading officials who advised Mr. Eisenhower on foreign policy during the first years of his tenure of office were opposed to the policies which the President had been pursuing in the Far East. That majority was composed of two groups. By far the larger of these groups wanted to advance toward a more aggressive position, even at the risk of a limited war with Communist China; by far the smaller one would have liked to retreat into less exposed positions. The actual policy of the United States was able to maintain an intermediate position between those two extremes, which followed the line of least resistance by trying neither to advance nor to retreat but to maintain the status quo.

Yet a rational examination of the forces opposing each other in the Far East and their probable dynamics cannot but lead to the conclusion that a policy of the status quo was not likely to be tenable in the long run. Both the United States and Communist China would have to go forward or backward, but they were not likely to remain indefinitely where they were then. Why, then, was the policy of the United States based upon an assumption that cannot be supported by rational argument? The answer is to be found in the surrender, in reasoning if not in policy, to an opposition whose reasoning, contradictory in itself, does not provide the basis for a rational policy, but which has been able to mold public opinion by default of the executive branch.

Public opinion with regard to Communist China was dominated by two strong contradictory emotions: to make somehow good the defeat which the United States suffered through the defection of China to the Communist camp, and to do so without getting involved in a major war on the continent of Asia. The opposition presented a program designed to meet these two emotional preferences. It promised the overthrow of the Communist regime of China and the restoration of Chiang Kai-shek's rule through aerial bombardment and a naval blockade, using Formosa as a springboard. Yet a careful reading of the minutes of the joint congressional committee investigating in 1951 the dismissal of General MacArthur can leave no doubt in the mind of the unbiased reader about the military and political emptiness of the Far Eastern policies of the opposition. For the opposition was not able to devise the policies the United States would have had to pursue short of all-out war if the Communist regime of China should have been able to withstand the limited measures of war proposed, if the conflict should not have been limited to China, and if the Chinese people should not have been waiting to be liberated from their Communist government. In one word, the program of the opposition served as an effective instrument for the demagogue to achieve an illusory reconciliation of policy with popular emotional preferences which cannot be reconciled in action. Hence, that program offered no basis for a rational policy which any responsible government would have been able to pursue.

Nevertheless, the Eisenhower administration, frightened like its predecessor by this specter of public opinion, at least appeared to have accepted the objectives and expectations of the opposition and thus allowed its own policies to be judged by the standards of the opposition. Judged by these standards, its policies could not help being found wanting. For, on the one hand, it was responsible enough not to embark upon military adventures; yet, on the other, it committed itself at least to the defense of Formosa, whose indispensability for the defense of the United States was accepted as a dogma by government and opposition alike. In consequence, the executive branch found itself continuously on the defensive, apologizing, as it were, for not living up to its own standards and feeling compelled from time to time to substitute for policy a momentous announcement or a grandiose gesture suggesting the imminence of forceful action. The executive branch had thus become the prisoner of the opposition. Too responsible to do what the opposition wanted it to do and prevented by its fear of public opinion from substituting a positive policy of its own for that of the opposition, the executive branch was reduced to having no positive policy at all, while trying to make it appear as though it were following in the footsteps of the opposition, however cautiously.

The Eisenhower administration was handicapped not only by its misunderstanding of public opinion, a misunderstanding it shares with its predecessor, but it added to that error one which is peculiarly its own: the misunderstanding of the nature of the "opposition" as it operates under the conditions of the American constitutional and political system. President Eisenhower's thinking on this matter was dominated by two basic assumptions: that of the two-party system in which the President's party supports the executive branch while the other party opposes it, and the assumption of the equality, in separation, of the executive and the legislative branch with regard to the conduct of foreign policy. Both assumptions are completely at odds with the constitutional principles and political practices of the American government. It can safely be said that diametrically opposite assumptions come closer to reflecting the actual facts of American political life.

On any controversial issue of United States foreign policy no Republican President can count upon the support of all members of his party. A Republican President, pursuing a rational foreign policy in a responsible manner, cannot help having at least a third of the Republican party in Congress against him, and on many a crucial issue he cannot count upon the support of even a bare majority. This seeming paradox is the result not of accident but of the political revolution which has transformed the American political scene in the last twenty-five years.

The general political and social outlook and the specific policies which this revolution has pushed to the fore are supported by a solid majority of the people but not by a majority of the Republican party in Congress. It follows that a Republican President, to be elected and to be re-elected, must identify himself with this outlook and these policies supported by the majority of the people. Yet he will have the support of his own party without major defections only between his nomination as a presidential candidate and his election, but neither before nor after. For the revolution which has transformed the political life of the United States has split the Republican party right down the middle. Its left wing has accepted, at least as inevitable, the results of that revolution, while its right wing lives in a prerevolutionary age, pursuing prerevolutionary policies with the fanaticism and irresponsibility of desperation.

The core of the opposition to a Republican President's foreign policies lies here, and it is against that opposition that the President must make his foreign policies prevail. A Republican President who thinks and operates in terms of party discipline and looks at the Republican party as his own and the Democratic party as the opposition confounds the American political system with the British and completely misreads the lines which divide both Congress and the people with regard to foreign policy. When it comes to foreign policy a Republican President has no party of his own to rely on, but must rely upon a bloc composed, at best, of the main bulk of the Democratic and a tenuous majority of the Republican party and, at worst, of a majority of the Democratic and a minority of the Republican party.

A Republican President who, like Mr. Eisenhower, conducts foreign policy with a view to maintaining the unity of his own party can do so only at the price of his own paralysis or of his own surrender. For political compromise is possible among groups that have certain basic assumptions in common and are at one in the desire to reconcile their formulation in a particular instance and to adjust their application for practical purposes. However, there can be no compromise with a group that denies the very assumptions of the foreign policy which the United States has pursued in the last decade and a half and regards the very principles of that foreign policy as an intellectual and moral aberration, if not close or tantamount to treason.

Misunderstanding what "opposition" means in American political life, the Eisenhower administration continuously and vainly tried to appease its real opposition which is within the Republican party, and it at the same time blessed, if not actively participated in, the attempts of that very opposition to stigmatize as the perpetrators and condoners of treason that very group within Congress and within the country which in terms of numbers and conviction provides the most solid support for the foreign policies the Eisenhower administration would have liked to pursue. This misunderstanding was symbolized in the paradoxical position of Senator Knowland who, as majority and minority leader in the Senate, had the official function to rally his party to the support of the President's foreign policies and who by conviction was the most outspoken critic of them. Even the most dexterous of politicians cannot at the same time be the chief spokesman for the executive branch and the leader of the opposition.

As the President has misjudged the meaning of "opposition" within the American political system, so has he misunderstood the relation the Constitution establishes between the President and Congress with regard to the conduct of foreign policy. Here again, the President has thought in terms of peaceful co-operation, while conflict is foreordained in the nature of things. The Constitution nowhere assigns the ultimate responsibility for the conduct of foreign policy to a particular office. It assigns certain functions to the President, others to Congress, and others still to the President and the Senate to be discharged in co-operation. Apart from these specific grants, the Constitution limits itself to an over-all distribution of powers between the President and Congress by vesting in the former the executive power and making him commander-in-chief of the armed forces and by vesting all legislative powers and the power of appropriations in Congress.

This silence of the Constitution as to where the ultimate responsibility for the conduct of American foreign policy rests is, in the words of Professor Corwin, "an invitation to struggle for the privilege of directing American foreign policy." This invitation has been accepted by all Presidents from Washington to Truman; for it could have been declined only at the price of surrendering the powers of the Presidency to a Congress which, in the nature of things, could not have discharged them. President Eisenhower was in large measure willing to pay that price, without, however, buying the peace with Congress he sought. Quite to the contrary, each surrender of executive powers to Congress called forth congressional demands for more, and, when the President retreated, he did not retreat into a prepared position from which to fight back but simply yielded to congressional pressure, waiting for renewed pressure to push him farther back. He resisted those pressures only when the issue of peace or war was directly at stake, not realizing that paralysis or surrender on other issues greatly complicated his task to defend his position against the advocates of war within his own administration and party.

It is at this point that the problem of the "opposition," discussed before, and the problem of the relations between the President and Congress merge. For when it is said that the President surrendered some of the prerogatives of his office in the conduct of foreign policy to Congress, the issue is oversimplified. It is not Congress as such, acting as a collective body by majority rule, which took over functions which by tradition and logic are the President's. It is to the opposition within his own party that the President surrendered them. While the more spectacular raids of the congressional opposition upon the executive preserve abated from 1955 onward, the impact which the opposition made upon both the substantive foreign policies and the personnel of the Eisenhower administration has been lasting and destructive of those very policies.

It stands to reason that a foreign policy which must be carried on under such conditions of domestic politics can leave little room for the initiative of even the greatest of statesmen. One might pause for a moment and imagine Sir Winston Churchill in his policies toward Egypt endeavoring to satisfy not only the military and political interests of Great Britain and the Egyptian aspirations for the evacuation of the Suez Canal Zone but also the opposition within his own party to that evacuation. Confronted with the choice between the national interest of Great Britain and considerations of domestic politics, he did not hesitate to choose the former. Yet the Eisenhower administration, confronted with similar choices, short of the ultimate choice between peace and war, invariably tended to choose the latter. In this it went far beyond those concessions which the requirements of democratic control and the peculiarities of the American constitutional and political system make inevitable.

Yet it is a tribute to President Eisenhower's innate good sense and a manifestation of the narrow limits within which objective circumstances confine initiative in foreign policy that the Eisenhower administration was by and large able, during the first years of its tenure of office, to continue the foreign policies of its predecessor, preserving its strong points, perpetuating and aggravating its weaknesses. It suffered its severest defeat on the plane of the imponderables of moral leadership and political prestige. And their drastic decline during the first two years of the Eisenhower administration can be directly traced to the ascendancy, during that very same period, of a kind of domestic politics that is incompatible not only with good foreign policy but with democratic government itself.

PART II

The Impasse
of American
Foreign Policy

9 *A Reassessment of United States Foreign Policy*

Of all the great issues which you are discussing, none is greater and more fraught with possibilities for good and evil than the issue of the foreign policy of the United States. The foreign policy of the United States will in good measure determine not only the future of the United States but the future of civilization itself. The great issue which confronts American foreign policy today can be summarized in an oversimplified form by saying that the United States is forced today to pursue its perennial interest in the world under radically changed conditions without being able to adapt its policies completely and with complete success to those new conditions.

The United States from the beginning of its history has had two great interests in foreign policy. You may even say one great interest of which the second one is a mere auxiliary. The United States from the very beginning pursued a policy seeking to maintain at first its security and very soon its predominance in the Western Hemisphere. The policies of Washington, recommended primarily by Hamilton, served the purpose of making the new nation secure, surrounded as it was by the colonies of European powers. Once that safety was secured and the United States had become the predominant nation in the Western Hemisphere, it then became the purpose of the United States to maintain that paramountcy among the nations of the Americas. The early American statesmen realized very soon that the interests of the United States could not be challenged by any ·American nation or combination of nations. No nation or possible combination of nations within the Western Hemisphere was strong enough to challenge the power of the United States. A threat to the safety of the United States could only come from outside the Western Hemisphere. If a European

Lecture given in the Great Issues Course at Dartmouth College, February 10, 1958.

nation would make common cause with an American nation, using the latter as an instrument of its own policies, then indeed the interests of the United States, in particular its security, might be in jeopardy.

Under what conditions was it likely that a non-American, which meant under the circumstances a European, nation would make common cause with a Latin American nation against the United States? It was only possible under one condition, that is, if the European balance of power ceased to operate. For as long as that balance of power operated, no European nation was safe enough in Europe to be able to dare starting on an adventure in the Western Hemisphere. Thus, from the very beginning, the main interest of the United States outside the Western Hemisphere, however subordinated to the American interest within it, was the maintenance, or if need be the restoration, of the European balance of power. Or, to put it in a different way, the United States, from the very beginning, was unalterably opposed to any one European nation trying to gain a hegemony over the European continent.

It is interesting to note how, for instance, Jefferson, in his verbal utterances generally not very sensitive to the balance of power and generally opposed to Great Britain, in his private letters during the Napoleonic Wars continually changed his position according to the fortunes of war. Whenever Napoleon seemed to have the upper hand he wished for the success of Great Britain; whenever Great Britain seemed to succeed against Napoleon he wished for the success of Napoleon. In other words, his opinions changed according to the changes of the balance of power.

The interventions of the United States in the two world wars can be well understood in terms of the same perennial interest. The United States entered the First World War in order to counter the hegemonic aspirations, nearing success, of Germany. It entered the Second World War, regardless of what the ideological justifications might have been, again in the conviction that the triumph of one nation in Europe, the conquest by one nation of all Europe, would put the very safety of the United States in the Western Hemisphere in jeopardy. The Cold War which we are waging against the Soviet Union today is another instance of the same general consideration. For again we are countering through our political and military policies the mortal threat to Europe emanating from the hegemonic aspirations of one nation, the Soviet Union. Again we are persuaded that the very safety of the United States in the Western Hemisphere would be in jeopardy if a nation of the power of the Soviet Union would conquer all of Europe, adding the resources of Europe to her own, and were free from all effective checks outside the Western Hemisphere.

From the turn of the century onward, a third interest joins the two I have mentioned. That is the interest in the maintenance or restoration of the balance of power in the Far East. The policy serving that interest initially went by the name of the "open door in China." While this policy in the beginning had a predominantly commercial connotation, it very soon took on a military and political connotation as well. For in the same way in which the United States was convinced that the hegemony of one nation over Europe would endanger the security of the United States, so was the United States convinced that the addition of the power potential of China, or a substantial part or all of it, to one of the great powers would again endanger the security of the United States. So the United States has been consistently opposed to the attempt of any great power to incorporate all of China into its sphere of domination, and it is a measure of the defeat which the interests of the United States have suffered in the communization of China that with it the balance of power in the Far East has drastically changed in favor of the Soviet Union. Those are in brief outline the perennial interests which the United States has been pursuing in part from the beginning of its history and in part from the turn of the century onward.

From the beginning of its history to the end of the Second World War, the United States was able to pursue those interests within the framework of the traditional state system. This system has since the beginning of the century been undergoing more and more drastic transformations so that today hardly anything is left of it. This system had its center in Europe. The main weights of the balance of power were located in Europe and whatever happened in Africa or in large parts of Asia or in the Western Hemisphere was a mere reflection of the struggles for power going on in Europe. The changes in sovereignty over the American colonies among Spain, Great Britain, and France, for instance, were a mere reflection of the relative standing of those powers in Europe. In other words, the political system was essentially a European political system.

This system has been transformed in two different respects. It has become a world system both qualitatively and quantitatively. Quantitatively, this development started at the turn of the century and made all nations of the world active participants in one great political system. Second, since the First World War the main weights of the system have shifted to an even greater extent into non-European spaces so that today the two great powers on earth are no longer European or no longer predominantly European in so far as one can consider the Soviet Union a European power. Today Europe has sunk to the same position relative to the United States and the Soviet Union which in former times the non-European spaces occupied vis-à-vis Europe. Europe has become a theater of operations for the two superpowers, one of the theaters within which the contest between the United States and the Soviet Union is fought out.

This radical change in the general structure of the world political system has also led to a radical change in its functions. Throughout modern times, from Henry VIII to Sir Edward Grey on the eve of the First World War, Great Britain performed a decisive, vital, and beneficial function for the balance of power because she was the holder of the balance; that is to say, she was both detached and powerful enough to shift her weight from one scale into the other for the purpose of maintaining the balance of power. In consequence, she could impose upon the conflicts among the European nations a restraint both in the means committed and the objective sought, which in good measure was responsible for the limited character of war and of foreign policy itself during the classic period of that system. Today Great Britain has lost that position, and, what is more important, there is no nation or combination of nations which can occupy the place vacated by Great Britain. As a matter of fact, the place no longer exists. The idea of a third force, such as the Afro-Asian block or a united Western Europe, as a successor to the position of the balancer, which Great Britain occupied before, is entirely utopian. For there is neither the power in any of those possible combinations nor that detachment in terms of interest which qualified Great Britain to perform that function.

In consequence, we have today what is generally called a bipolar system of world power. We have two power centers of the first rank with the other nations having been reduced to the second or third rank. There is no combination of other nations which all by itself could challenge the strength of either of the superpowers.

This political revolution, which has radically changed the structure and functions of world politics, has also deeply affected the position of the United States. It is, of course, superfluous to dwell upon the obsolescence of isolationism. But the very fact that isolationism in the Washingtonian sense or in the sense it was used in the twenties and thirties has unquestionably become obsolete shows the enormous change which has occurred in the position which the United States occupies in world politics. This change is in good measure due to the revolution which has occurred in the field of technology. It is not by accident that the two superpowers, the two powers of the first rank which are left in the world, are also the most advanced nations in the technological field. No nation which is technologically backward can today aspire to considerable power in international affairs. Technological advancement, in other words, is a precondition for political power on the international scene. By virtue of these changes in technology, political power has become to a much greater extent than ever before a mere function of technological potential.

What is even more important, the technological revolutions through which we have been passing have radically changed the relationship between force and foreign policy which has existed from the beginning of history to the beginning of the atomic age. For throughout history there has existed a perfectly rational relationship between violence and foreign policy. Violence was used as an instrument of foreign policy according to the rational calculations of statesmen who would ask themselves whether they could achieve their objectives by peaceful means or whether they should pursue them by military force. According to their calculations, they would choose one or the other, and that choice was rational because the risks and liabilities of violence were proportional to the objectives sought. In other words, nations acted like gamblers who would commit a tolerable fraction of their fortune to the game. If they won, then the risks taken were justified by winning the game. If they lost, the losses generally were not of a fatal nature. The atomic revolution has made an end to this rational relationship between violence and foreign policy; for under the conditions of all-out atomic war the use of all-out violence is a contradiction in terms, making war a perfectly irrational, senseless, self-defeating, and self-destructive enterprise. I shall come in a moment to the consequences of this revolution for the foreign policy of the United States.

Before I do this, let me say a word about the third revolution which has changed the face of the political world, and that is a moral revolution. You are all familiar with the phrase, "This is one world," which is one of those half-truths which conceal and distort as much as they explain; for this is one world only in terms of its technological possibilities, but it is far from one world in terms of the moral values which actually move men to political action on the international scene. This is obvious from a comparison between the situation in which we find ourselves today in this respect and the situation which has existed from the beginning of modern times through the Second World War, with the two significant exceptions of the religious and the Napoleonic wars; for in the preceding period of history, international conflicts were, as it were, imbedded in the common ground of one way of life, one set of moral principles, one kind of political philosophy. In other words, the struggles of the European nations during the eighteenth and nineteenth centuries, with the exception again of the Napoleonic Wars, were in the nature of family squabbles in which nations, holding essentially to the same values of civilization, fought over limited objectives, such as a province, a frontier, or a succession to a throne.

Today, we are in the presence of an ideological conflict, of a conflict between two political religions which parallels the political conflict. In other words, Washington and Moscow are not only the two poles of predominant political and military power, but they are also the centers of two incompatible and hostile ways of life, moral systems, and political philosophies and institutions. In consequence, the political conflict between East and West takes on a bitterness, a sharpness, and a resistance to conciliation of which purely political and military conflicts are generally free. If the conflict between the United States and the Soviet Union were considered simply in terms of a conflict of interests, it would not be impossible from the outset to settle it through diplomatic negotiation. But in so far as any specific conflict, say over the Middle East or Berlin or Korea, is also the manifestation of a conflict between good and evil, between two hostile and incompatible ways of life and political philosophies, it becomes virtually intractable in terms of a diplomatic settlement.

What are the consequences of these revolutions for the foreign policy of the United States, conceived as the instrument of protecting and promoting those perennial interests to which I have referred. The first and the overriding consequence of those revolutions for the foreign policy of the United States is to be found in the enormous limitation which those revolutions, and more particularly the technological revolution, impose on the freedom of action of the United States. The United States did not feel it could any longer use in the late forties or beginning of the fifties the enormous advantage it then had in terms of atomic superiority for the purposes of its foreign policy. In any previous period of history, any nation in its senses, endowed with that enormous and fleeting advantage in military power which the United States enjoyed immediately after the Second World War, would have used it for the purpose of settling its accounts with its enemies. The United States did not and could not do that in view of its own philosophy and interests in the world; for a preventive atomic war would have settled the issue of communism in Russia, it would have solved the problem of Russian imperialism, but it would not have solved the problem of how to govern a radioactive territory covering one-sixth of the globe. Considerations such as these moved the government of the United States, which weighed this alternative at the time, as was its duty, against a serious consideration of its feasibility. But the fact that it could not seriously consider this alternative is a reflection not primarily of moral virtue, as some of us might want to think, but of the uncontrollable and terrible consequences of the modern technology of warfare. If the United States had had the same superiority over the Soviet Union in conventional military weapons, it could have put it to much better use for the purposes of its foreign policy than it was able to when its superiority resided in its monopoly of the atomic bomb.

What was true ten years ago is still true today: the United States, and for that matter the Soviet Union, cannot afford to consider seriously the use of all-out atomic weapons for the purposes of its foreign policies. This being so, the United States is confronted with a second issue. How is it going to defend and promote its interests? If it cannot afford to use its most potent weapons, what weapons can it afford to use and what weapons does it have at its disposal for that use? Here we are in the presence of a real dilemma which a number of statesmen and writers have tried to solve in different ways. The most simple and, because of its simplicity, the most popular solution is what is generally called massive retaliation at times and places of our own choice, that is to say reliance upon the deterrent power of atomic weapons. This deterrent power is indeed the very foundation upon which the peace and the order of the world, such as it is, have rested since the end of the Second World War. But this deterrent power is, as it were, an umbrella under which the daily business of foreign policy must be carried on. It cannot be actually used for the purposes of our foreign policies except as an exercise in verbal "brinkmanship." No nation has dared seriously to threaten atomic war in order to defend this ally or that, this position or that, because no nation could afford to make good this bluff.

Another doctrine relies upon preparedness for what is called limited war, and here two different versions of limited war must be distinguished. One doctrine maintains that the United States must have at its disposal two different military establishments, one never to be used, serving the purposes of the all-out deterrent, and another composed of conventional forces and pre-atomic weapons with high mobility for the purpose of protection in a traditional way against traditional infringments upon the interests of the United States. The other version of the doctrine of limited war proposes the use of tactical atomic weapons for the purpose just mentioned. In other words, there should be a division, according to this version, not between atomic and non-atomic weapons but between atomic weapons strategically employed and atomic weapons used only for tactical purposes. Thus, for the defense of Western Europe against the Soviet Union, we would use small conventional forces armed with tactical atomic weapons. This version of limited war is indeed the one which is at present the official doctrine of the United States.

But this doctrine of limited war fought with tactical atomic weapons faces right away the dilemma, which is not limited to atomic weapons, of distinguishing between strategic and tactical purposes, a dilemma which has confused the writers of military doctrine since the time of Clausewitz. This dilemma is aggravated by the specific and, it seems to me, insuperable difficulties of distinguishing in a practical case between tactical and strategic atomic weapons. Let us consider for a moment a concrete case. Consider a civil war breaking out between East and West Germany, each side supported surreptitiously or openly by its respective allies, the Soviet Union and the United States. The United States would furnish the West German government with tactical atomic weapons to be aimed at Russian or East German troop concentrations, railroad stations, road crossings, ammunition dumps, and so on. The Soviet Union and East Germany, acting, let us suppose, on the same assumption of limited nuclear war, would have to try to intercept the logistic support of the West German troops by bombing the North Sea ports of West Germany, such as Hamburg and Bremen. Once the East German or Soviet troops have used atomic weapons against West German cities, the West would retaliate by dropping atomic weapons on East German cities, and before anyone knew what happened, if any people were left to know what happened, a tactical atomic war would have degenerated by virtue of its own logic into an all-out atomic war.

This is the great dilemma which confronts the United States today. Would we dare start or engage in any kind of war if this war were bound to be, as it actually is, a limited nuclear war, with the chance that such a war could not remain limited. The alternative to this choice is an equally unbearable alternative. It is the alternative of not defending the interests of the United States when only force or the threat of force can defend them.

Another dilemma, which in the long run is perhaps even more serious, confronts the foreign policy of the United States today, and it is also in the realm of technology. The time is close at hand, if no measures are taken to reverse the trend, when more than two or three nations, the United States, Great Britain, and the Soviet Union, will have atomic weapons. It is relatively easy and cheap to transform waste material from atomic reactors into atomic weapons. Thus if the trend is not reversed, if the governments concerned, especially the government of the United States, remain blind to the danger, then inevitably within five or ten years' time ten or twelve or fifteen nations will have atomic weapons. The mutual deterrent restraining the United States and the Soviet Union, which to this day has preserved the peace and the very existence of the civilized world, will then no longer operate. For today, if an atomic bomb should explode in New York, everybody knows who alone could have placed it, say, in a suitcase in Grand Central Station and retaliation will be swift and certain. Ten years from now when perhaps fifteen nations will have atomic bombs and an atomic bomb explodes in Grand Central Station, against whom are you going to retaliate? Are you going to drop atomic bombs on all nations which have atomic bombs? If this situation should be allowed to materialize, we will probably be faced with a terror and an insecurity in comparison with which the first decade of the atomic age will look like a kind of golden age when the nuclear deterrent preserved at least a modicum of peace and order in the world. And indeed to prevent this eventuality from coming to pass is the main task for American foreign policy today. It is not only a great issue of American foreign policy; it is its greatest issue: to prevent a dispersal of atomic weapons into many hands, some of which are bound to be foolish and irresponsible.

The United States is also confronted with a peculiar and unprecedented task in the form of the parallelism between political and ideological conflict, a task that is particularly acute in the so-called underdeveloped regions of the world, that is, primarily the former colonial and semicolonial territories; for it is here that the traditional measures of foreign policy—diplomatic negotiations and the threat or the use of military force—cannot work. The conflict over the control of these territories has been correctly called a struggle for the minds of men; for here the issue is not primarily acquisition of territory through physical conquest or the inducement, by diplomatic means, of a certain government to support the policies of another government. What is here at stake is the allegiance of hundreds of millions of peoples to one or the other of the competing and conflicting ideologies and ways of life. Are the nations of Asia, for instance, who are still uncommitted going to follow the examples of Moscow or Peiping, or are they going to choose another alternative? Is Africa going to follow the Communist line, or is it going to choose another alternative? These are the issues, presented necessarily in an oversimplified form, which confront the foreign policy of the United States.

In order to prevent communism from triumphing in those regions of the world, the United States must fashion policies entirely different from those on which it could rely throughout its history and even during the first years of the Cold War. Two such instruments have been fashioned, propaganda, which is called by the more polite name of information, and foreign aid. Again I have no time to do more than scratch the surface of these problems. Let me say only that we have misconceived in good measure, if not almost completely, the task of propaganda as an advertising campaign for goods to be sold. We have tried to sell the American way of life, and the very metaphor taken from commercial life indicates the fundamental mistake of our conception of political propaganda. Political propaganda is a function of foreign policy; it is not the self-sufficient technical enterprise of selling something to somebody who would otherwise not buy it. Propaganda cannot be better than the foreign policy it seeks to support; however, it can be much worse, and we have proven both points.

As far as foreign aid is concerned we have again fallen into the mistake, and I should add this applies to our military policy as well, to consider it as a self-sufficient technical enterprise, undertaken for its own sake or preferably for humanitarian purposes. But like propaganda, foreign aid is a political weapon, supporting a political policy, being at the service of a political policy in the same way in which military policy is at its service. The Russians have been much smarter, you might say if you wish, more cynical or more Machiavellian in this respect. When we are asked for economic aid by an underdeveloped nation, we supply it with economic experts who examine the economic feasibility of the project according to the best principles of economic thought. If we arrive at the conclusion that this project is not sound economically, we will reject it, and no one seems to care about the political consequences. When we and the Russians were asked by the Afghan government to pave the streets of Kabul we said no, and from an economic stand of view we were right. Why should the Afghan camels walk on asphalt instead of sand? But the Russians said yes; and now the streets of Kabul are covered with asphalt furnished by the Soviet Union, and the Afghans, if not the Afghan camels, are eternally grateful to the Soviet Union. This, I think, is a classic example of how to approach foreign aid as an instrument of political policy and how to approach it in terms of a self-sufficient and non-political technical undertaking.

. . . .

Let me then say in conclusion that the great tasks which the United States must perform if it wants to serve not only the interests of America but the interests of humanity itself cannot be performed without the active support of the American people. It is in this that the foreign policy of the United States differs from the foreign policy of the Soviet Union. Perhaps if my talk had been about the foreign policy of the Soviet Union, I could have stopped here; since I am talking about the foreign policy of the United States, I cannot stop here. I must point to this ultimate problem which confronts the foreign policy of the United States, a problem which does not concern foreign policy proper but rather the relationships between foreign policy and domestic politics, for domestic politics has been the one great limiting factor which has impeded the flexibility of American foreign policy. The stagnation that many of us have noted in the foreign policy of the United States in recent years is in good measure the result of this fear of domestic politics which limits the initiative of those who frame our foreign policy. For, indeed, if you are afraid of Congress, if you are afraid of public opinion, you play safe by not starting on a new initiative, by not taking the risks of an untried policy, by doing what has been done before, doing it perhaps a little bit better or perhaps a little bit worse and preferably doing it a little bit more unobtrusively, but doing essentially the same thing all over again. In a world that is in a revolutionary turmoil on all levels of social interaction, it is fatal for the policy of a great nation to stand still and remain sterile. To give American foreign policy a new impulse, a new vision, a new sense of direction is indeed a task not only and perhaps not even primarily for the makers of American foreign policy but for every citizen of the United States.

10 *National Security Policy*

To do justice to the topic of the basic considerations which go into the making of national security policy, one would really have to survey the whole gamut of reflections and arguments which go into the making of the foreign and military policies of the United States. Of course, within the short span of this meeting nobody could do that. What I shall do, then, is to give the general framework within which the formulation of policy in the United States must operate and perhaps dig out a few of what seem to me to be the crucial problems with which the interest and national security policy of the United States must come to terms.

A rational security policy of any great nation must first of all be aware of the over-all national purpose. What is the over-all national purpose which this policy is supposed to serve? What is it that the United States stands for in the world? What is the common purpose that the different and multifarious policies the United States is pursuing are supposed to serve?

This question, of course, is not asked every time explicitly, but if it is not in the back of the minds of the policy makers, if the policy makers are not, as it were, instinctively aware of the over-all national purpose that their activities are supposed to serve, more likely than not the national security policy will be composed of a number of fragmentary, isolated acts which have no coherence, which have no organic connection with each other. Thus, the first requirement of a rational national security policy is an awareness, however inarticulate and almost instinctive it may be, of the over-all purpose which the nation is supposed to serve by its very existence.

The second consideration, of a more concrete nature, concerns the over-all interests which the nation has throughout the world. The national interest, the concrete interests, let me say, which the United States has in the Western Hemisphere, in Asia, in Africa, in Europe, are different from the over-all national purpose. You might

Lecture given at the National War College, October 13, 1959.

want to define the over-all national purpose in terms of the integrity of the national territory and of its institutions. What we call the American way of life within the traditional territory of the United States is the over-all purpose which the foreign and military policies of the United States are supposed to serve.

Beneath this overarching purpose there are concrete interests which, in turn, are supposed to serve this over-all purpose. Take, for instance, the national interest as it is defined in the Monroe Doctrine, the maintenance, the protection, of the security of the United States and the Western Hemisphere, the quasi-hegemonic position which the United States has in the Western Hemisphere. Take the traditional interest which the United States has pursued in Europe, the maintenance or, if need be, the restoration of the balance of power in Europe. Those national interests, those concrete interests which the United States pursues throughout the world, receive their justification from the over-all purpose, the preservation of the American way of life, the protection of the American institutions within the American territory.

The national security policy must constantly keep in mind those great national objectives, and while the national purpose may not generally be articulated, the national interests must constantly be articulated and must be related to the concrete issues of the day. The history of the United States, especially its more recent history, provides, unfortunately, a number of examples which make clear the disastrous consequences of a national security policy which is not fully aware of those concrete national interests.

Take, for instance, the policy which we pursued in the last year or so of the Second World War in Europe when we conceived of our national interest in terms of the unconditional surrender of the enemy, when we thought that the destruction of the power of Nazi Germany would solve once and for all the political and military problems which confronted us in Europe, that it would satisfy our national interest in Europe, and that afterward we could go back to the Western Hemisphere and forget about Europe. If we had kept in mind that our national interest in Europe has constantly been —from the very beginning of the Republic, starting in 1793 with the Neutrality Declaration of Washington and the War of the First Coalition against Napoleon—not the defeat of a particular enemy, but the maintenance or restoration of the balance of power in Europe, we would have asked ourselves in 1944 and 1945 what the distribution of power in Europe was likely to be after the defeat of Germany and what measures the United States would have to take in order to meet the military and political situation which was likely to arise. If we had raised this issue, we would have realized, as Churchill for instance realized very clearly, that after the defeat of Germany the millennium would not dawn upon us, that another threat to the balance of power would occur by virtue of the political and military vacuum which would exist in Eastern and Central Europe, that we would have to meet that threat, and that we would meet it with full success only if we prepared for it before it became acute. Thus it is clear that a national security policy which is intent upon maximizing its chances for success must constantly keep in mind the perennial interests which that policy is supposed to serve in a particular region of the world.

I have mentioned Europe as an example. I could have mentioned the Far East, where the lack of a relationship between a clearly conceived and defined national interest and our military and political policies again shows by its negative results the vital importance of such a relationship. Once this relationship has been established, the field of national security policy is narrowed down to what we call the policy-making process; and the fundamental questions of policy-making—What resources do you have, and what resources can you get which are most likely to lead to a successful pursuit of those interests—must be asked. In Europe after 1945, for example, it was necessary to ask, as we at long last did, What resources do we have, what political and military means do we have at our disposal, to pursue successfully the national interest of restoring the balance of power in Europe? And if at present we don't have the resources necessary for that purpose, what resources can we create out of our own material and human resources to satisfy that interest? Because of considerations such as these, we embarked upon a political and military policy which committed the fraction of human and material resources necessary for the satisfaction of that national interest, the restoration of the balance of power in Europe.

If you look back at the way in which the policy of containment of the Soviet Union was fashioned in 1946 and 1947, you will realize that this was exactly the way in which the government of the United States operated once it had become belatedly aware of the need to stand firm, to counteract the power of the Soviet Union, that is to say, to commit the resources of the United States in Europe in order to restore a viable balance of power. In other words, in terms of policy formation, the first necessity and also the first problem is to create a balance between the objectives of policy and the resources available to the nation. No particular problem arose with regard to the restoration of the balance of power in Europe after the Second World War because the resources of the United States were clearly sufficient to support the policy embarked upon with a good chance for success.

The happy balance between the objectives of policy and the resources available is not always successfully established, and, in failing to establish it, a nation can err in two different ways. It can either choose objectives of a magnitude far superior to the resources available, or else it can set its sights too low, choosing objectives far below the resources available. The first kind of error is typical of the great imperial ventures of an Alexander or a Napoleon or a Mussolini or a Hitler, leaders who set themselves objectives of world conquest—or of limited conquest, as in the case of Mussolini— for which the national resources available were not sufficient. Since there then exists an imbalance between the objectives of policy and the resources available, the policy is bound to fail. The United States, on the other hand, during the interwar period, for instance, set its national political objectives far below the resources which it had at its disposal. The United States emerged from the First World War as potentially the most powerful nation on earth; but in the interwar period it pursued policies, it set itself objectives, it tried to pursue aims on the international scene, which were far below its resources. In other words, if the United States had been aware of its power potential, if it had been aware of its interests in Asia and Europe, it could have pursued much more forceful policies. It could have set its sights much higher and would have had a good chance to pursue successfully objectives which it thought were out of its reach.

Therefore, a rational national security policy must be careful not to fall into either of those two errors, either to underestimate its resources in view of its national objectives or, what is more likely in the long run, to overestimate its resources, to set its sights too high, and thereby to squander its national resources in unsuccessful enterprises beyond its capacity.

The second great issue with which a rational national security policy must come to terms is the establishment of a balance among the different types of resources available to the nation. Once you have arrived at the conclusion that the over-all resources available are sufficient to pursue your national objectives with a good chance for success, you have to ask yourself, How am I going to allocate the different types of resources available to the nation for the different objectives which I have resolved to pursue? The famous slogan, "guns or butter," illustrates one of the basic decisions which has to be made in this field of policy determination. How much of the economic resources of the nation can the government afford to commit to military objectives or to military policies, and what is the very minimum which must remain for the pursuit of civilian activities? What, in other words, is the economic structure of the nation capable of bearing in order to maximize the chances for success of the policy agreed upon.

The problem which has confronted the United States continuously in recent years, the problem of the balanced budget, is another manifestation of the same over-all issue. That is to say, where is the point at which the commitment of the national resources for purposes of foreign and military policy becomes counterproductive in that it destroys or threatens to destroy the very economic basic upon which the over-all structure of national security policy rests? Opinions, as you well know, differ as to where that point is, whether we have reached it or whether we are far from reaching it. In any case, upon the correct, or at least the approximately correct, decision in this matter depend the chances for success or failure of the policy you are pursuing. And again, if you underestimate the productive capacity of the nation, you will commit fewer resources to the national objectives than you could afford, thereby decreasing the chance for attaining your objectives, and perhaps even jeopardizing the national security, or at least not maximizing the chances for the security of the nation.

On the other hand, if you overestimate the potential economic capacity of the nation, and commit more of its economic resources to military and foreign policy than you should, you may create inflation or economic dislocation, which will get in the way of your political and military policies and thereby conjure up the specter of failure of your national security policies. So the policy maker must strike a delicate balance, not only between the objectives of policy, on the one hand, and the over-all resources, on the other, but also within the field of resources itself. I don't need to tell you how important and how difficult and how delicate and how uncertain this problem is within the military establishment itself. How much, for instance, of the total resources of the nation should be allocated to the over-all retaliatory nuclear capacity of the armed forces; how much should be allocated to the tactical atomic capacity of the nation; how much should be allocated to its conventional capacity.

Here, you are in the field not only of uncertainty with regard to what the economic potential of the nation is capable of supporting, but of the much greater uncertainty with regard to the technological possibilities of the future in a period of history when one technological revolution, especially in the field of military technology, succeeds the other. Here we can only resort to a number of hunches, one series of which the future will prove to be more accurate than the other. But again, success or failure depends upon maximizing the chances that one series of hunches is likely to turn out to be more correct than the other.

These considerations point to another besetting error which we have often made in this field, especially at the beginning of our participation in the Second World War: that is, to think of the economic and over-all resources of the nation in static rather than dynamic terms. Some of you will remember the shock of unbelief and incredulity which went through the nation when the President at the beginning of 1942 set as the national goal the annual production of 50,000 or 60,000 airplanes. It was a staggering number which nobody believed the United States would be able to manufacture. Certainly with the base of the industrial establishment which the United States had at the end of 1941 this was a preposterous figure to shoot at. It was not at all preposterous in terms of the potential capacity of the American people and the American economy. I think there is a great danger that the artificially and necessarily limited goals and means of national security policy will encourage thinking in the static terms of what exists at present rather than in the dynamic terms of what could happen tomorrow if the sights were higher.

So far we have dealt with the material aspects of national security policy. We have talked about purposes, national interests, national resources, as though there were no human factor without which purposes, interests, and resources do not exist or do not operate at all. A rational national security policy must, of course, always be aware of the human factor which stands behind those material objectives, animating them and in the last analysis determining whether they will be achieved. In other words, the maker of national security policy must constantly have in mind a picture of the character of the people with which he deals, especially in terms of national morale. How much of a burden can I impose upon the nation in times of peace? How much of a burden can I impose upon the nation in times of war? What kind of policy, what kind of sacrifices, is the nation willing to bear? How will the national morale stand up under the shock of this or that kind of effort? What kind of foreign or military policy will find the support of public opinion?

Those questions must be uppermost in the mind of the policy maker, not only in a democracy like ours, but in any nation, for there is a point beyond which no nation, regardless of its institutions and political system, will support the policies of the government. It may submit to them, but it will not actively support them. There is a breaking point for national morale as there is a breaking point for individual morale; and it is part, and a vital part, of the policy-making process in the field of national security to ask oneself constantly, Where is the breaking point in the national morale of our people likely to be? How will it stand up under an all-out atomic attack? Would it break, or would the United States survive as an integral nation, as a going concern? How much taxation will the nation support for purposes of national security policy? Again it may be said, whether you underestimate or overestimate the character and morale of the nation under different conditions will in good measure determine the success or failure of your national security policies, or at least will determine whether you are able to maximize your national security.

Take, for instance, the argument which has frequently been advanced in recent years against those who call for a greater national effort in view of the new challenge of Soviet communism that the American people will not support, say, higher taxes, that we have reached the maximum of taxes, or that a greater national effort will interfere to such an extent with the standard of living to which the American people are accustomed that they will not support any greater national effort, any greater commitment of national resources, which, instead of going into the civilian economy, would support military or political policies.

Now, in so far as this estimate of the character of the American nation and of American national morale is correct, the policy based upon it is also correct; that is to say, we have reached the maximum of what we can afford to commit for the competitive struggle with communism. If this is not enough to safeguard our national security, then it is just too bad. If, however, this estimate of the American national character and morale is not correct, as I personally believe, we could make a greater national effort in order to meet the challenge of communism without endangering the human foundation upon which the whole structure of American government and American policy is based.

Here again you see to what extent the estimate of the human national resources determines the character not only of a particular military or political policy, but of the over-all design of national security policy. For if you start with the assumption—for instance, in the military field—that we cannot afford a dual military capability, a conventional and a nuclear one, that we have to make a choice between them but cannot have both at the same time, then you are bound to arrive at a particular type of national security policy, not only in the military field, but in the over-all aspects of the grand strategy the nation pursues. For, obviously, if you limit yourself, by and large, to one particular kind of military establishment, you limit your own policies, political and military; you preclude certain actions from even being considered because you do not have the military capability to put them through.

There is a classic example of this relationship in our negative policy concerning the Hungarian revolution of 1956. While it is an open question whether or not it was wise for us to say from the very outset of the revolution that we would have nothing to do with it, that we would not intervene, objectively it must be noted that we had no capability to intervene with any degree of effectiveness because we lacked the military resources to do so. In other words, the specter of an all-out atomic war, which arose right away out of the consideration of any active involvement in the Hungarian revolution, precluded such an involvement from the very outset. Thus a limitation upon the commitment of resources for the national objectives limits, in a very real and important sense, the choices of the objectives of the national policy.

So this is not a mere means-end relationship—you choose your end and then commit certain resources to that end. It is the other way around: the choice of your resources, the mental picture you have of the resources—human and material—available to you, determines your ends. With those resources available you can only pursue certain ends. If you have more resources available, you could pursue other, more important ends. And thus the estimate of the resources is not a mere subordinate activity, but determines in good measure the ends you are capable of choosing.

In a democracy such as the United States, there is another overriding factor which determines national security policy. This factor is what is generally referred to as public opinion. That is to say, a government which governs with the consent of the governed and, more particularly, which cannot stay in power without having the consent of the governed, whose national security policies therefore are bound to be oriented toward not losing the consent of the governed, must strike still another balance. This is the balance between considerations of domestic politics and considerations of national security policy. In other words, no democratic government can afford to ask itself simply what is the best policy for the United States to pursue and then decide to pursue it. It must also ask itself how appropriate is this national security policy, however rational in its own terms, to the requirements of domestic politics? What effect will the choice of this policy have upon the domestic political situation in view of my party or myself staying in power? In view of the necessity of domestic politics, an American government is bound to water down to some degree the rational requirements of good foreign and military policy.

Someone has said that American foreign policy is 90 per cent domestic politics. I think this is a slight exaggeration, which points, however, to a real problem. A balance must be struck between what is required in terms of good national security policy and what is required by domestic politics. By striking the wrong balance, especially by following the natural tendency to let considerations of domestic politics prevail, a government may well jeopardize the national security in the long run in order to gain a very temporary and fleeting domestic political advantage.

Therefore, those charged with the formulation and execution of national security policy must have very good judgment as to what is absolutely indispensable in terms of national security and what is required in terms of domestic political considerations. There is a natural tendency in a democracy to sacrifice the long-run objectives of national security for the sake of temporary political advantage. It is a measure of the greatness and of the competence and moral stamina of the statesman in a democracy that he is capable of resisting those domestic political pressures in order to safeguard the perennial interests and purposes of the nation; and it is a measure of his flexibility and his subtlety that he is capable of yielding to those pressures to such an extent as to satisfy the requirements of domestic politics without jeopardizing the perennial interests and purposes, the very existence, of the nation.

11 *The Fortieth Anniversary of the Bolshevist Revolution*

It is a revealing coincidence that the fortieth anniversary of the Bolshevist Revolution follows closely upon the Russian firing of an intercontinental ballistic missile and the placing of a Russian satellite in space as though it had been planned as the culmination of these momentous achievements. This time the Bolshevists have really something more substantial to celebrate than the memory of an ancient historic event and the disappointments and miseries following it. By connecting this anniversary with the great technological achievements of contemporary Russia, the Russian people will give a verdict on the Bolshevist Revolution which history is likely to bear out; for while history most certainly will not confirm the Communist claim that the October Revolution of 1917 has put an end to the class division of society, the domination and exploitation of man by man, imperialism and war, it is likely to prove correct Lenin's definition of bolshevism as "the Soviets plus electrification." What the Bolshevist Revolution has actually achieved is to open the door to the transformation, within the span of a few decades interrupted by a devastating war, of a backward, half-feudal, and predominately agrarian Russia, a kind of Spain of the East, into a modern industrial society of the first rank, the other great power on the face of the earth.

It has been argued that Russia would have developed on similar lines if the Bolshevist Revolution had not occurred. This may or may not be so. In any event, the argument is beside the point, for the Bolshevist Revolution has occurred and is responsible for this development.

By demonstrating how quickly and radically a Communist society, which does not count the cost in human lives and happiness, can jump from backwardness into modernity, Russian bolshevism has set an example for other backward countries to follow. What the Russians have been able to do, we can do, the Chinese are saying,

From the *Chicago Sun-Times*, November 3, 1957.

and these words echo in the vast expanses of Asia and Africa and are openly expressed in unlikely places such as Spain. The Bolshevists have given the world a lesson in how to make a backward nation powerful, and many of the nations which, as colonies, have been for so long the object of the power of others are eager to try that lesson out for themselves. They are at one with the leaders of bolshevism in not counting the hecatombs of dead, the miseries and degradation of whole generations, upon which that power has been built. They are on familiar terms with violent death and misery and know from their colonial experience what degradation means. For them, as for the masters of bolshevism, only the result counts.

While the Bolshevist Revolution has thus become the actual foundation for a successful experiment in rapid industrialization and for great domestic and international power, communism also claims for the Bolshevist Revolution that it provides experimental proof for the correctness of the Communist philosophy as revealed in the teachings of Marx and Lenin. Nothing could be further from the truth. If the Bolshevist Revolution and its consequence in the form of the Soviet Union teach anything, they teach the irrelevance of the teachings of Marx and, to a lesser degree, of Lenin for what has happened in Russia in the last forty years.

To begin with, if Marx was right, Russia was about the last country where the Bolshevist Revolution should have occurred; for according to Marx, the historic process has its own inner logic, and one historic epoch follows with objective necessity from its predecessor, creating within itself the conditions for the birth of the succeeding one. The proletarian revolution ushering in the socialist society is ineluctably caused by the inner contradictions of capitalism culminating in a succession of ever more severe crises until finally the desperate mass of impoverished proletarians confronts a small group of desperate monopoly capitalists and their mercenaries. At this point in the historic process, the proletarian revolution, according to Marx, becomes inevitable. Yet, what were the conditions of Russia in October, 1917? Capitalism was in its infancy, and the economic problem that faced the masses was agrarian and not industrial. The issue over which the Bolshevist Revolution broke out and which led to the downfall of the social-democratic Kerensky government was not economic and was not even primarily domestic. It was the question of war or peace, the Kerensky government being committed to the continuation of the war, the Bolshevists to its termination.

The Bolshevist Revolution was no more Marxist in its consequences than it was in its origin. Marx saw in the very fact of government an expression of the class division of society, the apparatus of the state being the instrument by which the exploiting minority establishes and maintains its power over the exploited majority. Consequently, a socialist society, being by definition classless, would no longer be in need of an apparatus of coercion, and the state would, in the famous phrase of Engels, "wither away." Man would at long last be liberated from political domination altogether and in complete freedom develop his faculties, living in harmony with himself and his fellow men. Yet the "classless society" of bolshevism created and has maintained to this day a system of totalitarian control and suppression, covering one-sixth of the globe, superior in efficiency and equal in ruthlessness to any instrument of domination and violence a class society ever produced. The slavery it brought to hundreds of millions of people is more oppressive than the enslavement on which past societies lived because it aims not only at the body but the mind and soul as well. It amounts to that very mutilation of man for which Marx reproached the capitalistic system and to which he thought communism would put an end.

Bolshevism has given the lie to the Marxist prophecies in foreign policy as well. Marx and Lenin claimed that imperialism and war were instigated by profit-hungry capitalists, and only recently Khrushchev, in his interview with James Reston of the *New York Times*, has again hammered on that theme. The corollary to this argument is, of course, that the destruction of capitalism is needed to bring peace and freedom to suffering mankind. Yet count the wars, not of self-defense but of aggression, the Soviet Union has fought during the four decades of its existence. No capitalistic country has such a record. Or take a look at the map and compare the limits of Russian power today with what they were in 1920, at the end of the civil war, and in 1914 under the tsars. Not only has the Soviet Union recovered the empire of the tsars, but she has added vast spheres of influence in Europe and the Middle East which the tsars were only able to dream of dominating. Yet this imperialistic expansion of the Soviet Union took place while the great capitalistic nations of the West liquidated their empires.

What the Bolshevist Revolution of 1917 actually achieved—the industrialization of a backward country and its transformation into one of the two great world powers—is something entirely different from what communism has claimed for it and will claim again on this fortieth anniversary. It has turned out to be an instrument of power and not of freedom, of war and not of peace, of degradation of man and not of his dignity, of industrial progress, and of political barbarism. How, then, is it that in the face of all these obvious facts, the myth of the Bolshevist Revolution persists among its friends and foes alike, in the East as well as in the West and probably more here than there—more, say, in France than in Hungary?

The reason lies in the character of the Bolshevist Revolution itself, which was not only a political event of the first importance but also a quasi-religious occurrence. It was the culmination of the eschatological expectations not only of the Marxists but of many liberals as well. Many non-Marxists welcomed it, clinging to the belief, common in the nineteenth century and the first decades of the twentieth, that man can attain salvation, especially from the evil of political domination, through his own unaided efforts here and now. The Bolshevist Revolution was for them the Armageddon destroying the old rotten order and laying the foundation for a new perfect one. A succession of disappointments opened the eyes of many; yet many others continue to believe in the saving powers of the Bolshevist Revolution and expect the millennium sooner or later to follow it.

Those of us, for instance, who cling to the hope that the Soviet Union would be less of a menace to the West if she became less Communist confound the actual and the mythological meaning of the Bolshevist Revolution; for what the Soviet Union is today and what she portends for the West, she owes primarily not to the Communist myth of the revolution but to its reality: that it has made Russia a powerful part of the modern world. Communism may have strengthened that power, but it has not created it. What the West is threatened with as the fifth decade of the Soviet Union begins is not primarily the Communist myth but the power of Russia. If the West finally learns that lesson, it will not have reminded itself in vain of this fortieth anniversary of the Bolshevist Revolution.

12 *Khrushchev's New Cold War Strategy*

According to Plutarch, Julius Caesar announced his victory at Zela in 47 B.C. to his friend Amintius with the words, "*Veni, vidi, vici*—I came, I saw, I conquered." Is it likely that Khrushchev similarly described his American visit to his friends in the Kremlin; and, if so, did he have a point? There can be no doubt that Khrushchev came here, although, as one watched, listened, and read about this extraordinary voyage, which the London *Economist* properly called a "coast to coast riot," it was sometimes hard to believe that it was real. There can be no doubt, either, that Khrushchev saw something—although it was not much and for the most part not what he ought to have seen. But did Khrushchev conquer? Did he achieve what he set out to achieve? I am afraid that the answer must be in the affirmative, judging by Khrushchev's actions during his trip and our reactions to them, as seen in the context of the Soviet Union's new foreign policy.

The novelty of Soviet foreign policy, in both its aims and its methods, is the overriding fact of the present era in Soviet-American relations. The inception of this new policy and its successful execution thus far constitute Khrushchev's historic contribution to the development of the Soviet Union as a world power and of communism as a world movement. Khrushchev's foreign policy marks a drastic break with the foreign policy of Stalin and reverts, at least in its aims, to Lenin's conception of the roles of the Soviet Union and of communism in world affairs. Khrushchev, however, has devised new methods to achieve Lenin's goals. His trip to the United States was one of them.

Lenin saw in Russian bolshevism the doctrinal and political fountainhead of the Communist world revolution, and in the success of that revolution the precondition for the survival of the Bolshevik regime in Russia. Russian bolshevism was the "base" of world revolution; that was its historic function and justification in Marxist terms, as world revolution was Russian bolshevism's inevitable sequel and the guarantee of its success. On this doctrinal foundation,

From *Commentary*, November, 1959.

as developed in Lenin's *"Left-wing" Communism: An Infantile Disorder*, the Soviet Union stood in its earliest years as the guide and instigator of violent revolution throughout the world.

Both the consolidation of bolshevism within Russia and the collapse of the world revolutionary movement gave birth to Stalin's policy of "socialism in one country." Stalinist foreign policy was essentially traditional in its objectives and, appearances to the contrary notwithstanding, even in its methods. The subservience of foreign Communist parties to the Soviet Union was enforced and justified in terms of Lenin's doctrine; yet the opportunities for espionage and subversion which that subservience provided were exploited with complete cynicism as means to the traditional ends of Russian power.

Russian foreign policy in the 1930's and 1940's was in the classic tradition of power diplomacy. The temporary reliance upon the League of Nations, the Franco-Russian alliance of 1935, the Molotov-Ribbentrop pact of 1939, the support of Chiang Kai-shek during and just after the Second World War, the conquest of Eastern Europe, the attempts to gain a foothold on the eastern shores of the Mediterranean and in Iran and to draw all of Germany into the Russian orbit, owed nothing to communism; they followed the traditional objectives and techniques of Russian foreign policy. Exploitation of the loyalty of foreign Communists made it easier for the Soviet Union to attain some of these objectives, but neither the choice of the objectives nor their attainment was determined by the fact that Stalin professed the political philosophy of communism and pretended to act in its name. This, then, was the paradox of Stalin's foreign policy, which must have been congenial to his sardonic sense of humor: although he spoke the language of doctrinaire Marxism-Leninism and founded his charismatic leadership upon the pretense of executing and developing the teachings of Marx and Lenin, in fact the objectives and techniques of his foreign policy owed everything to the Russian tradition going back to Peter the Great and Ivan the Terrible. Aside from improvements in technical efficiency, communism provided Stalin's foreign policy only with ideological justifications and rationalizations.

The foreign policy of Khrushchev presents a paradox of a différent sort. Much less a doctrinaire Communist than his predecessors, he has set out to accomplish the world-wide triumph of communism, not as the heir of Marx and Lenin, but as the pragmatic competitor of the United States. He means to do what Lenin and Stalin never attempted: to defeat the foremost capitalist nation at its own game of technology and production. In the measure that Khrushchev succeeds in this endeavor, the foreign policy of the Soviet Union takes on an ideological complexion different from the ritual verbal tributes which Stalin used to pay to the infallibility of Marx and Lenin. Khrushchev's Communist truth is derived from an experience whose reality is beyond doubt: the truly impressive fact of Russian technological and productive achievements. And these achievements he attributes to the superiority of the Communist organization of society.

Lenin bent Marxist philosophy to his will to power; he used it as an instrument for gaining and maintaining power; Marxism was an integral part of the power structure of Lenin's state. Stalin used Marxist philosophy as a mere ideology, as the justification and rationalization of a power structure resting on the quite different foundation of Oriental despotism. For Khrushchev, Marxism is neither an instrument nor an ideology of power, but the self-evident and unquestioned body of truth from which the reality of Soviet power receives its meaning. Khrushchev, in his way, is as serious about communism as was Lenin. Lenin used Marxism as a hammer with which to slay his enemies and reassure himself of his own strength; Marxism was as important to him as revolutionary cadres and machine guns. Khrushchev's Marxism is not a dynamic and flexible weapon in the struggle for power, but an ossified set of intellectual assumptions which give meaning to the actual triumphs of the Soviet Union and receive plausibility from them. Khrushchev does not need Marxism to transform the world, as Lenin did, but to make the actual transformation of the world intelligible. It may well be that, because of this intellectual need, he is more beholden to Marxism than was either Lenin or Stalin, whose Marxist convictions, real or pretended, had to be adapted to the ever changing exigencies of the political struggle.

Thus communism as a universal principle of social organization gains from actual performance a prestige which neither Lenin's use of Marxism as an instrument for the seizure and consolidation of power nor Stalin's barren exercise in dialectic theology could give it. The Communist prophets from Marx to Stalin had to argue philosophically for the foreordained triumph of communism, the Communist salvation of mankind which would inevitably occur, in however distant a future. Khrushchev can point to what has already occurred as a token of the correctness of that prophecy.

This radical change in the relationship between Communist promise and Communist performance has brought forth a radical change in Soviet foreign policy. Soviet imperialism, which in Stalin's day was, and had to be, of a limited military character—for here lay its only opportunities—has become under Khrushchev both demilitarized and unlimited. Khrushchev's new imperialism seeks to win the world neither by military might nor with the gospel of Marx and Lenin, but through the technological and productive capacity of the Soviet Union. Khrushchev proposes to fight that battle on three different fronts:

1. He offers the Soviet Union as a model for the other nations of the world to emulate, especially the underdeveloped and uncommitted nations.

2. He seeks to spread the influence of the Soviet Union through foreign aid and trade.

3. By overtaking the United States in technological and productive achievements, he aims to reduce the United States to the status of a second-rank power.

Khrushchev means to conquer the world not by force of arms or through world revolution but with the prestige which the Soviet Union acquires through its unsurpassed achievements and invincible power. His is indeed the most comprehensive and single-minded policy of prestige in modern times, reducing the traditional autonomous instruments of foreign policy—diplomacy and force—to mere handmaidens of that policy. Whatever increases the prestige of the Soviet Union and diminishes that of its opponents, then, is a calculated gain for Khrushchev's policy.

Four immediate objectives of that policy become intelligible in the light of this over-all goal: avoidance of war, with the Soviet Union taking credit for it; relaxation of tensions; termination of the Cold War; bi- and multi-lateral summit meetings. The success Khrushchev has achieved in realizing these immediate objectives by coming to the United States is a measure of the success of his trip.

By coming to the United States as the apostle of peace, Khrushchev carried the traditional Soviet peace propaganda, clothed in the highest authority, to the territory of the enemy. Khrushchev was good enough to admit that President Eisenhower wanted peace, too, even though that could not be said of "certain circles" in the United States; and American public opinion was good enough to avow that Khrushchev was "sincere" in his desire for peace. This innocuous-sounding exchange of apparent platitudes was, in truth, a great victory for Khrushchev's new policy. Not only can Khrushchev claim to have taken the initiative in preserving peace, attested to by the United States; but also, and more important, he has been able to impose his standards of action upon the United States, with untoward consequences for American freedom of action which only the future can reveal.

The issue of peace and war has consistently been presented by the Soviet Union in terms both false and advantageous to itself. Now, in the fall of 1959, that presentation has been accepted by the United States, just as a similar presentation was accepted and acted upon by Great Britain in the fall of 1938. It stands to reason that any government, unless it is dominated by a madman, will prefer peace to war, especially in the atomic age, if it can get what it wants by peaceful means. The crucial question, then, is not whether it prefers peace to war, but whether its goals can be attained by peaceful means. To answer that question, one must examine not a statesman's "sincerity" in the pursuit of peace, but the statesman's policies in the light of their compatibility with the preservation of peace. Khrushchev has left no doubt about his intention to communize the world, and he is no doubt sincere, especially in view of the present distribution of military power, in wanting to achieve this end by peaceful means. But what will he do if it should become obvious that the world cannot be communized by peaceful means, and if he should come to believe, however mistakenly, that the distribution of military power has decisively changed in favor of the Soviet Union? That is the crucial question, and it seems to have been lost in the general satisfaction about Khrushchev's "sincerity" in wanting peace.

By returning from his American trip as the champion of peace—

by general acclamation—Khrushchev has won another even more subtle and ominous victory. Whether or not a nation protects and promotes its interests by peaceful means is not necessarily a matter of choice, but may well be determined by objective conditions, especially those created by its enemy, over which it has no control. My neighbor may ruin my property and make life intolerable for me by peaceful means, and my only defense may be resort to force. If my neighbor is cunning and I am naïve, he may well get me to express my confidence in his peaceful intentions and agree that neither he nor I will ever resort to force on behalf of our interests. Thus I will either stand disarmed before his trespasses or be guilty of the violation of a solemn pledge. In other words, the symmetry of a bilateral pledge to forswear force, eminently equitable in appearance, can be deceptive and hide an asymmetry of interests, disadvantageous if not disastrous to the party which must either defend itself by force or else not defend itself at all.

Such asymmetry of interests is obvious in the relations between the United States and the Soviet Union. It is obvious in their over-all relations, as well as with regard to the specific issue of Berlin, which provided the occasion for the agreement betwen Eisenhower and Khrushchev not to resort to force. Khrushchev's new foreign policy of communizing the world through the prestige of the Soviet Union does not require the use of force; it even precludes it. Violent conflict, even of a limited character, might require the commitment of Soviet resources needed for the spectacular achievements upon which the Soviet policy of prestige rests. Furthermore, violent conflict, incalculable in its dimensions and outcome, might not only add nothing to Soviet prestige, but might even diminish it. As long as the Soviet Union can bank on a succession of spectacular achievements to be exploited on behalf of the expansion of Soviet influence, it can have no interest in trying to attain by force what it is capable of attaining without it.

The same considerations do not necessarily apply to the United States. The United States could not remain indifferent to the communization of uncommitted or allied nations by the peaceful means of economic domination, military infiltration, and political subversion. Can it be maintained that the United States must forego the threat or use of force, however limited, if no other remedy is available against such a threat? That question applies with particular poignancy to Berlin. The Soviet Union obviously has it in its power to make life intolerable for the Western garrisons without openly resorting to force. Could the United States protect its presence in Berlin in the face of such a Soviet policy of "peaceful strangulation" without the threat or use of force? If it should resort to this extreme remedy, Khrushchev, having persuaded us to accept his standards of action, can blame the "warmongers" who have prevailed over the "sincere" or "treacherous" President, as the case may be. If in these circumstances the United States does not resort to this remedy, it will have lost the battle for Berlin.

Similarly, Khrushchev's insistence upon relaxation of tensions is a weapon in the armory of the new Soviet foreign policy. My neighbor who is out to ruin me has good reason to dwell upon the desirability of relaxing tensions and upon the ease with which this could be done if I only wanted to. What my neighbor has omitted to say is that it is not I, but he, who is responsible for the existence of tensions; that if he would only mind his own business there would be no tensions; and that the existence of tensions is due to his regarding not only his back yard as his business, but mine and everybody else's as well. If Khrushchev were willing to change by one iota the aims and methods of Soviet foreign policy from which the tensions have arisen, the United States could afford to relax tensions to the degree that the modification of Soviet foreign policy had removed the causes of those tensions. With that policy remaining substantially unchanged, relaxation of tensions is for the United States tantamount to disarming psychologically. A nation which has been advised of its forthcoming burial cannot afford not to be tense—if it wants to survive.

What holds true of the relaxation of tensions as a psychological state, also applies to the Cold War as the objective condition of political hostilities threatening armed conflict. The Cold War did not come into being because the United States decided to have one; hence, it cannot be ended by the United States deciding to call it off. The Cold War is the result of the expansionist policies the Soviet Union has pursued since the end of the Second World War and of American resistance to these policies. To end the Cold War, the Soviet Union would have to stop trying to expand. Khrushchev, far from calling a halt to the expansionist tradition of Soviet foreign policy, has restored Lenin's unlimited objectives. Since the Cold War is the result of the unresolved political conflict between Soviet expansionism and American resistance to it, Khrushchev's appeal to the United States to call off the Cold War, in the absence of even the slightest progress toward the settlement of the political conflict, is tantamount to inviting the United States to stop resisting the expansion of the Soviet Union.

The insistence of Khrushchev upon peace, relaxation of tensions, and ending the Cold War aims at weakening the resistance of the United States to the foreign policy of the Soviet Union. It also seeks to break down the psychological barriers which, under the influence of American resistance, have grown in allied and uncommitted nations against Soviet encroachments and blandishments. So long as tensions and the Cold War pit the United States against the Soviet Union, the uncommitted nations will take care to remain uncommitted, and the allies of the United States will continue to seek protection from the powerful nation which alone can hold the Soviet Union in check. But once the United States agrees to the relaxation of tensions and a decrease in the intensity of the Cold War, it issues to the Soviet Union, as it were, a certificate if not of good, at least of improved, conduct. It is no longer necessary, the United States would seem to be saying, to oppose the Soviet Union with the same degree of determination as before; the Soviet Union, far from wanting to attack us, wishes only to compete. This is what many uncommitted nations and many people within the allied nations have been longing to hear, and they are likely to relax with a vengeance and see vistas of "peace in our time."

Khrushchev's insistence on a visit to the United States and on a summit meeting serves the same purpose as do professions of peaceful intentions, of his desire to relax tensions and end the Cold War. Khrushchev must know that the procedural question of who meets where is less important than the substantive terms of a settlement, say, of the Berlin issue. If he had wanted to settle that issue short of the surrender of the Western position, he could have given his terms to our ambassador in Moscow or to his ambassador in Washington to be transmitted to our government, or he could have instructed his foreign minister to negotiate with the Western foreign ministers a settlement acceptable to them. There are, it is true, extraordinary issues of transcendent importance with which only the heads of state might be able to cope. The Berlin issue is not one of them.

Why, then, has Khrushchev been so insistent on meeting at the summit? The answer to that question has nothing to do with any of the substantive issues outstanding between the United States and the Soviet Union. Summit meetings are the most direct and spectacular attempt at making Khrushchev's new foreign policy respectable throughout the world, at disarming the Western alliance in the face of it, and at opening the gates for its success in the allied and uncommitted nations.

How this three-stage mechanism—Soviet challenge to relax tensions, American acceptance, allied and neutral relaxation—operates has already become apparent in the aftermath of Khrushchev's visit. Obviously, so the reasoning runs, Khrushchev and his policies cannot be as bad as all that if the most powerful and thus far implacable enemy of the Soviet Union organizes a continental circus for him and receives him as a respectable statesman with whom—in contrast to Stalin—it is possible to do business. If the United States can do business with Khrushchev, why not Japan? And so, immediately following the Khrushchev visit, leading members of the Japanese government party rushed to Moscow and Peiping. President Sukarno of Indonesia replied to the critics of his address to a Communist rally that, if the United States can talk to Khrushchev, he can talk to the Indonesian Communists. The government of Iran has raised similar questions in its relations with the Soviet Union. The tone and arguments of the British press of September, 1959, resemble those of September, 1938, to such an extent that, as an official who made a study of it commented, they could be interchanged, save for the names, without anyone noticing.

If Khrushchev can now view the over-all world scene with satisfaction, he can also feel triumphant and a bit contemptuous when he beholds the disarray of American foreign policy and public opinion which his visit left in its wake. For that honorable desire to be done with preparations for war and to have peace once and for all, which from Demosthenes' Athens to Chamberlain's Britain has darkened the judgment of the democracies, threatens again to confuse our thoughts and emasculate our actions.

It is indeed awkward for those who, like myself, have for more than ten years advocated a negotiated settlement with the Soviet Union as the only alternative to war now to have to disassociate themselves from a diplomatic initiative which, thus far at least, has honored the principle of negotiations in appearance rather than substance. Negotiations are an attempt at reconciling divergent interests through a process of give-and-take in which either both sides concede minor points while leaving the substance of their interests intact or else one side receives through compensations from the other at least the equivalent of what it concedes. Negotiations, then, require first of all objective conditions conducive to a negotiated settlement; there must be room for maneuver, for retreat, advance, and side-stepping, for mutual concessions. When neither side can afford to yield an inch, negotiations are a priori impossible. Given the objective conditions conducive to a negotiated settlement, both sides, in order to negotiate successfully, must be strong enough to support their negotiating positions with promises of benefits and threats of disadvantages. In other words, they must be able, in Dean Acheson's famous phrase, to negotiate from strength.

The American position with respect to these two requirements of successful negotiations has, as a result of the Khrushchev visit, been rendered, at the very least, ambiguous and has thus been weakened. What is being hailed as the beginning of a negotiated settlement appears rather to be, at this stage at least, the beginning of a softening-up process which, if it is not stopped, can only end in the surrender of the Western position. The claim that we have started on the road to a genuine negotiated settlement has from the outset been made doubtful by the aura of vulgarity and frivolity which enveloped this visit. Here are two men, Eisenhower and Khrushchev, who hold the fate of the world in their anxious hands, and one visits the other with the declared purpose of halting the drift toward war. Can one imagine a more incongruous setting for so noble and weighty a task, a setting less conducive for the concentrated thought required for its accomplishment, than this traveling circus with its clowning and obscenities to which the brief confrontation at Camp David was attached almost as an afterthought? The visit was indeed a modern equivalent of Nero fiddling while Rome burned. And it is testing our credulity to try to make us believe, as Khrushchev did, that the purpose of such an exhibition of levity was to lay the foundations for an honorable and enduring peace.

The manner in which our government conceived the Khrushchev

trip, and its timing, helped assure that the trip would turn out to be a propaganda success for the Soviet Union rather than a step toward peace for the world. When the President reversed his position of long standing, for which the late Secretary Dulles was mainly responsible, and invited Khrushchev, he acted from a position of weakness and in a mood of despair. The negotiations about Berlin had failed and the United States, unable to fight a conventional war of more than small dimensions, faced the prospect of either backing down or measurably raising the stakes in that continuous poker game of the mutual nuclear deterrent. Unwilling to face either alternative squarely, the government resorted in desperation to the one device which had never been tried before: an encounter between Eisenhower and Khrushchev in the United States. This encounter was conceived by our government not as part of a well thought-out plan to negotiate in earnest on the outstanding issues, but rather as a gimmick, a gesture, a stalling device, which would gain time and at least postpone a showdown. And it was carefully timed for a maximum effect on the British elections.

We have indeed gained time, but for what? Are we still holding fast to the essential distinction between the two types of negotiations, one affecting secondary issues since the primary interests themselves cannot be reconciled, the other exchanging interest for interest? The Berlin issue is clearly of the former type. The Soviet Union wants us to leave Berlin, and we want to stay; no compromise can bridge these two positions. Neither we nor the Soviet Union can accommodate the other side without surrendering its very position. We can negotiate about the conditions of our presence in Berlin, not about that presence itself. Rather, our presence in Berlin is the incontestable foundation upon which negotiations concerning the conditions can proceed. We have said we will negotiate with the Soviet Union—but from what position and about what?

The West has begun the process of giving way while Khrushchev has not given an inch. Much has been made of Khrushchev's alleged concession in removing the time limit for negotiations. In truth, no time limit could have been removed at Camp David because none existed. Whatever time limit there had been lapsed when the Soviet Union allowed its original six month time limit to expire in May, 1959, without taking action. From then on, negotiations were carried on in a normal fashion, as they will be carried on from now on. Furthermore, and most important, Khrushchev is free, even in the absence of a time limit, to stop negotiations and take action whenever he sees fit, and the Camp David communiqué emphasized his freedom by stipulating that the negotiations should not be protracted indefinitely.

Yet while Khrushchev has conceded nothing either in substance or procedure, Eisenhower has begun to concede the substance of the Western position by calling the situation in Berlin "abnormal." A situation that is abnormal must be made normal by being changed. In fact, there is nothing abnormal in the Berlin situation, in view of Western interests and assumptions; for if the division of the German capital is symbolic of the division of Germany, then the removal of the Western presence in Berlin is contingent upon the removal of the Soviet presence in East Germany. The division of Germany, maintained by the armed forces of the Soviet Union, is symbolically duplicated in Berlin; one ought not to disappear without the other. What is abnormal is the presence of the Red Army a hundred miles east of the Rhine, preventing the East German population from joining their compatriots in the West, except by migration. As a counterfoil to that abnormality, the Western presence in Berlin is perfectly normal. To call it something else is to give the game away, at least in words.

Negotiations are no more an end in themselves than are peace, relaxation of tensions, and the termination of the Cold War. What are decisive are the unsettled substantive issues which disturb peace, create tensions, and must be settled by negotiations. None of these issues was brought closer to an acceptable settlement by the Khrushchev visit, and they have all been beclouded by it. We co-operated with Khrushchev in creating a fog of distortion and illusion—we out of thoughtlessness, he by design. From within that fog the cunning, determined vulgarian from the East watches the giant from the West, aimless in complacency, sleepy from past success. We can believe Khrushchev when he tells us that, for the time being, he brings us peace, not a sword. But sword or no sword, he has made perfectly clear what he means by peace; it is the peace of the burial ground. Whatever he says and does is designed to hasten that peace.

13 *Germany's New Role*

The London conference was successful in that it did what it set out to do: to establish legal obligations and institutional devices to which M. Mendès-France could agree as a framework for the rearmament of West Germany. However, the hyperbolic self-congratulations of some of the participants should not blind us to the narrow limits within which the London conference has actually been a success.

First of all, much of what was agreed upon in London is in the nature of general principles and declarations of intention rather than of definitive, binding obligations and settlements and, hence, must await elaboration. Furthermore, the success of the conference appears to be greater than it actually is because its frame of reference excluded the more important of the two issues which the rearmament of Germany presents. Thus, even if there should be agreement on the many points still outstanding and the agreements thus reached should be ratified by the parliaments concerned, only one of the two basic issues which threatened European Defense Community from its very inception and finally destroyed it—and the less important one—will have been brought closer to solution.

That less important issue is posed by the fact that France, facing Germany alone, finds itself in a position of irremediable inferiority. Two examples will serve to illustrate. Since 1870 the population of France has increased by approximately four million and that of Germany by twenty-seven million; in 1800 every seventh European was a Frenchman, in 1930 only every thirteenth; in 1940 Germany had at its disposal about fifteen million men fit for military service, and France had only five million. In the last elections one out of every four Frenchmen voted for a Communist candidate, and, hence, 25 per cent of the French people support directly or indirectly, wittingly or unwittingly, a foreign and hostile government and are

From *Commonweal*, November 12, 1954.

alienated in different degrees from the purposes of France. For France, conscious of this drastic and hopeless inferiority, to join Germany in a continental supranational combination would have required either extraordinary faith in the intentions of Germany or extraordinary despair about the future of France. France had neither, and thus E.D.C. failed. E.D.C. frightened France, not because it threatened another German attack, but because it threatened to swallow France up in a supranational organization dominated by an unchecked and uncheckable Germany, which might draw it into military adventures of incalculable scope.

For France the problem of German rearmament presents itself as the age-old problem of the balance of power in a novel setting. Where can France find additional power which would provide a counterweight to that of Germany? That was the question which had worried Richelieu and Mazarin, Delcassé and Poincaré, as it is worrying now Herriot and Mendès-France. It is the great historic achievement of the London conference that, for the first time in modern history, this perennial concern of France has met with a response which is more than a mere legal commitment, but changes permanently the distribution of power on the continent. The British commitment to station four divisions and a tactical air force on the continent has made Great Britain a continental military power in permanence. This revolutionary transformation constitutes the momentous British contribution to Franco-German reconciliation and makes the London pact a political instrument superior to E.D.C. By adding its military power permanently to that of France, Great Britain has made it easier for France to reconcile itself to the ascendancy of Germany.

Yet while the London conference has been successful in this respect, it has failed to understand, let alone solve, the central problem posed by a renascent Germany, which is how to deny the new power of Germany to the Soviet Union. By posing it in the military terms of rearmament, we have missed the political significance of the problem. The issue has never been whether or not Germany would rearm. German rearmament being a foregone conclusion, the real issue is for what political purposes German arms will be used. Yet, obsessed with the military contribution which West Germany could make to Western defense, the participants in the London conference have based their policies upon two assumptions, both unsound: one, that a German military contribution is essential for the successful defense of Western Europe; the other, that some sort of organizational integration of the German army into the Western alliance and the exchange of legal commitments will prevent Germany from using that army for purposes at variance with those of the Westrn alliance or hostile to the interests of one or the other of its members.

It is tedious, at least for this writer who has made the same argument within and outside the government since 1949, to state again that Western Europe cannot be defended on land against the two hundred Russian and satellite divisions even if twelve German divisions arc added to the twenty Western divisions now available. What has defended Western Europe in the past, and what will defend it in the future, is the certainty that a military attack upon Western Europe means the beginning of the third world war, bringing the retaliatory atomic power of the United States to bear upon the aggressor. This being so, twelve German divisions will at best be able to perform the same function which the European army as a whole is able to perform: to contribute to internal stability and slow down the Russian advance on land, allowing our air bases in Western Europe to accomplish their strategic task. As a deterrent factor against aggression in the over-all balance of power, the German army is bound to be negligible. What frightens the Russians—and there is little doubt that the fears they profess so often and so loud are real—is not the military damage which those twelve German divisions could do to them, but the political and military turbulence they could create in the heart of Europe in the absence of a political settlement. It so happens that our overriding concern with German rearmament not only makes the Russians afraid; it also gives them hope, for it provides them with a great political opportunity: to strike a bargain with an armed, yet politically dissatisfied, Germany.

The real problem which Germany presents to the Western world has been obscured and perverted by the illusion of the decisiveness of the German military contribution. That problem is not military but political. It is posed by the fact that West Germany, which is already, even without an army, the most powerful nation on the continent, cannot forever remain under the tutelage of the occupying powers. How can an independent Germany be prevented from making common cause with the Soviet Union? That is the momentous question which confronts the Western world. The real problem, then, is not German rearmament but German sovereignty.

Attempts have been made to solve this problem within the context of German rearmament, and that very context has condemned these attempts, as it will future ones, to futility. All these attempts, from E.D.C. to the London solution, have endeavored to deprive a sovereign German government of the free use of its armed forces. E.D.C. has attempted to achieve this through the establishment of a multinational army under truly supranational control. The London solution seeks to accomplish the same end through the international controls provided by NATO and the Brussels treaty. However, the legalistic concern with degrees of integration and of control is misplaced; for the history of both multinational armies and alliances shows clearly that their cohesion does not depend primarily on the degree of integration and the quantity of legal ties, but is determined by the community of interests which holds out more advantages to the component parts if they stand together than if they go their separate ways.

No sovereign German government can be expected not to use its armed forces in support of its own interests, let alone to use them against those interests. Yet the political interests of Germany, with which our policy has shown an amazing unconcern, are in the long run irreconcilable with the military integration of West Germany into the Western alliance. Our often repeated official assertions to the contrary impress nobody in Germany and certainly not the German man-in-the-street. For it stands to reason that the reunion of a West Germany, militarily integrated into the Western alliance, with Soviet-occupied East Germany would be tantamount to the military integration of all of Germany into the Western alliance and, hence, would presuppose the capitulation of the Soviet Union.

West Germany can be firmly integrated into the Western alliance only at the price of the renunciation of its elemental national objective of making an end to the division of Germany. No great nation, especially one so proudly conscious of its newly won power as West Germany is today, will consent to such renunciation. It is this fundamental incompatibility between organizational devices and legal ties, on the one hand, and national interest, on the other, which dooms any attempt at integration, however ingeniously devised. Yet the legalistic obsession with integrating devices is not only useless in its own military frame of reference; it also tends to obstruct our basic political objective of making West Germany a reliable partner of the West and of withholding its political and military support from the Soviet Union. For it discredits American policy and those German political forces supporting it and, at the same time, strengthens those German forces which are hostile both to the ideas and to the interests of the West and which are by tradition, predilection, and political logic likely to seek Eastern orientation in order to satisfy the aspirations of Germany.

Any observer of the German scene who listens, not to official spokesmen, but to the man-in-the-street must be struck by the unpopularity of German rearmament, the drastic decline in American influence and prestige, and the indifference—tolerant or intolerant as the case may be—to the Bonn regime. On a recent trip to Germany I raised the question of German rearmament with scores of all kinds of people. I found only one man who came out in favor of it, and he is closely identified with the Adenauer government.

The arguments from which that opposition derives are three, and they are in order of priority: the threat to peace, the threat to German democracy, and the threat to unification.

Revulsion from war and desire for peace at virtually any price constitute at present the basic German attitudes toward international affairs, a truly revolutionary departure from the traditional German militarism. Rightly or wrongly, the opinion is prevalent in Germany that a German army would be used for the same purposes for which armies have been used in the past, that is, to make war. Rightly or wrongly, it is widely believed that the integration of a German army into the Western alliance will not diminish but increase the danger of war; for throughout Europe, what a few years ago was nothing more than a prop of Communist propaganda has now become a widely, if not generally, accepted belief: that the

Western alliance is at least as much an instrument of war as the Red Army.

What frightens the German man-in-the-street in the short run even more than the threat of war is the threat to democracy which he sees implicit in German rearmament. Germans remember the preponderant role which the German army has played as a social and political force throughout German history, a role which became well-nigh decisive, however carefully disguised, during that brief period of history from 1919 to 1933, when German political life operated within a constitutional framework and through the institutions of democracy. Germans are also dimly aware of the weakness of German democracy, a weakness which in many respects ominously resembles that of the Weimar Republic. The Bonn regime is accepted not because it evokes the active loyalties of the people, but because there exists no feasible alternative, especially as long as Germany is occupied by foreign troops. People vote for the parties of the Bonn regime, not out of enthusiasm, but *faute de mieux*.

An army will provide a new focus for active loyalties, especially when it seems to be hamstrung by foreign controls against which it struggles surreptitiously and successfully. If it follows the traditions established by its predecessors, it will become a political force in its own right, with domestic and foreign policies of its own. Unification might well provide an issue which would establish the army as the protector of the national interest against an indifferent, if not treacherous, civilian government, acting in concord with the foreign enemy.

Suspicion is widespread in Germany that neither the Bonn regime nor the Western powers are really interested in unification. The Bonn regime is suspected not to be interested because unification would deprive the governing coalition of its parliamentary majority and would radically change the social and religious complexion of West Germany. The Western powers, and more particularly France, are suspected on that count because, not being able to obtain military integration and unification at the same time, they have obviously chosen military integration as the goal to be obtained, while paying lip service to the ultimate objective of unification. This conclusion is strengthened by the impression of intransigence which the foreign policy of the United States is making not only in Germany but in Europe at large. The clumsiness and confusions of our foreign policy and the deterioration of professional competence and morale of our diplomatic representatives have not been lost on the Germans, and our friends in Bonn in particular react to them with indignation, derision, and despair. Russian tactics, with considerable aid and comfort from our own, exploit these weaknesses of both policy and diplomacy and have maneuvered us into a position in which we appear as a stumbling block to peace and national aspirations.

This being so, the demonstrative espousal of Adenauer as "our man" and the placing of all the bets of our German policy on him have tended to discredit rather than strengthen him in German eyes. Many have come to believe or suspect that he owes his position of authority to his support of Western designs, inimical to the interests of Germany, and that he keeps himself in power through his subservience to these designs. The Bonn regime, then, appears to many as the prolonged arm of the Western powers, putting Germany into the chains of "integration" in order to prevent it from achieving its destiny. It is against the background of such sentiments that one must judge the defections of important officials of the Bonn regime to the East. Their treason to the Bonn regime appears to nationalistic Germans as an ambiguous act in which treason to legal authority is mixed with loyalty to a greater Germany to which the legal authority seems at best indifferent. It is against this same background that one must evaluate the fact that recently all four living ex-chancellors of Germany, representing the most diverse colors of the political spectrum from the extreme right of Papen to the extreme left of Wirth, have declared their opposition to the Western orientation of the Bonn regime and their support for an independent policy which envisages an understanding with the Soviet Union.

Yet while our military policies appear to be incompatible with the fulfilment of the national aspirations of Germany, those very same policies assign to West Germany an essential role in the defense of the West. "Europe cannot be defended without twelve German divisions," has been the refrain dinned into the ears of thus far unreceptive Germans. The first reaction was one of *Schadenfreude*, and *"ohne mich"* was the answer. This negative mood still exists, but it is strongly mingled today with pride in the restored power of Germany and the rightness of its past policies; for, so ask many Germans, "Didn't we tell the Americans ten years ago what they are telling us now? And what was the answer then?" Thus, our insistence upon the vital importance of German rearmament for the Western world cannot fail to stimulate German nationalism and so strengthen those antidemocratic forces which have no regrets about past policies except their lack of success. Yet our simultaneous insistence upon military integration with its concomitant controls and limitations makes us appear as the enemy of the aspirations of that very same nationalism which we are nourishing with the most potent argument of German military indispensability. Thus we will find ourselves caught in a vicious circle; for the nationalism which we are doing so much to keep alive will be turned by our military policies into a force hostile to our political aims.

If you want to make Germany a reliable member of the Western alliance, then you must persuade the Germans that their national interests can best be satisfied with your support. If you persuade them only that your own interests cannot be defended without their military support, you force upon them a key position in the balance of power between East and West and make them the center of attraction for both—an opportunity which only fools would not wish to exploit.

Such are the results of a policy which neglects fundamental political interests in its obsession with obsolete military considerations. The simple truth is that we have placed our bets on Germany rather than France and that we have replaced our traditional French orientation with a German one. There are men in the councils of our government who are convinced that the unification of Europe under German auspices is both desirable and inevitable, and who deplore Hitler's attempt for its methods and failure rather than its objective. The idea of German supremacy in Europe as being both desirable and inevitable must come naturally to men who are able to think only in terms of combat-ready divisions. Yet those of us who try to put military problems in their political context cannot fail to see that this conception defeats not only the political purposes of our German policy, but tends to have the same negative effect upon our French policies and thus upon our European policies. In short, that conception raises the specter of the dissolution of the Atlantic alliance.

Paradoxical as it may seem, the rise of Germany restores to France much of the freedom of action which it has possessed traditionally and of which it has been deprived since the end of the Second World War. Economic weakness and the intransigence of Stalinist policies left France hardly any freedom of movement, even within the limits of the Western alliance. Today trade with the Soviet bloc looms as an alternative to American economic support, and the flexibility of the foreign policy of Stalin's successors is not likely to require adherence to the Bolshevist gospel according to Malenkov as a precondition for close political and military association. That loosening of the two-bloc system offers France an alternative to the American orientation. After all, the traditional Russian orientation of France, with a superior Germany, did not grow from the whims of some individuals, but was a natural outcome of the distribution of power in Europe.

Once before, in 1919, France sought assurance against a German hegemony from the United States and Great Britain. It did not get it. At London, France obtained that assurance from Great Britain, but it received at best an equivocal answer from the United States, for the commitment of leaving American troops in Europe, weakened as it is by the recurrent talk about "agonizing reappraisal," is equivocal in its political purposes. Certainly its primary purpose is to deter the Russians, but what is its purpose with respect to the Germans? If to deter them, to deter them from what? If to encourage them, to encourage them for what? Here again it becomes obvious that a military policy operating in a political vacuum can only have pernicious results. Such a result has materialized at London.

For the first time, and contrary to a tradition which has remained unbroken since the First World War, France has not tried to draw the United States deeper into the affairs of Europe but to limit American influence. M. Mendès-France has insisted that the Brussels powers, and not NATO, control the rearmament of Germany. The political purpose of this insistence has been to exclude from this control the United States, which is a member of NATO but not a signatory of the Brussels Pact. This is a revolutionary development, equaling in its potentialities Great Britain's transformation into a continental military power. The British commitment mitigates the inferiority of France vis-à-vis Germany; it does not restore a healthy balance of power between the two countries. Thus France has traditionally sought still another counterweight to German power and has looked for it to Russia or the United States or both. If the United States should make itself unacceptable to France as such a counterweight by committing itself permanently to a German orientation, France would be forced by the very logic of its position to look East again.

There can be no doubt that the Soviet Union would pay a high price for a political and military understanding with either Germany or France or both. To France it can offer assurance against German hegemony and the transformation of the French Communist party into the mainstay of the national interest of France. To Germany it can give unification and the recovery of all or part of the eastern provinces. The vision of a united Europe under Russian auspices, without its concomitant bolshevization and even accompanied by the decline of domestic communism as a Russian fifth column, is no doubt farfetched today, and must seem fantastic to those whose own rigidity of mind is a mere ineffectual and obsolescent response to the self-defeating rigidity of Stalin's policies.

Yet here lies the real threat to American interests, which our fascination with twelve German divisions does nothing to counter but much to aggravate. How could that threat have been countered before the London conference, and how can it be countered now? The actual alienation of France from the United States and the prospective alienation of Germany from the West are both the result of the German orientation of our military policies to the neglect of political considerations. The subordination of the former to the latter, then, is the precondition for a reform of our European policies which does at least not carry from the outset the seeds of failure.

If we had established in our thinking this proper relationship between military and political policy before the London conference met, we would have restored the sovereignty of West Germany pure and simple without imposing either rearmament or ineffectual controls upon an unwilling country. We should have let the Germans use their sovereignty for their own political and military ends as they saw fit—which they will do anyhow, controls or no controls, integration or no integration. We should have abstained from trying to control what cannot be controlled and instead exerted our influence where it might count, that is, for unification without military strings attached. By doing this, we would have minimized the political liabilities which the restoration of German sovereignty would have created for us in any case in both Germany and France, and we would at the same time have maximized our political opportunities in appealing to the Germans as the disinterested champion of German unity.

However, the freedom of action of nations, as that of individuals, is narrowly circumscribed both by circumstances and by the limits which their own previous actions have erected. The circumstance which drastically limits the German policies of the United States lies in the unmatchable freedom of action which the Soviet Union enjoys vis-à-vis Germany; for the Soviet Union, controlling both Poland and East Germany like satrapies, can decree whatever arrangement—political or territorial—it sees fit to make in order to attract all of Germany to its side, or at least to detach West Germany from the Western alliance. By committing itself irrevocably to the controlled rearmament of West Germany, the United States has on its own volition narrowed even more its freedom of political action. Nations, like men, can cross the Rubicon, and after the point of no return is passed, there remains only to mitigate the consequences of folly and to hope for the best. This is about the situation in which we find ourselves today. The best we can do under the circumstances is to pursue within the framework of the London accords policies which restore as much as possible the ascendancy of political over military considerations. Concretely that would mean, on the one hand, to play down both the indispensability of the German military contribution and the importance of integration and controls and, on the other hand, to emphasize the identity of our objectives with the German aspirations for unification. The forthcoming implementation of the London accords presents us with an opportunity to change at least the emphasis of our policies.

Without such a change and with our military obsession continuing unabated, we are apt to see a new political vacuum develop in the heart of Europe which promises to the Soviet Union a political and military harvest even richer than that which it reaped from another political vacuum created by our preoccupation with military matters and the neglect of political considerations at the end of the Second World War. Of the policies responsible for that political vacuum, from which most of our present troubles stem, General Bradley has said in retrospect: ". . . we looked naïvely on this British inclination to complicate the war with political foresight and nonmilitary objectives." Let us beware lest a sad reflection such as this become an appropriate motto for the memoirs of Mr. Dulles.

14 *The Problem of German Reunification*

German reunification is like the weather. Everybody talks about it, but nobody does anything about it. The analogy does not end there. For nobody does anything about the weather because nobody can do anything about it; and to a very great degree, especially in so far as the Western world is concerned, we do not do anything about German unification because we are unable to do anything about it. There is, then, a great gap between the verbal professions of interest in German unification and the actual unwillingness and inability to do anything about it. The reasons for this hopeless situation—hopeless in terms of German unification —lie deep in the very nature of the German problem as it presents itself not only to the Soviet Union and the nations of Eastern Europe but to the Western world as well.

In order to do justice to the German problem and the policies of the nations regarding it, it is necessary to take into account certain objective facts. First of all, even the truncated West Germany of today has already become the third most powerful nation on earth. This is one fact. Furthermore, and this fact goes back into history at least to the first unification of Germany in 1870, the other nations of Europe have regarded and still regard today a powerful, independent Germany as a threat to their interests, if not to their existence. And third, the other nations of Europe have tried to counter this threat of a powerful, independent Germany, and this goes back even to the seventeenth century, by dividing Germany.

The present attitude of both the Soviet Union and the United States toward Germany was established immediately after the Second World War and has remained constant to this very day because of the objective interests which both powers must pursue with regard to Germany. Considering the actual and potential power of Germany, neither side has been willing to contemplate all of Ger-

From the *Annals of the American Academy of Political and Social Science*, July, 1960.

many joining the other side as an ally or a satellite. Of this unwillingness, the division of Germany has been the logical result. In other words, what has happened in Korea and Vietnam has also happened with regard to Germany. Since neither side could accept the falling of the whole country into the orbit of the other side and since neither side had enough power to draw all of the country to its side, the division of these countries was a natural consequence of the actual balance of power, of the military and political stalemate, between East and West. The negotiations between East and West which have been carried on over the unification of Germany in innumerable conferences since 1947 all ended in complete failure. They were bound to end so because they were not real negotiations at all. Either side could have had no doubt but that what it proposed was unacceptable to the other side or was acceptable only on the condition of unconditional surrender. . . .

It is in the context of this hopeless and entirely negative situation that one must consider the current issue of Berlin, for the issue of Berlin has not been created by Mr. Khrushchev for his own amusement. The issue is intimately connected not only with the issue of Germany but more particularly with the long-range objectives of Soviet foreign policy. In order to understand more clearly the significance of the Berlin issue as it was raised by Mr. Khrushchev in November, 1958, one has to go back to the objectives of Stalinist foreign policy.

The major objective of Stalin in Europe was the stabilization of the status quo. During the Second World War, he conceived of the postwar world and, more particularly, Europe being divided between the United States and the Soviet Union into two gigantic spheres of influence, with both superpowers governing the rest of the world in unison and the Soviet Union advancing whenever the opportunity arose. Stalin made numerous proposals, either directly or indirectly through neutral diplomats, for an arrangement with the United States by which at least Europe would be divided into two spheres of influence with the military line of demarcation of 1945 constituting the boundary of the two empires. The United States has consistently refused even to consider such an arrangement. The United States has always regarded the line of military demarcation of 1945 as a provisional line which after a final settlement would run much farther to the east than it runs now. Here again, of course, the division of Germany is the outward manifestation of this stalemate over the territorial settlement of the Second World War, which one side regards as provisional and the other side wants to have recognized as definitive.

Khrushchev has revived this Stalinist objective by raising the issue of Berlin in an acute and threatening form. He has created the Berlin issue as a symbolic manifestation of the over-all German issue, and here lies its significance; for as long as part of Berlin—that is to say, the capital of a once united Germany, the potential capital of a reunited Germany—is occupied by the Western powers, that occupation symbolizes the provisional character of the division of Germany. If the Western powers were to leave Berlin, making it first a so-called "free city" and then allowing it to become a truly "free" city in the Communist sense—that is to say, a Communist city—they would relinquish that symbolic foothold. . . .

Furthermore, from the Russian point of view, as long as the Western powers are in Berlin by right and not merely by sufferance of the Soviet Union, a point to which I intend to return in a minute, the division of Germany is only provisional, for the status quo of Berlin implies paradoxically enough an instability in the status quo of all of Germany. . . . Once the Western powers have weakened their foothold in Berlin, in that measure the division of Germany is on the way to becoming permanent. And this is exactly what Khrushchev is aiming at. Through the instrumentality of the Berlin issue, he tries to force the West to recognize what it has refused to recognize for the last fifteen years, that is, the definitive division of Europe, with the Russian army standing one hundred miles east of the Rhine and staying there for an indefinite future. So the issue that Khrushchev has raised is by no means limited to whether there ought to be eleven or eight or six or five or four thousand Western troops in Berlin, or whether they ought to be in Berlin by virtue of this kind of arrangement or another kind of arrangement; the issue Mr. Khrushchev has raised is the fundamental issue of who shall rule what, and whether what is ruled now by the Soviet Union shall be ruled by it in perpetuity, recognized in its legitimacy by the West. In order to make the over-all status quo in Europe more secure for the Soviet Union, he has called into question the status quo of Berlin.

Thus the issue of Berlin in its true dimensions by far transcends the legal modalities of the Western presence in Berlin. The Western presence in Berlin and its modalities are a mere symbolic manifestation of the underlying issue from which the Cold War between the Soviet Union and the United States arose in the first place and which divides the Soviet Union and the United States today, that is, the legitimacy of the status quo. That issue will continue to divide them as long as both sides defend their interests as they see them.

It has been said that the issue of Berlin is not negotiable. Mr. Adenauer has said it in the name of Germany, and Mr. Acheson has said it as a citizen of the United States, but speaking also for a considerable body of American opinion. They have said that the Berlin issue cannot be negotiated, and I must say that in so far as the substance of the issue is concerned, I agree with them; for if you live in your house and your neighbor tells you to get out, you cannot reply "let's negotiate about it." Either you stick to your right to stay in your house and that is that, or your very willingness to negotiate implies that you are not quite sure that you have the right to be where you are. You cannot insist on your right and make it the subject of debate at the same time.

Mr. Khrushchev is a much more subtle man than Mr. Stalin was, and by trying to change the legal foundation of the Western presence in Berlin, he really tries to undermine the legal right of the West to be in Berlin. At present, the West is in Berlin not by leave of the Soviet Union, not by virtue of a contract with the Soviet Union, but by the right of the conqueror. Now Mr. Khrushchev says, on the face of it in a most reasonable manner—statesmen that try to separate you from what belongs to you often appear very reasonable—"The Second World War has ended fifteen years ago. Isn't it time to liquidate the war? Oughtn't we to have peace now?" What could be more sensible than this? And so he says: "Let's change the legal foundation for the Western presence in Berlin. Let's give up the right of the conqueror and you, the United States, Great Britain, and France, make a treaty with the Soviet Union, and we will allow you to stay in, and to have access to, Berlin." However, there is a great deal of difference between being in Berlin on the basis of conquest and being in Berlin because the Soviet Union allows you to be there; for what the Soviet Union allows you today it can deny you tomorrow, and international treaties have a way of being left by the wayside when the situation under which they have been concluded changes. The Soviet Union has shown itself particularly adept, as have other nations, at making treaty stipulations conform to changing circumstances. This innocent-looking change in the legal right of the West to be in Berlin would really put the West at the mercy of the Soviet Union with regard to that right.

However, to say that you cannot negotiate about the substance of your right to be in Berlin does not mean that you cannot negotiate about the modalities of your presence. Certainly you can manipulate that right, you may debate the decorations of the house, the roof, the paint, the driveway. You can agree to building a different fence—say, a United Nations fence—if your neighbor does not like the fence you have. Or we can diminish our troops in a moderate way, or we can stop hostile propaganda. We can pledge ourselves not to have atomic weapons in Berlin, which we would not want to have there anyway, and so forth. But you cannot sit down and negotiate about your right to be where you are without by implication casting doubt on that right.

If this is the nub of the Berlin issue, then the struggle over Berlin is really a struggle for Germany, and we should realize its significance. And those in our midst, and more particularly in Great Britain, who say that the Berlin issue is not worth bothering about and is not worth fighting for, if they face the issue squarely, are really saying that Germany is not worth bothering about and Germany is not worth fighting for. And this is exactly what Mr. Khrushchev wants us to believe. For once we have retreated in Berlin, we have not only started to give up Berlin, but we have started to give up much more.

This leads me to a point which is again part of the objective conditions with which all policy must come to terms, regardless of what it aims at and what measures it proposes. That is the basic fact that with regard to the unification of Germany and to the future allegiance of Germany the Soviet Union has an enormous advantage over the West; for the Soviet Union can unify Germany tomorrow if it wants to, simply by throwing the East German government overboard. . . . What has kept West Germany thus far on the Western side is its mistrust of the ultimate objectives of the Soviet Union and its confidence in the objectives and power of the West. In the measure that this mistrust and this confidence should diminish, West Germany will be tempted to try to obtain from the Soviet Union what it wants, that is, unification and the restoration of the former eastern frontiers. The only hope the West has to prevent this from happening is to keep West Germany from becoming disillusioned with the West and to make it crystal-clear that the West will not accede to the Soviet Union's demands either with regard to Berlin or with regard to any other issue in which Germany has an interest; for if West Germany should believe, rightly or wrongly, that it cannot rely upon the West for support in the pursuit of its national objectives, it will naturally turn elsewhere, and the natural direction in which it will turn is the Soviet Union.

Mr. Khrushchev, who is a subtle but also a blunt man, has taken this possibility into account. He has said to one of his Western visitors that one of these days he will make a bargain with West Germany, and the West will then be left empty-handed. This is a real danger. It is not yet an acute danger, but it is a real danger because it is inherent in the objective conditions of interest and power. Hence, the West must be on guard lest it is lured into policies which will give both the Soviet Union and West Germany an incentive for bringing to pass what would be a real catastrophe for the interests and the power position of the West. It is obvious that the prospects for German unification are dim as long as both sides keep their positions. There is no chance for the unification of Germany under Western auspices as long as the power and interests of the Soviet Union are what they are today. It is also obvious, it seems to me, that the prospects for German unification under Russian auspices will be greatly improved if the West should weaken in its resistance to changing the status quo in Berlin in order to stabilize, for the time being, the status quo in all of Germany.

So far I have spoken primarily of American and Soviet policies. Ten years ago it would have been sufficient to do that, and I could have stopped here. But today it is, of course, necessary to speak of German policies as well. For, as I pointed out before, Germany has already become one of the great powers—economically and politically strong and in the process of becoming militarily strong again. Here lies another factor which strengthens the hand of the Soviet Union. For nobody fears the military power of Germany more than the countries of Eastern Europe, such as Czechoslovakia and Poland, who remember what happened to them fifteen and twenty years ago when Germany was very powerful indeed. And the support of the nations of Eastern Europe for the German policies of the Soviet Union is primarily motivated by that fear. Here is another problem and, I think, another opportunity for the West.

It is interesting to note that President de Gaulle, alone of all the Western statesmen, has seen this opportunity by declaring himself in favor of the Oder-Neisse line as the permanent eastern frontier of Germany. If all nations would make such a declaration—in other words, if all nations would make it appear a hopeless undertaking for any German government ever to recover the regions east of the Oder-Neisse line—the present community of interests between the Soviet Union and the nations of Eastern Europe would be thereby weakened, if not destroyed, in so far as their policies toward Germany are concerned. And, I think, the nations of the West would also greatly contribute to the stabilization of order in all of Europe and to the promotion of freedom in Eastern Europe.

These considerations have, of course, but an indirect and negative bearing upon my topic, the unification of Germany. They deal with policies and conditions which would make the continuing division of Germany bearable for all concerned, for unification cannot be brought about in the foreseeable future by diplomatic negotiations. Given the continuation of the present balance of military power, it cannot be brought about by force. It can only be brought about by the Soviet Union, which, as I have said, occupies the key position in this situation, realizing that it is more to its advantage to relinquish East Germany than to keep it indefinitely.

The last question I want to raise then is how can one create an interest in the Soviet Union to yield East Germany? Two proposals have been made to create such an interest; one has been the neutralization of Germany—which was widely debated in the late forties —the other, more recently discussed, has been disengagement. Neutralization might have been possible perhaps ten or twelve years ago when Germany was both impotent and antimilitaristic. But a great power which is aware of its power and which is rapidly regaining its military strength, primarily under Western instigation and auspices, cannot be neutralized from the outside. It can be neutral if it wants to be neutral, but no other power or group of powers will be able to impose neutrality upon it against its will. Thus nobody, I suppose, seriously thinks of the neutralization of Germany today. The idea of disengagement, on the other hand, implies a retreat of the armed forces which face each other in the center of Europe at the line of demarcation of 1945, so that a zone free of the armed forces of both West and East would be created, comprising at least all of Germany and some adjacent territories to the east and west. I have always had difficulty in seeing the virtue of this proposal in strictly military terms, for obviously the danger of war does not arise from armed forces opposing each other in physical proximity in Europe. It arises rather from intercontinental ballistic missiles poised in readiness on both sides. This danger would not be affected by disengagement. This anticipated benefit of disengagement, if I understand it correctly, is really political. It is intended to create an incentive for the Soviet Union, by paying it a price, to loosen its military grip on Eastern Europe.

In the abstract, this is indeed a sensible proposition. But as a practical matter, it has become obvious from Mr. Khrushchev's words and deeds that he does not intend to strike a bargain for such a price. Being aware of the inner weakness of the Russian empire, on the one hand, and, on the other, being much more committed than Stalin ever was to the dynamic expansion of communism, he intends to stabilize, not to dismantle, that empire. The Russian government cannot afford, in view of both his weakness and this dynamism, to retreat from any forward position, such as East Germany, without endangering its empire altogether, for once it starts retreating there will be no way of knowing where the retreat will stop. Once the East Germans have regained their freedom, will not the Poles and Hungarians try to regain theirs? Furthermore, a political movement which claims to bring salvation to all mankind and looks forward to burying the non-Communist world cannot afford to retreat; it cannot afford to stop advancing. At the very least, it must stay where it is and must try to advance; for by retreating, it denies its very claim of being the "wave of the future," the ideal organization of society in whose image sooner or later the whole world will be organized. Thus it is impossible to visualize at present a price sufficient to induce the Soviet Union to forsake East Germany and thereby create the essential precondition for German unification.

This is obviously, in terms of German unification, a hopeless outlook. But it is not necessarily a hopeless outlook in terms of the objective interests of all concerned. We and everybody else can live with a divided Germany, provided we can convince the West Germans that they also must live for the time being with a divided Germany. Knowing that Germany cannot at present be united, we must nevertheless keep up their hope that one day it will. And we must convince them that their hope to see their country united on tolerable terms lies in co-operation with the West. This task requires a great measure of statesmanship, of subtlety, of courage, and of caution, and it carries within itself a formidable danger. That danger poses the real problem for Western policy: how to prevent the West Germans from becoming desperate about unification and making a bargain with the Soviet Union.

15 *The Immaturity of Our Asian Policy*

The American position in the world, as it appears at the beginning of 1956, suggests that we have not learned or forgotten enough; we have sometimes learned the wrong lessons and forgotten what we just seemed to have learned. We have learned that in our age world politics is being fought with the weapons not only of diplomacy and military might but also of psychological warfare; it has become in good measure a struggle for the minds of men. Yet in practice we conceive that struggle for the minds of men primarily as a kind of philosophic debate, far removed from the concrete, specific concerns of living men.

We have also learned that in order to protect and promote one's interests in a world of competing and hostile nations a nation must be strong. Yet we have defined strength primarily in military terms. In doing so, we have fallen into the same error which cost us the political reward of victory in two world wars: divorcing military policy from political objectives it is meant to serve.

We have also learned that there exists a relation between the economic and technological advancement of underdeveloped countries and the objectives of our foreign policy. Yet in practice we have not been able to correlate our economic and technical aid to our political objectives, beyond discriminating between our allies and the uncommitted nations. The main standard by which we have judged our aid has been its soundness in technical terms; the correlation between aid and political stability has by and large escaped us—in theory and practice.

These different policies—psychological, military, economic—are not operationally oriented toward common political objectives. That missing common orientation has been supplied by a peculiar type of political oratory which correlates these different policies both to the highest ideals of mankind and to our ability to wage war successfully. It is typical of this oratory, singularly unrevealing

From the *New Republic*, March 12, 19, 26, and April 16, 1956.

about the real issues confronting the United States, that it is hardly ever followed by action, political or military. It seeks not to justify and explain action, but to provide a substitute for it. Thus official pronouncements on foreign policy, self-advertisement, bluff, and hoax tend to become indistinguishable.

This combination of mechanical military measures and similarly mechanical economic aid—with the propensity to think about foreign policy in terms of philosophic abstractions and to talk about it like a huckster—has been the bane of our foreign policy. It leaves unattended that intermediate sphere of political maneuver where a peaceful foreign policy finds the opportunity of bringing its imagination, inventiveness, and flexibility to bear upon the concrete political issues of the day. It is in that sphere that the political battles are won and lost.

What ails American foreign policy today—and what has ailed it during the better part of the last half-century—is not primarily clumsiness in execution here, weakness in administration there, improvidence at another place—even though it is no stranger to these ailments either—but an all-pervading deficiency of understanding. *The foreign policy of the United States is not based upon the threat that faces it and, hence, is not capable of countering this threat.* The uncertainties and blunders of many of our concrete moves have their roots in that basic misunderstanding.

The negative political effects of that deficiency of understanding are less obvious in Europe than they are in Asia, for the conflict in Europe can indeed be defined in good measure in strictly military and purely ideological terms. The military security of Western Europe is threatened by Russian imperialism, as is its intellectual and moral identity by the advance of communism. It is true that by placing these two issues in a political vacuum and divorcing them thereby from the concrete, specific interests of the individual nations of Western Europe, we have done more than has our enemy to jeopardize our position in Europe.

But it is in Asia that the weakness of our thinking on foreign policy becomes fully apparent, for here both the extremes of philosophic generalities and local military preparations completely miss the point. The ideological cannonade, as it were, soars far above the advancing enemy, and military pacts, far from stopping him, actually help him to advance. Nowhere in Asia, with the exception of Japan, is the conflict between communism and democracy relevant or even intelligible as a philosophic contest between tyranny and freedom, between the total state and the individual. Nowhere in Asia does either the Soviet Union or Communist China advance under the banner of Marxism, calling upon the masses to assume the historic role which Marx had assigned them. Instead, communism advances by identifying itself with the concerns and, more particularly, the grievances, of different groups.

All Asians are afraid of atomic war; thus the Soviet Union poses as the defender of peace. All Asians are opposed to colonialism; thus the Soviet Union poses as the enemy of colonialism. The educated classes throughout Asia seek economic advancement and technological development; thus the Soviet Union poses as the champion of that, too. The political leaders of the uncommitted nations—and the leaders of the nations committed to the United States as well—want to be on the winning side; thus both the Soviet Union and Communist China claim that the future belongs to them.

All educated Asians remember with awe or pride the past greatness of China as a culture and a state. Thus Communist China impresses the unceasing stream of visitors from all over Asia—estimated for 1955 at close to 100,000—not with the Communist qualities of its philosophy and institutions, but with the restored dignity and power of a great nation. Similarly, the delegations, books, magazines, and movies which Communist China is sending all over Asia make their impact by identifying themselves not with Chinese communism but with the great tradition of Chinese culture.

The Communist victory in Vietnam was a victory of anticolonialism, for which communism supplied effective leadership and organization. Communist infiltration in Malaya and Singapore is accounted for in part by the specific need of a Chinese majority for protection against a Malay minority; British rule has provided that protection thus far, but its impending disappearance compels the Chinese to look elsewhere, and they look naturally to the restored power of China. Besides, here and elsewhere, grievances of Chinese labor provide a vehicle for the advance of communism. And everywhere in Asia, China and, through it, communism attract the gifted youth of the Chinese communities because they find in China the only opportunities for study and work, commensurate with their ambitions and abilities.

Conversely, the relative lack of success of communism in certain parts of Asia, such as Cambodia, Thailand, and Hong Kong, is due to nothing else but the lack of grievances which communism could exploit. The three major reverses which communism has suffered in Asia are likewise the result not, as we have been led to believe, of a revolt against Communist philosophy and the Communist way of life, but of specific and thus far unique circumstances. First, the Chinese soldiers who refused to return to Communist China after they had been captured by United Nations forces in the Korean War were members of former units of the Nationalist army who had most recently been captured by the Communists and whom, for want of sufficient indoctrination, the Chinese Communists considered as expendable. Second, the overwhelming majority of the approximately 800,000 refugees who left the Communist part of Vietnam for the South are Catholics who had lived in the North in compact communities and left in a body under the leadership of their priests; the balance is composed of the families of soldiers of the army of South Vietnam who happened to live north of the demarcation line. And third, the main bulk of the refugees who streamed into Hong Kong in 1949 and 1950 did so for the traditional economic reasons, and the small-scale reverse movement from Hong Kong to Communist China is motivated by similar considerations.

The Soviet Union and Communist China have joined the battle on the level of the actual, specific aspirations and grievances of the peoples of Asia, and their success has been spectacular and consistent. This success has been in part inevitable; for the restored power of China—to give only one example—makes an unanswerable case for Chinese influence in Asia. In good measure, however, that success is due to the inadequacy of our own policies, derived from a philosophy which has no bearing at all upon the actual issues at stake.

That philosophy has just been codified in a document which will certainly go down in history as one of the most extraordinary state papers of all times. It is called "Militant Liberty"; its author is John C. Broger, president of the Far East Broadcasting Company, consultant in the Office of the Joint Chiefs of Staff, and an officer in the Naval Reserve. It offers a blueprint for United States psychological warfare together with a quantitative method to evaluate its effects. It was approved last summer by a conference of a score of distinguished public figures convened by the secretary of defense. Admiral Radford, the chairman of the Joint Chiefs of Staff, has been its most enthusiastic champion, and last fall the Joint Chiefs approved it. Many and various activities carried on by our government are based on it.

"Militant Liberty" is hardly remarkable in itself. It is one of those documents which come from time to time across one's desk, impressing one by the combination of enthusiasm, ignorance, and naïveté. "Militant Liberty" has these three qualities in the extreme. No description and analysis can convey the full flavor of its illiteracy.

What makes "Militant Liberty" remarkable is the faithfulness, undiluted by even the shadow of a doubt, with which it reflects the philosophy which dominates our understanding of the Asian problem and the policies devised to cope with it. What makes "Militant Liberty" a sensation and a scandal is the fact that the government of a great and civilized country sees fit to identify itself with so unmistakably misguided and incompetent an effort. In itself, "Militant Liberty" is laughable. As a state paper endorsed by the Government of the United States of America, it is nothing short of shocking, reflecting as it does upon the judgment of our leaders in matters of basic policy.

"Militant Liberty" starts with the sound observation that communism has been more successful than democracy in the struggle for the minds of men. Yet the conclusions it draws from this observation are unsound. It defines the conflict between democracy and communism in terms of "individual personality and conscience" versus "class conscience" or "conscience of the masses," which it regards to be the "hard-core of Communist philosophy." It assumes that "experience has demonstrated that aspects of Militant Liberty," defined as individual conscience, "will have a practical appeal to many individuals of every race, color or creed, irrespective of cultural, social, economic or political background." What, then, ought to be done?

The concept of Militant Liberty is designed as a program to be developed on a country-by-country basis to make available to peoples of the free world the ideas and ideals of individual liberty which are basic to a free society in a manner which will motivate indigenous leaders to seek training in and to foster these ideals within their own countries, insofar as local conditions will permit. . . . Therefore, the concept consists of motivating people everywhere to be collectively demonstrative of a positive philosophy of freedom. For this purpose, training must be available in the meaning of freedom, and the methodology of communication and persuasion.

Nations can be evaluated "with reasonable accuracy" as to the degree of liberty attained through a quantitative analysis of discipline, religion, civics, education, social order, and economic order. To each of these six categories a numerical value can be assigned ranging from zero to plus or minus one hundred according to a trend toward or away from liberty.

In the light of what has been said before, it is hardly necessary to point out that "Militant Liberty" has no bearing upon the situation in Asia. Neither liberty nor communism has a universal appeal, irrespective of the circumstances under which the individual appealed to lives. Communism has been successful wherever its tenets of social, economic, and political equality have appealed to people for whom the removal of inequality has been the most urgent aspiration. On the other hand, the appeal of liberty has succeeded wherever in popular aspiration political liberty has taken precedence over all other needs. For this reason, communism has largely lost the battle for the minds of men in Central and Western Europe, and democracy has by and large been defeated in Asia.

Little needs to be said to show that "Militant Liberty" is also defective in its own abstract philosophic terms, for it is obvious that it has hardly an inkling of the nature of Marxist philosophy. Marxism does not deny the existence of an individual conscience; it denies only that the content of this conscience derives either from supranatural or autonomous individual sources. Instead, it maintains that the consciousness of the proletarian class, as that of any other class, gives content to the individual conscience. In consequence, universal morality is transformed into class morality, determined by the consciousness of the class to which the individual happens to belong. The problem as to where the content of the individual conscience comes from is certainly different from the question of whether an individual conscience exists at all. By confounding the Marxist "consciousness" with "conscience," "Militant Liberty" offers a caricature of Marxist thought.

Its ignorance is as glaring in what it does not say about Marxism as in what it says. It would certainly be fortunate for us if there were nothing more to Marxism than this emphasis upon the collective consciousness. But must one really point out to the Joint Chiefs of Staff that Marxist philosophy contains a few other "hard-core" elements which are politically relevant and without which the persistent intellectual attraction of Marxism could not be explained?

Such is the quality of the weapon with which the Joint Chiefs of Staff intend to win the battle for the minds of men throughout the world. They might as well divine their military strategy from the flight of birds and fashion our economic policy after the Townsend Plan.

Our policies in Asia are irrelevant to the political problems confronting us. At best, they are ineffective, as are our propaganda and economic policies. At worst, the political damage they do is out of all proportion to whatever intrinsic merits they may have; this is true of our military policies.

Our military policies in Asia owe their existence to the shock of the Korean War. The North Korean attack demonstrated the need for local military defenses wherever a similar attack was likely to occur. Our commitment to defend South Korea, Formosa, and South Vietnam meets that obvious military requirement. However, the Korean War gave rise to a broad interpretation of the Asian problem in primarily military terms. The North Korean attack was interpreted to have been planned by the Soviet Union as the opening move in a series of military aggressions likely to occur anywhere in Asia. The Soviet Union was believed to have changed its policy radically from peaceful penetration and subversion to open warfare. If that interpretation was correct, a corresponding shift of our policies was obviously in order.

Yet that interpretation was intrinsically implausible at the time and has been discredited further by subsequent events. The evidence, both intrinsic and explicit, points strongly toward a different interpretation. According to it, the Russian role in the outbreak of the Korean War was one of acquiescence rather than of instigation, resulting from a miscalculation of our intentions and capabilities. However, our military policies have never recovered from the shock of that original assumption of Communist determination to launch military aggression at any time anywhere in Asia. Our military policies remain oriented toward this assumption. They have taken two different forms: in our rearmament policy for Japan, and our alliance policy in south Asia. In both instances the military advantages have been negligible, while the political results have been disastrous.

The only legitimate military interest we have in Japan is the availability of air bases. Whatever Japan will do to increase that availability must be welcome to, and supported by, American policy. Thus we must welcome and support Japanese measures of internal security. However, over-all rearmament of Japan, with which our policy has identified itself, does not meet that test. For no contingency can be visualized which would require the traditional armed forces of Japan to protect our bases. These traditional forces would be useless as defense against an atomic attack, and Japan is protected against an invasion by the threat of American atomic retaliation and not by whatever traditional forces she could put into the field. As far as Japan herself is concerned, the availability of our air bases rests primarily not on military but on political foundations. It is exactly these political foundations that our rearmament policy tends to undermine.

For rearmament is unpopular in Japan. It is so per se and as an instrument of American policy. Japan has drawn from the Second World War the lesson that militarism does not pay, especially when you are on the losing side. Rearmament and militarism are largely equated by the popular mind; and since militarism stands for defeat, devastation, and degradation, the shadow of these stigmas falls upon rearmament as well. For many Japanese, impressed in particular by the pacifist provisions of the MacArthur constitution, democracy in turn has come to mean disarmament, peace, and a new deal.

Thus it is not by accident that the democratic and pro-American elements of the Japanese population oppose rearmament while the conservative and reactionary forces, potentially hostile to the United States, support it. Some support it halfheartedly and cynically as a means for getting the American forces out of the country. Others support it as a symbol of national sovereignty. Still others—at present a small minority—favor it as the instrument of an independent foreign policy.

One attitude unites both the foes and friends of rearmament: the bewilderment and resentment at the about-face of the United States. Defeat and occupation made a deep impression upon the Japanese mind. The Japanese were ready to follow the lead of, and imitate, a nation whose victory had proved its superiority in war and whose occupation policies seemed to prove its political superiority as well. The sudden reversal of our position on the rearmament issue has had a drastic psychological effect. It has darkened the image of the United States in the minds of precisely those Japanese upon whom the hope for a peaceful Japan, friendly to the West, has largely rested. To these Japanese, the United States appears now selfish, fallible, unreliable, and, more particularly, bent upon letting Japanese fight their wars.

It hardly needs emphasis that this political devastation, inflicted upon us not by the enemy but by ourselves, has not occurred in a political vacuum. Our rearmament policy is being exploited for all it is worth by Marxists of all shades of opinion. More detrimental by far has been the connection which many Japanese have established between our insistence upon their rearmament and our entanglement with Communist China over the island of Formosa. While there is hardly a Japanese who does not favor the establishment of normal political and economic relations with Communist China, I have not found a single one who supports our Formosa policy. It is in this political and military context that we must put the rearmament of Japan, for it is in that context that the Japanese themselves see it. The coincidence of our China and rearmament policies suggests to them the ominous possibility of their involvement in a war against their will and their interests.

There are indeed situations in which a nation must take great political risks and incur great political liabilities for the sake of greater military advantage. The rearmament of Japan, however, is not one of them. It is the tragedy of our Japanese policy and the crowning monument to our folly that by identifying ourselves with the rearmament of Japan, we have created political conditions adverse to that very rearmament. Our very insistence upon it has made Japan reluctant to go on with it. It is hardly open to doubt that a sovereign Japan—conscious of her power, aware of her interests, and free to decide her own course of action in this as in other matters— would in the long run have rearmed, in one form or the other, much more willingly than she does now and without being able to blame the United States for a step which she would have taken on her own initiative.

The same pattern of the payment of an exorbitant political price for insignificant or illusory military advantages is repeated in south Asia. Neither the Southeast Asia Treaty Organization (SEATO) nor the Baghdad Pact adds anything material to the strength of the West. All the nations concerned, with the exception of Iran, Pakistan, and Thailand, were already members of one or the other Western military alignment before the conclusion of these pacts. Nothing needs to be said of the obvious military insignificance of Iran and Thailand, which would be liabilities rather than assets for whatever side they would join in case of actual war. A few words, however, need to be said about Pakistan, which is the strongest ally the United States has on the continent of Asia.

The military power of Pakistan is the measure of America's military power on that continent. Pakistan has a good army of more than 200,000 men and a population of close to 100 million. As a member of both the Baghdad Pact and SEATO she is the connecting link between the two defense organizations. Her government is as reliable and co-operative as that of any of our Asian allies.

But beneath these appearances of strength there is enormous and, so it seems, irremediable weakness. Pakistan is not a nation and hardly a state. It has no justification in history, ethnic origin, language, civilization, or the consciousness of those who make up its population. They have no interest in common save one: fear of Hindu domination. It is to that fear, and to nothing else, that Pakistan owes its existence, and thus far its survival, as an independent state. When India gained her independence and the civil war between Hindus and Moslems ended, two regions, the western and easternmost parts of India, remained with a predominantly Moslem population. These two regions, West Pakistan, with the capital Karachi, and East Bengal form the state of Pakistan. It is as if after the Civil War Louisiana and Maryland had decided to form a state of their own with the capital in Baton Rouge. In fact, it is worse than that.

The two parts of Pakistan are separated not only by 1,200 miles of Indian territory, but even more by language, ethnic composition, civilization, and outlook. West Pakistan belongs essentially to the Middle East and has more in common with Iran or Iraq than with East Bengal. East Bengal, in turn, with a population which is one-third Hindu is hardly distinguishable from West Bengal, which belongs to India, and gravitates toward the latter's capital, Calcutta; the major labor unions in East Bengal, for instance, are run from Calcutta. The man in the street in West Pakistan speaks any one of four languages—none of which enables him to communicate with the Bengali-speaking inhabitants of East Bengal. A politician in Karachi who is able to address an East Bengal audience in its own tongue has a rare political asset. While 84 per cent of the total population of Pakistan is illiterate, the literacy rate is much higher in East Bengal, which is also much more politically conscious and active than its western counterpart.

Even Jinnah, the creator of this strange state, did originally not believe in its viability, and there are few politicians in Karachi today who really believe in it. If there are solutions which could assure the future of Pakistan, only extraordinary wisdom and political skill will find them and put them into effect. If there is such wisdom and skill in Pakistan, it is not to be found among the politicians of Karachi. Thus it is hard to see how anything but a miracle, or else a revival of religious fanaticism, will assure Pakistan's future.

Against whom and how is an army likely to fight, which is built upon so tenuous a political foundation? Aside from the fact that the Karachi government may well need its army to maintain its rule over the two disparate territories of Pakistan, geography allows of military operations only against two countries: Afghanistan and India. While the Pakistani army could easily take care of Afghanistan and might perhaps be able to defend West Pakistan against India at the price of the surrender of East Bengal, such capabilities are obviously meaningless in view of the over-all political and strategic situation on the continent of Asia as it appears from the vantage point of the United States. A local war between Pakistan and one or the other of its neighbors would not necessarily affect the interests of the United States to the point of requiring its intervention. A general war into which Pakistan would be drawn should set the United States on the side where her interests lie, which might or might not be the side of Pakistan.

In such a general war it is not very likely that the main issue would be joined where the Pakistani army happens to be. Geography makes it impossible for that army in case of war to give effective assistance to any of its allies under either the Baghdad Pact or SEATO or receive such assistance from them. The SEATO treaty appears to take that impossibility into account by stipulating in case of military attack against a member state, not automatic military assistance (as NATO does), but only consultation, which would be likely to occur even without a formal legal commitment.

The absurdity of these military alignments is surpassed only by the absurdity of their political consequences. By allying ourselves with Thailand, we have alienated Burma, which is militarily and in view of the social and political dynamics of Asia infinitely more important than a stagnant country—bypassed by the Asian revolution—such as Thailand, which has been traditionally misgoverned to the satisfaction of its population. By allying ourselves with Pakistan, we have alienated India, which for identical reasons is infinitely more important than our ally. The Baghdad Pact, far from erecting a barrier against Russian penetration of the Middle East, has given Egypt and the other Arab countries hostile to Iraq the incentive and the pretext to come to terms with each other and with the Soviet Union.

The political bankruptcy of this military policy is indeed complete. Yet the origins of that military policy, at least in so far as SEATO is concerned, shed a revealing light upon the general character of our foreign policy. It can be stated on excellent authority that when SEATO was conceived in the fall of 1954, it was intended not as a measure of military policy but of psychological warfare. It was intended to counteract the psychological damage which the partition of Vietnam at the Geneva Conference of 1954 had inflicted upon the prestige of the West, the United States included. It was intended as a gesture of defiance, as an act which would convey the appearance of initiative and strength where actual initiative and strength were lacking. As such, SEATO was slated to take its place in that series of portentous yet hollow pronouncements which range from liberation and the unleashing of Chiang Kai-shek through agonizing reappraisal and the "new look" to the brink of war.

Yet while SEATO is militarily hollow and politically pernicious, it is more than a unilateral pronouncement of the Secretary of State of the United States. It is a solemn undertaking to which the representatives of the member states have put their signatures. This circumstance imposes upon the United States additional liabilities, both economic and political. Our Asian allies make no bones about their intention to use SEATO as an entering wedge into the treasury of the United States. Since they are our allies, they must have first claim upon American financial support. As one of the most astute of our representatives in Asia put it to me: "This is like the Community Chest. Two agencies acting in concert can collect more than two agencies acting alone."

SEATO, thus having become an instrument of economic pressure, transforms itself in the hands of its Asian members into a political weapon directed against the United States. Since whatever economic and political support these allies receive can never be enough, they are in a position of threatening the United States with looking for support elsewhere. The success of Egypt in playing one side against the other has impressed Thailand and Pakistan. Strong neutralist tendencies have recently come to the surface in both countries. On his recent visit to Burma, the prime minister of Thailand went so far as to equate his country's membership in SEATO with membership in the United Nations. And on December 26 of last year the Karachi Provincial Muslim League called upon the government to revise its foreign policy, declaring it "a failure on the whole." The government of Pakistan has echoed these sentiments by complaining that the government of the United States does not support Pakistan strongly enough against India.

Thus in every respect our military policy in Asia is a failure. It is a failure in its own military terms, and it is a failure in the political consequences it has had for the relations with our potential friends and actual allies.

The immaturity of our foreign-aid policy is strikingly illustrated by the way in which the current debate concerning it is carried on. The principal point at issue is the amount of money to be spent, not the substance of the policy to be pursued. Both camps assume that one can, as it were, buy the objectives of foreign aid through the outlay of a certain amount of money; the more money one spends, the more objectives one is going to buy; and the only point of difference is how many objectives one needs and can afford to buy. This monetary conception of foreign aid has dominated our policy since the days of the Marshall Plan. Yet it has been mistaken from the beginning, and many of the frustrations and futilities of our foreign-aid policy can be attributed to this misplaced emphasis.

For the objectives of economic or technical aid are not economic or technical per se but political and social, and these objectives have to be attained through the intermediary of a foreign government which may or may not be willing and able to attain them. This twofold complication of the problem of foreign aid was obscured by the stark urgency with which the economic decay of Western Europe in the aftermath of the Second World War posed the problem for American policy. The problem was further obscured by the spectacular success which American policy achieved, measured by the requirements of the immediate emergency.

The Marshall Plan restored the productivity of Western Europe and advanced it to record heights. However, the Marshall Plan sought to restore not only the economic but also the social and political health of Western Europe. Communism has not been able to take over Western Europe, and the Marshall Plan deserves part of the credit for that victory. Yet communism is far from defeated in Western Europe, and the Marshall Plan is partly to blame for that failure; for while the Marshall Plan has regenerated the productive capacity of Western Europe, it has left its economic, social, and political structure by and large intact. The dangers to the stability and strength of Western Europe which have grown in the past from the defects of that structure have continued to grow because those defects were not repaired. The Marshall Plan almost completely lost sight of those roots of instability and unrest which antedated the emergency and were bound to operate after it was over.

In Asia, the choices for our foreign-aid policy have as a rule not been as simple as the European ones. In Europe, an emergency had to be met, and in meeting it we had to decide whether we wanted to deal also with the economic, social, and political problems transcending it. We decided not to meet them, primarily because we did not dare intervene actively in the domestic affairs of other nations. So, as a matter of principle, we gave aid "without strings attached." In Asia, the choices of objectives and of policies have been more varied and their probable consequences more difficult to assess. Rarely, as in Korea and Vietnam, were we faced with an emergency which left us little leeway in the choice of objectives and policies. Generally, in view of our over-all objective of withholding the uncommitted nations of Asia and those committed to us from Communist domination, we have had a multitude of choices on different levels of decision.

First of all, we have had a choice between action and non-action in terms of foreign aid. Some of the Asian nations might be so firmly committed to our side or else so determinedly uncommitted that their policy does not need to be supported by foreign aid. Other nations might have economic, social, and political systems of such a nature as to make them impervious to influence by foreign aid. Others still might be susceptible to political or military measures rather than to those of foreign aid. Or foreign aid might create such social, economic, and political instability as to make us prefer the preservation of the status quo to change.

Once we decided that none of these four reasons for non-action in terms of foreign aid applied, we had then to select from the many areas of action at our disposal: military, political, economic, technological, and prestige. The choice of a particular sphere of action is dictated by the expectation that through it the desired objective is most easily attainable. However, the attainment of the objective depends also upon the willingness and ability of the foreign nation to put the necessary measures into effect; for it is, as we have seen, a peculiarity of foreign aid that it must become effective through the intermediary of a foreign agent.

The foreign government is the natural first choice. Yet it is quite possible that foreign aid, in order to be effective, requires a political change either in the composition of the government or in the over-all political structure. There must be a policy then on how to inter-fere with the political processes of the foreign country and how to choose between government and private auspices.

Our policy of foreign aid to Asia shows hardly a trace of such thought processes. The four principles by which it is guided are, by contrast with the subtlety actually required, simplicity itself. First, it defines success and failure of a measure of foreign aid not in terms of its political objective but in its own technical terms; an economic measure, for instance, is judged not by its political conse-quences, but by its economic results. Second, the political objective of defense against communism tends to become equated with mili-tary preparedness per se; in consequence, military rather than po-litical objectives tend to provide the standard and goal for American policy. Third, as recipients of foreign aid we tend to select coun-tries which are friendly to us, defining friendliness in military terms and, hence, attaching visible or invisible military strings to our aid. Fourth, we prefer to give aid to the government in power, thereby contributing toward keeping it in power regardless of whether or not an available political or private alternative would be preferable in view of our interests.

Thus our policy of foreign aid has virtually lost sight of the over-all objective of our Asian policy. Instead, it has tended to become either an auxiliary of military policy, performing technical func-tions for it, or else a self-sufficient technical operation, to be judged solely in terms of the technical rules proper to it, that is, whether it will aid in the improvement of port facilities here, the increase of the agricultural yield there, and the modernization of accounting procedures elsewhere. In consequence, its operations have, at best, largely become irrelevant to the purposes of our political policy.

For an act of foreign aid is a political act, regardless of whether we want it to be so or whether we are even aware of it. In so far as our foreign aid is, or only appears to be, an auxiliary of our mili-tary policy, it partakes of necessity of the political liabilities of that policy, to which we have referred above. As such, it raises the spec-ter of Western imperialism, of militarism, and of the exploitation of the human and material resources of the recipient country for alien purposes, especially those of war. Far from creating good will for the United States, it becomes a potent weapon in the Communist arsenal.

We are giving military aid to the countries which we have selected not in view of our political and military interests, but in view of their willingness to accept it. It is not we who have selected our allies to serve our interests, it is they who have selected us to serve theirs as a supplier of goods and money. Since our military aid has no rational political objective, it is invalid not only in political but also in military terms. We are training and equipping foreign armies with apparently no thought being given to the political purposes to which those armies might be put, to the political consequences our support for them might call forth, and to the military context within which these armies might have a chance to operate successfully.

Wherever foreign aid is a self-sufficient technical operation, it tends to strengthen the status quo, without regard for the effects which the strengthening of the status quo may have upon the political interests of the United States. The increase in the productivity of a politically and socially unsound economic system is likely to accentuate unsolved social and political problems rather than bring them closer to solution. A team of efficiency experts and public accountants might well have improved the operations of the Al Capone gang; yet by doing so, it would have aggravated the social and political evils which the operations of that gang brought forth.

However, the lack of an organic connection between foreign aid and a clearly defined, consistent political policy tends to defeat foreign aid even if it is narrowly defined as a self-sufficient technical operation; for the very possibility of successful foreign aid thus defined may well depend upon the existence of a political and social environment conducive to it. In the absence of such an environment and with the aiding nation being oblivious to it, foreign aid, perfectly rational in its own terms, becomes a waste of human and material resources. Thus we sent the complete modern equipment for a tuberculosis hospital to East Pakistan where it remains unused because the interest and skill to use it are not available. Thus we established in South Vietnam a school for radio repairmen without a sufficient number of radios available to be repaired. In some countries of Asia we have duplicated segments of the government bureaucracy with teams of experts which form a virtual shadow government; and so has the United Nations.

As a general phenomenon the wastefulness of our foreign-aid operations is intimately connected with the political aimlessness of our policy. That policy is lacking in the practical discipline which is the reflection, in the field of action, of the discipline of the intellect. When I am sure in the knowledge of what I seek to achieve and how to go about achieving it, that certain knowledge will give all my actions a common direction and all my plans a common standard for evaluation, and the smallest detail of my planning and action will be informed by it.

The absence of a political discipline which could give intellectual standards and political direction to our foreign-aid policy in Asia has harmed our interests in yet another way. We have mentioned before the problem of prestige in connection with foreign aid. This is the tendency toward what may be called "conspicuous industrialization," an industrialization spectacular for producing the symbols of industrial advancement rather than sound in the technical terms of economics. A policy of foreign aid which is technically rather than politically oriented must make it almost a point of professional honor to disparage considerations of prestige and press for compliance with the principles of sound economics. While we have sometimes yielded, haphazardly and ineffectually, to the former considerations, we have generally been too "honest," too much devoted to the standards of the economic engineer, to sacrifice the principles of sound economics to political expediency.

By doing so, we have sacrificed political advantage. By insisting on sound economic grounds, on going slow with industrialization, we have earned the resentment of countries which want to go fast and who suspect our insistence to be inspired by competitive, if not monopolistic, motives. By emphasizing aid rather than trade, an emphasis dubious from a strictly economic point of view, we wound the self-respect of the recipient nation, and by appearing to neglect its obvious short-range economic needs through our concern with long-range and less obvious benefits, we lay ourselves open to similar suspicions of selfish policies carried on under altruistic guise. By carrying on our policy of economic aid against the overpowering background of our military concerns, all our economic aid becomes suspect of being a mere auxiliary of our military policy.

Until the fall of 1955, the main immediate liabilities which the United States suffered from the immaturity of its foreign-aid policy in Asia were its futility and wastefulness; it was only the long-range prognosis which suggested the possibility of political disaster. For having the field of foreign aid virtually to ourselves, we could afford failing in our foreign-aid policy without, in the short-run at least, losing the political battle for Asia. The entrance of the Soviet Union in the competition has changed all that.

We have it on very high authority that this is all to the good, that the Russians are imitating us, thus bearing witness to the success of our foreign-aid policy, and that it ought to be easy for us to beat them at that game. It would indeed be a comfort to believe that this were so and that the Russians were taking a leaf out of our own book, intending to play the game according to our own rules and trying to outspend us. What a triumph it would indeed be for American policy if we had persuaded the Soviet Union by our example that they can win the battle for Asia by being as futile, as wasteful, and as politically unaware as we have been!

Unfortunately, this "authoritative" analysis bears no relation whatever to the actual facts. The Russian initiative owes nothing to our example, but everything to the awareness that the Cold War of position has changed to one of movement and maneuver, requiring new methods on all levels of policy. Everywhere in Asia and the Middle East the Soviet Union has completely, one might even say ruthlessly, subordinated foreign aid to the requirements of high political policy.

The Soviet Union does not ask what do these countries need in view of their economic and technical development? Rather, it asks what do they want and what should they have in view of the political objectives of the Soviet Union? Thus in Afghanistan and Egypt, in India and Burma, the Russians aid and trade oblivious of the rules of economics but fully aware of the rules of the political game.

To that aid the Russians attach no strings, military or other. More particularly, they promise and deliver arms without asking for what purpose they might be used. Nor do they try to reward their friends and punish those who refuse to exclude the enemies of the Soviet Union from their friendship. The difference between our dealings with India and the Russian treatment of Pakistan illuminates the basic difference in conception and method. We have been reluctant and grudging in giving aid to India because she has refused to become an ally of the United States. On the other hand, the Soviet Union has offered aid and trade to Pakistan, which as an ally of the United States is certainly more hostile to the Soviet Union than India is to the United States. Finally, the Soviet Union has everywhere available at least two levers for action: the established government and the Communist party. It can use one or the other or both of them in concert or against each other.

Such are some of the methods of foreign aid against which the United States must contend. It can no more afford to imitate the Russian methods than the Russians are imitating ours. Yet it can and must bring the fulness of its human and material resources to bear upon problems which are as vital for the future of the United States and of the non-Communist world as they are difficult to grasp and solve.

This task we have hardly begun to tackle because the United States has no more understood the political function of foreign aid than it has understood the political function of psychological warfare and military policy. This lack of understanding has indeed been the besetting sin of our foreign policy both in Asia and Europe.

The United States once believed that the Kellogg-Briand Pact was an efficient instrument for the preservation of peace; later, that the Stimson doctrine of non-recognition of territorial changes brought about by force could stop the imperialism of Japan; and still later that a piece of domestic legislation forbidding loans to belligerents and the transportation of war materials in American boats could keep the United States out of the Second World War. Today, we look back on these policies and the state of mind from which they sprang with wonderment and almost with disbelief. What shall we and those who come after us say of our present Asian policies, once the distance of time or reflection has revealed their kinship in futility to their predecessors of the twenties and thirties?

The futility of all these policies stems from a thinking which is unable to come to terms with political reality and seeks substitutes in legal and moral abstractions or in self-sufficient technical operations. Sound political thinking requires answers to four fundamental questions: What do we want? Can we get what we want at a price commensurate with the objectives sought? If the answer to this question is negative, how must we revise our objective in order to bring it in line with what is possible and with the price we can afford to pay? Finally, how do we go about getting what we want?

Our Asian policy has given a satisfactory answer to the first of these questions; it has given a partially satisfactory answer to the second and third, and it has largely missed the fourth and most important question.

The immediate objective of our Asian policy is the containment of Russian and Chinese imperialism. Since the Soviet Union and China have used communism as the main vehicle for the expansion of their power, this objective is of necessity identical with the containment of communism. It can be sought in two different ways: through the destruction of the Russian and Chinese ability to expand, or by putting an end to their willingness to expand. The destruction of the ability to expand means to strike at the roots of the political and military power of the Soviet Union and China. This can only be accomplished by all-out war, a course of action which the atomic stalemate rules out as suicidal. We are necessarily limited, then, to depriving Russian and Chinese communism of opportunities to expand in Asia and creating liabilities and risks which are likely to outweigh the advantages to be gained through expansion. This creation of liabilities and risks can proceed on two different levels of action: military and political.

On the military level we can deprive the prospective enemy of the incentive to attack the vital interests of the United States by way of general deterrence, or we can create local balances of military power where there is the danger of local expansion by military means. We are employing both military techniques successfully. Our ability to counter a military attack upon our vital interests through all-out atomic war has forestalled such an attack. Likewise our ability and willingness to wage local wars in the Formosa Strait, Korea, and Vietnam have thus far prevented their outbreak.

What is needed beyond these measures is not a hodgepodge of military alliances concluded regardless of their military worth and political consequences. Instead, we need the actuality of military power capable and ready to aid in the defense of exposed areas. Such a military policy, in order to have even a chance for success, must have as its instrument a mobile force-in-being stationed outside the Asian continent, and it must not be committed to intervene everywhere or anywhere in particular.

Any localized military policy in Asia which is likely to avoid the two extremes of defeat and general war must be conscious of the very narrow limits within which it has a chance to succeed. These conditions are the facts of geography and of the over-all distribution of military power, which are impervious to change short of a general war. For a nation which has ruled out such a general war as a deliberate instrument of national policy, these conditions of geography and military power are the preconditions of policy, not its object.

The experience of the Korean and Vietnamese wars has clearly shown the narrow limits which circumscribe even defensive military action undertaken by Western powers against an Asian nation supported by the Soviet Union or China. The military defense of any piece of territory located at the rim of the Asian continent by a non-Asian power against one or the other or both of the great Asian land powers is possible only on condition that the latter limit their commitment regardless of the outcome. If the latter press their geographic and local military advantage to the full, local defense becomes impossible, and the alternative is either defeat or a general war.

On the military plane, our actions, if not our words, have taken into account the narrow limits within which successful action is possible; for the consequences of not taking them into account were so obviously fraught with danger that even the most vociferous supporters of forceful action had to shrink from them. It has been different in the political sphere, for here failure and disaster do not of necessity follow foolish and improvident action as immediate consequences. Thus circumstances have allowed us to act in the political sphere with unconcern for the long-range consequences of specific failures.

Yet our freedom of political action is hemmed in by four circumstances which either cannot be eliminated at all or else can be
eliminated only by a general war ruled out by our over-all policy.
These circumstances are the impact of the emancipation and restoration of China, the opportunity for Communist subversion, the
suspicion of Western intentions, and the domestic politics of the
United States.

Nobody who has recently traveled through Asia with his eyes
open can fail to be impressed by the impact which the emancipation
of China from Western dependence and the restoration of her
power as a nation and as a civilization is making upon all of Asia
from Japan to Pakistan. What Asians admire and respect in China is
what seems to them the fulfilment of the aspirations of all of Asia:
to be masters in their own house and to prove themselves to be the
equal, if not the superior, of the West. When Japan in 1942 drove
the Western powers from Southeast Asia, she established herself for
a fleeting moment, the echoes of which are still audible enough
throughout Asia, as the liberator rather than the conqueror of Asia
and dealt the prestige of the white man a blow from which it should
never recover. Similarly, China, in the teeth of the opposition of
the most powerful nation on earth, has given herself a political, social, and economic order of her choosing and has defied with a considerable measure of success what appeared to Asia as the combined
military strength of the Western world.

This being so, it is impossible for the United States to square a
policy of implacable enmity to China with the first objective of its
Asian policy: the containment of Communist imperialism. For in
the way that this enmity forces China to the side of the Soviet Union, even if other circumstances would not do so anyhow, the very
same enmity forces virtually all of Asia to the side of China. Our
enmity toward China becomes a hindrance to the attainment of our
objectives in Asia. Yet so strong is China's position that even if we
should recognize the Communist government of China and extend
the hand of friendship to it, we would only strengthen those very
factors which are responsible for China's strong position in Asia in
the first place. Thus we are here faced with a condition which our
policy must take into account but cannot change, short of the destruction of the Communist government of China.

The same is true of the opportunities for domestic subversion which throughout Asia are at the disposal of Communist China and, to a lesser extent, of the Soviet Union. We have pointed above to the spectacular success the Soviet Union and China have had in using the general aspirations and specific grievances of the peoples of Asia for their own purposes. These successes are not primarily due to Communist astuteness, but to the objective conditions which made the exploitation of these aspirations and grievances by communism almost inevitable while they largely preclude the West from exploiting them. First of all, the Soviet Union and China can count everywhere in Asia upon the support of Communist parties which they control. Furthermore, China, regardless of her ideological coloration and system of government, has traditionally had unique opportunities for exerting influence in the overseas-Chinese communities. When the Chinese of Malaya and Singapore need protection, to whom should they look if not to China? When the intellectual youth of the overseas-Chinese communities seek an outlet for their abilities and ambitions, where can they seek it if not in China? China has here an advantage which no competing nation can hope to match.

The West faces another disadvantage which it is not able to change, at least in the short run: the Asian suspicion of Western intentions. A Western nation coming to Asia comes branded with the stigma of Western colonialism, no matter what its purposes and actions. The wall of hostility and suspicion which dismayed General William Dean when he begged food and shelter from the Koreans whom he had come to liberate and protect constitutes a barrier, insurmountable at least for the time being, to Western influence and policy in Asia.

The intentions and policies of Western nations are doubly suspect in Asia by virtue of their domestic politics. All of Asia is extremely sensitive to the issue of racial equality; and in its relations with the West, the aspiration to be free from contempt takes precedence over all other issues. Every case of racial discrimination in the United States takes on in Asia the aspects of a *cause célèbre*. One has to travel in Asia for some length of time, reading nothing but Asian newspapers, in order to realize to what extent the Asian picture of America is determined by the American attitude on racial equality. For days on end, the only news about America the reader will find deals with racial discrimination and racial violence. Since the elimination of racial discrimination in the United States will inevitably be slow, our policies suffer from a handicap which they, at least in the short run, cannot escape.

Asians also resent the fact that we take for granted the superiority of democracy as a form of government. Suspicious of all such Western professions of superiority, they are eager to put our sincerity to the test of actual performance. Since the performance cannot fail to fall short of the professed ideal, Asia tends to doubt the United States and all its work. Here, then, we face yet another limitation which domestic policies may diminish but cannot completely erase.

What follows from all this for the Asian policies of the United States?

1. Our Asian policies, on different levels of action, must be subjected to continuous examination in view of our over-all objectives, instead of being examined only in terms of their technical self-sufficiency.

2. No action may be vastly preferable to any kind of action and, more particularly, to action for action's sake.

3. Flexibility, both as to the kind of action and the country to be chosen, must be substituted for the doctrinaire rigidity of our present policies.

It is a peculiarity of the situation in Asia, resulting from the limiting factors mentioned above, that a Western policy, even though successful in its own technical terms, may still fail to bring us closer to the containment of communism, or may even do the opposite. A military action, successful and even necessary in its own terms, may hold the advance of communism at the particular spot where it was undertaken, while the very fact of its success and of its having been undertaken by a Western nation brings all of Asia closer to the Communist camp. Nothing needs to be added here to what has been said of the negative political effects which can follow from alliance and foreign-aid policies, successful in their own terms. What is true of all technical policies is true with particular force of our Asian policies: they stand and fall not with their success in their own technical terms, but with the service they render to the attainment of the over-all objective of political policy. Whatever we do or do not do in Asia must answer to this ultimate test: does it serve the immediate objective of our Asian policy, the containment of communism?

There is no doubt an element of hyperbole in Mr. Acheson's famous statement that we should let the dust settle in Asia. Yet it contains also a great unrecognized truth; for given the insurmountable barriers within which any Western policy is confined in Asia, many an action undertaken by a Western nation is bound to be futile, if not self-defeating, for no other reason than that it is a Western nation which undertakes it. There is not only waste but positive harm in that frenzied activity which is unaware of those insurmountable barriers confining it and feeds on the illusion that ever more and bigger actions cannot fail to surmount them. A passive policy of patient, watchful waiting goes against the grain of the American genius. Yet there is no escape from the necessity to learn how to tread cautiously the narrow path between the Scylla of failure and the Charybdis of universal destruction.

Where there is an aspiration which we can meet or a grievance which we can redress in Asia, we should do so. Where we can extend our military protection with a chance of success and without undue political liabilities, we should do so. But we should stop offering alliances, military support, and economic and technical aid to all who will take them. We should select our allies and the recipients of our aid in view of our interests, rather than suffer to be selected by them in view of theirs.

We must select the place and nature of our Asian policies in view of the opportunities for successful action, and our policies must change with them. Opportunities for politically successful economic aid may disappear in one country, which may instead offer a chance for military support. A chance for a spectacular political or military move may suddenly open up here, to vanish as quickly as it appeared. The statesman must take a leaf out of the book of the military commander who, having at his disposal a great variety of weapons, uses them in ever changing combinations for the attainment of his over-all objective.

There is nothing spectacular in these principles of a sound Asian policy, nothing that is likely to make good copy for the public-relations expert, nothing that lends itself to a flamboyant oratorical demonstration. Yet considering the narrow limits within which we can act in Asia with any chance of success at all, the delicacy of our psychological relations with the peoples of Asia, and sometimes the incompatibility of our policies, it may not be amiss to question whether the interests of the United States are not served best by an Asian policy which is discreet rather than spectacular, restrained rather than indiscriminately active, cautious, pragmatic, and humble rather than confident in its superior principles and technical ability, and not caring who knows it.

16 *The Formosa Resolution of 1955*

The Formosa resolution which has just been passed by Congress presents an extraordinary paradox to the American people and to the world. In the context of the measures which have preceded it and which are likely to follow it, it constitutes a decisive change in the Far Eastern policies of our government, an important step toward a peaceful settlement of the Far Eastern crisis. Yet, in its most spectacular provision and in the dramatic measures and gestures accompanying it, it raises up the specter of an impending armed conflict. By doing this it gets in the way of the very purposes our government is pursuing in the Far East.

When the Communists had driven Chiang Kai-shek from the mainland in 1949, the American people were united in assessing this event as a catastrophic defeat for the United States; for this event brought to pass what America's traditional policy of the "open door" had been able to prevent: that all of China would fall in the orbit of another great power. However, the American people and their government were divided, and have remained so to this day, over the policies to pursue vis-à-vis Communist China.

By far the more articulate group, of which Admiral Arthur W. Radford, the chairman of the Joint Chiefs of Staff, has recently been the most eminent spokesman, maintains that the United States cannot live securely with Communist China in the same world, that the Communist regime of China can and ought to be overthrown, and that this can be done now with a relatively small commitment of American air and naval forces.

The other group, by no means negligible in either size or influence (General Matthew B. Ridgway is probably its most prominent representative in the councils of government) but hardly audible in public, assume that the Communists are in firm control of the mainland and can be overthrown only by a military effort of the first magnitude. From this estimate of the military situation, it follows

From the *Chicago Sun-Times*, January 30, 1955.

logically that the United States ought to make the best of a bad situation by recognizing a fact, however distasteful and dangerous in itself, which could be changed only at an exorbitant price and at enormous risks.

Until recently the present administration, as its predecessor, has tried to strike an uneasy balance between those two positions. By refusing to recognize the Communist government of China, it has by implication denied its right to govern China and its ability to do so permanently. By promising to unleash Chiang Kai-shek for an invasion of the mainland, it has given the appearance of encouraging and supporting such an undertaking. On the other hand, in its actual policies our government has been very careful to minimize armed conflict between the two Chinas and to preserve the status quo. Recent statements and measures make it obvious that the administration is moving decisively away from the counterrevolutionary attitude implicit in its non-recognition policy.

The defense treaty with Formosa, concluded in December, 1954, and now before the Senate for ratification, and more particularly the notes exchanged between Mr. Dulles and the Formosan Foreign Minister on the conclusion of that treaty make it perfectly clear that our government has reconciled itself to the Communist domination of the Chinese mainland and seeks the preservation of the territorial status quo in the short run and an over-all Far Eastern settlement in the long run. The recent statements by the President and the Secretary of State in support of a cease-fire to be arranged under the auspices of the United Nations are part and parcel of that new policy. And so is the resolution which has just been passed by Congress. It, too, serves the purpose of maintaining the territorial status quo in the Formosa Strait by peaceful means; and the President's statement of last Thursday to this effect expresses faithfully the peaceful and defensive purposes of our policy.

Why, then, have these purposes been obscured by flights of jet planes, navy concentrations, and talk about preventive war? As so often before, the sound purposes of our foreign policy have been sacrificed to the requirements, generally apparent rather than real, of psychological warfare and political pressures, foreign and domestic.

There can be no doubt that the drastic military and political measures taken during the last week have the primary purpose of impressing upon the Chinese Communists our determination to defend Formosa even at the risk of a general war. Nothing in the present military situation suggests that the Seventh Fleet would not be strong enough to meet any immediate emergency without drastic reinforcements, and the constitutional authority of the President to commit the armed forces of the United States to the defense of Formosa has not been challenged since President Truman so committed them at the beginning of the Korean War. Thus the resolution considered by Congress only confirms what needed no confirmation on constitutional grounds.

A good case can be made in support of a policy which leaves the prospective enemy in no doubt about one's own intentions. Yet there is a difference between making it unmistakably clear that one has a loaded gun ready for use under certain conditions and waving a loaded gun under somebody's nose or aiming it at somebody's head, even though without any intention to pull the trigger. In the latter case, the psychological effects might well be the exact opposite from those intended. Instead of deterring a prospective enemy from taking a certain step you might provoke him into committing one because your dramatic demonstrations have filled him with the fear, however unfounded, of drastic action. In short, in psychological warfare one can do too little and one can do too much, and one can only hope that we have not done too much.

The measures of the last week also show the obvious marks of a political compromise with Chiang Kai-shek and the supporters of his counterrevolution in this country. We have attempted for months to persuade Chiang Kai-shek to evacuate the outlying islands which are of minor military importance for the defense of Formosa and untenable in case of serious attack. We have now succeeded in persuading Chiang Kai-shek to evacuate the Tachen Islands, and we have committed ourselves in return for this concession to defend, at least for the time being, the island groups of Quemoy and Matsu. A look at the map will show that, while the Pescadores are indeed essential for the defense of Formosa, Matsu and the Quemoys are not. Anything the Communists could do to Formosa from these islands they could also do from the mainland. These islands are not stepping stones from the mainland to Formosa, but they are stepping stones from Formosa to the mainland. From them, a determined enemy can harass the port of Foochow and paralyze the port of Amoy.

It is true that in this fashion the Communists can be prevented from using these ports to stage the invasion of Formosa. But another look at the map will show that an invasion force, even if it controlled these islands, would have to cross a large body of water, and it would be a reflection on the prowess of the Seventh Fleet to assume that it would be unable to intercept such a force. Given the defensive purposes of our policy, the commitment to defend these islands for the time being must then derive from political rather than military considerations.

Yet while our purposes are defensive, the purposes of Chiang Kai-shek are not and cannot be. Chiang Kai-shek's regime stands and falls with the expectation to return victoriously to the mainland. The policies upon which our government has embarked in recent months preclude such a return by freezing the status quo. Chiang Kai-shek knows this, and so do the advocates of his counterrevolution in this country. Yet neither of them can fail to note the splendid opportunity which last Friday's resolution offers them to maneuver the government of the United States into supporting policies which run counter to its own purposes.

It would not be the first time that the Formosan tail has wagged the American dog. The islands of Quemoy and Matsu, lying in close proximity to the Chinese mainland, cannot be defended against actual assault. They can be defended only by preventing an assault from being staged in the first place. In order to defend these islands, we cannot allow the enemy to fire the first shot; we must fire it ourselves in order to prevent the enemy from firing any shot.

In other words, the philosophy underlying last Friday's resolution calls for our carrying the war to the Asiatic mainland in order to defend Formosa. Yet to carry the war to the Asiatic mainland is exactly what Chiang Kai-shek and his American supporters want our government to do. Only their purpose is not the defense of Formosa, but the reconquest of the mainland.

The President's statement of last Thursday that any decision to use United States forces other than in immediate self-defense or in direct defense of Formosa and the Pescadores would be a decision which he would take and the responsibility for which he has not delegated does little to dispel the misgivings which the supporter of the President's own policies must feel. For it is Chiang Kai-shek, and not the President's subordinates, who controls the Quemoy and Matsu islands. Hence, it is Chiang Kai-shek who can create in the proximity of the Chinese mainland a situation calling for Communist countermeasures in the form of concentrations of troops and war material. No military intelligence is smart enough to distinguish between the defensive and aggressive purposes of such a concentration, and all military intelligence is prone to find what it would like to find. A military commander, itching for action, will more likely than not find in the intelligence reports evidence for the need for action, especially if failure to act might cause defeat. Yet it is upon such intelligence that the President must base his final decision.

The implications of last Friday's resolution, then, run counter to the present purposes of our foreign policy. A case—and in our opinion an unanswerable one—can be made for the policies President Eisenhower has embarked upon. A case also can be made for the policies Admiral Radford has been advocating. But no case can be made for a policy which tries to achieve the purposes of one with the methods appropriate for the other.

PART III

The Restoration
of American
Politics

17 *Love and Power*

The proposition that power and love are organically connected, growing as they do from the same root of loneliness, must appear to the modern mind paradoxical, if not completely absurd. For power as the domination of man by man, pleasurable to one and painful to the other, and love as the voluntary and pleasurable surrender of two human beings to each other, seem not only to have nothing in common but to be mutually exclusive. Where two human beings are in the relation of power, they cannot be, so it seems to the modern mind, in the relation of love. The inability of the modern mind to see this connection between love and power is the measure of its inability to understand the true dimensions of either love or power. As Paul Tillich put it in the introductory chapter to *Love, Power, and Justice*, "It is unusual to take the word 'confusion' into the title of a chapter. But if one has to write about love, power, and justice the unusual becomes natural."

The modern mind, both in its Marxist and non-Marxist expressions, sees in the power of man over man not an ineluctable outgrowth of human nature but only an ephemeral phenomenon, the product of a peculiar historic configuration, bound to disappear with the disappearance of that configuration. According to Marx, the lust for power and its political manifestations are a mere by-product of the class division of society. In the classless society, the domination of man by man will be replaced by the administration of things. In liberal thought, power politics is regarded as a kind of atavism, a residue from the less enlightened and civilized era of autocratic rule, which is destined to be superseded by the institutions and practices of liberal democracy.

While the modern mind denies the intrinsic relation between the lust for power and human nature, transcending all historic configurations, antedating them, as it were, and even determining them, it does not understand the nature of love at all. Love as the reunion of

From *Commentary*, March, 1962.

two souls and bodies which belong together or, in the Platonic mythology, once were united, is reduced in the modern understanding
to sex and gregariousness, the togetherness of the sexes on dates, in
marriage, and in other associations, tending to be of a more or less
fleeting nature. What the modern understanding misses is the totality
of the commitment that characterizes the pure phenomenon of love.
It is aware only of surface phenomena which may or may not be
manifestations of love, because it is unaware of that very element in
man on which love is built: his soul. And it is unaware of that quality
of human existence which is the root both of the lust for power and
the longing for love: loneliness.

Of all creatures, only man is capable of loneliness because only he
is in need of not being alone, without being able in the end to escape
being alone. It is that striving to escape his loneliness which gives
the impetus to both the lust for power and the longing for love, and
it is the inability to escape that loneliness, either at all or for more
than a moment, that creates the tension between longing and lack
of achievement, which is the tragedy of both power and love. In that
existential loneliness man's insufficiency manifests itself. He cannot
fulfill himself, he cannot become what he is destined to be, by his
own effort, in isolation from other beings. The awareness of that
insufficiency drives him on in search of love and power. It drives
him on to seek the extension of his self in offspring—the work of his
body; in the manufacture of material things—the work of his hands;
in philosophy and scholarship—the work of his mind; in art and literature—the work of his imagination; in religion—the work of his
pure longing toward transcendence.

Love and power both try to overcome loneliness, and the sense of
man's insufficiency stemming from this loneliness, through duplica-
tion of his individuality. Through love, man seeks another human
being like himself, the Platonic other half of his soul, to form a union
which will make him whole. Through power, man seeks to impose
his will upon another man, so that the will of the object of his power
mirrors his own. What love seeks to discover in another man as a
gift of nature, power must create through the artifice of psychological manipulation. Love is reunion through spontaneous mutuality,
power seeks to create a union through unilateral imposition.

It is the common quality of love and power that each contains an element of the other. Power points toward love as its fulfilment, as love starts from power and is always threatened with corruption by it. Power, in its ultimate consummation, is the same as love, albeit love is corrupted by an irreducible residue of power. Love, in its ultimate corruption, is the same as power, albeit power is redeemed by an irreducible residue of love.

Love is a psychological relationship which in its pure form is marked by complete and spontaneous mutuality. *A* surrenders himself to *B*, as *B* surrenders himself to *A;* and both do so spontaneously, in recognition of their belonging together. Both are lover and beloved; what *A* is, feels, and wants, *B* is, feels, and wants, too. Love is the most perfect union two human beings are capable of, without losing their respective individualities. Aristophanes has given in the *Symposium* the classic description of the nature of pure love:

And when one of them meets with his other half, the actual half of himself . . . the pair are lost in an amazement of love and friendship and intimacy, and one will not be out of the other's sight, as I may say, even for a moment: these are the people who pass their whole lives together; yet they could not explain what they desire of one another. For the intense yearning which each of them has towards the other does not appear to be the desire of lover's intercourse, but of something else which the soul of either evidently desires and cannot tell, and of which she has only a dark and doubtful presentiment . . . this meeting and melting into one another, this becoming one instead of two, was the very expression of his ancient need. And the reason is that human nature was originally one and we were a whole, and the desire and pursuit of the whole is called love.

Love in its purest form is the rarest of experiences. It is given to few men to experience it at all, and those who experience it do so only in fleeting moments of exaltation. What makes love as commonly experienced fall short of its pure form is the element of power with which love begins in triumph and ends in defeat and which corrupts it throughout. Love typically begins with *A* trying to submit *B* to his will, that is, as a relationship of power, and frequently it does not progress beyond it. As Socrates puts it in the *Phaedrus:* "As wolves love lambs so lovers love their loves." And it is significant that Socrates, in his first speech in that dialogue, in parodying Lysias' conception of love, presents a picture of the love relation which is tantamount to what we would call a relationship of power.

What makes the lover behave like a master and the beloved like the object of the master's power, what makes, in other words, the love relationship similar to the power relationship is the inevitable frustration of love. For if love is a reunion of two human beings who belong together, that reunion can never be complete for any length of time. For, except in the *Liebestod,* which destroys the lovers by uniting them, it stops short of the complete merger of the individualities of the lovers. It is the paradox of love that it seeks the reunion of two individuals while leaving their individualities intact. *A* and *B* want to be one, yet they must want to preserve each other's individuality for the sake of their love for each other. So it is their very love that stands in the way of their love's consummation.

That inner contradiction the lovers endeavor to overcome by letting power do what love is unable to do by itself. Power tries to break down the barrier of individuality which love, because it is love, must leave intact. Yet in the measure that power tries to do the work love cannot do, it puts love in jeopardy. An irreducible element of power is requisite to make a stable relationship of love, which without it would be nothing more than a succession of precarious exaltations. Thus without power love cannot persist; but through power it is corrupted and threatened with destruction. That destruction becomes actual when *A* and *B,* by trying to reduce each other to an object of their respective wills, transform the spontaneous mutuality of the love relationship into the unilateral imposition of the relationship of power.

Thus the lust for power is, as it were, the twin of despairing love. Power becomes a substitute for love. What man cannot achieve for any length of time through love he tries to achieve through power: to fulfill himself, to make himself whole by overcoming his loneliness, his isolation. As Shakespeare's Richard III puts it:

> And this word "love," which greybeards call divine,
> Be resident in men like one another
> And not in me: I am myself alone. . . .
> And am I then a man to be belov'd?
> O, monstrous fault, to harbor such a thought!
> Then, since this earth affords no joy to me,
> But to command, to check, to o'erbear such
> As are of better person than myself,
> I'll make my heaven to dream upon the crown. . . .

Yet of what love can at least approximate and in a fleeting moment actually achieve, power can only give the illusion.

Power is a psychological relationship in which one man controls certain actions of another man through the influence he exerts over the latter's will. That influence derives from three sources: the expectation of benefits, the fear of disadvantages, the respect or love for men or institutions. It may be exerted through orders, threats, promises, persuasion, the authority or charisma of a man or of an office, or a combination of any of these.

It is in the very nature of the power relationship that the position of the two actors within it is ambivalent. *A* seeks to exert power over *B*; *B* tries to resist that power and seeks to exert power over *A*, which *A* resists. Thus the actor on the political stage is always at the same time a prospective master over others and a prospective object of the power of others. While he seeks power over others, others seek power over him. Victory will fall to him who marshals the stronger weapons of influence with greater skill.

Yet a political victory won with the weapons of threats and promises is likely to be precarious; for the power relation thus established depends upon the continuing submissiveness of a recalcitrant will, generated and maintained by the master's continuing influence. The will of the subject reflects the will of the master but incompletely and tenuously as long as the will of the master is imposed upon the will of the subject from without and against the latter's resistance. How to overcome that resistance and make the will of the subject one with the will of the master is one of the crucial issues with which all political orders must come to terms. It is the issue of political stability. The political masters, actual and potential, and on all levels of social interaction from the family to the state, have sought to meet that issue by basing their power upon the spontaneous consent of the subject. If the subject can be made to duplicate spontaneously within himself the master's will so that what the master wills the subject wills, too, not through inducement from without but through spontaneous consent from within, then the will of the master and the will of the subject are one, and the power of the master is founded not upon the master's threats and promises but upon the subject's love for the master.

So it is not by accident that the political philosophies which emphasize the stability of power relationships, such as those of monarchies and autocracies, make a point of appealing to the love of the subject for the ruler. The philosophy and ritual of absolute monarchy, in particular, are full of references to the love of the subject for the monarch as the foundation of the monarch's power. That foundation has perhaps nowhere been more clearly revealed than in a letter which John Durie, Scotch Presbyterian and worker for Protestant unity, wrote in 1632 to the British Ambassador, Thomas Roe, explaining the decline of the power of Gustavus Adolphus of Sweden, then fighting for the Protestant cause in Germany:

> The increase of his authority is the ground of his abode; and love is the ground of his authority; it must be through love; for it cannot be through power; for his power is not in his own subjects but in strangers; not in his money, but in theirs; not in their good will, but in mere necessity as things stand now betwixt him and them; therefore if the necessity be not so urgent as it is; or if any other means be shown by God (who is able to do as much by another man as by him) to avoid this necessity; the money and the power and the assistance which it yieldeth unto him will fall from him and so his authority is lost, and his abode will be no longer: for the love which was at first is gone. . . .

In recent times, the continuous references to "our beloved leader" in the literature and ritual of Naziism and Stalinism point to the same relationship between ruler and subject—in the case of Naziism in good measure as an actual fact, however corrupted by power and hate; in the case of Stalinism as something to be desired but unattainable.

Obviously, this transformation of the unilateral imposition of the power relationship into the mutuality of love is in the political sphere, at least in its modern secular form, an ideal rather than an attainable goal. Thus the great political masters, the Alexanders and Napoleons, while painfully aware of the love that is beyond their reach, seek to compensate for the love they must miss with an ever greater accumulation of power. From the subjection of ever more men to their will, they seem to expect the achievement of that communion which the lack of love withholds from them. Yet the acquisition of power only begets the desire for more; for the more men the master holds bound to his will, the more he is aware of his loneliness. His success in terms of power only serves to illuminate his failure in terms of love.

There is then in the great political masters a demoniac and frantic striving for ever more power—as there is in the misguided lovers, the Don Juans who mistake sex for love, a limitless and ever unsatiated compulsion toward more and more experiences of sex—which will be satisfied only when the last living man has been subjected to the master's will. " 'More! More!' " in the words of William Blake, "is the cry of a mistaken soul; less than all cannot satisfy man." Thus the heights of the master's power signal the depths of his despair. For the world conqueror can subject all inhabitants of the earth to his will, but he cannot compel a single one to love him. The master of all men is also the loneliest of all men; for his loneliness, in spite of the totality of his power, proves that it cannot be cured by power. That fruitless search for love through power leads in the most passionate of the seekers of power from a despair, impotent in the fulness of power, to a hate, destructive of the objects of their successful power and frustrated love. Thus the Genghis Khans, Hitlers, and Stalins lash out with unreasoning fury at their subjects whom they can dominate but whose love they cannot command and, hence, whom they cannot afford to love.

Yet while the subjects may not love the master and the master may impose his will with bloody tyranny, there is even in the crudest of power relationships an irreducible element of love. What both master and subject seek is that union which remedies the awareness of insufficiency born of loneliness and which only love can give. But they have chosen the wrong track of power and are doomed to failure. Thus they—master and subject—must search forever and in vain for that other human being to whom they could say, I love you, to hear the reply, I love you, too.

The power relationship is, then, in the last analysis, a frustrated relationship of love. Those who must use and suffer power would rather be united in love. Master and subject are at the bottom of their souls lovers who have gone astray. The hostility of their relationship carries a trace of that frustrated love which is at the root of a type of hate. Napoleon, in his conversations with De Las Cases on Saint Helena, and Hitler, in his harangues to his generals, have bemoaned their fate that in the fulness of their power they could trust nobody and found nobody worthy of their love. Many of the powerful have throughout history sought the illusion of love in the promiscuous enjoyment of sex. Beneath that artificial community which power builds as a substitute for, and a spite to, love, there remains at least a glimmer of an aspiration which longs for that reunion only love can give. It manifests itself in the sometimes sudden emergence of charity, pity, and forgiveness in the relations between master and subject. Nowhere has that kinship of power and love been expressed with simpler profundity than in the two words which Homer makes Achilles speak when he is about to slay Lykaos: "Die, friend."

The loneliness of man is, then, impervious to both love and power. Power can only unite through the unilateral imposition of subjection, which leaves the master's isolation intact. Behold that master whom the wills of millions obey and who cannot find a single soul with which to unite his own. Love can unite only in the fleeting moments when two souls and bodies merge in spontaneous mutuality. The lovers bear the dual burden of Adam and Eve and of Moses. They see the promised land in their longing's imagination and enter it only to be expelled from it. Behold the lovers who find in their embrace the illusion of complete union and in fleeting moments even its reality, only to awaken alone in the embrace of another lover.

Thus in the end, his wings seared, his heart-blood spent, his projects come to nought—despairing of power and thirsting for, and forsaken by, love—man peoples the heavens with gods and mothers and virgins and saints who love him and whom he can love and to whose power he can subject himself spontaneously because their power is the power of love. Yet whatever he expects of the other world, he must leave this world as he entered it: alone.

18 *Death in the Nuclear Age*

It is obvious that the nuclear age has radically changed man's relations to nature and to his fellow men. It has enormously increased man's ability to use the forces of nature for his purposes and has thus concentrated unprecedented destructive powers in the hands of governments. That concentration of power has fundamentally altered the relations which have existed throughout history between government and people and among governments themselves. It has made popular revolution impossible, and it has made war an absurdity. Yet, less obvious and more important, the nuclear age has changed man's relations to himself. It has done so by giving death a new meaning.

Death is the great scandal in the experience of man; for death—as the destruction of the human person after a finite span of time—is the very negation of all man experiences as specifically human in his existence: the consciousness of himself and of his world, the remembrance of things past and the anticipation of things to come, a creativeness in thought and action which aspires to, and approximates, the eternal. Thus man has been compelled, for the sake of his existence as man, to bridge the gap between death and his specifically human attributes by transcending death. He has done so in three different ways: by making himself, within narrow limits, the master of death; by denying the reality of death through the belief in the immortality of his person; by conquering the reality of death through the immortality of the world he leaves behind.

Man can make himself the master of death by putting an end to his biological existence whenever he wishes. While he cannot live as long as he wants to, he can stop living whenever he wants to. While he cannot choose life over death when his life has reached its biological limits, he can choose death over life regardless of these limits. He can commit suicide; or he can commit what Nietzsche has called "suicide with a good conscience" by seeking out death, especially at

From *Commentary*, September, 1961.

the hand of someone else. He is capable of sacrificial death. In his self-chosen death for a cause in particular, on the battlefield or elsewhere, man triumphs over death, however incompletely. He triumphs because he does not wait until his body is ready to die, but he offers his life to death when his chosen purpose demands it. Yet that triumph is incomplete because it cannot overcome the inevitability of death but only controls its coming.

Man also denies the reality of death by believing in the immortality of his person. This belief can take two different forms. It may take the form of the assumption that the finiteness of man's biological existence is but apparent and that his body will live on in another world. It can also take the form of the assumption that what is specifically human in man will survive the destruction of his body and that man's soul will live on forever, either separated from any body or reincarnated in someone else's. This belief in personal immortality, in defiance of the empirical evidence of the finiteness of man's biological existence, is of course peculiar to the religious realm. It presupposes the existence of a world which is not only inaccessible to the senses but also superior to the world of the senses in that what is truly human in man is there preserved forever.

It is a distinctive characteristic of our secular age that it has replaced the belief in the immortality of the human person with the attempt to assure the immortality of the world he leaves behind. Man can transcend the finiteness of his biological existence either in his consciousness or in objective reality by adding to that existence four different dimensions which are in one way or another independent of that finiteness. They are different dimensions of immortality. He can extend his consciousness into the past by remembering it. He can extend his consciousness into the future by anticipating it. As *homo faber*, he imbeds his biological existence within technological and social artifacts which survive that existence. His imagination creates new worlds of religion, art, and reason that live after their creator.

By thus bestowing immortality upon the past, man assures himself of immortality to be granted by future generations who will remember him. As the past lives on in his historic recollection, so will he continue to live in the memory of his successors. The continuity of history gives the individual at least a chance to survive himself in the collective memory of mankind. Those who are eminent, or believe themselves to be so, aspire to posthumous fame which will enable them to live on, perhaps forever.

The ability to remember and the aspiration to be remembered call for deliberate action to assure that remembrance. The assurance of his life after death becomes one of man's main concerns here and now. Man on all levels of civilization is moved to create monuments which testify to his existence and will live after him. He founds a family and lives on in his sons, who bear his name as he bears his father's. He leaves an inheritance of visible things not to be consumed but to be preserved as tangible mementos of past generations. Over his grave he causes a monument of stone to be erected whose durability, as it were, compensates for the impermanence of what lies beneath. Or he may even refuse to accept that impermanence altogether and have his body preserved in the likeness of life. At the very least, he will have pictures made of himself to perpetuate his physical likeness.

This concern with immortality in this world manifests itself on the highest level of consciousness in the preparation of man's fame. He lives in such a way as to make sure that his fame will survive him. All of us, from the peasant and handicraft man to the founders of churches, the architects of empires, the builders of cities, the tamers of the forces of nature, seek to leave behind the works of our wills and hands to testify to our existence. "*Roma eterna*," "the Reich of a thousand years" are but the most ambitious attempts to perpetuate man in his deeds. The tree that he has planted, the house that he has built, have been given a life likely to last longer than his own. At best, he as a person will live on in his works; at worst, he has the satisfaction of living on anonymously in what he has created.

It is, however, in the works of his imagination that man conquers the mortality of his body in the most specifically human way. The artists and poets, the philosophers and the writers, can point with different degrees of assurance to their work and say, with Horace: "I have finished a monument more lasting than bronze and loftier than the Pyramids' royal pile, one that no wasting rain, no furious north wind can destroy, or the countless chain of years and the ages' flight. I shall not altogether die. . . ." In the works of his mind it is not just his physical existence, the bare fact that he once lived, that is remembered. Rather, what is rememberd is the creative quality that sets him apart from all other creatures, that is peculiar to him as a man. What is remembered is not only the specifically human quality, but also and most importantly the quality in which he lives on as a unique individual, the like of whom has never existed before or since. In the works of his mind, man, the creator, survives.

Yet why are those works a "monument more lasting than bronze," and why can their creator be confident that "on and on shall I grow, ever fresh with the glory of after time"? Because the man endowed with a creative mind knows himself to be a member in an unbroken chain emerging from the past and reaching into the future, which is made of the same stuff his mind is made of and, hence, is capable of participating in, and perpetuating, his mind's creation. He may be mortal, but humanity is not, and so he will be immortal in his works. This is the triumphant message of Horace.

Our life, then, receives one of its meanings from the meaning we give to death. What we make of life is shaped by what we make of death; for we live in the presence of the inevitability of death and we dedicate our lives to the proof of the proposition that death is not what it seems to be: the irrevocable end of our existence. We search for immortality, and the kind of immortality we seek determines the kind of life we lead.

The significance of the possibility of nuclear death is that it radically affects the meaning of death, of immortality, of life itself. It affects that meaning by destroying most of it. Nuclear destruction is mass destruction, both of persons and of things. It signifies the simultaneous destruction of tens of millions of people, of whole families, generations, and societies, of all things that they have inherited and created. It signifies the total destruction of whole societies by killing their members, destroying their visible achievements, and therefore reducing the survivors to barbarism. Thus nuclear destruction destroys the meaning of death by depriving it of its individuality. It destroys the meaning of immortality by making both society and history impossible. It destroys the meaning of life by throwing life back upon itself.

Sacrificial death has meaning only as the outgrowth of an individual decision which chooses death over life. The hero who risks his life or dies for a cause is bound to be one man, an identifiable individual. There is meaning in Leonidas falling at Thermopylae, in Socrates drinking the cup of hemlock, in Jesus nailed to the cross. There can be no meaning in the slaughter of the innocent, the murder of six million Jews, the prospective nuclear destruction of, say, fifty million Americans and an equal number of Russians. There is then, a radical difference in meaning between a man risking death by an act of will and fifty million people simultaneously reduced— by somebody switching a key thousands of miles away—to radioactive ashes, indistinguishable from the ashes of their houses, books, and animals. Horace could say, thinking of the individual soldier ready to die, "It is sweet and honorable to die for one's country." Yet Wilfred Owen, describing the effects of a gas attack in the First World War, could call Horace's famous phrase "The old Lie," and beholding a victim of modern mass destruction, could only bewail the futility of such a death and ask in despair, "Was it for this the clay grew tall? O what made fatuous sunbeams toil to break earth's sleep at all?" The death of the Horatian soldier is the assertion of man's freedom from biological necessity, a limited triumph over death. The death of Owen's soldier and of his prospective successors in the nuclear age is the negation not only of man's freedom but of his life's meaning as well.

Man gives his life and death meaning by his ability to make himself and his works remembered after his death. Patroclus dies to be avenged by Achilles. Hector dies to be mourned by Priam. Yet if Patroclus, Hector, and all those who could remember them were killed simultaneously, what would become of the meaning of Patroclus' and Hector's deaths? Their lives and deaths would lose their meaning. They would die, not like men but like beasts, killed in the mass, and what would be remembered would be the quantity of the killed—six million, twenty million, fifty million—not the quality of one man's death as over against another's.

Of their deeds, nothing would remain but the faint hope of remembrance in distant places. The very concept of fame would disappear, and the historians, the professional immortalizers, would have nothing to report. What had been preserved and created through the mind, will, and hands of man would be dissolved like man himself. Civilization itself would perish. Perhaps in some faraway place some evidence would be preserved of the perished civilization and of the men who created it. Nothing more than that would be left of the immortality man had once been able to achieve through the persistence of his fame and the permanence of his works.

And what would become of life itself? If our age had not replaced the belief in the immortality of the individual person with the immortality of humanity and its civilization, we could take the prospect of nuclear death in our stride. We could even afford to look forward to the day of the great slaughter as a day on which the preparatory and vain life on this earth would come to an end for most of us and the true, eternal life in another world begin. Yet a secular age, which has lost faith in individual immortality in another world and is aware of the impending doom of the world through which it tries to perpetuate itself here and now, is left without a remedy. Once it has become aware of its condition, it must despair. It is the saving grace of our age that it has not yet become aware of its condition.

We think and act as though the possibility of nuclear death had no bearing upon the meaning of life and death. In spite of what some of us know in our reason, we continue to think and act as though the possibility of nuclear death portended only a quantitative extension of the mass destruction of the past and not a qualitative transformation of the meaning of our existence. Thus we talk about defending the freedom of West Berlin as we used to talk about defending the freedom of the American colonies. Thus we talk about defending Western civilization against communism as the ancient Greeks used to talk about defending their civilization against the Persians. Thus we propose to die with honor rather than to live in shame.

Yet the possibility of nuclear death, by destroying the meaning of life and death, has reduced to absurd clichés the noble words of yesterday. To defend freedom and civilization is absurd when to defend them amounts to destroying them. To die with honor is absurd if nobody is left to honor the dead. The very conceptions of honor and shame require a society that knows what honor and shame mean.

It is this contrast between our consciousness and the objective conditions in which we live, the backwardness of our consciousness in view of the possibility of nuclear death, that threatens us with the actuality of nuclear death. It would indeed be the height of thoughtless optimism to assume that something so absurd as a nuclear war cannot happen because it is so absurd. An age whose objective conditions of existence have been radically transformed by the possibility of nuclear death evades the need for a radical transformation of its thought and action by thinking and acting as though nothing of radical import had happened. This refusal to adapt thought and action to radically new conditions has spelled the doom of men and civilizations before. It is likely to do so again.

19 *The Problem of the National Interest*

We have suggested that a theory of politics, domestic or international, requires a central concept. For a general theory of politics, the concept of interest defined as power serves as the central focus, while a theory of international politics must be focused on the concept of the national interest. The controversy which has arisen since the end of the Second World War around the concept of the national interest differs from the great historical debates on American foreign policy in that it raises not necessarily a specific issue of American foreign policy but the fundamental issue of the nature of all foreign policy and of all politics as well.

The great debates of the past, such as the one over intervention versus neutrality in 1793, expansion versus the status quo before the Mexican and after the Spanish-American War, international cooperation versus isolation in the twenties, intervention versus abstention in the late thirties—all evolved around clear-cut issues of foreign policy. In 1793 you were in favor of going to war on the side of France or of remaining neutral. In the 1840's you approved of the annexation of Texas or you did not. At the turn of the century you supported overseas expansion or you were against it. In the twenties you advocated joining the League of Nations or staying out of it. In the late thirties you wanted to oppose the Axis Powers by all means short of war or you wanted to abstain from intervening. While what separates the two schools of thought, the "utopian" and the "realist," which have developed around the concept of the national interest can sometimes be expressed in terms of alternative foreign policies, more often it cannot. Frequently and typically, the very same policies can be and are being supported by both schools of thought. What sets them apart is not necessarily a matter of practical judgment but of philosophies and standards of thought.

The issue the present debate raises concerns the nature of all politics and, more particularly, of the American tradition in foreign

From the *American Political Science Review*, December, 1952.

policy. The history of modern political thought is the story of a contest between two schools which differ fundamentally in their conception of the nature of man, society, and politics. One believes that a rational and moral political order, derived from universally valid abstract principles, can be achieved here and now. It assumes the essential goodness and infinite malleability of human nature and attributes the failure of the social order to measure up to the rational standards to lack of knowledge and understanding, obsolescent social institutions, or the depravity of certain isolated individuals or groups. It trusts in education, reform, and the sporadic use of force to remedy these deficiencies.[1]

The other school believes that the world, imperfect as it is from the rational point of view, is the result of forces inherent in human nature. To improve the world one must work with those forces, not against them. This being inherently a world of opposing interests and of conflict among them, moral principles can never be fully realized, but at best approximated through the ever temporary balancing of interests and the ever precarious settlement of conflicts. This school, then, sees in a system of checks and balances a universal principle for all pluralist societies.[2] It appeals to historic precedent rather than to abstract principles and aims at achievement of the lesser evil rather than of the absolute good.

The conflict between two basic conceptions of man and politics is at the bottom of the present controversy. It provided in the sixteenth, seventeenth, and eighteenth centuries the issue for the debate on the reason of state of which Friedrich Meinecke has given the definitive account. It separated on the occasion of the neutrality proclamation of 1793 Washington and Hamilton from their opponents, and Hamilton has indeed given in the "Pacificus" and "Americanus" letters the classic American formulation of the philosophy

[1] This is the ideal type of the utopian position rather than the empirical description of any particular historic type. In actuality, and this is true particularly of the present, the utopian position in international affairs is not always consistent with its philosophic premises.

[2] It ought not to need special emphasis that a principle of social conduct, in contrast to a law of nature, allows of, and even presupposes, conduct in violation of the principle. Robert W. Tucker, in "Professor Morgenthau's Theory of Political 'Realism,'" *American Political Science Review*, XLVI (March, 1952), 214–24, has missed this and many other points in his zeal to find contradictions where there are none.

of the national interest. In general philosophic terms it found its classic expression in the polemic of Burke against the philosophy of the French Revolution.

In order to refute a theory which pretends to be scientific, it is first necessary to understand what a scientific theory is. A scientific theory, as pointed out before, is an attempt to bring order and meaning to a mass of phenomena which without it would remain disconnected and unintelligible. Anyone who disputes the scientific character of such a theory either must produce a theory superior in these scientific functions to the one attacked or must, at the very least, demonstrate that the facts as they actually are do not lend themselves to the interpretation that the theory has put upon them. When a historian tells us that the balance of power is not a universal principle of politics, domestic and international, that it was practiced in Europe only for a limited period and never by the United States, that it ruined the states that practiced it,[3] it is incumbent upon him to tell us how we can dispose by means of theory of the historic data by which, for instance, David Hume demonstrated the universality of the balance of power and Paul Scott Mowrer[4] and Alfred Vagts[5] its practice by the United States; what Kautilya was writing about in the fourth century B.C. when he summarized the theoretical and practical tradition of Indian statecraft in terms of the balance of power; what the Greek city-states, the Roman republic, and the medieval emperors and popes were doing if they did not apply the principles of the balance of power; and how the nations that either neglected these principles or applied them wrongly suffered political and military defeat and even extinction, while the nation that applied these principles most consistently and consciously, that is, Great Britain, enjoyed unrivaled power for an unparalleled length of time.

The historian who wishes to replace the balance of power as the guiding principle of American foreign policy with the "humani-

[3] Tannenbaum in "The Balance of Power versus the Coördinate State," *Political Science Quarterly*, LXVII (June, 1952), 173, and in "The American Tradition in Foreign Relations," *Foreign Affairs*, XXX (October, 1951), 31–50.

[4] *Our Foreign Affairs* (New York: E. P. Dutton & Co., 1924), pp. 246 ff.

[5] "The United States and the Balance of Power," *Journal of Politics*, III (November, 1941), 401–49.

[6] Tannenbaum, "The Balance of Power versus the Coördinate State," p. 173.

tarian and pacific traditions" of the "coördinate state"[6] must first of all explain how it has come about that the thirteen original states expanded into the full breadth and a good deal of the length of a continent, until today the strategic frontiers of the United States run parallel to the coastline of Asia and along the River Elbe. If such are the results of policies based upon "humanitarian and pacific traditions," never in the history of the world has virtue been more bountifully rewarded! Yet our historian must explain not only the great sweep of American expansion but also the specific foreign policies which in their historic succession make up that sweep. Is it easier to explain the successive shifts of American support from Great Britain to France and back again from the beginning of King George's War in 1744 to the War of 1812 in terms of the "coördinate state" than in terms of the balance of power? The same question might be asked about the postponement of the recognition of the independence of the Spanish colonies until 1822, when the Floridas had been acquired from Spain and Spain had thereby been deprived of the ability to challenge the United States from within the hemisphere. The same question might be asked about the Monroe Doctrine itself, about Lincoln's policies toward Great Britain and France, and about our successive policies with regard to Mexico and the Caribbean. One could go on and pick out at random any foreign policy pursued by the United States from the beginning to the First World War, and one would hardly find a policy, with the exception perhaps of the War of 1812, that could not be made intelligible by reference to the national interest defined in terms of power—political, military, and economic—rather than by reference to the principle of the "coordinate state." This inevitable outcome of such an inquiry is well summarized in these words:

Ease and prosperity have made us wish the whole world to be as happy and well to do as ourselves; and we have supposed that institutions and principles like our own were the simple prescription for making them so. And yet, when issues of our own interests arose, we have not been unselfish. We have shown ourselves kin to all the world, when it came to pushing an advantage. Our action against Spain in the Floridas, and against Mexico on the coasts of the Pacific; our attitude toward first the Spaniards, and then the French, with regard to the control of the Mississippi; the unpitying force with which we thrust the Indians to the wall wherever they stood in our way, have suited our professions of peacefulness and justice and liberality no better than the aggressions of other nations that were strong and not to be gainsaid. Even Mr. Jefferson, philanthropist and champion of peaceable and modest government though he was, exemplified this double temper of the people he ruled. "Peace is our passion," he had declared; but the passion abated when he saw the mouth of the Mississippi about to pass into the hands of France. Though he had loved France and hated England, he did not hesitate then what language to hold. "There is on the globe," he wrote to Mr. Livingston at Paris, "one single spot the possessor of which is our natural and habitual enemy. The day that France takes possession of New Orleans seals the union of two nations, who, in conjunction, can maintain exclusive possession of the sea. From that moment we must marry ourselves to the British fleet and nation." Our interests must march forward, altruists though we are; other nations must see to it that they stand off, and do not seek to stay us.

This realist appraisal of the American tradition in foreign policy was published in 1901 in the *Atlantic Monthly*. Its author was a professor of jurisprudence and political economy at Princeton by the name of Woodrow Wilson.[7]

Nothing more needs to be said to demonstrate that facts do not support a revision of American diplomatic history that tries to substitute "humanitarian and pacifist traditions" and the "coördinate state" for power politics and the balance of power as the guiding principle of American foreign policy. What, then, does support it? Three things: the way American statesmen have spoken about American foreign policy; the legal fiction of the "coördinate state"; finally, and foremost, an emotional urge to justify American foreign policy in humanitarian, pacifist terms.

It is elementary that the character of a foreign policy can be ascertained only through the examination of the political acts performed and of the foreseeable consequences of these acts. Thus we can find out what statesmen have actually done, and from the foreseeable consequences of their acts we can surmise what their objectives might have been. Yet examination of the facts is not enough. To give meaning to the factual raw material of history, we must approach historical reality with a kind of rational outline, a map which suggests to us the possible meanings of history. In other words, we put ourselves in the position of a statesman who must meet a certain problem of foreign policy under certain circumstances and ask ourselves: what are the rational alternatives from which a statesman

---

[7] "Democracy and Efficiency," *Atlantic Monthly*, LXXXVII (March, 1901), 293–94.

may choose who must meet this problem under these circumstances, presuming always that he acts in a rational manner, and which of these rational alternatives was this particular statesman, acting under these circumstances, likely to choose? It is the testing of this rational hypothesis against the actual facts and their consequences which gives meaning to the facts of history and makes the scientific writing of political history possible.

In the process of writing the history of foreign policy the interpretations by statesmen of their own acts, especially if they are made for public consumption, must needs have a strictly subsidiary place. The public self-interpretation by actors on the political scene is itself, of course, a political act which seeks to present a certain policy to its presumed supporters in terms of their moral and political folklore and to those against which it is directed in terms which intend to embarrass and deceive. Such declarations may indeed shed light upon the character and objectives of the policy pursued if they are considered in conjunction with, and in subordination to, rational hypotheses, actions, and likely consequences. Yet it is quite a different matter to interpret the American tradition of foreign policy in the light of a collection of official statements which, like most such statements, present humanitarian and pacifist justifications for the policies pursued. If anybody should be bold enough to write a history of world politics with so uncritical a method he would easily and well-nigh inevitably be driven to the conclusion that from Timur to Hitler and Stalin the foreign policies of all nations were inspired by the ideals of humanitarianism and pacifism. The absurdity of the result is commensurate with the defects of the method.

It is only from a method that accepts the declarations of statesmen as evidence of the character of the policies pursued that the principle of the "coördinate state" receives a semblance of plausibility. Statesmen and international lawyers have been wont to speak of the "equal dignity" of all states, regardless of "wealth, power, size, population or culture,"[8] which I take the principle of the "coördinate state" to mean. It is also referred to as the principle of "federalism in international relations."[9] As its prime examples are cited the relations amongst the states of the Union, the states of the American

[8] Tannenbaum, "The Balance of Power versus the Coördinate State," p. 177.
[9] *Ibid.*

system, the members of the Commonwealth of Nations, and the members of the Swiss Confederation. If the whole world were organized in accordance with this principle, as are already these four political entities, it is assumed that the freedom, dignity, and peace of all nations would then be assured.

There is no need to examine the theoretical and practical merits of the principle of the "coördinate state," because for none of the four political entities mentioned does the idea of the "coördinate state" provide the principle of political organization. The equality of the states as the political foundation of the United States became obsolescent when Chief Justice Marshall's Supreme Court resolved the ambiguity of the Constitution in favor of the federal government, and it became obsolete when the Civil War proved Chief Justice Marshall's point. The equality of the states survives today only in the shadow and by virtue of the federal government's political supremacy, and without the cohesive force of that supremacy there would be no union of equal states to begin with. That these powers of the federal government are limited and qualified by the principle of federalism, that is, by the constitutionally granted powers of the states, is quite a different matter; it concerns the distribution of powers between federal government and states within a general system of checks and balances, but has nothing to do with the equality of the states as the alleged political foundation of the American system of government. With the exception of the equality of senatorial representation, the principle of the equality of the states is today, as it has been for almost a century, devoid of political content. It serves only as a principle of regional organization, of administrative decentralization, and, above all, of constitutional rhetoric. What it really signifies was pointed out more than fifty years ago by W. A. Dunning when he summarized his answer to the question "Are the states equal under the Constitution?" by saying that "the theory of equal states falls to the ground."[10]

Similarly, the federalism of Switzerland is the result of a long series of civil wars, the last one fought a little more than a century ago, which established the predominance of the German-speaking cantons within the confederation. Here too, it is the existence of

[10] William Archibald Dunning, *Essays on the Civil War and Reconstruction and Related Topics* (New York: P. Smith, 1931), p. 351.

predominant power, located in one segment of the federal system, which makes federalism possible in the first place.

By the same token, the unchallengeable supremacy of the United States within the Western Hemisphere has throughout been the backbone of the system of American states. As long as this supremacy is secure, there is, on the one hand, no need for the United States to assert it in the political and military sphere, and, taking it for granted, the United States can well afford to pursue a policy of the Good Neighbor; and there is, on the other hand, no opportunity for the other members of the system to challenge that supremacy effectively. This is what the principle of the "coördinate state" amounts to in the Western Hemisphere. Consequently, whenever there was even a remote possibility that the supremacy of the United States might be challenged, generally through instigation from outside the hemisphere, the United States asserted its superior power within the hemisphere and acted as all states must act under similar conditions.

Whatever possibility for common political action there remains among the members of the Commonwealth of Nations is the result of the interests which these members may have in common. In other words, the member states may work together or each of them may work with other nations, as their interests dictate. Their membership in the Commonwealth, as the examples of India, South Africa, Australia, and New Zealand clearly show, has no influence upon this decision; that membership is but a faint remembrance of the times when Great Britain could secure co-operation among the member states on its terms by virtue of its superior power.

What, then, have these four examples of the "coördinate state" in common which would establish them as a distinct type of interstate relationship, and what conclusions can be drawn from them for the organization of the world? The only thing that these four examples seem to have really in common is the legal stipulation of the equality of the members of the respective systems, and this characteristic is not peculiar to them, but a general principle of international law applicable to all sovereign states. In the political sphere they seem to have nothing in common at all. What they tend to show, however, is the decisive importance of the distribution of political power for the operation of federal and egalitarian relations among states. The political cohesion of a federal system is the result of superior power located in some part of it. It is by virtue of its superior power that the predominant part can afford to grant the other members of the federal system a measure of equality in the non-political sphere. These observations bring us back to power politics and the balance of power to which the principle of the "coördinate state" was supposed to be the alternative.

In truth, it is not the disinterested consideration of facts which has given birth to the theory of the "coördinate state." That theory is rather the response to an emotional urge, and since this emotion is not peculiar to a particular author but typical of a popular reaction to the new role which the United States must play in world affairs, it deserves a brief analysis.

One of the great experiences of our time which have impressed themselves upon the American mind is the emergence of the United States as a nation among other nations, exposed to the same opportunities, temptations, risks, and liabilities to which other nations have been traditionally exposed. This experience becomes the more shocking if it is compared with the expectation with which we fought the Second World War. We expected from that war a reaffirmation of the secure, detached, and independent position in world affairs which we had inherited from the founding fathers and which we had been successful in preserving at least to the First World War. By avoiding what we thought had been Wilson's mistakes, we expected to emerge from that war if not more independent, certainly more secure than we were when we entered it. In fact, not even in the early days of the Republic were we more exposed to danger from abroad than we are today, and never had we less freedom of action in taking care of our interests than we have today.

It is naturally shocking to recognize that a happy chapter in the history of the nation and in one's own way of life has come to an end. There are those who reconcile themselves to the inevitable, albeit with sorrow rather than with glee, and try to apply the lessons of the past to the tasks at hand. There are others who try to escape from a disappointing and threatening reality into the realm of fantasy. Three such escapist fantasies have arisen in our midst in response to the challenge of American world leadership and power: the fantasy of needless American participation in war, the fantasy of American treason, and the fantasy of American innocence.

The first of these fantasies presumes that the present predicament is a result not of necessity but of folly, the folly of American statesmen who needlessly intervened in two world wars. The second of these fantasies attributes the present predicament to treason in high places whereby the fruits of victory were handed to the enemy. The third of these fantasies denies that the predicament is real and prefers to think of it as an intellectual fraud perpetrated upon the American people. To support this fictional denial of the actualities of the present, it draws upon a fictional account of the past. The United States does not need to bear at present the intellectual, moral, and political burdens which go with involvement in power politics and the maintenance of the balance of power; for it has never borne them in the past, never having been thus involved. The golden age of past political innocence sheds its glow upon a but seemingly less innocent present and promises a future in which all the world will follow the example of America, forswear power politics and the balance of power, and accept the principle of the "coördinate state." Our alliances, we are told, have nothing to do with the balance of power but aim at the "organization of as much of the world as we can upon the basis of the coördinate state. . . . It may prove impossible under present conditions to build such a system without having to fight a war with Russia, but then at least we will be fighting, as we did before, for the thing we consider worth defending with our lives and treasure."[11] Thus a fictional account of the American past, begun as an act of uncalled-for patriotic piety, issues in an ideology for a third world war. Escape we must from the unfamiliar, unpleasant, and dangerous present, first into the political innocence of the past and from there into the immediate future of a third world war, beyond which the revived and universalized innocence of the more distant future will surely lie.

We have said that to present the American tradition in foreign policy as having been free from concern with power politics and the balance of power is not warranted by the facts of American history. Yet it might still be argued, and it is actually being argued, that, regardless of the evidence of history, the American people will not be reconciled to power politics and the balance of power and

[11] Tannenbaum, "The Balance of Power versus the Coördinate State," pp. 195–96.

will support only policies based upon abstract moral principles. While in the past the United States might have pursued balance-of-power policies and while it might be a good thing if it did do so again, the American people will not stand for it. Here the emotional appeal to patriotic piety is joined by calculations of political expediency. Yet the case for misrepresenting American history has nothing to gain from either.

There is a strong tendency in all historiography to glorify the national past, and in popular presentations that tendency takes on the aspects of the jingoist whitewash. Even so penetrating a mind as John Stuart Mill's could deliver itself of an essay in which he proved, no doubt to the satisfaction of many of his English readers but certainly of few others, that Great Britain had never interfered in the affairs of European nations and had interfered in those of the Indian states only for their own good.[12] Yet it is the measure of a nation's maturity to be able to recognize its past for what it actually is. Why should we not admit that American foreign policy has been generally hardheaded and practical and at times ruthless? Why should we deny Jefferson's cunning, say, in the Puget Sound affair, the cruelty with which the Indians were treated, and the faithlessness with which the treaties with the Indians were cast aside? We know that this is the way all nations are when their interests are at stake—so cruel, so faithless, so cunning. We know that the United States has refrained from seeking dominions beyond the seas not because it is more virtuous than other nations but because it had the better part of a continent to colonize.

As has been pointed out elsewhere at greater length, the man in the street, unsophisticated as he is and uninformed as he may be, has a surer grasp of the essentials of foreign policy and a more mature judgment of its basic issues than many of the intellectuals and politicians who pretend to speak for him and cater to what they imagine his prejudices to be. During the Second World War the ideologues of the Atlantic Charter, the Four Freedoms, and the United Nations were constantly complaining that the American soldier did not know what he was fighting for. Indeed, if he was fighting for

---

[12] "A Few Words on Non-Intervention," *Dissertations and Discussions: Political, Philosophical, and Historical* (London: Longmans, Green, Reader and Dyer, 1875), pp. 153–78.

some utopian ideal, divorced from the concrete experiences and interests of the country, then the complaint was well grounded. However, if he was fighting for the territorial integrity of the nation and for its survival as a free country where he could live, think, and act as he pleased, then he had never any doubt about what he was fighting for. Ideological rationalizations and justifications are indeed the indispensable concomitants of all political action. Yet there is something unhealthy in a craving for ideological intoxication and in the inability to act and to see merit in action except under the stimulant of grandiose ideas and far-fetched schemes. Have our intellectuals become, like Hamlet, too much beset by doubt to act and, unlike Hamlet, compelled to still their doubts by renouncing their sense of what is real? The man in the street has no such doubts. It is true that ideologues and demagogues can sway him by appealing to his emotions. But it is also true, as American history shows in abundance, that responsible statesmen can guide him by awakening his latent understanding of the national interest.

Yet what is the national interest? How can we define it and give it the content which will make it a guide both for understanding and for action? This is one of the relevant questions to which the current debate has given rise.

It has been frequently argued against the realist conception of foreign policy that its key concept, the national interest, does not provide an acceptable standard for either thought or action. This argument is in the main based upon two grounds: the elusiveness of the concept and its susceptibility to interpretations, such as limitless imperialism and narrow nationalism, which are not in keeping with the American tradition in foreign policy. The argument has substance as far as it goes, but it does not invalidate the usefulness of the concept.

The concept of the national interest is similar in two respects to the "great generalities" of the Constitution, such as the general welfare and due process. It contains a residual meaning which is inherent in the concept itself, but beyond these minimum requirements its content can run the whole gamut of meanings that are logically compatible with it. That content is determined by the political traditions and the total cultural context within which a nation formulates its foreign policy. The concept of the national interest, then, contains two elements, one that is logically required and in that sense necessary, and one that is variable and determined by circumstances. The former is, then, of necessity relatively permanent while the latter will vary with circumstances.

The relative permanency of what one might call the hard core of the national interest stems from three factors: the nature of the interests to be protected, the political environment within which the interests operate, and the rational necessities which limit the choice of ends and means by all actors on the stage of foreign policy. Any foreign policy that operates under the standard of the national interest must obviously have some reference to the physical, political, and cultural entity which we call a nation. In a world where a number of sovereign nations compete with and oppose each other for power, the foreign policies of all nations must necessarily refer to their survival as their minimum requirement. Thus all nations do what they cannot help but do: protect their physical, political, and cultural identity against encroachments by other nations.

The nature of the threat to which the national interest is exposed remains equally constant over long periods of history. Throughout the centuries the main threat to Great Britain has come from the hegemonic aspirations of one or the other of the European nations. Russia has traditionally been threatened by a great power having access to the plains of eastern Europe. France and Germany, regardless of their changing political forms, have threatened each other throughout the ages.

The relative permanency of interest and threat is surpassed by the virtual immutability of the configurations through which the reason of man transforms the abstract concept of the national interest into foreign policy. Faced with the necessity to protect the hard core of the national interest, that is, to preserve the identity of the nation, all governments have resorted throughout history to certain basic policies, such as competitive armaments, the balance of power, alliances, and subversion, intended to make of the abstract concept of the national interest a viable political reality. Governments might have been wise or unwise in their choice of policies, successful or unsuccessful in their execution; they could not have escaped the rational necessity of selecting one of a limited number of avenues through which to bring the power of their nation to bear upon the power of other nations on behalf of the national interest.

The possibility both to reconstruct past foreign policies through the writing of history and to understand the contemporary foreign policies of one's own and other nations derives from this rational character of the national interest. If one could not assume that this rationality is identical throughout history and ubiquitous on the contemporary scene, however diminished and distorted by the irrationality of men and nations, one would be lost in a maze of unconnected data, to be explained perhaps in terms of psychology and sociology but not in terms conducive to the understanding of foreign policy. It is this assumption of the universality of the national interest in time and space which enables us to understand the foreign policies of Demosthenes and Caesar, of Kautilya and Henry VIII, of the statesmen of contemporary Russia and China. Regardless of all the differences in personality, social environment, convictions, and preferences, their thinking was predetermined and their actions could take place only within a narrow range, when they were faced with the task of protecting and promoting the rational core of the national interest. By thinking as they must have thought we can understand their thoughts, and by putting their thoughts into the context of their personalities and social environment we can understand their actions as well.

It has been suggested that this reasoning erects the national state into the last word in politics and the national interest into an absolute standard for political action. This, however, is not quite the case. The idea of interest is indeed of the essence of politics and, as such, unaffected by the circumstances of time and place. Thucydides' statement, born of the experiences of ancient Greece, that "identity of interest is the surest of bonds whether between states or individuals" was taken up in the nineteenth century by Lord Salisbury's remark that "the only bond of union that endures" among nations is "the absence of all clashing interests." The perennial issue between the realist and utopian schools of thought over the nature of politics, to which we have referred before, might well be formulated in terms of concrete interests versus abstract principles. Yet while the concern of politics with interest is perennial, the connection between interest and the national state is a product of history.

The national state itself is obviously a product of history and as such is destined to yield in time to different modes of political organization. As long as the world is politically organized into nations, the national interest is indeed the last word in international politics. When the national state has been replaced by another mode of organization, foreign policy must then protect the interest in survival of that new organization. For the benefit of those who insist upon discarding the national state and constructing supranational organizations by constitutional fiat, it must be pointed out that these new organizational forms will either come into being through conquest or else through consent based upon the mutual recognition of the national interests of the nations concerned; for no nation will forego its freedom of action if it has no reason to expect proportionate benefits in compensation for that loss. This is true of treaties concerning commerce or fisheries as it is true of the great compacts, such as the European Coal and Steel Community, through which nations try to create supranational forms of organization. Thus, by an apparent paradox, what is historically conditioned in the idea of the national interest can be overcome only through the promotion in concert of the national interest of a number of nations.

These reflections have been made particularly relevant by the atomic age. It has been said that the atomic age has rendered obsolete the idea of the national interest and the conception of foreign policy derived from it. This is too sweeping a statement to be correct. What has become obsolete is the historically conditioned connection between interest and a passing historic phenomenon, the nation state; what has not, and could not have, become obsolete is the logically required connection between interest and foreign policy. The point can indeed be made that the technological revolutions of our age, of which the atomic revolution is the most spectacular one, have made the political organization of the world into nation states as obsolete as the first industrial revolution did the political organization based upon the feudal state. Yet the techniques by which new and wider interest must be given a politically viable expression have not been affected by those revolutionary changes. Thus the supranational control of atomic energy is today in the national interest of all nations; for while the present bipolarity of atomic power is dangerous to all nations, the acquisition of uncontrolled atomic power by an indefinite number of nations is likely to prove fatal to civilized life on this planet. In consequence, the nations of the world are faced with, and must overcome, the dilemma that the pursuit of their interests, conceived in national terms, is incompatible with modern technology, which requires supranational political organization.

The survival of a political unit, such as a nation, in its identity is the irreducible minimum, the necessary element of its interests vis-à-vis other units. Taken in isolation, the determination of its content in a concrete situation is relatively simple; for it encompasses the integrity of the nation's territory, of its political institutions, and of its culture. Thus bipartisanship in foreign policy, especially in times of war, has been most easily achieved in the promotion of these minimum requirements of the national interest. The situation is different with respect to the variable elements of the national interest. All the crosscurrents of personalities, public opinion, sectional interests, partisan politics, and political and moral folkways are brought to bear upon their determination. In consequence, the contribution which scientific analysis can make to this field, as to all fields of policy formation, is limited. It can identify the different agencies of the government which contribute to the determination of the variable elements of the national interest and assess their relative weight. It can separate the long-range objectives of foreign policy from the short-term ones which are the means for the achievement of the former and can tentatively establish their rational relations. Finally, it can analyze the variable elements of the national interest in terms of their legitimacy and their compatibility with other national values and with the national interest of other nations. We shall address ourselves briefly to the typical problems with which this analysis must deal.

The legitimacy of the national interest must be determined in the face of possible usurpation by subnational, other-national, and supranational interests. On the subnational level we find group interests, represented particularly by ethnic and economic groups, which tend to identify themselves with the national interest. Charles A. Beard has emphasized, however one-sidedly, the extent to which the economic interests of certain groups have been presented as those of the United States.[13] Group interests exert, of course, constant pressure upon the conduct of our foreign policy, claiming their identity with the national interest. It is, however, doubtful that, with the exception of a few spectacular cases, they have been successful in determining the course of American foreign policy. It is much more likely, given the nature of American domestic politics, that American foreign policy, in so far as it is the object of pressures by sectional interests, will normally be a compromise between divergent sectional interests. The concept of the national interest, as it emerges from this contest of conflicting sectional interests as the actual guide for foreign policy, may well fall short of what would be rationally required by the over-all interests of the United States. Yet this concept of the national interest is also more than any particular sectional interest or their sum total. It is, as it were, the lowest common denominator where sectional interests and the national interest rationally conceived meet in an uneasy compromise which may leave much to be desired in view of all the interests concerned.

The national interest can be usurped by other-national interests in two typical ways. The case of treason by individuals, either out of conviction or for pay, needs only to be mentioned here; for in so far as treason is committed on behalf of a foreign government rather than a supranational principle, it is significant for psychology, sociology, and criminology but not for the theory of politics. The other case, however, is important not only for the theory of politics but also for its practice, especially in the United States.

National minorities in European countries, ethnic groups in the United States, ideological minorities anywhere may identify themselves, either spontaneously or under the direction of the agents of a foreign government, with the interests of that foreign government and may promote these interests under the guise of the national interest of the country whose citizens they happen to be. The activities of the German-American Bund in the United States in the thirties and of Communists everywhere are cases in point. Yet the issue of the national interest versus other-national interests masquer-

---

[13] *The Idea of National Interest: An Analytical Study in American Foreign Policy* (New York: Macmillan Co., 1934).

ading as the national interest has arisen constantly in the United States in a less clear-cut fashion.

A country that had been settled by consecutive waves of "foreigners" was bound to find it particularly difficult to identify its own national interest against alleged, seeming, or actual other-national interests represented by certain groups among its own citizens. Since virtually all citizens of the United States are, as it were, "more or less" foreign born, those who were "less" so have frequently not resisted the temptation to use this distinction as a polemic weapon against latecomers who happened to differ from them in their conception of the national interest of the United States. Frequently, this rationalization has been dispensed with, and a conception of foreign policy with which a writer happened to disagree has been attributed outright to foreign sympathy or influence or worse. British influence and interests have served as standard arguments in debates on American foreign policy. Madison, in his polemic against Hamilton on the occasion of Washington's neutrality proclamation of 1793, identified the Federalist position with that of "the foreigners and degenerate citizens among us, who hate our republican government, and the French revolution,"[14] and the accusation met with a favorable response in a majority of Congress and of public opinion. However, these traditional attempts to discredit dissenting opinion as being influenced by foreign interests should not obscure the real issue, which is the peculiar vulnerability of the national interest of the United States to usurpation by the interests of other nations.

This problem has become in our time particularly acute in the form of Communist subversion. The transference of an individual's allegiance from his own nation to another one, the Soviet Union, is here made peculiarly attractive by the identification of the interests of the Soviet Union with the interests of humanity, that is, the supranational interest par excellence. As the testimony before the royal commission investigating the Gouzenko case clearly shows, the sincere Communist identifies the interests of the Soviet Union with those of humanity and, hence, experiences his betrayal of the

---

[14] "Helvidius, in Answer to Pacificus, on President Washington's Proclamation of Neutrality," in *Letters and Other Writings of James Madison* (Philadelphia: J. B. Lippincott Co., 1867), I, 611.

interests of his own nation not as treason but rather as the establishment of the correct priority between lower and higher interests, the
lower one having to yield in case of conflict to those that are superior.

The genuine usurpation of the national interest by supranational
interests can derive in our time from two sources: religious bodies
and international organizations. The competition between church
and state for determination of certain interests and policies, domestic and international, has been an intermittent issue throughout the
history of the nation state. Here, too, the legitimate defense of the
national interest against usurpation has frequently, especially in the
United States, degenerated into the demagogic stigmatization of dissenting views as being inspired by Rome and, hence, being incompatible with the national interest. Yet here, too, the misuse of the
issue for demagogic purposes must be considered apart from the
legitimacy of the issue itself.

The more acute problem arises at the present time from the importance which the public and government officials, at least in their
public utterances, attribute to the values represented and the policies
pursued by international organizations either as alternatives or supplements to the values and policies for which the national government stands. It is frequently asserted that the foreign policy of the
United States pursues no objectives apart from those of the United
Nations, that, in other words, the foreign policy of the United
States is actually identical with the policy of the United Nations.
This assertion cannot refer to anything real in actual politics to
support it. For the constitutional structure of international organizations, such as the United Nations, and their procedural practices
make it impossible for them to pursue interests apart from those of
the member states which dominate their policy-forming bodies. The
identity between the interests of the United Nations and the United
States can only refer to the successful policies of the United States
within the United Nations through which the support of the United
Nations is being secured for the policies of the United States. The
assertion, then, is mere polemic, different from the one discussed
previously in that the identification of a certain policy with an assumed supranational interest does not seek to reflect discredit upon
the former but to bestow upon it a dignity which the national interest
pure and simple is supposed to lack.

The real issue in view of the problem that concerns us here is not whether the so-called interests of the United Nations, which do not exist apart from the interests of its most influential members, have superseded the national interest of the United States, but for what kind of interests the United States has secured United Nations support. While these interests cannot be United Nations interests, they do not need to be national interests either. Here we are in the presence of that modern phenomenon which has been variously described as "utopianism," "sentimentalism," "moralism," the "legalistic-moralistic approach." The common denominator of all these tendencies in modern political thought is the substitution for the national interest of an assumed supranational standard of action which is generally identified with an international organization. The national interest is here not being usurped by subnational or supranational interests which, however inferior in worth to the national interest, are nevertheless real and worthy of consideration within their proper sphere. What challenges the national interest here is a mere figment of the imagination, a product of wishful thinking, which is postulated as a valid norm for international conduct, without being valid either there or anywhere else. At this point we touch the core of the present controversy between utopianism and realism in international affairs; we shall return to it later.

The national interest as such must be defended against usurpation by non-national interests. Yet once that task is accomplished, a rational order must be established among the values which make up the national interest and among the resources to be committed to them. While the interests which a nation may pursue in its relation with other nations are of infinite variety and magnitude, the resources which are available for the pursuit of such interests are necessarily limited in quantity and kind. No nation has the resources to promote all desirable objectives with equal vigor; all nations must therefore allocate their scarce resources as rationally as possible. The indispensable precondition of such rational allocation is a clear understanding of the distinction between the necessary and variable elements of the national interest. Given the contentious manner in which in democracies the variable elements of the national interest are generally determined, the advocates of an extensive conception of the national interest will inevitably present certain variable elements of the national interest as though their attainment were necessary for the nation's survival. In other words, the necessary elements of the national interest have a tendency to swallow up the variable elements so that in the end all kinds of objectives, actual or potential, are justified in terms of national survival. Such arguments have been advanced, for instance, in support of the rearmament of West Germany and of the defense of Formosa. They must be subjected to rational scrutiny which will determine, however tentatively, their approximate place in the scale of national values.

The same problem presents itself in its extreme form when a nation pursues, or is asked to pursue, objectives that are not only unnecessary for its survival but tend to jeopardize it. Second-rate nations which dream of playing the role of great powers, such as Italy and Poland in the interwar period, illustrate this point. So do great powers which dream of remaking the world in their own image and embark upon world-wide crusades, thus straining their resources to exhaustion. Here scientific analysis has the urgent task of pruning down national objectives to the measure of available resources in order to make their pursuit compatible with national survival.

Finally, the national interest of a nation that is conscious not only of its own interests but also of that of other nations must be defined in terms compatible with the latter. In a multinational world this is a requirement of political morality; in an age of total war it is also a condition for survival.

Two mutually exclusive arguments have been brought to bear upon this problem. On the one hand, it has been argued against the theory of international politics here presented that the concept of the national interest revives the eighteenth-century concept of enlightened self-interest, presuming that the uniformly enlightened pursuit of their self-interest by all individuals, as by all nations, will of itself be conducive to a peaceful and harmonious society. On the other hand, the point has been made that the pursuit of their national interest by all nations makes war the permanent arbiter of conflicts among them. Neither argument is well taken.

The concept of the national interest presupposes neither a naturally harmonious, peaceful world nor the inevitability of war as a consequence of the pursuit by all nations of their national interest.

Quite to the contrary, it assumes continuous conflict and threat of war, to be minimized through the continuous adjustment of conflicting interests by diplomatic action. No such assumption would be warranted if all nations at all times conceived of their national interest only in terms of their survival and, in turn, defined their interest in survival in restrictive and rational terms. As it is, their conception of the national interest is subject to all the hazards of misinterpretation, usurpation, and misjudgment to which reference has been made above. To minimize these hazards is the first task of a foreign policy that seeks the defense of the national interest by peaceful means. Its second task is the defense of the national interest, restrictively and rationally defined, against the national interests of other nations which may or may not be thus defined. If they are not, it becomes the task of armed diplomacy to convince the nations concerned that their legitimate interests have nothing to fear from a restrictive and rational foreign policy and that their illegitimate interests have nothing to gain in the face of armed might rationally employed.

We have said before that the utopian and realist positions in international affairs do not necessarily differ in the policies they advocate, but that they part company over their general philosophies of politics and their way of thinking about matters political. It does not follow that the present debate is only of academic interest and without practical significance. Both camps, it is true, may support the same policy for different reasons. Yet if the reasons are unsound, the soundness of the policies supported by them is a mere coincidence, and these very same reasons may be, and inevitably are, invoked on other occasions in support of unsound policies. The nefarious consequences of false philosophies and wrong ways of thinking may for the time being be concealed by the apparent success of policies derived from them. You may go to war, justified by your nation's interests, for a moral purpose and in disregard of considerations of power; and military victory seems to satisfy both your moral aspirations and your nation's interests. Yet the manner in which you waged the war, achieved victory, and settled the peace cannot help reflecting your philosophy of politics and your way of thinking about political problems. If these are in error, you may win victory on the field of battle and still assist in the defeat of both your moral principles and the national interest of your country.

Any number of examples could illustrate the real yet subtle practical consequences which follow from the different positions taken. We have chosen two: collective security in Korea and the liberation of the nations that are captives of communism. A case for both policies can be made from both the utopian and the realist positions, but with significant differences in the emphasis and substance of the policies pursued.

Collective security as an abstract principle of utopian politics requires that all nations come to the aid of a victim of aggression by resisting the aggressor with all means necessary to frustrate his aims. Once the case of aggression is established, the duty to act is unequivocal. Its extent may be affected by concern for the nation's survival; obviously no nation will commit outright suicide in the service of collective security. But beyond that elemental limitation no consideration of interest or power, either with regard to the aggressor or his victim or the nation acting in the latter's defense, can qualify the obligation to act under the principle of collective security. Thus high officials of our government have declared that we intervened in Korea not for any narrow interest of ours but in support of the moral principle of collective security.

Collective security as a concrete principle of realist policy is the age-old maxim, "Hang together or hang separately," in modern dress. It recognizes the need for nation A under certain circumstances to defend nation B against attack by nation C. That need is determined, first, by the interest which A has in the territorial integrity of B and by the relation of that interest to all the other interests of A as well as to the resources available for the support of all those interests. Furthermore, A must take into account the power which is at the disposal of aggressor C for fighting A and B as over against the power available to A and B for fighting C. The same calculation must be carried on concerning the power of the likely allies of C as over against those of A and B. Before going to war for the defense of South Korea in the name of collective security, an American adherent of political realism would have demanded an answer to the following four questions: First, what is our interest in the preservation of the independence of South Korea;

second, what is our power to defend that independence against North Korea; third, what is our power to defend that independence against China and the Soviet Union; and fourth, what are the chances for preventing China and the Soviet Union from entering the Korean War?

In view of the principle of collective security, interpreted in utopian terms, our intervention in Korea was a foregone conclusion. The interpretation of this principle in realist terms might or might not, depending upon the concrete circumstances of interest and power, have led us to the same conclusion. In the execution of the policy of collective security the utopian had to be indifferent to the possibility of Chinese and Russian intervention, except for his resolution to apply the principle of collective security to anybody who would intervene on the side of the aggressor. The realist could not help weighing the possibility of the intervention of a great power on the side of the aggressor in terms of the interests engaged and the power available on the other side.[15]

The Truman administration could not bring itself to take resolutely the utopian or the realist position. It resolved to intervene in good measure on utopian grounds and in spite of military advice to the contrary; it allowed the military commander to advance to the Yalu River in disregard of the risk of the intervention of a great power against which collective security could be carried out only by means of a general war, and then refused to pursue the war with full effectiveness on the realist grounds of the risk of a third world war. Thus Mr. Truman in 1952 was caught in the same dilemma from which Mr. Baldwin could extricate himself in 1936 on the occasion of the League of Nations sanctions against Italy's attack upon Ethiopia only at an enormous loss to British prestige. Collective security as a defense of the status quo short of a general war can be effective only against second-rate powers. Applied against a major power, it is a contradiction in terms, for it means necessarily a major war. Of this self-defeating contradiction Mr. Baldwin

[15] The difference in these two attitudes is well illustrated by the following passage from a Moon Mullins cartoon. An elderly representative of the utopian school asks little Kayo: "Remember the golden rule. Now, supposing that boy slapped you on the right cheek, what would you do?" Whereupon Kayo replies realistically: "Jest how big a boy are you supposin'?"

was as unaware in the thirties as Mr. Truman seemed to be in 1952. Mr. Churchill put Mr. Baldwin's dilemma in these cogent terms: "First, the Prime Minister had declared that sanctions meant war; secondly, he was resolved that there must be no war; and thirdly, he decided upon sanctions. It was evidently impossible to comply with these three conditions." Similarly Mr. Truman had declared that the effective prosecution of the Korean War meant the possibility of a third world war; he resolved that there must be no third world war; and he decided upon intervention in the Korean War. Here, too, it was impossible to comply with these three conditions.

Similar contradictions are inherent in the proposals which would substitute for the policy of containment the liberation of the nations presently the captives of Russian communism. This objective can be compatible with the utopian or realist position, but the policies designed to secure it will be fundamentally different according to whether they are based upon one or the other position. A clear case for the utopian justification of such policies was made by Representative Charles J. Kersten of Wisconsin, who pointed to these four "basic defects" of the "negative policy of containment and negotiated coexistence":

It would be immoral and unchristian to negotiate a permanent agreement with forces which by every religious creed and moral precept are evil. It abandons nearly one-half of humanity and the once free nations of Poland, Czechoslovakia, Hungary, Rumania, Bulgaria, Albania, Lithuania, Latvia, Esthonia and China to enslavement of the Communist police state.

It is un-American because it violates the principle of the American Declaration of Independence, which proclaims the rights of all people to freedom and their right and duty to throw off tyranny.

It will lead to all-out World War III because it aligns all the forces of the non-Communist world in military opposition to and against all the forces of the Communist world, including the 800,000,000 peoples behind the Iron Curtain.

The policy of mere containment is uneconomic and will lead to national bankruptcy.[16]

This statement is interesting for its straightforwardness and because it combines in a rather typical fashion considerations of abstract morality and of expediency. The captive nations must be liberated not only because their captivity is immoral, unchristian,

[16] *New York Times,* August 14, 1952, p. 1.

and un-American, but also because its continuation will lead to a third world war and to national bankruptcy. To what extent, however, these considerations of expediency are invalidated by their utopian setting will become obvious from a comparison between the utopian and the realist positions.

From the utopian point of view there can be no difference between the liberation of Estonia or Czechoslovakia, of Poland or China; the captivity of any nation, large or small, close or far away, is a moral outrage which cannot be tolerated. The realist, too, seeks the liberation of all captive nations because he realizes that the presence of the Russian armies in the heart of Europe and their cooperation with the Chinese armies constitute the two main sources of the imbalance of power which threatens our security. Yet before he formulates a program of liberation, he will seek answers to a number of questions such as these: While the United States has a general interest in the liberation of all captive nations, what is the hierarchy of interests it has in the liberation, say, of China, Estonia, and Hungary? And while the Soviet Union has a general interest in keeping all captive nations in that state, what is the hierarchy of its interests in keeping, say, Poland, East Germany, and Bulgaria captive? If we assume, as we must on the historic evidence of two centuries, that Russia would at present not give up control over Poland without being compelled by force of arms, would the objective of the liberation of Poland justify the ruin of Western civilization, that of Poland included, which would be the certain result of a third world war? What resources does the United States have at its disposal for the liberation of all captive nations or some of them? What resources does the Soviet Union have at its disposal to keep in captivity all captive nations or some of them? Are we more likely to avoid national bankruptcy by embarking upon a policy of indiscriminate liberation with the concomitant certainty of war or by continuing the present policy of containment?

It might be that in a particular instance the policies suggested by the answers to these questions will coincide with Representative Kersten's proposals, but there can be no doubt that in its over-all character, substance, emphasis, and likely consequences a utopian policy of liberation differs fundamentally from a realist one.

The issue between liberation as a utopian principle of abstract morality versus the realist evaluation of the consequences which a policy of liberation would have for the survival of the nation has arisen before in American history. Abraham Lincoln was faced with a dilemma similar to that which confronts us today. Should he make the liberation of the slaves the ultimate standard of his policy even at the risk of destroying the Union, as many urged him to do, or should he subordinate the moral principle of universal freedom to considerations of the national interest? The answer Lincoln gave to Horace Greeley, a spokesman for the utopian moralists, is timeless in its eloquent wisdom. "If there be those," he wrote on August 22, 1862,

who would not save the Union unless they could at the same time save slavery, I do not agree with them. If there be those who would not save the Union unless they could at the same time destroy slavery, I do not agree with them. My paramount object in this struggle *is* to save the Union, and is *not* either to save or to destroy slavery. If I could save the Union without freeing *any* slave I would do it, and if I could save it by freeing *all* the slaves, I would do it; and if I could save it by freeing some and leaving others alone I would also do that. What I do about slavery, and the colored race, I do because I believe it helps to save the Union; and what I forbear, I forbear because I do *not* believe it would help to save the Union. I shall do *less* whenever I shall believe what I am doing hurts the cause, and I shall do *more* whenever I shall believe doing more will help the cause. I shall try to correct errors when shown to be errors; and I shall adopt new views so fast as they shall appear to be true views.

I have here stated my purpose according to my view of *official* duty; and I intend no modification of my oft-expressed *personal* wish that all men everywhere could be free.

The foregoing discussion ought to shed additional light, if this is still needed, upon the moral merits of the utopian and realist positions. This question, more than any other, seems to have agitated the critics of realism in international affairs. Disregarding the voluminous evidence, some of them have picked a few words out of their context to prove that realism in international affairs is unprincipled and contemptuous of morality. To mention but one example, one eminent critic summarizes my position, which he supposes to deny the possibility of judging the conduct of states by moral criteria, in these words: "And one spokesman finds 'a profound and neglected truth,' to use his words, in the dictum of Hobbes that 'there is neither morality nor law outside the state.' "[17] These are indeed my words, but not all of them. What I actually said was this: "There is a profound and neglected truth hidden in Hobbes's extreme dictum that the state creates morality as well as law and that there is neither morality nor law outside the state. Universal moral principles, such as justice or equality, are capable of guiding political action only to the extent that they have been given concrete content and have been related to political situations by society."[18]

It must be obvious from this passage and from all my other writings on the subject that my position is the exact opposite from what this critic makes it out to be.[19] I have always maintained that the actions of states are subject to universal moral principles, and I have been careful to differentiate my position in this respect from that of Hobbes. Five points basic to my position may need to be emphasized again.

The first point is what one might call the requirement of cosmic humility with regard to the moral evaluation of the actions of states. To know that states are subject to the moral law is one thing; to pretend to know what is morally required of states in a particular situation is quite another. The human mind tends naturally to identify the particular interests of states, as of individuals, with the moral purposes of the universe. The statesman in the defense of the nation's interests may, and at times even must, yield to that tendency; the scholar must resist it at every turn. For the lighthearted assumption that what one's own nation aims at and does is morally good and that those who oppose that nation's policies are evil is morally

[17] A. H. Feller, "In Defense of International Law and Morality," *Annals of the American Academy of Political and Social Science,* CCLXXXII (July, 1952), 80.

[18] *In Defense of the National Interest: A Critical Examination of American Foreign Policy* (New York: Alfred A. Knopf, 1951), p. 34.

[19] See, for instance, "The Machiavellian Utopia," *Ethics,* LV (January, 1945), 145–47; "Ethics and Politics," in *Approaches to Group Understanding* (Sixth Symposium of the Conference on Science, Philosophy and Religion), ed. Lyman Bryson *et al.* (New York, 1947), pp. 319–41; *Scientific Man vs. Power Politics* (Chicago: University of Chicago Press, 1946), chaps. 7, 8; "Views of Nuremberg: Further Analysis of the Trial and Its Importance," *America,* LXXVI (December 7, 1946), 266–67; "The Twilight of International Morality," *Ethics,* LVIII (January, 1948), 79–99; *Politics among Nations* (2d ed.; New York: Alfred A. Knopf, 1954), chap. 16; "National Interest and Moral Principles in Foreign Policy: The Primacy of the National Interests," *American Scholar,* XVIII (Spring, 1949), 207–12. See also above, chap. 2.

indefensible and intellectually untenable and leads in practice to that distortion of judgment, born of the blindness of crusading frenzy, which has been the curse of nations from the beginning of time.

The second point which obviously needs to be made again concerns the effectiveness of the restraints which morality imposes upon the actions of states.

A discussion of international morality must guard against the two extremes either of overrating the influence of ethics upon international politics or else of denying that statesmen and diplomats are moved by anything else but considerations of material power.

On the one hand, there is the dual error of confounding the moral rules which people actually observe with those they pretend to observe as well as with those which writers declare they ought to observe. . . .

On the other hand, there is the misconception, usually associated with the general depreciation and moral condemnation of power politics, discussed above, that international politics is so thoroughly evil that it is no use looking for ethical limitations of the aspirations for power on the international scene. Yet, if we ask ourselves what statesmen and diplomats are capable of doing to further the power objectives of their respective nations and what they actually do, we realize that they do less than they probably could and less than they actually did in other periods of history. They refuse to consider certain ends and to use certain means, either altogether or under certain conditions, not because in the light of expediency they appear impractical or unwise, but because certain moral rules interpose an absolute barrier. Moral rules do not permit certain policies to be considered at all from the point of view of expediency. Such ethical inhibitions operate in our time on different levels with different effectiveness. Their restraining function is most obvious and most effective in affirming the sacredness of human life in times of peace.[20]

In connection with this passage we gave a number of historic examples showing the influence of moral principles upon the conduct of foreign policy. An example taken from contemporary history will illustrate the same point. There can be little doubt that the Soviet Union could have achieved the objectives of its foreign policy at the end of the Second World War without antagonizing the nations of the West into that encircling coalition which has been the nightmare of Bolshevist foreign policy since 1917. It could have mitigated cunning for its own sake and the use of force with persuasion, conciliation, and a trust derived from the awareness of a partial community of interests and would thereby have minimized the dan-

[20] Morgenthau, *Politics among Nations,* pp. 210–16.

gers to itself and the rest of the world which are inherent in the objectives of its policies. Yet the Soviet Union was precluded from relying upon these traditional methods of diplomacy by its general conception of human nature, politics, and morality. In the general philosophy of Bolshevism there is no room for honest dissent, the recognition of the intrinsic worth of divergent interests, and genuine conciliation between such interests. On all levels of social interaction opposition must be destroyed by cunning and violence, since it has no right to exist, rather than be met halfway in view of its intrinsic legitimacy. This being the general conception of the political morality of Bolshevism, the foreign policy of the Soviet Union is limited to a much more narrow choice of means than the foreign policies of other nations.

The United States, for instance, has been able, in its relations with the nations of Latin America, to replace military intervention and dollar diplomacy with the policy of the Good Neighbor. That drastic change was made possible by the general conception of political morality which has been prevalent in the United States from its very inception. The United States is a pluralist society which presupposes the continuing existence and legitimacy of divergent interests. These interests are locked in a continuing struggle for supremacy to be decided by force only as a last resort but, normally, through a multitude of institutions which are so devised as to allow one or the other interest a temporary advantage but none a permanent supremacy at the price of the destruction of the others. This morality of pluralism allows the United States, once it is secure in that minimum of vital interests to which we have referred above, to transfer those principles of political morality to the international scene and to deal with divergent interests there with the same methods of genuine compromise and conciliation which are a permanent element of its domestic political life.

The third point concerns the relations between universal moral principles and political action. I have always maintained that these universal moral principles cannot be applied to the actions of states in their abstract universal formulation but that they must be, as it were, filtered through the concrete circumstances of time and place. The individual may say for himself: *Fiat justitia, pereat mundus;* the state has no right to say so in the name of those who are in its care.

Both individual and state must judge political action by universal moral principles, such as that of liberty. Yet while the individual has a moral right to sacrifice himself in defense of such a moral principle, the state has no moral right to let its moral disapprobation of the infringement of liberty get in the way of successful political action, itself inspired by the moral principle of national survival. There can be no political morality without prudence, that is, without consideration of the political consequences of seemingly moral action. Classical and medieval philosophy knew this and so did Lincoln when he said: "I do the very best I know how, the very best I can, and I mean to keep doing so until the end. If the end brings me out all right, what is said against me won't amount to anything. If the end brings me out wrong, ten angels swearing I was right would make no difference." The issue between utopianism and realism, as it bears on this point, has been put most succinctly by Edmund Burke, and what he has to say in the following passage about revolution, that is, civil war, may well be applied *mutatis mutandis* to all war.

Nothing universal can be rationally affirmed on any moral or any political subject. Pure metaphysical abstraction does not belong to these matters. The lines of morality are not like the ideal lines of mathematics. They are broad and deep as well as long. They admit of exceptions; they demand modifications. These exceptions and modifications are not made by the process of logic, but by the rules of prudence. Prudence is not only the first in rank of the virtues political and moral, but she is the director, the regulator, the standard of them all. Metaphysics cannot live without definition; but Prudence is cautious how she defines. Our courts cannot be more fearful in suffering fictitious cases to be brought before them for eliciting their determination on a point of law than prudent moralists are in putting extreme and hazardous cases of conscience upon emergencies not existing. Without attempting, therefore, to define, what never can be defined, the case of a revolution in government, this, I think, may be safely affirmed—that a sore and pressing evil is to be removed, and that a good, great in its amount and unequivocal in its nature, must be probable almost to a certainty, before the inestimable price of our own morals and the well-being of a number of our fellow-citizens is paid for a revolution. If ever we ought to be economists even to parsimony, it is in the voluntary production of evil. Every revolution contains in it something of evil.[21]

21 *The Works of The Right Honorable Edmund Burke* (4th ed.; Boston: Little, Brown & Co., 1871), IV, 80–81. Cf. also Burke, "Speech on a Bill for Shortening the Duration of Parliaments, May 8, 1780," *ibid.*, VII, 73: "I must see

Fourth, the realist recognizes that a moral decision, especially in the political sphere, does not imply a simple choice between a moral principle and a standard of action which is morally irrelevant or even outright immoral. A moral decision implies always a choice among different moral principles, one of which is given precedence over others. To say that a political action has no moral purpose is absurd; for political action can be defined as an attempt to realize moral values through the medium of politics, that is, power. The relevant moral question concerns the choice among different moral values, and it is at this point that the realist and the utopian part company again. If an American statesman must choose between the promotion of universal liberty, which is a moral good, at the risk of American security and, hence, of liberty in the United States, on the one hand, and the promotion of American security and of liberty in the United States, which is another moral good, to the detriment of the promotion of universal liberty, on the other, which choice ought he to make? The utopian will not face the issue squarely and will deceive himself into believing that he can achieve both goods at the same time. The realist will choose the national interest on both moral and pragmatic grounds; for if he does not take care of the national interest nobody else will, and if he puts American security and liberty in jeopardy the cause of liberty everywhere will be impaired.

Finally, the political realist distinguishes between his moral sympathies and the political interests which he must defend. He will distinguish with Lincoln between his "*official* duty" which is to protect the national interest and his "*personal* wish" which is to see universal moral values realized throughout the world.

The issue has been admirably put by Father Wilfred Parsons of Catholic University in defending Mr. Kennan's position:

Mr. Kennan did not say state behavior is not a fit subject for moral judgment, but only that it should not sway our realization of the realities with

---

to satisfy me, the remedies; I must see, from their operation in the cure of the old evil, and in the cure of those new evils which are inseparable from all remedies, how they balance each other, and what is the total result. The excellence of mathematics and metaphysics is, to have but one thing before you; but he forms the best judgment in all moral disquisitions who has the greatest number and variety of consideration in one view before him, and can take them in with the best possible consideration of the middle results of all."

which we have to deal. Msgr. Koenig continues: "Should we accept power realities and aspirations without feeling the obligation of moral judgment?" And he appeals to the present writer and other political scientists to say whether this doctrine agrees with Pope Pius XII's messages on peace.

I am sure that most political scientists, and also Mr. Kennan, would agree with the Monsignor that we should not accept those realities "without feeling the obligation of moral judgment." But there is a difference between *feeling* this obligation (and even expressing it) and allowing this feeling to sway our actions in concrete negotiations that deal with the national or world common good. We can still feel and yet deal.

To make my meaning clearer, I understood Mr. Kennan to hold that we went off the beam with Woodrow Wilson, when we began to make our moral disapprobation an *essential part* of our foreign relations, even sometimes at the expense of our own and the world's common good Logically, such an attitude would inhibit our dealing with Britain, France and a host of countries. Pius XI, speaking of Mussolini after the Lateran Treaty, said he would deal with the devil himself if he must. Here was moral disapprobation, but it was not "carried over into the affairs of states."

This relative position, and not the absolute one of Msgr. Koenig (with which in itself I agree), is, I think, the issue raised by Mr. Kennan, and it is worth debating on that basis.[22]

The contest between utopianism and realism is not tantamount to a contest between principle and expediency, morality and immorality, although some spokesmen for the former would like to have it that way. The contest is rather between one type of political morality and another type of political morality, one taking as its standard universal moral principles abstractly formulated, the other weighing these principles against the moral requirements of concrete political action, their relative merits to be decided by a prudent evaluation of the political consequences to which they are likely to lead.[23]

[22] *America,* LXXXVI (March 29, 1952), 700. See also Algernon Cecil, "The Foreign Office," in *The Cambridge History of British Foreign Policy, 1783–1919* (Cambridge: Cambridge University Press, 1923), III, 605, concerning Lord Salisbury: "Always, however, the motive of his policy was to be found in the political interests as opposed to the political sympathies of Great Britain; and in this way his treatment of Foreign Affairs is at the opposite policy from that of Palmerston and Gladstone." Cf. also the general remarks in Alexander H. Leighton, *Human Relations in a Changing World* (New York: E. P. Dutton & Co., 1949), pp. 155 ff.

[23] See, on this point, Shirley R. Letwin, "Rationalism, Principles, and Politics," *Review of Politics,* XIV (July, 1952), 367–93; L. Susan Stebbing, *Ideals and Illusions* (London: Watts & Co., 1951); Vernon H. Holloway, *Religious Ethics and the Politics of Power* (New York: Church Peace Union and World Alliance for International Friendship through Religion, 1951); and Dorothy Fosdick,

These points are re-emphasized by the foregoing discussion. Which attitude with regard to collective security and to the liberation of the captive nations, the utopian or the realist, is more likely to safeguard the survival of the United States in its territorial, political, and cultural identity and at the same time to contribute the most to the security and liberty of other nations? This is the ultimate test—political and moral—by which utopianism and realism must be judged.

"Ethical Standards and Political Strategies," *Political Science Quarterly*, LVII (1942), 214 ff.

20 *The State of Political Science*

    In Plato's *Theaetetus* Socrates develops the character of the philosopher, the man of knowledge, in contrast to the atheoretical, practical man. He endeavors to demonstrate the distinctive qualities of the philosopher by emphasizing his peculiar attitude toward the political sphere.

First, the philosopher has no political ambitions, and he does not care about what is going on in the political sphere. The philosophers have never, from their youth upwards, known their way to the Agora, or the dicastery, or the council, or any other political assembly; they neither see nor hear the laws or decrees, as they are called, of the State written or recited; the eagerness of political societies in the attainment of offices—clubs, and banquets, and revels, and singing-maidens—do not enter even into their dreams. Whether any event has turned out well or ill in the city, what disgrace may have descended to any one from his ancestors, male or female, are matters of which the philosopher no more knows than he can tell, as they say, how many pints are contained in the ocean.

Second, the philosopher is ignorant about political matters and incapable of acting effectively on the political plane. He "is wholly unacquainted with his next-door neighbor; he is ignorant, not only of what he is doing, but he hardly knows whether he is a man or an animal. . . . His awkwardness is fearful, and gives the impression of imbecility. When he is reviled, he has nothing personal to say in answer to the civilities of his adversaries, for he knows no scandals of anyone, and they do not interest him. . . ."

Third, the philosopher is morally uncommitted and indifferent to the values of politics.

When he hears a tyrant or king eulogized, he fancies that he is listening to the praises of some keeper of cattle—a swineherd, or shepherd, or perhaps a cowherd, who is congratulated on the quantity of milk which he squeezes from them; and he remarks that the creature whom they tend, and out of whom they squeeze the wealth, is of a less tractable and more

From the *Review of Politics.* October, 1955; Roland Young (ed.), *Approaches to the Study of Politics* (1958); and a book review in the *American Political Science Review,* March, 1952.

insidious nature. Then again, he observes that the great man is of necessity as ill-mannered and uneducated as any shepherd—for he has no leisure, and he is surrounded by a wall, which is his mountain-pen. Hearing of enormous landed proprietors of ten thousand acres and more, our philosopher deems this to be a trifle, because he has been accustomed to think of the whole earth; and when they sing the praises of family, and say that some one is a gentleman because he can show seven generations of wealthy ancestors, he thinks that their sentiments only betray a dull and narrow vision in those who utter them and who are not educated enough to look at the whole, nor to consider that every man has had thousands and ten thousands of progenitors, and among them have been rich and poor, kings and slaves, Hellenes and barbarians, innumerable. And when people pride themselves on having a pedigree of twenty-five ancestors, which goes back to Heracles, the son of Amphitryon, he cannot understand their poverty of ideas. Why are they unable to calculate that Amphitryon had a twenty-fifth ancestor, who might have had a fiftieth, and so on? He amuses himself with the notion that they cannot count, and thinks that a little arithmetic would have got rid of their senseless vanity.

This political indifference and incapacity is the reflection of the philosopher's positive nature. The philosopher's

outer form . . . only is in the city. His mind, disdaining the littlenesses and nothingnesses of human things, is "flying all abroad" as Pindar says, measuring earth and heaven and the things which are under and on the earth and above the heaven, interrogating the whole nature of each and all in their entirety, but not condescending to anything which is within reach. . . . He is searching into the essence of man, and busy in enquiring what belongs to such a nature to do or suffer different from any other. . . .

This commitment to the search for the truth for its own sake and, concomitant with it, his divorcement—morally and intellectually, in judgment and action—from the political sphere makes the man of theory a scandal in the eyes of the multitude. He "is laughed at for his sheepishness. . . . He seems to be a downright idiot." He "is derided by the vulgar, partly because he is thought to despise them, and also because he is ignorant of what is before him and always at a loss." Socrates tells "the jest which the clever witty Thracian handmaid is said to have made about Thales, when he fell into a well as he was looking up at the stars. She said, that he was so eager to know what was going on in heaven, that he could not see what was before his feet." And Socrates adds: "This is a jest which is equally applicable to all philosophers."

Yet the philosopher has his revenge.

But, O my friend, when he draws the other into upper air, and gets him out of his pleas and rejoinders into the contemplation of justice and injustice in their own nature and in their difference from one another and from all other things; or from the commonplaces about the happiness of a king or a rich man to the consideration of government, and of human happiness and misery in general—what they are, and how a man is to attain the one and avoid the other—when that narrow, keen, little legal mind is called to account about all this, he gives the philosopher his revenge; for dizzied by the height at which he is hanging, whence he looks down into space, which is a strange experience to him, he being dismayed, and lost, and stammering broken words, is laughed at, not by Thracian handmaidens or any other uneducated persons, for they have no eye for the situation but by every man who has not been brought up a slave.

We may well recognize in this juxtaposition of the philosopher with the practitioner the archetypes of a perennial conflict between the theoretical man who thinks for the sake of finding the truth and the practical man who thinks for the sake of finding solutions to practical problems. Yet neither can we fail to recognize the limitations of the Platonic analysis, which is too neat, too "Greek" in its classical simplicity to satisfy us. While what Plato says is true, it is not the whole truth of the matter. There is, as we shall see, in the political thinker's place within the society about which he thinks an ambiguity—intellectual and moral—of which the ancients knew—and perhaps were bound to know—nothing. Yet with all its limitations Plato's statement conveys an insight into the nature of philosophy, theory, and science which, in turn, sheds an illuminating light upon the state of political science in America.

The impulse to which American political science owes its existence was overwhelmingly practical. It was nourished from two roots, one of which it has in common with all of modern political science, while the other is peculiar to itself.

Political science as an academic discipline everywhere in the Western world owes its existence to the disintegration, after their last flowering in the early nineteenth century, of the great philosophic systems which had dominated Western thought and to the concomitant development of the empirical investigation of the social world. All the social sciences are the fruit of the emancipation of the Western mind from metaphysical systems which had made the social world primarily a subject for metaphysical speculation and ethical postulates. In certain fields, such as economics, that emancipation occurred early; in others, such as political science, it occurred relatively late (for reasons which, as we shall see, are inherent in the nature of political science).

This antispeculative and empirical tendency of Western thought, as it developed in the second half of the nineteenth century, could not but find a ready and, as it were, natural response in the propensities of the American mind. Yet, while European political thought continued to combine an antimetaphysical position with concern for theory, American political science was overwhelmed by the practical promises of the new discipline. The first departments of political science were established in America in the eighties of the last century, not for the purpose of theoretical understanding, let alone philosophic speculation, but primarily for the purpose of meeting the practical exigencies of the day.

It is illuminating in this context, and it is in a sense a moving experience, to read the address that was delivered on October 3, 1881, at the opening of the School of Political Science at the University of Michigan by its first dean, Charles Kendall Adams.[1] Of the perennial problems of politics, such as power, legitimacy, authority, freedom, forms of government, natural law, sovereignty, revolution, tyranny, majority rule, this address makes no mention. The only problems which concern it are the practical problems of the day, and the case it tries to make for political science in America rests exclusively upon the contribution the new discipline promises to make to the solution of these problems. Looking abroad, Dean Adams finds that the rapid recovery of France after 1871 was primarily due to the instruction in political science. "The close of their war was six years later than the close of ours; and yet long before we had gained our financial equilibrium, France was the most prosperous nation in Europe." In England, "political instruction . . . has been given by men, some of whom have been thought worthy of high places in Parliament, in the diplomatic service, and in the Cabinet. . . . Their pupils are all about them in Parliament and in the diplomatic service." In diplomacy and, more particularly, in economic reform the influence of university instruction has been persuasive. Dean Adams finds the same beneficial results in Germany. "Graduates of these schools [of political

[1] *The Relations of Political Science to National Prosperity* (Ann Arbor, 1881).

science] found their way into administration positions of influence in all parts of Germany. . . . Commissioner White . . . uses these words: 'In conversation with leading men in Southern Germany I have not found one who did not declare this and similar courses of instruction the main cause of the present efficiency in the German administration.' "

Having thus made a case for the advantages that political science has brought to the practice of European governments, Dean Adams must now dispose of the argument that American political institutions are superior to those of Europe and that, therefore, America has no need of political science. The argument is revealing in its exclusive emphasis upon the practical benefits to be expected.

Is it certain that our municipal governments are better than theirs? Are our systems of taxation more equitably adjusted than theirs? Do our public and private corporations have greater respect for the rights of the people than theirs? Can we maintain that our legislatures are more free from corruption and bribery than theirs? Was our financial management at the close of our war wiser than that of France at the close of hers? If these questions can be answered in the affirmative, and without the shadow of a doubt, I concede that an argument may be built upon them in favor of what may be called intuitive methods.

After passing in systematic review the operations of the three branches of government which are in need of improvement, Dean Adams turns to "several other fields of activity in which great influence is exerted." He singles out journalism and speechmaking, which political science can help to improve. He sums up his argument in favor of political science by saying:

It is for the purpose of aiding in the several directions that have been hinted at, and in others that would be mentioned if there were time, that the School of Political Science in the University of Michigan has been established. It finds its justification where the other schools of the University find theirs: in the good of the people and the welfare of the State.

This exclusive concern with practical improvements is by no means an isolated instance. It dominates the virtually simultaneous establishment of a School of Political Science at Columbia University. The objective of that school was as practical as that of Michigan; yet while the latter's appeal was one of boundless vocationalism, the former's practical interests were narrowly confined to a particular profession, that of the civil servant. When President

Barnard submitted the proposal for the establishment of the school to the trustees of Columbia University, he called it "Proposed School of Preparation for the Civil Service." Reflecting the philosophy of John W. Burgess, the driving spirit behind the proposal, we find the purpose of the school defined as "to prepare young men for public life whether in the Civil Service at home or abroad, or in the legislatures of the States or of the nation; and also to fit young men for the duties and responsibilities of public journalists."[2]

The first departments of political science in this country, then, did not grow organically from a general conception as to what was covered by the field of political science, nor did they respond to a strongly felt intellectual need. Rather they tried to satisfy practical demands, which other academic disciplines refused to meet. For instance, in that period the law schools would not deal with public law. It was felt that somebody ought to deal with it, and thus it was made part of political science. There was a demand for instruction in journalism, but there was no place for it to be taught; thus it was made part of political science. There was a local demand for guidance in certain aspects of municipal administration; and thus a course in that subject was made part of the curriculum of political science.

In other words, political science grew, not by virtue of an intellectual principle germane to the field, but in response to pressures from the outside. What could not be defined in terms of a traditional academic discipline was defined as political science. This inorganic growth and haphazard character of political science is strikingly reflected in the curriculums of the early departments of political science, such as those of Michigan, Columbia, and Harvard. In the address from which we have quoted, Dean Adams mentions the following subjects which were to form part of the curriculum of the School of Political Science: General History, The History of Political Institutions, The Recent Political History of Europe, The Political and Constitutional History of England, The Political and Constitutional History of the United States; several courses in political economy; under the general heading of "Sanitary Science": The Laws of Physiological Growth and Decay, The Varieties and

[2] R. Gordon Hoxie *et al., A History of the Faculty of Political Science, Columbia University* (New York: Columbia University Press, 1955), p. 13.

Adaptabilities of Foods, The Best Methods of Supplying Pure Water and Air, The Causes of Infectious Diseases, The Proper Disposal of Decomposing Matter, The Proper Functions of Boards of Health and Health Officers; under the general heading of "Social Science": The Prevalence of Crime and the Most Efficient Means of Diminishing and Preventing It, The Best Methods of Treating our Criminals, The Care of the Insane and the Management of Asylums, The Proper Treatment of the Poor and the Proper Superintendence of Almshouses, The Place and the Proper Equipment and Control of Hospitals; courses in forestry and political ethics; and finally "crowning the whole": The Idea of the State; The Nature of Individual, Social, and Political Rights; The History of Political Ideas; The Government of Cities; Theories and Methods of Taxation; Comparative Constitutional Law; Comparative Administrative Law; Theories of International Law; and The History of Modern Diplomacy. "Such," Dean Adams concludes, "in the briefest outline, is what it is the purpose of the school at present to teach. Additions to the corps and the courses of instruction will be added, from time to time, as the necessity is revealed."

While this program is but an extreme example of the practicality of early American political science, the list of courses which formed the curriculum of the School of Political Science of Columbia University from 1880 to 1887 is typical of its eclecticism. According to Burgess, the "School of Political Science" was "the collective name which we give the graduate or university courses in history, philosophy, economy, public law, jurisprudence, diplomacy, and sociology."[3] These are the courses which were then taught: Physical and Political Geography, Ethnology, General Political and Constitutional History of Europe, Political and Constitutional History of England, Political and Constitutional History of the United States, Bibliography of the Political Sciences, History of Roman Law to the Present Day, Comparative Constitutional Law of the Principal European States and of the United States, Statistical Science—Methods and Results, Comparative Jurisprudence of the Principal European Systems of Civil Law, Comparative Constitutional Law of the Several Commonwealths of the American Union,

[3] John W. Burgess, "The Study of the Political Sciences in Columbia College," *International Review,* XII (1882), 348.

History of Diplomacy, Comparative Administrative Law of the Principal States of Europe and of the United States, Comparative Administrative Law of the Several Commonwealths of the American Union, Private International Law; social sciences: Communistic and Socialistic Theories; political economy: History of Politico-Economic Institutions, Taxation and Finance; philosophy: History of Political Theories from Plato to Hegel.[4]

Similarly, the courses differentiated in 1892–93 at Harvard under the heading of "Government" comprised: Constitutional Government; Elements of International Law (which included history of diplomacy); History and Institutes of Roman Law; Federal Government—Historical and Comparative; Leading Principles of Constitutional Law—Selected Cases American and English; History of Political Theories, with particular reference to the origin of American institutions; Government and Political Methods in the United States; and International Law as Administered by the Courts.[5]

In its further development political science as an academic discipline has undergone a process of both contraction and expansion. On the one hand, new schools and departments have absorbed much of the subject matter that was formerly taught in departments of political science because there was no other place in the university to teach them. On the other hand, however, new practical interests have continued to call for the inclusion of new subjects of instruction in the curriculum.

Thus today the curriculum of political science still bears the unmistakable marks of its haphazard origin and development. To pick out at random some courses from two departments of political science with which I am familiar, what have "Plato's Political Philosophy and Its Metaphysical Foundation" and "The Politics of Conservation" in common, or "General Principles of Organization and Administration" and "International Law," or "Conduct of American Foreign Relations" and "Introduction to Jurisprudence," or "Nationalism" and "Political Behavior and Public Policy," or "Russian Political and Economic Institutions" and "Public Personnel Administration"? The only common denominator which

[4] Hoxie *et al., op. cit.*, pp. 305–6.

[5] Anna Haddow, *Political Science in American Colleges and Universities, 1636–1900* (New York: Appleton-Century, 1939), p. 175.

now ties these courses loosely together is a general and vague orientation toward the nature and activities of the state and toward activities which have in turn a direct bearing upon the state. Beyond that orientation toward a common subject matter, defined in the most general terms, contemporary political science has no unity of method, outlook, and purpose.

As concerns method, political science is split five ways, and four of these methodological positions have hardly anything in common. Their disparity is such that there is hardly even a possibility of fruitful discourse among the representatives of the different approaches beyond polemics which deny the very legitimacy of the other approaches. These approaches can be classified as philosophic theory, empirical theory, empirical science, description, and practical amelioration.

These five methodological approaches are not peculiar to political science. They have appeared in other social sciences as well—such as psychology, economics, and sociology—yet with two significant differences. First of all, the other social sciences have traditionally shown a much greater awareness of the existence, nature, and separate functions of these approaches than has political science. Second, they have been able, at least at times, to rid themselves in good measure of the ameliorative and vocational approach which has by itself only a minimum of intellectual relevance. Political science, on the other hand, has never squarely faced the methodological problem in terms of the intrinsic character of these different approaches and the functions which they are able to perform for the understanding of its subject matter. These five approaches have rather coexisted without clear distinction within the departments of political science, one to be emphasized over the others at different times and places according to the pressures of supply and demand. Here, too, the development has been haphazard and subject to accident rather than guided by certain fundamental requirements of theory.

Thus political science has not generally been able to make that distinction which is a precondition for the development of any true science: the distinction between what is worth knowing intellectually and what is useful for practice. It is this distinction which economics and sociology accomplished some decades ago when schools of business, home economics, retailing, social work, and the like took over the practical concerns which at best develop practical uses for theoretical knowledge or else have but the most tenuous connection with it. Political science has taken a similar step in some instances by organizing the practical uses of political science for the amelioration of government activities in schools of administration and the like. But not only has this separation been exceptional rather than typical, it has also been made as a matter of convenience rather than in application of a generally accepted theoretical principle. In consequence, improvement of the processes of government is still generally considered not only a worthwhile activity to be engaged in by political scientists but also a legitimate, and sometimes even the only legitimate, element of political science as an academic discipline, to be taught under any of the course headings composing its curriculum.

It should be pointed out in passing that we are dealing here not with a specific subject matter but with a particular method, a particular intellectual approach. This approach will naturally manifest itself most frequently and typically in those fields of political science which have a direct relevance to the operations of government, such as public administration, but it is by no means limited to them. The other fields of political science, such as international relations, American government, constitutional law, and parties, have at times been dominated by the practical approach seeking practical remedies for conditions regarded as being in need of amelioration.

Yet it is exactly this commitment of modern political science to practical ends which has powerfully contributed to its decline as theory. Modern political science has been largely committed to the practical goals of liberal reform. Each major achievement in the direction of one of these goals was expected to bring society that much closer to solving once and for all one of the perennial problems of politics, such as inequality, insecurity, conflict, violence, power itself—and none ever did. The old problems reappeared in a new garb, mocking the scientific pretenses and eschatological expectations of liberal political science, and yesterday's hope and today's achievement became tomorrow's illusion. To this succession of blows which liberal politics suffered at the hands of experience must be attributed in good measure its disenchantment with reform and its decline in creative thought and action. The grand ameliorative schemes of liberal political science petered out in proposals for piecemeal improvements from which no great things can be expected.

Thus description is today the method most widely used in political science. Factual information arranged according to certain traditional classifications still dominates most of the textbooks in the field. While it is unnecessary to argue the case for the need for factual information, it ought to be no more necessary to argue that factual description is not science but a mere, however indispensable, preparation for the scientific understanding of the facts. It may, however, point toward a theoretical awakening that descriptive political science tends to dress up descriptive accounts of facts in theoretical garb and to use fancy classifications and terminologies in order to conceal the mere descriptive character of its substance. While the theoretical pretense of factual accounts shows an awareness of the need for theoretical understanding, that understanding itself requires more than the demonstrative use of an elaborate apparatus of classification and terminology.

With this last type of descriptive political science which overlays its descriptive substance with theoretical pretense, we are in the borderland where description and empirical science merge. Empirical science is today the most vigorous branch of political science and tends to attract many of the abler and more inventive students. Taking its cue from the natural sciences, or what it thinks the natural sciences are, it tries to develop rigorous methods of quantitative verification which are expected in good time to attain the same precision in the discovery of uniformities and in prediction to which the natural sciences owe their theoretical and practical success.

I have argued elsewhere against this analogy between the social and the natural sciences,[6] and this is not the place to resume the controversy. It must suffice here to state dogmatically that the object of the social sciences is man, not as a product of nature but as both the creature and the creator of history in and through

[6] *Scientific Man vs. Power Politics* (Chicago: University of Chicago Press, 1946).

which his individuality and freedom of choice manifest themselves. To make susceptibility to quantitative measurement the yardstick of the scientific character of the social sciences in general and of political science in particular is to deprive these sciences of that very orientation which is adequate to the understanding of their subject matter.

The inadequacy of the quantitative method to the subject matter of political science is demonstrated by the limitation of its success to those types of political behavior which by their very nature lend themselves to a certain measure of quantification, such as voting, and the barrenness of the attempts to apply the quantitative method to phenomena which are determined by historic individuality, rational or moral choice. As concerns these phenomena, the best quantification can achieve is to confirm and refine knowledge which theory has already discovered. It will not do to argue that this limitation is due to the "backwardness" of political science which could be overcome if only more and better people would spend more time and money for quantification. For that argument to be plausible, the limitation is too persistent, and it becomes ever more spectacular as more and better people spend more time and money to make it a success.

Once quantification has left that narrow sphere where it can contribute to relevant knowledge, two roads are open to it. Either it can try to quantify phenomena which in their aspects relevant to political science are not susceptible to quantification, and by doing so obscure and distort what political science ought to know; thus much of quantitative political science has become a pretentious collection of trivialities. Or, dimly aware of this inadequacy, quantification may shun contact with the empirical phenomena of political life altogether and try to find out instead what the correct way of quantifying is. Basic to this methodological concern is the assumption that the failure of quantification to yield results in any way proportionate to the effort spent follows from the lack of a correct quantitative method. Once that method is discovered and applied, quantification will yield the results in precise knowledge its adherents claim for it.

However, it is obvious that these methodological investigations, patently intended for the guidance of empirical research, have hardly exerted any influence upon the latter. This divorce of methodology from empirical investigation is not fortuitous. For it points not only to the inadequacy of the quantitative method for the understanding of much of the subject matter of political science, an inadequacy which must become particularly striking when quantification is confronted in its pure theoretical form with the actuality of political life. That divorce also illuminates a tendency, common not only to all methodological endeavors in the social sciences but to general philosophy as well, to retreat ever more from contact with the empirical world into a realm of self-sufficient abstractions. Logical positivism and general semantics owe their existence as independent branches of philosophy to this "new scholasticism," as it has been aptly called.[7] General sociological theory is dominated by it, and it has left its impact also upon political science. The new scholastic dissolves the substance of knowledge into the processes of knowing; he tends to think about how to think and to conceptualize about concepts, regressing ever further from empirical reality until he finds the logical consummation of his endeavors in mathematical symbols and other formal relations. And it is not fortuitous that the apparent precision of his formal categories tends to go hand in hand with an often shocking imprecision of his vestigial substantive thought; for, to the extent that objective reality demands qualitative evaluation, formalism either misses the point altogether or else distorts it.

A remarkable example of this new political science—remarkable by virtue of the reputation of its authors and of its own claims—is Lasswell and Kaplan, *Power and Society: A Framework for Political Inquiry*.[8] This book claims to be "a book of political theory, not an analysis of the contemporary or impending political situation" (p. ix). Critical of the German *Staatslehre* and of De Tocqueville and Bryce, it finds itself "much closer to the straightforward empirical standpoint of Machiavelli's *Discourses* or Michels' *Political Parties*" (p. x). "The present work is an attempt to formulate the basic concepts and hypotheses of political science" (p. xi). Its purpose is "to provide a framework for political science" (p. xiii). There can

[7] Barrington Moore, Jr., "The New Scholasticism and the Study of Politics," *World Politics,* VI (1953), 122–38.

[8] New Haven: Yale University Press, 1950.

be no doubt that the authors present this work as a major contribution to political theory.

The book consists of a series of definitions and propositions, with commentary, under the following headings: persons, perspectives, groups, influence, power, symbols, practices, functions, structures, process. What do these definitions and propositions contribute to knowledge? We open the book at random and read on page 13 the following definitions: "A *personality trait* is a kind of act characteristic of a self. The *personality* is the totality of the personality traits pertaining to an actor. A person is an actor characterized as to personality." This is hardly more meaningful than Gertrude Stein's "Rose is a rose is a rose is a rose," and does not have even its primitive phonetic charm. On page 154, we read the following proposition: "Acquisition and maintenance of leadership is a function of the prestige of the leaders." On page 187, the rulers are defined as "those supreme in the body politic." On page 218, information is conveyed in the form of the following definition: "*Autocracy* is the form of rule in which the weight of power is chiefly in the hands of one person; *oligarchy*, in the hands of a group of rulers; a *republic*, distributed throughout the domain." On page 234, democracy and despotism are defined as follows: "A *democracy* is a libertarian, juridical commonwealth; a *despotism* is a nondemocratic rule." These definitions are obviously either platitudinous, circular, or tautological, and at best convey information which Aristotle would have taken for granted.

However, what vitiates this book as a major contribution to political theory is a thorough misunderstanding of the nature of political theory and of its relationship to empirical research. The authors believe that political science can be "straightforward empirical" and that Machiavelli and Michels so conceived it. We shall not deal here with the case of Michels. But do the authors not recognize the fact that Machiavelli was a political philosopher steeped in the ancient tradition, that his empirical inquiry is inclosed within a philosophical framework resting upon the pillars of *fortuna* and *virtu*, concepts which come straight from classical antiquity, and that his work, far from being "straightforward empirical," is a philosophic protest against the scholastic tradition in an attempt to reassert the political philosophy of the ancients? Are the authors unaware of the fact that in this sense Machiavelli is no more an empiricist in politics than Raphael and Michelangelo are naturalists in art? Their purpose, as that of the Renaissance as a whole, was philosophic and not merely descriptive. Are the authors unfamiliar with the literature which has uncovered the philosophic system behind the seemingly empirical surface of Machiavelli's writings?

One error, perhaps inconsequential in itself, but characteristic of the authors' method, will illustrate the point. The authors express their criticism of the metaphysical speculation of the "German *Staatslehre* tradition, so influential at the turn of the century" (p. x). As an example they quote J. K. Bluntschli and give as the date of his *Theory of the State* the year 1921. It so happens that Bluntschli was a Hegelian who died in 1881 and whose work, referred to by the authors, was published in 1851 and 1852. What the authors cite is the third edition of the English translation, the first of which appeared in 1885 (the year of the last German one), the second in 1895. Neither Bluntschli's organismic brand of Hegelianism nor metaphysical speculation in general had any considerable influence on German political thought at the turn of the century, having been replaced by the theories of social and legal historians such as Gierke, or of constitutional and comparative lawyers such as Laband, Gneist, and Jellinek. In 1921 Bluntschli and his metaphysical speculations were a mere historic recollection, and the epic struggle between Kelsen, the philosopher of the pure theory of law, and his politically oriented enemies provided the great issues in political science.

The authors are not only careless about the incontestable facts of political theory; they are also given to sweeping judgments barely supported by evidence. Let us examine the following statement: "Many of the most influential political writings—those of Plato, Locke, Rousseau, the *Federalist*, and others—have not been concerned with political inquiry at all, but with the justification of existent or proposed political structures. We say such works formulate *political doctrine* rather than propositions of *political science*" (p. xi). What is correct in this statement is that the great writings of political theory had as their ultimate purpose the justification of a certain political system. This is true of Plato and Locke, as it is of Machiavelli and Michels. There have been thinkers who were "not concerned with political inquiry at all," as there were and are those who are concerned with nothing but political science conceived in "straightforward empirical" terms; most of them for that very reason have been, and will be, forgotten. What makes it today worth reading Plato, Locke, Rousseau, the *Federalist,* and above all Aristotle (whom the authors have omitted from their list) is exactly that, within the framework of a political doctrine, they have given us the results of political inquiry in the form of propositions of political science, more profound and more illuminating by far than anything that a "straightforward empirical standpoint" has to offer. The authors are unable to see that a political science inclosed in nothing but an empirical framework is a contradiction in terms and a monstrosity. The intellectual barrenness of the present work, its logical aimlessness and diffuseness, and its excessive concern with verbal artifices are the results of this fundamental misunderstanding.

Every student approaches the political scene, whether as a thinker or as an actor, with certain intellectual and moral preconceptions regarding it. His thoughts and actions are determined by those preconceptions. In other words, he looks at the political scene from a perspective which is determined by his philosophy and which he will share with some but not with other observers. Whether or not he approves of it, whether or not he realizes it, he is a political philosopher before he is a political scientist. All observers of politics, then, bring to their observations a framework of political philosophy, however inarticulate and fragmentary it may be. It is only within such a philosophical framework that an empirical framework of political inquiry can have meaning and that empirical inquiry can become fruitful. Of the realization in theory and practice of that necessary relationship between political philosophy and empirical inquiry, Aristotle provides the unrivaled example.

Our authors have subjected Aristotle to a kind of content analysis and have found, on the basis of a sample of three hundred sentences, that the proportion of "political philosophy (demand statements and evaluations) to political science (statements of facts and empirical hypotheses)" (p. 118 n.) is 25 to 75. We shall not compete with the authors in a mechanical exercise of this kind and shall not even raise the question of whether the three hundred sentences chosen were "representative samples." We only call attention to the basic proposition that in politics empirical inquiry without a philosophic framework must needs be blind, as political philosophy without empirical verification must needs be wholly speculative. To have understood this makes Aristotle a great political scientist, regardless of the quantitative proportions of different kinds of statements in his work.

We have said that all men dealing with the political realm bring of necessity to their field of inquiry or action a political philosophy, and our authors are no exception. Their philosophy is that of freedom (pp. xiii–xxiv). Yet the difference between the layman and the dilettante, on the one hand, and the political scientist worthy of the name, on the other, is determined by whether the individual has made his political philosophy articulate and whether he has brought it into organic relationship with his empirical inquiry. In this respect all the great political thinkers of the past, from Plato and Aristotle onward, stand on one side; our authors, together with many academic political scientists of the day, stand on the other. The latter take the democratic values of freedom for granted and do not ask themselves what the content of those values and what the relations among those values and between them and other values of a nondemocratic character must be under the conditions of the contemporary world. Nor are they aware—and they cannot be, in view of their preconceptions—of the necessary relationship between those questions of political philosophy and the framework and content of empirical political inquiry. As their political philosophy is inarticulate and fragmentary, so their empirical inquiry is bound to be without direction and barren of meaning.

This spectacle of two superbly endowed minds failing so thoroughly in spite of great ability and great effort contains an element of tragedy. That tragedy is not so much the tragedy of two men as the tragedy of political science and of philosophy in America. For as Mr. Lasswell is the product of a school of political science which was, if not hostile, in any case indifferent, to the necessary contribution which political philosophy must make to empirical inquiry, so Mr. Kaplan is the product of a school of philosophy which sees in the history of philosophy primarily a history of errors. These authors are among the most gifted representatives of schools which at present ride the crest of the wave. Yet in truth they represent an obsolescent point of view. This book perhaps constitutes the most extreme, and therefore self-defeating, product of the fundamental errors of those schools. It may well contribute to their demise by virtue of its own absurdity.

There is a revealing similarity, pointing to a common root in the disorders of our culture, between abstract modern political science and abstract modern art. Both retreat from empirical reality into a world of formal relations and abstract symbols, which either on closer examination reveal themselves to be trivial or else are unintelligible, except to the initiated. Both share in the indifference to the accumulated achievements of mankind in their respective fields; Plato and Phidias, St. Thomas and Giotto, Spinoza and Rembrandt have no message for them. That divorcement from reality, contemporary and historic, deprives both of that wholesome discipline which prevents the mind from indulging its fancies without regard to some relevant objective standards. Thus one fashion, intellectual or artistic, follows the other, each oblivious of what has gone before, each relegated to limbo by its successors. Both abstract political science and abstract modern art tend to become esoteric, self-sufficient, and self-perpetuating cults, clustered around a "master," imitating his "style," and conversing in a lingo intelligible only to the members. Yet common sense, trying to penetrate the mysteries of these abstractions, cannot help wondering whether even the initiated understand each other and themselves. Perhaps, common sense continues wondering, some of the "masters" are just pulling the legs of their followers, who must pretend to understand in order to remain intellectually "up to date." "Enlightened people," to quote Georges Sorel, "dare not admit that they cannot understand arguments that are presented in very sophisticated language by an illustrious writer."

With this emphasis upon theoretical abstractions which have no relation to political reality, the methodology of political science joins a school which from the beginning to this day has occupied an honored but lonely place in the curriculum of political science: political theory. Political theory as an academic discipline has been traditionally the history of political philosophies in chronological succession, starting with Plato and ending, if time permits, with Laski. As an academic discipline, political theory has been hardly more than an account of what writers of the past, traditionally regarded as "great," have thought about the traditional problems of politics, with hardly a systematic attempt being made to correlate that historic knowledge to the other fields of political science and to the contemporary political world. "The danger," in the words of Sir Ernest Barker, "of some subjects of speculation—I would cite in evidence literary criticism as well as political theory—is that they may be choked, as it were, by the history of their own past."[9] Thus political theory as an academic discipline has been intellectually sterile, and it is not by accident that some of the most important contributions to contemporary political theory have been made not by professional political scientists but by theologians, philosophers, and sociologists.

Political theory remained an indispensable part of the curriculum, not because of the vital influence it was able to exert upon our thinking, but rather because of a vague conviction that there was something venerable and respectable in this otherwise useless exercise. Thus the academic concern with political theory tended to become an intellectually and practically meaningless ritual which one had to engage in for reasons of tradition and prestige before one could occupy one's self with the things that really mattered.

The awareness of this contrast between the prestige of political theory and its actual lack of relevance for the understanding of contemporary political problems has led theory closer to the contemporary political world. On the other hand, the awareness of the meagerness of the insights to be gained from strictly empirical investigations has made empirical political science search for a theoretical framework. Avoiding the limitations of the traditional approaches and fusing certain of their elements, contemporary political science is in the process of reviving a tradition to which most of the classics of political science owe their existence and influence. The intent of that tradition is theoretical: it wants to understand political reality in a theoretical manner, that is, by bringing to bear upon it propositions of both objective and general validity. These propositions claim to be objective in that their validity is not affected by the subjective limitations of the observer. They claim to be general in that their validity is not affected by the peculiar circumstances of time and place of the subject matter.

[9] *The Study of Political Science and Its Relation to Cognate Studies* (Cambridge: Cambridge University Press, 1929), pp. 25–26.

The subject matter of this theoretical concern is the contemporary political world. This branch of political science, which we call empirical theory, reflects in theoretical terms upon the contemporary political world. The political world, however, poses a formidable obstacle to such understanding. This obstacle is of a moral rather than an intellectual nature. Before we turn to the requirements of such an empirical theory and its central concept, we have to dispose of the moral problem with which political science must come to terms.

21 *The Commitments of Political Science*

The moral position of the political scientist in society is ambivalent; it can even be called paradoxical. For the political scientist is a product of the society which it is his mission to understand. He is also an active part, and frequently he seeks to be a leading part, of that society. To be faithful to his mission he would, then, have to overcome two limitations: the limitation of origin, which determines the perspective from which he looks at society, and the limitation of purpose, which makes him wish to remain a member in good standing of that society or even to play a leading role in it.

The mind of the political scientist is molded by the society which he observes. His outlook, his intellectual interests, and his mode of thinking are determined by the civilization, the national community, and all the particular religious, political, economic, and social groups of which he is a member. The "personal equation" of the political scientist both limits and directs his scholarly pursuits. The truth which a mind thus socially conditioned is able to grasp is likewise socially conditioned. The perspective of the observer determines what can be known and how it is to be understood. In consequence, the truth of political science is of necessity a partial truth.[1]

Upon a mind which by its very nature is unable to see more than part of the truth, society exerts its pressures, which confront the scholar with a choice between social advantage and the truth. The stronger the trend toward conformity within the society and the stronger the social ambitions within the individual scholar, the greater will be the temptation to sacrifice the moral commitment to the truth for social advantage. It follows that a respectable political science—respectable, that is, in terms of the society to be investi-

From the *Review of Politics*, October, 1955; and Roland Young (ed.), *Approaches to the Study of Politics* (1958).

[1] Cf. below, pp. 268 ff., the comment on the changing perspectives of political science. The views, expressed here necessarily in an aphoristic form, develop further what was said in *Scientific Man vs. Power Politics* (Chicago: University of Chicago Press, 1946), pp. 166–67.

gated—is in a sense a contradiction in terms. For a political science which is faithful to its moral commitment of telling the truth about the political world cannot help telling society things it does not want to hear. The truth of political science is the truth about power, its manifestations, its configurations, its limitations, its implications, its laws. Yet one of the main purposes of society is to conceal these truths from its members. That concealment, that elaborate and subtle and purposeful misunderstanding of the nature of political man and of political society, is one of the cornerstones upon which all societies are founded.[2]

In his search for truth, the political scientist is hemmed in by society in three different ways: with regard to the objects, the results, and the methods of his inquiry. In so far as the political scientist yields to these pressures, he violates his moral commitment to discovering the truth of society.

In all societies certain social problems cannot be investigated at all, or only at grave risk to the investigator. The basic philosophic assumptions by which a society lives are beyond scientific investigation. For to question them is tantamount to questioning the worth of society itself, its justice, its rationality, its very right to exist. Thus a theocratic society cannot permit the scientific investigation of its religious beliefs. A Marxist society cannot tolerate scientific inquiry into dialectic materialism. In a society based upon racial discrimination, race problems are beyond the ken of social science. The profit motive and free enterprise are taboo in capitalistic societies, and the popular control of government will be taken for granted rather than questioned in democracies.

Similarly, in all societies certain results are beyond the reach of scientific inquiry, or they can be reached only at great personal risks. No Russian economist is likely to conclude publicly that capitalism is superior to communism, nor is an American professor of economics likely to maintain the reverse position. Social scientists in monogamic societies are not likely to see virtue in polygamy, and in a scientific civilization, they will emphasize the advantages of science rather than its liabilities.

What is true of the objects and results of scientific investigation

[2] For an elaboration of this theme see *ibid.*, pp. 155 ff.; *Politics among Nations* (2d ed.; New York: Alfred A. Knopf, 1954), pp. 80 ff.

is true likewise of its methods. In a humanistically or religiously oriented society, quantitative methods and experimental methods in general will be at a disadvantage. The same fate will befall the methods of philosophic inquiry and rational deduction in a scientifically oriented society. Thus different societies put the stamp of social approval or disapproval upon different methods of inquiry, and the political scientist is again confronted with a dilemma between his commitment to the truth and his concern with social convenience and advancement.

No lengthy explanation is needed to show that those different pressures against which the political scientist must maintain his moral commitment are multiplied in the actual situation in which he must make his decisions. For the political scientist to be a member of a pluralistic society, such as America, means actually to be a member of a multiplicity of sectional societies of a religious, political, social, and economic character, all exerting parallel or contradictory pressures upon him. All these groups are committed to a particular social "truth," and the political scientist cannot help deviating from one or the other of these "truths," if he does not want to forego his moral commitment to discovering *the* truth of society altogether.

These pressures account for the enormous positive and negative influence which foundations exert upon the objects, results, and methods of research. They reward certain types of research by supporting them and stimulate more research of the same type by promising to support it. On the other hand, they thwart or make impossible other types of research by not supporting them. The political scientist who wants to share in these rewards and, by doing so, gain prestige and power within the profession cannot help being influenced by these positive and negative expectations in his concept of the social truth, of the methods by which to seek it, and of the relevant results to be expected from it.

A political science that is true to its moral commitment ought at the very least to be an unpopular undertaking. At its very best, it cannot help being a subversive and revolutionary force with regard to certain vested interests—intellectual, political, economic, social in general. For it must sit in continuous judgment upon political man and political society, measuring their truth, which is in good part a social convention, by its own. By doing so, it is not only an embarrassment to society intellectually, but it becomes also a political threat to the defenders or the opponents of the status quo or to both; for the social conventions about power, which political science cannot help subjecting to a critical—and often destructive—examination, are one of the main sources from which the claims to power, and hence power itself, derive.

It stands to reason that political science as a social institution could never hope even to approach this ideal of a completely disinterested commitment to the truth. For no social institution can completely transcend the limitations of its origin; nor can it endeavor to free itself completely from its commitments to the society of which it forms a part, without destroying itself in the attempt. Only rare individuals have achieved the Socratic distinction of unpopularity, social ostracism, and criminal penalties, which are the reward of constant dedication to the relevant truth in matters political. Yet while political science as a social institution cannot hope to approach the ideal, it must be aware of its existence; and the awareness of its moral commitment to the truth must mitigate the limitations of origin as well as the compromises between the moral commitment and social convenience and ambition, both of which no political scientist can fully escape. It is the measure of the degree to which political science in America meets the needs of society rather than its moral commitment to the truth that it is not only eminently respectable and popular, but—what is worse—that it is also widely regarded with indifference.

A political science that is mistreated and persecuted is likely to have earned that enmity because it has put its moral commitment to the truth above social convenience and ambition. It has penetrated beneath the ideological veil with which society conceals the true nature of political relations, disturbing the complacency of the powers-that-be and stirring up the conscience of society. A political science that is respected is likely to have earned that respect because it performs useful functions for society. It helps to cover political relations with the veil of ideologies which mollify the conscience of society; by justifying the existing power relations, it reassures the powers-that-be in their possession of power; it illuminates certain aspects of the existing power relations; and it contributes to the improvement of the technical operations of government. The relevance of this political science does not lie primarily in the discovery of the truth about politics but in its contribution to the stability of society.

A political science that is neither hated nor respected, but treated with indifference as an innocuous pastime, is likely to have retreated into a sphere that lies beyond the positive or negative interests of society. The retreat into the trivial, the formal, the methodological, the purely theoretical, the remotely historical—in short the politically irrelevant—is the unmistakable sign of a "non-controversial" political science which has neither friends nor enemies because it has no relevance for the great political issues in which society has a stake. History and methodology, in particular, become the protective armor which shields political science from contact with the political reality of the contemporary world. Political science, then, resembles what Tolstoi said modern history has become: "a deaf man answering questions which no one has asked him."

By being committed to a truth which is in this sense irrelevant, political science distorts the perspective under which the political world is seen. Certain eminent exceptions notwithstanding, it tends to pass in silence over such burning problems as the nature of power and of the truth about it, political ideologies, the political power of economic organizations, alternative foreign policies, the relations between government and public opinion, between tyranny and democracy, between objective truth and majority rule, as well as most of the other fundamental problems of contemporary democracy. By doing so, it makes it appear as though these problems either did not exist or were not important or were not susceptible to theoretical understanding. By its predominant concern with the irrelevant, it devaluates by implication the really important problems of politics.

Thus the political scientist, oblivious of his moral commitment, has completed his descent. The custodian of the truth and disturber of society's complacent conscience first descends to the role of the ideologue of society and mollifier of its conscience. This role still requiring a social commitment, not to the truth but to society as it is, and, hence, implying a long-term risk, the political scientist who wants to play absolutely safe must take another downward step. In this final role, concerning himself with issues in which nobody has a stake, he avoids the risk of social disapproval by foregoing the chance of social approbation. In the end, then, the concern with social convenience triumphs over social ambition. The commitment to the truth in matters political is dangerous all the time, while carrying within it the promise of ultimate triumph and spiritual perfection. The commitment to society as it is may be dangerous in the long run, carrying within it the promise of social rewards. Retreat from any commitment, to truth or to society, is free of danger, carrying within it no other reward but that freedom from danger itself.

What, then, ought a political science to be like, which does justice both to its scientific pretense and to its subject matter? The answer to this question, in so far as it concerns the scientific pretense of political science, derives from three basic propositions: the importance of political philosophy for political science, the identity of political theory and political science, the ability of political science to communicate objective and general truth about matters political.

Political science, like all science, is both in the general conception of its scope and method and in its particular concepts and operations a—largely unavowed—reflection of philosophic propositions. Even the most antiphilosophic science of politics is founded upon a philosophic understanding of the nature of man and society and of science itself. That understanding is philosophic in that its validity does not derive from its being capable of empirical verification (although it may be so verified) but rather from its logical consistency with certain general propositions which claim to present the true nature of reality. Political science needs neither to prove nor disprove the philosophic validity of these propositions but must assume the fallacy of some and the validity of others. The choice of these philosophic assumptions cannot but limit the scope, outlook, method, and purpose of political science. Political science is of necessity based upon, and permeated by, a total world view—religious, poetic as well as philosophic in nature—the validity of which it must take for granted.

During most of the history of Western political thought, the functions of political philosophy and political science were united in the same persons. The great political philosophers were also the great political scientists deriving concrete, empirically verifiable propositions from abstract philosophic ones. If the disintegration of the great political systems in the nineteenth century and the concomitant development of a separate political science to which we have referred above had led only to a division of labor between political philosophy and political science, no objection on principle would have been in order. However, the denial of the legitimacy and relevance of political philosophy for political science, prevalent in our day, is quite a different matter. For by denying that legitimacy and relevance, political science cuts itself off from the very roots to which it owes its life, which determine its growth, and which give it meaning. A political science that knows nothing but its own subject matter cannot even know that subject matter well. Contemporary political science, predominantly identified with a positivistic philosophy which is itself a denial of virtually all of the philosophic traditions of the West, has, as it were, mutilated itself by refusing itself access to the sources of insight available in the great philosophic systems of the past. Yet without that access it cannot even recognize, let alone understand, some of the perennial problems of politics which contemporary experience poses with almost unprecedented urgency.

Why is it that all men lust for power; why is it that even their noblest aspirations are tainted by that lust? Why is it that the political act, in its concern with man's power over man and the concomitant denial of the other man's freedom, carries within itself an element of immorality and puts upon the actor the stigma of guilt? Why is it, finally, that in politics good intentions do not necessarily produce good results and well-conceived plans frequently lead to failure in action, and why is it, conversely, that evil men have sometimes done great good in politics and improvident ones have frequently been successful? Here we are in the presence of the mystery, the sin, and the tragedy of politics. The problems that these questions raise are not scientific but philosophic in nature. Yet without the awareness of their legitimacy and relevance political science is precluded from even raising certain problems essential to the scientific understanding of politics.[3]

The same antiphilosophic position, prevalent in contemporary political science, is responsible for the common distinction between

[3] Cf. on this general problem the discussion on values in the social sciences in *America*, Vol. XCII (Oct. 9, 30, 1954).

political theory and political science. Theory, being by definition useless for practical purposes, was assigned that honorific but ineffectual position to which we have referred before, and main emphasis was placed upon science whose immediate usefulness for society the natural sciences seemed to have demonstrated.

Perhaps no event has had a more disastrous effect upon the development of American political science than this dichotomy between political theory and political science. For it has made political theory sterile by cutting it off from contact with the contemporary issues of politics, and it has tended to deprive political science of intellectual content by severing its ties with the Western tradition of political thought, its concerns, its accumulation of wisdom and knowledge. When American political science became sporadically aware of that impoverishment suffered by its own hands, it resorted to the remedy of adding more courses in political theory to the curriculum, or making them compulsory, or requiring knowledge of political theory in examinations. However, the remedy has been of no avail; for it derives from that very dichotomy between political theory and political science, which is at the root of the disease itself.

Of that disease, the plight of comparative government as an academic discipline provides a striking example. The comparison of different political institutions and systems requires logically a *tertium comparationis*, that is, a proposition which provides a standard for comparison. That standard, in order to be meaningful, cannot be merely empirical but must have a theoretical significance pointing to propositions of general validity. Comparative government, in order to be an academic discipline at all, then, requires a theory of politics that makes meaningful comparisons possible. In the absence of such a theory, it is not fortuitous that comparative government is hardly more than the description of, or at best a series of theories about, individual political institutions and systems without comparison.

The very distinction between political theory and political science is untenable. Historically and logically, a scientific theory is a system of empirically verifiable, general truths, sought for their own sake. This definition sets theory apart from practical knowledge, common-sense knowledge, and philosophy. Practical knowledge is interested only in truths which lend themselves to immediate practical application; common-sense knowledge is particular, fragmentary, and unsystematic; philosophic knowledge may be, but is not of necessity, empirically verifiable. What else, then, is scientific knowledge if not theory? It follows that political science cannot be made more theoretical by increasing emphasis upon the separate field of political theory but only by infusing all branches of political science susceptible of theoretical understanding with the spirit of theory.

The same philosophic position which has made political science disparage philosophy and separate itself from theory has also made it deny the existence and intelligibility of objective, general truths in matters political. That denial manifests itself in different ways on different levels of discourse. On the level of the general theory of democracy, it leads to the conclusion that the decision of the majority is the ultimate datum beyond which neither analysis nor evaluation can go. On the level of the analysis of political processes and decisions, it reduces political science to the explanation of the ways by which pressure groups operate and the decisions of government are reached. A political science thus conceived limits itself to the descriptive analysis of a complex of particular historic facts. Its denial of the existence and intelligibility of a truth about matters political that exists regardless of time and place implies a denial of the possibility of political theory both in its analytical and normative sense. What a political science of the past has discovered to be true, then, is true only in view of the peculiar and ephemeral historic circumstances of the time, carrying no lesson for us or any other period of history, or else is a mere reflection of the subjective preferences of the observer. The political science of the past is thus reduced, in so far as it seeks empirical analysis, to the description of an ephemeral historic situation and, as normative theory, becomes undistinguishable from political ideology.

This being so, contemporary political science is caught in the same relativistic dilemma and is no more able to transcend the limitations of time and place than were its predecessors. Either it will be tempted to overcome the limits of its relativist assumptions, whose nihilistic consequences it is unable to face, by taking flight in a subjective dogmatism that identifies the perspective and preferences of the observer with objective, general truth. Thus it becomes the ideology of a particular view of society, reflecting particular social interests. Or else political science will travel the relativistic road to the end and surrender the very concept of objective, general truth, concluding from the subjectivity of its own insights that there is nothing but opinion and that one opinion is as good as another, provided society does not object to it.

We cannot here enter into a detailed discussion of this fundamental problem; two observations must suffice. Political science, like any science, presupposes the existence and accessibility of objective, general truth. If nothing that is true regardless of time and place could be said about matters political, political science itself would be impossible. Yet the whole history of political thought is a living monument to that possibility. The relevance for ourselves of insights which political scientists of the past, reflecting upon matters political under the most diverse historic circumstances, considered to be true, points toward the existence of a store of objective, general truths which are as accessible to us as they were to our predecessors. If it were otherwise, how could we not only understand, but also appreciate, the political insights of a Jeremiah, a Kautilya, a Plato, a Bodin, or a Hobbes?

The content of political science is not to be determined a priori and in the abstract. A theory is a tool for understanding. Its purpose is to bring order and meaning to a mass of phenomena which without it would remain disconnected and unintelligible. There is a strong tendency in contemporary political science to force theory into a Procrustean bed by judging it by its conformity with certain pre-established methodological criteria rather than by its intrinsic contribution to knowledge and understanding. The result is an academic formalism which in its concern with methodological requirements tends to lose sight of the goal of knowledge and understanding which method must serve. One is reminded of the answer which Galileo is reported to have received when he invited some of his critics to look through a telescope at an astronomical phenomenon the existence of which they had denied; they said that there was no need for them to use this empirical instrument since according to Aristotle such a phenomenon could not exist. One is also reminded of the tendencies of the French literature of the seventeenth, the German literature of the eighteenth, and the French art of the nineteenth centuries to make the compliance with certain formal requirements the ultimate standard of literary and artistic value. And one takes heart from the impotence of such attempts to prevent for long the human mind from seeking and finding what is important in science, literature, and art.

The validity of a theory, then, does not depend upon its conformity with a priori assumptions, methodological or otherwise. It is subject to a purely pragmatic test. Does this theory broaden our knowledge and deepen our understanding of what is worth knowing? If it does, it is good, and if it does not, it is worthless, regardless of its a priori assumptions.

The content of theory, then, must be determined by the intellectual interest of the observer. What is it we want to know about politics? What concerns us most about it? What questions do we want a theory of politics to answer? The replies to these three questions determine the content of political science and the replies may well differ, not only from one period of history to another, but from one contemporaneous group of observers to another.

Hypothetically one can imagine as many theories of politics as there are legitimate intellectual perspectives from which to approach the political scene. But in a particular culture and a particular period of history, there is likely to be one perspective which for theoretical and practical reasons takes precedence over the others. At one time theoretical interest was focused upon the constitutional arrangements within which political relations take place; in view of the theoretical and practical problems to be solved, this was then a legitimate interest. At another time in the history of political science, theoretical interest was centered upon political institutions and their operations; in view of what was worth knowing and doing at that time, this theoretical interest was again legitimate. Thus political science is like a spotlight which, while trying to illuminate the whole political world, focuses in one period of history upon one aspect of politics and changes its focus in accordance with new theoretical and practical concerns.[4]

In our period of history, the justice and stability of political life is threatened, and our understanding of the political world is challenged, by the rise of totalitarianism on the domestic and international scene. The novel political phenomenon of totalitarianism

[4] Cf. the discussion of international relations below, pp. 309 ff.

puts in doubt certain assumptions about the nature of man and of society which we took for granted. It raises issues about institutions which we thought had been settled once and for all. It disrupts and overwhelms legal processes on which we had come to look as self-sufficient instruments of control. In one word, what has emerged from under the surface of legal and institutional arrangements as the distinctive, unifying element of politics is the struggle for power, elemental, undisguised, and all-pervading.[5] As recently as at the end of the Second World War, it was still held by conservatives, liberals, and Marxists alike either that the struggle for power was at worst a raucous pastime, safely regulated by law and channeled by institutions, or that it had been replaced in its dominant influence by economic competition, or that the ultimate triumph of liberal democracy or the classless society, which were expected to be close at hand, would make an end to it altogether. These assumptions and expectations have been refuted by the experience of our age. It is to the challenge of this refutation that political science must respond, as political practice must meet the challenge of that experience.

Yet while political science must thus come to terms with the problem of power, it must adapt its emphasis to the ever changing circumstances of the times. When the times tend to depreciate the element of power, it must stress its importance. When the times incline toward a monistic conception of power in the general scheme of things, it must show its limitations. When the times conceive of power primarily in military terms, it must call attention to the variety of factors which go into the power equation and, more particularly, to the subtle psychological relation of which the web of power is fashioned. When the reality of power is being lost sight of over its moral and legal limitations, it must point to that reality. When law and morality are judged as nothing, it must assign them their rightful place.

It may be pointed out in passing that all great contributions to political science, from Plato, Aristotle, and Augustine to *The Federalist* and Calhoun, have been responses to such challenges arising from political reality. They have not been self-sufficient theoretical developments pursuing theoretical concerns for their own sake.

[5] Cf. W. A. Robson, *The University Teaching of Social Sciences: Political Science* (Paris: UNESCO, 1954), pp. 17, 63.

Rather, they were confronted with a set of political experiences and problems which defied understanding with the theoretical tools at hand. Thus they had to face a new political experience, unencumbered by an intellectual tradition which might have been adequate to preceding experiences but which failed to illuminate the experience of the contemporary world. Thus they were compelled to separate in the intellectual tradition at their disposal that which is historically conditioned from that which is true regardless of time and place, to pose again the perennial problems of politics, and to reformulate the perennial truths of politics, in the light of the contemporary experience. This has been the task of political science throughout its history and this is the task of political science today.[6] There is, then, in political science what might be called a "higher practicality," which responds to practical needs not by devising practical remedies, but by broadening and deepening the understanding of the problems from which the practical needs arose.

By making power its central concept, a theory of politics does not presume that none but power relations control political action. What it must presume is the need for a central concept which allows the observer to distinguish the field of politics from other social spheres, to orient himself in the maze of empirical phenomena which make up that field, and to establish a measure of rational order within it. As economics is centered upon the concept of interest defined as wealth, its accumulation and distribution, so political science is centered upon the concept of interest defined as power, its accumulation, distribution, and control. A central concept, such as power, then provides a kind of rational outline of politics, a map of the political scene. Such a map does not provide a complete description of the political landscape as it is in a particular period of history. It rather provides the timeless features of its geography distinct from their ever changing historic setting. Such a map, then, will tell us what are the rational possibilities for travel from one spot on the map to another, and which road is most likely to be taken by certain travelers under certain conditions. Thus it imparts a measure of rational order to the observing mind and, by doing so, establishes one of the conditions for successful action.

[6] Cf. Alfred Cobban's important article, "The Decline of Political Theory," *Political Science Quarterly*, LXVIII (1953), 321–32.

A theory of politics, by the very fact of painting a rational picture of the political scene, points to the contrast between what the political scene actually is and what it tends to be, but can never completely become. The difference between the empirical reality of politics and a theory of politics is like the difference between a photograph and a painted portrait. The photograph shows everything that can be seen by the naked eye. The painted portrait does not show everything that can be seen by the naked eye, but it shows one thing that the naked eye cannot see: the human essence of the person portrayed. Thus a theory of politics must seek to depict the rational essence of its subject matter.

By doing so, a theory of politics cannot help implying that the rational elements of politics are superior in value to the contingent ones and that they are so in two respects. They are so in view of the theoretical understanding which theory seeks; for its very possibility and the extent to which it is possible depend upon the rationality of its subject matter. A theory of politics must value that rational nature of its subject matter also for practical reasons. It must assume that a rational policy is of necessity a good policy; for only such a policy minimizes risks and maximizes benefits and, hence, complies both with the moral precept of prudence and the political requirement of success. A theory of politics must want the photographic picture of the political scene to resemble as much as possible its painted portrait.

Hence, a theory of politics presents not only a guide to understanding but also an ideal for action. It presents a map of the political scene not only in order to understand what that scene is like but also in order to show the shortest and safest road to a given objective. The use of theory, then, is not limited to rational explanation and anticipation. A theory of politics also contains a normative element.

A curriculum of political science which would try to put such a theoretical understanding of politics into practice for the purposes of teaching would have to eliminate all those subjects which do not serve this theoretical understanding. It would also have to add subjects which at present are not included but which are essential to such understanding.

The process of elimination must move on two fronts. First, it must affect those subjects which have been traditionally included in the field but which have no organic connection with its subject matter or with the perspective from which contemporary political science ought to view it. In this category belong, for instance, all the legal subjects with which political science concerns itself because the law schools at one time did not. However, this practical consideration is unfounded today when law schools offer courses in jurisprudence and administrative, constitutional, and international law. Political science is not interested in any legal subject per se, yet it has indeed a vital interest in the interrelations between law and politics. It must look at law not as a self-contained system of rules of conduct, but rather as both the creation and the creator of political forces.

Second, there has been a strong tendency in political science to add to the curriculum subjects which happen to be of practical importance at a particular moment, regardless of their theoretical relevance. However, what is worth knowing for practical reasons is not necessarily worth knowing on theoretical grounds. A certain innovation in municipal administration or international organization may attract at one time wide attention by virtue of the practical results it promises, or the political developments in a certain area of the world may become a matter of topical interest for public opinion. It still remains to be shown on theoretical grounds that such topics ought to be included as independent subjects in the curriculum of political science. On a limited scale this problem raises again the issue of liberal versus vocational education.

The additions to the curriculum of political science, too, must be of two different kinds. On the one hand, the curriculum must take into account the fact that its central concept is a general social phenomenon which manifests itself most typically in the political sphere but is not limited to it. The phenomenon of power and the social configurations to which it gives rise play an important, yet largely neglected, part in all social life. A configuration, such as the balance of power, is a general social phenomenon to be found on all levels of social interaction. The theoretical understanding of specifically political phenomena and configurations requires the understanding of the extent to which these political phenomena and configurations are merely the specific instances of general social phenomena and configurations and the extent to which they grow out of their specific political environment. One of the cornerstones of the curriculum of political science, then, ought to be political sociology, which deals with the phenomenon of power and the social configurations to which it gives rise in general, with special reference, of course, to those in the political sphere.[7]

On the other hand, the contemporary political scene is characterized by the interaction between the political and economic spheres. This interaction runs counter to the liberal assumption and requirement of actual separation, which is reflected in the academic separation of the two fields. This interaction reverts to a situation which existed before political science was established as an academic discipline and which was reflected by the academic fusion of the two fields in the form of political economy. The curriculum of political science must take theoretical notice of the actual development of private governments in the form of giant corporations and labor unions. These organizations exercise power within their own organizational limits, in their relations to each other, and in their relations to the state. The state, in turn, exercises power over them. These power relations constitute a new field for theoretical understanding.[8]

Yet what political science needs above all changes in the curriculum—even though it needs them too—is the restoration of the intellectual and moral commitment to the truth about matters political for its own sake. That restoration becomes the more urgent in the measure in which the general social and the particular academic environment tends to discourage it. Society in general and that particular society of which he is a professional member pull and push the political scientist toward being useful here and now and playing it safe forever. If the political scientist cannot resist these pushes and pulls by repairing to the vision of the searcher for the political truth, which Plato brought to the world, and of the professor of the politi-

[7] Cf. the important but largely neglected monograph by Frederick Watkins, *The State as a Concept of Political Science* (New York: Harper & Bros., 1934), esp. pp. 81 ff.

[8] Morgenthau, "The New Despotism and the New Feudalism," *The Restoration of American Politics* (Vol. III of *Politics in the Twentieth Century*), chap. 10.

cal truth, which the prophets exemplified, what will become of him as a scholar, and what will become of a society which has deprived itself of the ability to measure the conflicting claims of interested parties against the truth, however dimly seen?

A society which has thus closed its eyes to the truth about itself has cut its tie with what connects it with the mainsprings of civilization. For without at least the assumption that objective, general truth in matters political exists and can be known, order and justice and truth itself become the mere by-products of ever changing power relations. In such a society the political scientist has still an important part to play: he becomes the ideologue who gives the appearance of truth and justice to power and the claim for it.

Political science, as we have tried to show before, can indeed not help performing such an ideological function. Yet it is the measure of the awareness and fulfilment of its mission as a science of politics that it is conscious of the existence of an objective, general truth behind ideological rationalizations and justifications and that it seeks the comprehension of that truth. In order to fulfil that mission the political scientist must live within the political world without being of it. He must watch it with intense interest and sympathy; yet the gaze of his mind and the impulse of his will must transcend it. He must understand it as well and better than does the politician, and yet his ambition has nothing in common with the latter's. His primary moral commitment is not to society but to the truth and, hence, to society only in so far as it lives up to the truth. Only so can he at least approach the ideal of political justice, he alone among those concerned with political matters; for in the words of Goethe: "The actor is always unjust; nobody has justice but the observer."

At such impracticality in action and ambivalence in moral commitment, the Socratic handmaids of all ages, the born servants of society, can only laugh. Of them, however clever and witty they may be, history reports nothing but laughter. Yet what they laugh at is the moral and intellectual outlook from which stems our heritage of political knowledge and wisdom.

22 The Commitments of a Theory of International Politics

          With the dilemmas discussed in the previous chapters, all attempts at a theoretical understanding of politics must come to terms. The intensity of the dilemma is proportional to the political involvement of the observer and to the political relevance of the subject matter. Under present conditions, it is likely to be greater in the field of economic policy than in the field of municipal government. That intensity is greatest in the sphere of international politics, and it is compounded by the presence of a dilemma which is peculiar to that sphere.

One basic fact distinguishes international politics from all other types of politics and exerts a persuasive influence on the practice of international politics as well as upon its theoretical understanding. That fact concerns the relationship between international society and its constituent members, the nation states. The constituent members of domestic society, individuals and subnational groups, live in an integrated society, which holds supreme power and is the repository of the highest secular values and the recipient of the ultimate secular loyalties. Yet these domestic societies are the constituent members of international society which must defer to them in terms of power, values, and loyalties. What sets international society apart from other societies is the fact that its strength—political, moral, social—is concentrated in its members, its own weakness being the reflection of that strength.

A theory of international politics has the task, in applying the general principles of politics to the international sphere, to reformulate, modify, and qualify these principles in the light of that distinctive quality of international politics. A theory of international politics plays, as it were, the tune which the general theory of politics provides, but it plays it in a key and with variations which stem from the peculiarities of international society. The national interest

From W. T. R. Fox (ed.), *Theoretical Aspects of International Relations* (Notre Dame, Ind.: University of Notre Dame Press, 1959).

defined in terms of power, the precarious uncertainty of the international balance of power, the weakness of international morality, the decentralized character of international law, the deceptiveness of ideologies, the inner contradictions of international organization, the democratic control of foreign policy, the requirements of diplomacy, the problem of war—of these phenomena and problems of international politics theory must take account in terms of the general principles of politics which reveal themselves on the international scene in peculiar manifestations, owing to the peculiar character of international society.

This is obviously not the place to attempt a demonstration of the correctness of this view; for such a demonstration would require the development of a substantive theory of international politics. Since the attempt to do this has been made elsewhere and since this chapter deals with the requirements and problems of such a theory rather than with its substance, it must suffice here to point to the great and peculiar difficulties which stand in the way of the development of such a theory and to the relatively narrow limits within which it seems to be possible. Two facts deserve special attention in this context: the implicit rather than explicit character of past attempts at a theory of international politics; and the peculiar difficulties impeding theoretical understanding which arise from the relationship of power, morality, and the national interest as it reveals itself on the international scene.

That men throughout the ages have thought little of a theory of international politics is borne out by the fact that but rarely an explicit attempt to develop such a theory has been made; as rare instances of such atempts, Kautilya and Machiavelli come to mind. Men have generally dealt with international politics on one of three levels, all alien to theory: history, reform, or pragmatic manipulation. That is to say, they have endeavored to detect the facts and meaning of international politics through the knowledge of the past; or they have tried to devise a pattern of international politics more in keeping with an abstract ideal than the empirical one; or they have sought to meet the day-by-day issues of international politics by trial and error.

Yet each of these approaches presupposes, and in actuality reveals, a theoretical conception of what international politics is all about, however fragmentary, implicit, and unavowed such a theoretical conception may be. In historians with a philosophic bent, such as Thucydides and Ranke, the history of foreign policy appears as a mere demonstration of certain theoretical assumptions which are always present beneath the surface of historical events to provide the standards for their selection and to give them meaning. In such historians of international politics, theory is like the skeleton which, invisible to the naked eye, gives form and function to the body. What distinguishes such a history of international politics from a theory is not so much its substance as its form. The historian presents his theory in the form of a historical recital using the historic sequence of events as demonstration of his theory. The theoretician, dispensing with the historical recital, makes the theory explicit and uses historic facts in bits and pieces to demonstrate his theory.

What holds true of the historian of international politics applies also to the reformer. He is, as it were, a "forward-looking" theoretician. His scheme of reform provides an explicit theory of what international politics ought to be, derived from an explicit or implicit theory of what international politics actually is. What has prevented William Penn, the Abbé de St. Pierre, or contemporary World Federalists from developing a complete theory of international politics is their primary concern with practical reform rather than the absence of theoretical elements in their thinking.

This same practical concern has prevented the practitioners of international politics from developing an explicit theory of what they are doing. Even a perfunctory perusal of the speeches, state papers, and memoirs of such diverse types of statesmen as Bismarck, Wilson, Churchill, and Stalin, shows that their relationship to theory is even closer than we found that of the historian to be. For the great statesman differs from the run-of-the-mill diplomatist and politician exactly in that he is able to see the issues confronting him as special cases of general and objective—that is, theoretical—propositions. Here again it is not the substance of his thinking but the form in which it manifests itself, which distinguishes the statesman from the theoretician of international politics. Here again it is his practical concern, not his alienation from theory as such, which prevents him from becoming a theoretician. Yet it illuminates the theoretical essence of the statesman's thinking that whenever practical concerns receded into the background or seemed best served by theoretical considerations, the four great statesmen mentioned above naturally transformed themselves from practitioners into theoreticians, making explicit in systematic or aphoristic form the theoretical foundations of their statecraft.

These observations support the case for the possibility and even the necessity of the theoretical understanding of international politics. However, by showing the scarcity of explicit, systematic theories of international politics, they point to the difficulties which stand in the way of the development of such a theory. The relationship of power, morality, and the national interest constitutes one of these difficulties.

On the domestic plane, the relationship of power, morality, and interest is so obvious as to be hardly open to controversy. In domestic politics, individuals pursue their interests defined in terms of power. These interests, in view of their relation to power, have three outstanding characteristics. First, the interests to which power attaches itself and which it serves are as varied and manifold as are the possible social objectives of the members of a given society. Second, these interests shift continuously from the center of political attention and emphasis to its margin until they may fade out of the political picture altogether, only to come back again when circumstances change. Third, measured by the interests of society as a whole, these interests are partial in nature, and their existence within a transcendent whole both limits their nature and the manner of their pursuit. The very nature of the interests with which the member of a domestic society may identify himself is determined by the "common good" as society as a whole understands it, and so are the means by which he may pursue those interests.

The relationship between interest and power is different on the international plane. Here power is wedded to the interests of a particular nation. And while it is true, as will be pointed out in the next chapter, that it has not always been so and it is not likely to be so forever, the relatively constant relationship between power and the national interest is the basic datum for purposes of both theoretical analysis and political practice. The content of the national interest is likewise constant over long periods of history. All the ideal and material elements which make up that content are subordinated at the very least to those requirements—not susceptible to rapid change—upon which the survival of the nation and the preservation of its identity depend. Finally—and most importantly—the national interest is not a fraction of a transcendent, comprehensive social interest to which it is subordinated and by which it is limited both as to content and to the means employed for its realization. The period of history when the national interest could be said to be so subordinated and limited has been replaced by one in which the nation has become the highest secular social organization and its interest the common focus of secular social interests.

However, it is not these characteristics of the national interest which make theoretical understanding difficult. Quite to the contrary, the constancy and supremacy of the national interest, taken by themselves, favor theoretical analysis. Theoretical complications arise from the relationship which exists between morality, on the one hand, power and the national interest, on the other. Here again it is revealing to trace the different manifestations of the same theoretical structure in the domestic and international sphere.

The relationship between morality, on the one hand, power and interest, on the other, is threefold. First, morality limits the interests that power seeks and the means that power employs to that end. Certain ends cannot be pursued and certain means cannot be employed in a given society within a certain period of history by virtue of the moral opprobrium that attaches to them. Second, morality puts the stamp of its approval upon certain ends and means which thereby not only become politically feasible but also acquire a positive moral value. These moral values, then, become an intrinsic element of the very interests that power seeks. Third, morality serves interests and power as their ideological justification.

In the domestic sphere morality performs all these three functions effectively. It directs the choice of the means and ends of power away from what society considers to be harmful to its purposes and toward what it regards to be beneficial to them. What we call a civilized political community is the result of the efficiency with which morality performs these negative and positive functions. Yet civilization requires more than the negative and positive limitations of the means and ends of politics. It also requires the mitigation of the struggle for power by glossing over power interests and power relations and making them appear as something different than what they actually are.

This ideological function, which morality performs on the domestic scene together with the other two, has become its main function for international politics. On the international scene, the individual nation is by far the strongest moral force, and the limitations which a supranational morality is able to impose today upon international politics are both fewer and weaker than they were almost at any time since the end of the Thirty Years' War. The individual nation, thus having become virtually the highest moral unit on earth, has naturally been tempted to equate its own moral values with morality as such, and especially the most powerful nations have found it hard to resist that temptation. In consequence, the main function which morality performs today for international politics is ideological. It makes it appear as though the interests and policies of individual nations were the manifestations of universal moral principles. The part aspires to become the whole, and there is very little to counteract that aspiration. It is not so much morality which limits individual interests, as it is the individual interests which identify themselves with morality.

This identification of the interests and power of the nation with universal morality confronts theoretical understanding with formidable difficulties. The distinction between ideology and morality becomes blurred as does the distinction between ideology and theory. The advocate of the national crusade appears not only to promote universal moral values but also to have discovered theoretical truth. By contrast, the theoretician who seeks the truth hidden beneath these veils of ideology cannot help being in an intellectually and morally awkward position. His very probing of the moral pretenses of national interest and national power in the name of a higher truth and a higher morality makes him suspect of being indifferent to all truth and all morality. Thus to write a theory of international politics is not an easy thing. Perhaps this is why we have so many ideologies, and so few theories, of international politics.

The difficulties which stand in the way of the theoretical understanding of international politics have grown more formidable with the ever more intensive identification of national purposes and policies with absolute truth and universal morality. Yet at the same time the need for such understanding has become paramount in an age in which the nation, deeming itself intellectually and morally self-sufficient, threatens civilization and the human race itself with extinction. To look in such circumstances at one's own nation and its relations with other nations objectively, dispassionately, critically has never been more difficult, hazardous, and necessary than it is today. This task presents a theory of international politics with its supreme intellectual and moral challenge. Its performance would constitute not only an intellectual and moral but a political triumph as well. For it would indicate that at least the mind of man has succeeded in mastering that blind and potent monster which in the name of God or history is poised for universal destruction.

23 *The Intellectual and Political Functions of a Theory of International Relations*

In the April, 1960, issue of *International Relations*, Professor Martin Wight, then of the London School of Economics and Political Science, published a paper with the title "Why Is There No International Theory?" While I cannot, of course, subscribe to the unqualified negativism of the title for both personal and professional reasons, I find the paper a most illuminating and penetrating discussion of the problem. Its fourteen pages contain more insights into the intellectual issues posed by theoretical concern with international relations than a whole shelf of books and articles which, following the fashion of the day, spin out theories about theories of international relations and embark upon esoteric methodological studies about how to go about theorizing about theories of international relations.

Professor Wight finds elements of an international theory in writings of international lawyers, such as Grotius and Pufendorf; the so-called "irenists," seekers after a peaceful international order, such as Erasmus, Sully, Campanella, Crucé, Penn, the Abbé de St. Pierre; the Machiavellians rediscovered by Meinecke; the *parerga* of political philosophers, philosophers, and historians, such as Hume's "The Balance of Power," Rousseau's *Project of Perpetual Peace*, Mably's *Principes des Négociations;* and finally the speeches, dispatches, memoirs, and essays of statesmen and diplomatists, such as Gentz's *Fragments on the Balance of Power*[1] or Bismarck's *Memoirs*. Professor Wight concludes that "international theory is marked, not only by paucity but also by intellectual and moral poverty. For this we must look to internal reasons. The most obvious are the intellectual prejudice imposed by the sovereign State, and the belief in progress."

An Address given at the University of Maryland, March, 1961; reprinted in Horace V. Harrison, ed., *Role of Theory in International Relations* (New York: Van Nostrand, 1964).

[1] Classified by Wight in the preceding category.

According to Professor Wight, the sovereign state has been the focus of Western political thought and experience since the Reformation. Almost all intellectual energies devoted to political studies have been absorbed by it. "It has been natural to think of international politics as the untidy fringe of domestic politics . . . and to see international theory in the manner of the political theory textbooks, as an additional chapter which can be omitted by all save the interested student." Political theory, centered upon the state and its survival within the existing state system, has prevailed over international theory, studying the state system itself as a phenomenon that owes its existence to the historic process and is destined to be superseded by it. This is what Wight calls "a small-scale field of political theory." International theorists "have not been attracted by the possibility of maximising the field of political theory through establishing a world State. Nor is it unfair to see the League and the United Nations as the expression of a belief that it may be possible to secure the benefits of a world State without the inconveniences of instituting and maintaining it." Wight finds it significant that none of the three most powerful influences on the development of the modern state system—Reformation and Counter Reformation, the French Revolution, and the totalitarian revolutions of the twentieth century—have brought forth a coherent body of international theory.

Professor Wight finds the other impediment to the development of an international theory in the fact that

the character of international politics is incompatible with progressivist theory. Thus international theory that remains true to diplomatic experience will be at a discount in an age when the belief in progress is prevalent. If Sir Thomas More or Henry IV, let us say, were to return to England and France in 1960, it is not beyond plausibility that they would admit that their countries had moved domestically towards goals and along paths which they could approve. But if they contemplated the international scene, it is more likely that they would be struck by resemblances to what they remembered. International politics is the realm of recurrence and repetition; it is the field in which political action is most regularly necessitous.

Yet when the modern mind comes face to face with this immutable character of international politics, it revolts and takes refuge in the progressivist conviction that what was true in the past cannot be true in the future; for, if it were, mankind would be in desperate

straits. This is what Wight calls "the argument from desperation."
Thus

> whereas political theory generally is in unison with political activity, international theory (at least in its chief embodiment as international law) sings a kind of descant over against the movement of diplomacy . . . international law seems to follow an inverse movement to that of international politics.

This tension between international theory and international reality is already obvious in the identification of international politics with a precontractual state of nature assumed by the classical international lawyers. Yet while the state of nature among individuals leads to the social contract establishing authority over, and peace and order among, them, international theory sees no need for a similar development among states.

Wight finds it odd

> that, while the acknowledged classics of political study are the political philosophers, the only counterpart in the study of international relations is Thucydides, a work of history. And that the quality of international politics, the preoccupations of diplomacy, are embodied and communicated less in works of political or international theory than in historical writings. There are out of date books like Seeley's *Growth of British Policy*, which were second-rate at best, that might be thought to convey the nature of foreign policy and the working of the State-system better than much recent literature concerned with the games theory, decision-making, politicometrics and psychological concepts.

Wight summarizes his position by pointing to

> a kind of recalcitrance of international politics to being theorized about. The reason is that the theorising has to be done in the language of political theory and law. But this is the language appropriate to man's control of his social life. Political theory and law are maps. of experience or systems of action within the realm of normal relationships and calculable results. They are the theory of the good life. International theory is the theory of survival. What for political theory is the extreme case (as revolution or civil war) is for international theory the regular case.

Thus in the end international theory "involves the ultimate experience of life and death, national existence and national extinction." What we call international theory, then, amounts to a kind of philosophy of history.

It hardly needs pointing out that my position coincides in large measure with that of Professor Wight.[2] I take indeed a more sanguine view of the possibility of international theory than he does, finding that possibility in the very fact that "international politics is the realm of recurrence and repetition." It is this repetitive character of international politics, i.e., the configurations of the balance of power, that lends itself to theoretical systematization. I would also hesitate to equate international theory with philosophy of history. Theory is implicit in all great historiography. In historians with a philosophic bent, such as Thucydides and Ranke, the history of foreign policy appears as a mere demonstration of certain theoretical assumptions which are always present beneath the surface of historical events to provide the standards for their selection and to give them meaning. In such historians of international politics, theory is like the skeleton which, invisible to the naked eye, gives form and function to the body. What distinguishes such a history of international politics from a theory is not so much its substance as its form. The historian presents his theory in the form of a historical recital using the chronological sequence of events as demonstration of his theory. The theoretician, dispensing with the historical recital, makes the theory explicit and uses historic facts in bits and pieces to demonstrate his theory.

Yet both Wight's and my orientation are historic, and it is this historic orientation that sets us apart from the presently fashionable theorizing about international relations. This theorizing is abstract in the extreme and totally unhistoric. It endeavors to reduce international relations to a system of abstract propositions with a predictive function. Such a system transforms nations into stereotyped "actors" engaging in equally stereotyped symmetric or asymmetric relations. What Professor Wight has noted of international law applies with particular force to these theories: the contrast between their abstract rationalism and the actual configurations of world politics.[3] We are here in the presence of still another type of

[2] I am referring of course primarily to *Politics among Nations* and, more particularly, to chaps. xi–xiv, xvii, xix, xxix, dealing with the balance of power, the nation-state, and world government, respectively.

[3] See, for instance, the special issue on "The International System" of *World Politics*, XIV, No. 1 (October, 1961), and the critique of this type of thinking in Irving Louis Horowitz, "Arms, Policies and Games," *The American Scholar*, XXXI, No. 1 (Winter, 1961–62), 94 ff. For criticism, see also P. M. S. Blackett,

progressivist theory. Its aim is not the legalization and organization of international relations in the interest of international order and peace, but the rational manipulation of international relations and, more particularly, of military strategy in the interest of predictable and controlled results. The ideal toward which these theories try to progress is ultimately international peace and order to be achieved through scientific precision and predictability in understanding and manipulating international affairs.

In view of their consistent neglect of the contingencies of history and of the concreteness of historic situations that all these theories have in common, they are destined to share the fate of their progressivist predecessors: they must fail both as guides for theoretical understanding and as precepts for action. However, the practical consequences of their theoretical deficiencies are likely to be more serious than those of their predecessors.

The straits in which the Western democracies found themselves at the beginning of the Second World War were in good measure the result of the reliance upon the inner force of legal pronouncements, such as the Stimson Doctrine of refusing to recognize territorial changes brought about by violence, and of legal agreements, such as the Kellogg-Briand Pact and non-aggression treaties, and of international organizations, such as the League of Nations, which were incapable of collective action. The scientist theories of our day pretend to be capable of manipulating with scientific precision a society of sovereign nations who use weapons of total destruction as instruments of their respective foreign policies. With that pretense, these theories create the illusion that a society of sovereign nations thus armed can continue the business of foreign policy and military strategy in the traditional manner without risking its destruction. They create the illusion of the viability of the nation-state in the nuclear age. If statesmen should take these theories at their pseudo-scientific word and act upon them, they would fail, as the statesmen of the interwar period failed when they acted upon the progressivist theories of their day.

"Critique of Some Contemporary Defence Thinking," *Encounter*, XVI (April, 1961), 9 ff., and Sir Solly Zuckerman, "Judgment and Control in Modern Warfare," *Foreign Affairs*, XL, No. 2 (January, 1962), 196 ff.

It is significant that until very recently no explicit theory of international relations has existed. Nobody until very recently considered even the possibility of writing a theory of international relations. This is a very significant fact which ought to give us pause. For certainly theoretically inclined, reflective people have been aware, since the beginning of the existence of international relations, of the facts of foreign policy, the fateful results of good and bad foreign policies, the significance of success or failure in foreign policy. And certainly we have not grown so much wiser in recent years or so much more acute in self-awareness that we have all of a sudden started to think in theoretical terms of one of the crucial facts of human existence, recognized as such by prophets, statesmen, historians, and political philosophers for thousands of years. There must be a profound reason why until very recently nobody has thought of writing an explicit theory of international relations. Certainly it cannot be the backwardness of Plato and Aristotle, Hobbes and Locke, which prevented them from developing such a theory.

The first reason why there has been no theory, but only history, of international relations is to be found in the philosophic outlook that prevailed until the end of the Napoleonic Wars. Until then, the relations among nations were regarded to be a fact of nature which was beyond the power of man to change. The relations among nations were regarded to be a datum of history, a state of nature, resulting from the nature of man; and nothing could be said in terms of a specific theory of international relations about their characteristics and about their manipulation. Given this outlook, the best theory could do was what political philosophy actually did, that is, to describe the state of nature and the rudimentary legal order existing, or assumed to exist, among nations.

As long as man believed that the relations among nations were beyond human control, beyond reform by the human will, there was no place in the intellectual scheme of things for a theory of international relations. International theory found itself in this respect in the same position as social theory in general. As long as people believed that poverty, for instance, was a natural state which man had to accept without being able to change it, social philosophy could do no more than affirm this natural condition. As long as this state of mind persisted, there was no possibility for the development of a social theory, a social theory of change at least. What *The Times* said in mid-nineteenth century of the misery of the unemployed: "There is no one to blame for this; it is the result of Nature's simplest laws!" people thought of international relations. Thus the intellectual possibility of a theory of international relations depended upon the recognition that the relations among nations are not something which is given to man, which has to be accepted as given, and which he must cope with as best he can, but rather that the relations among nations have been created by the will of man and therefore can be manipulated and changed and reformed by the will of man.

The second reason why theoretical concern with international relations was so late in emerging lies in the reformist orientation that characterized theoretical thinking on foreign policy in the nineteenth century and the first decades of the twentieth. The main. theoretical concern during that period was not with understanding the nature of international relations, but with developing legal institutions and organizational devices which would supersede the type of international relations then existing. "Power politics" itself as a synonym for foreign policy was then a term of opprobrium, referring to something evil, not to be understood but to be abolished. To take Woodrow Wilson's position during and after the First World War as a classic and most impressive example, he was interested not in understanding the operations of the balance of power but in getting rid of it, in reforming international relations in such a way that one did not need to resort any more to the balance of power.

Secretary of State Cordell Hull echoed the Wilsonian conception when, on his return from the Moscow Conference of 1943 where the establishment of the United Nations had been agreed upon, he declared that "there will no longer be need for spheres of influence, for alliances, for balance of power, or any other of the special arrangements through which, in the unhappy past, the nations strove to safeguard their security or promote their interests." And President Franklin D. Roosevelt did the same when on March 1, 1945, in his report to Congress on the Yalta Conference, he declared:

> The Crimean Conference . . . spells the end of the system of unilateral action and exclusive alliances and spheres of influence and balances of power and all other expedients which have been tried for centuries—and have failed.

We propose to substitute for all these a universal organization in which all peace-loving nations will finally have a chance to join.

As long as this negative orientation toward the very nature of international relations and foreign policy persisted, it was both intellectually and morally impossible to deal in a theoretical, that is, an objective, systematic manner with the problems of international relations.

The third and permanent factor, which does not make a theory of international relations altogether impossible, but strictly limits its development and usefulness, is to be found in the very nature of politics, domestic and international. There is a rational element in political action which makes politics susceptible to theoretical analysis, but there is also a contingent element in politics which obviates the possibility of theoretical understanding.

The material with which the theoretician of politics must deal is ambiguous. The events he must try to understand are, on the one hand, unique occurrences. They happened in this way only once and never before or since. On the other hand, they are similar, for they are manifestations of social forces. Social forces are the product of human nature in action. Therefore, under similar conditions, they will manifest themselves in a similar manner. But where is the line to be drawn between the similar and the unique? The political world appears to the theoretical mind as a highly complicated combination of numerous systems of multiple choices which in turn are strictly limited in number. The element of irrationality, insecurity, and chance lies in the necessity of choice among several possibilities multiplied by the great number of systems of multiple choice. The element of rationality, order, and regularity lies in the limited number of possible choices within each system of multiple choice. Viewed with the guidance of a rationalistic, blueprinted map, the social world is, indeed, a chaos of contingencies. Yet it is not devoid of a measure of rationality if approached with the modest expectations of a circumspect theory.

To take as an example three current situations, we can say that the situations in Laos, Cuba, and Berlin provide American foreign policy with a limited number of rational choices. For some strange reason these choices generally number three. What a theory of international relations can state is the likely consequences of choosing one alternative as over against another and the conditions under which one alternative is more likely to occur and be successful than the other. Theory can also say that under certain conditions one alternative is to be preferred over another. But all these theoretical analyses are contingent upon factors of whose occurrences we either know nothing or whose consequences we cannot foresee.

Take for instance so crucial a problem of international relations as the problem of nuclear war. It is possible to develop a theory of nuclear war, as Herman Kahn has done in his book *On Thermonuclear War*, which assumes nuclear war to be just another kind of violence, greater in magnitude but not different in kind than the types of violence with which history has acquainted us. It follows from this assumption that nuclear war is going to be much more terrible than pre-nuclear war, but not necessarily intolerable, provided we take the measures which will enable us to survive it. In other words, once you start with this theoretical assumption of the nature and the consequences of a nuclear war, you can logically arrive at Mr. Kahn's conclusion that the foreign policy of the United States does not need to limit itself to trying to avoid nuclear war, but that the United States must also prepare to survive it. And then it becomes perfectly legitimate to raise the question, provided 50 million Americans were to be killed in a nuclear war and 9/10 of the economic capacity of the United States were to be destroyed, how do we enable the surviving 130 million Americans to rebuild the United States with the remaining 1/10 of economic capacity?

The contingent element in this theory of nuclear war is its utter uncertainty, and this uncertainty is typical of all levels of theoretical analysis and prediction in the field of politics, domestic and international. Even if one were to accept all its estimates of deaths and material destruction and of the rate of material recovery, this theory would have to be uncertain about the human reaction to the kind of human and material devastation which nuclear war is likely to bring about. Obviously, if a highly complex human society could be visualized to operate like a primitive ant society, its recuperative ability could be taken for granted. If 1/3 of the ants of one ant hill have been destroyed together with 9/10 of the material of the ant hill, it is safe to conclude that the remaining ants will start all over again, building up the ant hill and reproducing until the next catastrophe will force them to start all over again.

But it is a moot question whether a human society has this type of mechanical recuperative ability. Perhaps societies have a breaking point as do individuals, and there may be a point beyond which human endurance does not carry human initiative in the face of such unprecedented massive devastation. Perhaps under the impact of such devastation civilization itself will collapse.

It is at this point that the theoretical understanding of international relations reaches its limits. It can develop different alternatives and clarify their necessary preconditions and likely consequences. It can point to the conditions which render one alternative more likely to materialize than the other. But it cannot say with any degree of certainty which of the alternatives is the correct one and will actually occur.

This is but an extreme example of the utter uncertainty of theorizing about foreign policy beyond the clarification of alternative policies, their possibilities and possible consequences. The Munich settlement of 1938 is another case in point. In retrospect, of course, we all know from practical experience that it was a great failure, and from that experience we have developed the theoretical categories which demonstrate that it was bound to be such a failure. But I remember very well the near-unanimity with which the Munich settlement was approved by theoreticians and practitioners of foreign policy and by the man in the street as well. The Munich settlement was generally regarded at the time of its conclusion as a great act of statesmanship, a concession made to a would-be conqueror for the sake of peace. E. H. Carr so regarded it then, and A. J. P. Taylor so regards it now. The flaw in that reasoning, which few people were—and perhaps could be—aware of at the time, was again the neglect of the contingencies inherent in political prediction. That which reveals itself as a simple truth in retrospect was either completely unknown in prospect or else could not be determined by anything but an uncertain hunch.

Apply the reasoning with which I have just analyzed the Munich settlement of 1938 to a hypothetical Berlin settlement of 1962. One of the alternatives for American foreign policy, which theoretical analysis can isolate, is to make certain concessions to the Soviet

Union which change the modalities of the West's presence in Berlin but leave that presence itself intact. Another alternative, also revealed by theoretical analysis, is to stand on the Western right to be in Berlin and to refuse to make any concessions because whatever concessions we make will of necessity be followed by other concessions, and so step by step our presence in West Berlin will be whittled down until it becomes untenable.

A third alternative assumes that our presence in Berlin is a priori untenable. It holds that the symbolic value of our presence in Berlin with regard to the unification of Germany has really been bypassed by history because the division of Germany has become definitive. Sooner or later, we must recognize this fact and adapt our policies to it. Especially in view of the risks involved and the odds against success, there is no point in maintaining a symbol which has no longer any active function to perform.

A theoretical argument can be made for any of those three alternatives, and nobody can say in advance with any degree of certainty which of the courses of action indicated by those three alternatives is correct in theory, sound in practice, or is likely to be chosen by actual policy. Only in retrospect, judging from the nature and the results of the action chosen, can we answer these questions. This limitation of theoretical analysis is inherent in the very subject matter of international relations, and this subject matter erects insuperable limits to the development of a rational theory of international relations. It is only within those limits that theoretical thinking on international relations is theoretically and practically fruitful. Within these limits, a theory of international relations performs the functions any theory performs, that is, to bring order and meaning into a mass of unconnected material and to increase knowledge through the logical development of certain propositions empirically established.

While this theoretical function of a theory of international relations is no different from the function any social theory performs, its practical function is peculiar to itself. The practical function of a theory of international relations has this in common with all political theory that it depends very much upon the political environment within which the theory operates. In other words, political thinking is, as German sociology puts it, "*standortgebunden*," that is to say, it is tied to a particular social situation. And we find that all great and fruitful political thought, which we still remember because of its greatness and fruitfulness, has started from a concrete political situation with which the political thinkers had to come to terms both for intellectual and practical reasons. Edmund Burke is a typical example of how great and fruitful political theory develops from concrete practical concerns. It is not being created by a professor sitting in his ivory tower and looking at a contract with his publisher, which stipulates the delivery of a manuscript on the "Theory of International Relations" by the first of January, 1962. It is developed out of the concern of a politically alive and committed mind with the concrete political problems of the day. Thus all great political theory, from Plato and Aristotle and from the biblical prophets to our day, has been practical political theory, political theory which intervenes actively in a concrete political situation with the purpose of change through action.

A theory of international relations can perform four different practical functions by approaching political reality in four different ways. I shall try to exemplify these four different ways with my own experience as a theoretician of international relations, attempting to come to terms with the issues of international relations and of American foreign policy in particular since the end of the Second World War.

I had my first experience as a theoretician of international relations under the Truman-Acheson administration of America's foreign policy. Theory then provided a theoretical justification for what the policy makers were doing, you may say, instinctively— what they were doing pragmatically, on a mere day-by-day basis.

By 1947 the new pattern of American foreign policy was set. It manifested itself in four political innovations: the Truman doctrine, containment, the Marshall Plan, and the American alliance system. These policies have in common the permanent assumption, by the United States, of responsibilities beyond the limits of the Western Hemisphere. The heart of that new policy was the policy of containment. Yet the policy of containment was never officially formulated. It grew as an almost instinctive reaction to the threat of Russian imperialism. It called a halt to the territorial expansion of Russian power beyond the line of military demarcation drawn at the end of the Second World War between the Soviet orbit and the Western world.

There was no theory in support of these new policies. It was only as an afterthought that theoreticians developed a doctrine in the form of a theoretical framework which gave rational justification to the new policies. The policy makers played it by ear; they did what they thought they needed to do under the circumstances; they embarked upon courses of action which at the time appeared to them almost inevitable in view of their knowledge of the threat and of their objectives. It was only as a kind of intellectual reassurance that a theory of American foreign policy was developed which put the stamp of rational approval upon policies already established.

The function of the theoretician of international relations under the two Eisenhower administrations, dominated by the foreign policy of John Foster Dulles, was of an entirely different nature. It was a function which has many precedents in the history of political thought. One can even go so far as to say that it is one which political theories have traditionally performed. Theory here developed a coherent system of thought which was supposed to embody the sound principles of foreign policy. The actual conduct of American foreign policy was judged by the standards of that theory and frequently found wanting. Criticism directed at that theory was similarly judged and justified or found wanting, as the case might have been, by the standards of the theory. I remember very vividly that, whenever I published an article critical of the foreign policy of Mr. Dulles, I found nowhere more enthusiastic approval of that criticism than in the Department of State. Theory here provided a rational framework for a non-orthodox, critical political position either within the government or outside it. Theory gave a rational justification to that position.

The situation in which the theoretician of international relations has found himself since January 20, 1961, when the Kennedy administration took office, is, of course, quite extraordinary. What is the function of the outside theoretician when the government itself is staffed on the command posts of foreign policy by theoreticians? It stands to reason that he has become in good measure technologically obsolete. I have, since January 20, 1961, reflected with a great deal of embarrassment upon this change of position. Hardly anybody asks my advice any more because the people in government know at least as much as I do, and probably some are convinced that they know much more—and perhaps they actually do.

What, then, is the function of the academic theoretician of international relations in a society in which foreign policy itself is determined by theoretically conscious policy makers? There is still a function to be performed. For it is in the very nature of the conduct of foreign policy in a democracy that what theoreticians regard to be the sound principles of foreign policy must be adapted to the preferences of public opinion and to the pressures of domestic politics, and thereby corrupted and distorted. I remember the statement I once heard a former secretary of state make to the effect that he had always regarded it as his function to give the President advice on the basis of what he thought the principles of a sound American foreign policy required, leaving it to the President to decide how much of those sound principles could be safely put into practice in view of the state of domestic public opinion and the pressures of domestic politics.

Thus the actual foreign policies pursued by a government staffed even by theoreticians are bound to fall short, from time to time, of the requirements of a pure theoretical understanding of what American foreign policy ought to be. It is here that the theoretician of foreign policy must perform the function of an intellectual conscience which reminds the policy makers as well as the public at large of what the sound principles of foreign policy are and in what respects and to what extent actual policies have fallen short of those principles.

There is a final task—and perhaps it is the most noble of all—which a theory of international relations can perform and which it must perform particularly in an age in which the very structure of international relations has radically changed. It is to prepare the ground for a new international order radically different from that which preceded it. Theoretical analysis, I think, can show that the principle of political organization which has dominated the modern world from the French Revolution of 1789 to this day is no longer valid. The sovereign nation-state is in the process of becoming obsolete. That is to say, the fact of nuclear power, which transcends the ability of any nation-state to control and harness it and render it both innocuous and beneficial, requires a principle of political organization transcending the nation-state and commensurate with the potentialities for good or evil of nuclear power itself. Theoretical analysis can show that the availability of nuclear power as an instrument of foreign policy is the only real revolution which has occurred in the structure of international relations since the beginning of history, because it has radically changed the relationship between violence as a means of foreign policy and the ends of foreign policy.

Until the end of the Second World War, there existed a rational relationship between violence as a means of foreign policy and the ends of foreign policy; that is to say, the policy maker could rationally ask himself whether he should pursue the aims of his country by peaceful means or whether he ought to go to war. If he chose the latter alternative and if he lost the war, his nation lost in general only a bearable fraction of its human and material resources. If he won, then the risks taken were justified by the victory gained. This rational relationship between violence as a means and the ends of foreign policy has been obliterated by the availability of nuclear power. Nuclear power provides governments with a destructive force transcending all possible rational objectives of the foreign policy of any nation. For all-out nuclear war is likely to obliterate the very distinction between victor and vanquished and will certainly destroy the very objective for which such a war would be fought. It is here that a theory of international relations has a creative and vital task to perform, a task which has been performed throughout history by the political theories of domestic politics. It is at this point that the realistic and utopian approaches to politics in general and to international relations in particular merge.

It is a legitimate and vital task for a theory of politics to anticipate drastic changes in the structure of politics and in the institutions which must meet a new need. The great political utopians have based their theoretical anticipation of a new political order upon the realistic analysis of the empirical status quo in which they lived. Today political theory and, more particularly, a theory of international relations, starting from the understanding of politics and international relations as they are, must attempt to illuminate the impact which nuclear power is likely to exert upon the structure of international relations and upon the functions domestic government performs and to anticipate in a rational way the intellectual, political, and institutional changes which this unprecedented revolutionary force is likely to require.

There is another function of international theory which is not so much intellectual as psychological in nature and is of interest primarily to the sociology of knowledge. It is to provide a respectable shield which protects the academic community from contact with the living political world. That function is performed by many of the methodological activities which are carried on in academic circles with sometimes fanatical devotion to esoteric terminology and mathematical formulas, equations, and charts in order to elucidate or obscure the obvious. These activities can be explained psychologically by the fear of many academicians to come into too close contact with the political world, to become controversial in consequence, and to become contaminated in their objective scholarship by contact with political reality. By engaging in activities which can have no relevance for the political problems of the day, such as theorizing about theories, one can maintain one's reputation as a scholar without running any political risks. This kind of international theory, then, is consummated in theorizing for theorizing's sake, an innocuous intellectual pastime engaged in by academicians for the benefit of other academicians and without effect upon political reality as it is unaffected by it.

In conclusion, It may be said that the nature of a theory of international relations and the intellectual and political functions a theory of international relations performs and ought to perform are not in essence different from the nature of general political theory and the functions which such theories have performed since the beginning of history. The fact that we have only in recent years turned toward explicit theoretical reflection about international relations is in good measure due to our recognition that international relations is something not to be taken for granted, but something to be understood and to be changed and, more particularly, to be changed beyond the present limits of its political structure and organization. Here lies indeed the ultimate theoretical and practical justification of our interest in a theory of international relations. Threatened by the unsolved political problems of the day, we have come to think more and more in terms of a supranational community and a world government, a political organization and structure which transcend the nation-state. Reflecting on a theory of international relations, the politically conscious theoretician cannot help reflecting upon the political problems whose solution requires such novel structures and types of organization.

24 International Relations as an Academic Discipline

The assumption that a central concept is necessary for the theoretical understanding of politics has been disputed implicitly through the development of theories of politics which are lacking in such a central concept and explicitly in the form of an attack upon the suggested central concept of power. The question of whether such a central concept is necessary at all and, if so, which one it ought to be has divided opinion on all levels of theory and practice. It has done so also on the level of academic curriculum and organization. The controversy about the nature and the proper place of international relations and area studies as academic disciplines is a manifestation of that division of opinion concerning the fundamental problem of understanding politics.

These two novel academic disciplines must solve the same basic problems. If one wants to put the issue in epigrammatic and, therefore, oversimplified form, one might say that the main problem, as yet unsolved, that confronts these two academic "disciplines" is that they have not been able to acquire intellectual discipline. They have no intellectually valid focus which could give unity to their intellectual endeavors, and they have no common method by which the results of their investigations could be tested. These deficiencies have been as obvious in the study of international relations as they are in area studies. They are the more obvious in the latter, since area studies have made integration their main claim for recognition as an academic discipline. Area studies are in the process of showing —and the most mature discussion of their problems shows it with particular clarity—that they stand and fall with the precise formulation of a relevant problem to which different academic disciplines are to contribute. If area studies can demonstrate in practice that success in international studies, area or otherwise, depends upon the precise definition of a common problem and the sharp focus of all relevant research upon that problem, they will indeed have made an outstanding contribution to the study of international relations.

From the *International Social Science Bulletin*, 1952, No. 4; and Bland Blanshard (ed.), *Education in the Age of Science* (1959).

When after the First World War the study of international relations gained recognition as an independent academic discipline, it had three main intellectual interests: history, international law, and political reform. It is not by accident that the first two occupants of the first chair of international politics, the one which was founded in 1919 at the University of Wales, were distinguished historians, Professors Zimmern and Webster. There can of course be no doubt that knowledge of history and, more particularly, of diplomatic history forms an indispensable element of international relations; but, as will be shown later, while the student of international relations must have a thorough knowledge of history, his intellectual interest is not identical with that of the historian.

Obviously, the intellectual interest of international relations is in the present and the future rather than in the past and, especially in the interwar years, that interest was conceived in terms of international law. International relations were considered to move on two different levels: the legal one which presented the rules by which states were supposed to act, and the empirical one which showed how they actually did act in view of the rules of international law. Thus general history, diplomatic history, and international law became three cornerstones of the study of international relations.

The fourth cornerstone of the study of international relations is less easy to identify. For it is formed by the aspirations for a better world, morally respectable in themselves but vaguely conceived and identified with whatever remedy seems to be fashionable at a particular time. Thus we find that the focus of academic interest changes continuously in accordance with the preferences of public opinion, centering on disarmament one day, the League of Nations or the United Nations another, world government or regional federation another again.

The interstices between those four cornerstones are filled in with an incoherent collection of fragmentary knowledge ranging the whole gamut of academic disciplines and having only one thing in common: that they transcend the boundaries of a particular nation. The tone is set in the letter offering in 1919 a chair of international politics to the University of Wales and describing its purposes as "the study of those related problems of law and politics, of ethics and economics, which are raised by the project of a League of Nations, and for the encouragement of a truer understanding of civilizations other than our own." Reading the voluminous proceedings of the International Institute of Intellectual Co-operation, which in the interwar years dedicated much of its work to the discussion of international relations as an academic discipline, one cannot but be struck by the amorphousness of the discussion and the vagueness of the results. One speaker seems to have well summarized the consensus of those meetings when he said:

The science of international relations has primarily a descriptive character. It is somewhat in the order of the contemporary history of nations, covering all fields: economics, trade, exchange, movement of production, of goods, of currency, as well as politics and culture.... The factor uniting the problems which form the science of international relations is their international character, that is to say, the tie which is created among all domains of social life when that life transgresses the limits of one single nation and influences the relations among nations.[1]

The same consensus is reflected in the ironic comment, rare in its critical detachment, of another speaker who expressed himself thus:

One can without doubt call international any phenomenon because it belongs to all countries. Anything one wants to then becomes international. From this point of view, seasickness is an international fact; not only does one experience it on all oceans; but there are societies against that disease, and one can conceive of an international league whose purpose it is to do research and compare the methods with which to combat the disease. Yet the question remains outside our field of inquiry until one concerns oneself with the conclusion of an international convention obligating vessels to equip themselves with certain medicines which are recognized as necessary for the protection against seasickness.

I beg your pardon for having chosen that imaginary example. I wanted only to indicate the need for a narrow definition of international studies.[2]

The organization of academic teaching and research in international relations has largely reflected the vagueness and eclecticism of the theoretical conception of international relations as an academic discipline. There has been a general tendency to divide the field of international relations into a number of subdivisions whose common denominator is their transcendence of national boundaries either geographically or functionally. These subdivisions were selected

---

[1] Antoni Deryng, in *Coopération intellectuelle*, No. 68–69 (Paris, 1936), p. 33. Translated from the French by the author.

[2] Paul Mantoux, in *Coopération intellectuelle*, No. 57–58 (Paris, 1935), p. 490. My translation.

from the traditional academic disciplines either *in toto*, such as international law and international economics, or rearranged through the selection of individual courses taken from different disciplines. Thus all the courses which, for instance, had a reference to Russia in their title would be grouped under the area heading of Russia.

It could not have passed unnoticed that the intellectual unity of an academic field, thus established, was bound to be of a most superficial nature and that where there occurred real integration and cross-fertilization among several academic disciplines, credit was due to the creative process occurring in the minds of outstanding students rather than to the academic organization of the field. Attempts have therefore been made to give international relations the unity of an academic discipline by buttressing the eclectic organization of the field with a general or "core" course or number of courses which are supposed to present the distinctive characteristics of international relations as an academic discipline. This core generally covers the fields of international law, international organization, international politics, international economics, international geography, American and European diplomatic history, with such additions as meet the preferences of individual institutions. Most textbooks in the field reflect the eclectic character of this core. For such a core, if it has no focus other than that of the "international" character of international relations, cannot help being as eclectic and disparate as the field itself.

The problems with which area studies must cope are similar, *mutatis mutandis*, to those with which the academic discipline of international relations has dealt thus far without spectacular success. The central problem is again that of focus and method. Area studies, both historically and analytically, form a part of the field of international relations. The type of area study which is prevalent today owes its existence to the practical need to prepare members of the armed forces for service in foreign countries during the Second World War. Those who were expected to take responsible positions in foreign countries had to get acquainted as quickly as possible with the language, geography, culture, and history of those countries. Not only were these training courses successful in their immediate purpose; they also put into sharp focus a foreign area not in terms of the traditional academic disciplines but, as it were, in terms of the characteristics and problems of the area itself upon which the methods of all the relevant disciplines would be brought to bear. The process by which this objective is to be accomplished is generally called "integration"; the effect of this process upon the minds of the student goes by the name of "cross-fertilization."

Practical needs, if on a higher intellectual level, still provide one of the major arguments in favor of area studies; they are also apparrent in the selection of the areas most frequently studied. Russia and Asia vie with each other for the attention of students and the commitment of resources. It is not by accident that it is with those areas that American foreign policy is primarily concerned and that knowledge of them is fragmentary and the supply of experts available for government service falls drastically below demand. Nor is it an accident that the areas around which area studies are centered are generally defined in terms which coincide with the areas of political interest.

Aside from the training of prospective government officials, area studies are frequently motivated by the recognition of America's predominant place in world affairs, which necessitates a knowledge of the world with which the United States must deal as friend or foe. This higher level of practicality entails the desire to learn all the facts about all the regions of the world. Since the regions of prime political importance seem already to be adequately covered, latecomers among university administrations have been known to search for empty spaces on the map which they might cover with an institute for area studies. Underlying this tendency is the conviction that knowledge of unknown areas is useful in itself and that the more knowledge of this kind there is, the better will we be able to understand the world and discharge our responsibilities toward it.

The purely intellectual objectives which are connected with area studies—generally in theory and sometimes also in practice—number three. One stands on the borderline between theory and practice, one is conceived from the perspective of the social sciences, and one from that of the humanities. Area studies are aimed at conveying the experience of cultural relativity which will enable us to do justice to foreign cultures in our intellectual judgment, moral evaluation, and aesthetic appreciation and will at the same time enable us to deal effectively with foreign areas, that is, on their own terms rather than through the imposition of our culture on theirs. Furthermore, area studies are expected to contribute to the development of a universal social science which will arise from the isolation, analysis, and comparison of similar phenomena in different cultures. Finally, they are supposed to provide the intellectual and aesthetic satisfaction that comes from the understanding of any culture in all its manifestations.

These different objectives of area studies are not necessarily incompatible with one another. Yet it is obviously impossible to plan for all of them with equal emphasis at the same time. If they are all achieved at once, some of them are bound to be the by-products of those for the sake of which the studies were undertaken. There can be little doubt that in practice, as concerns the delimitation and selection of areas as well as the development of concrete research projects, practical considerations have generally prevailed over purely intellectual ones.

An interdisciplinary science of areas, in order to be theoretically valid and practically useful, must be mindful of seven principles which apply to all social sciences but which have been insufficiently heeded by area studies in particular and by international relations in general:

First, a non-directive, "objective" social science is, as we have seen, a contradiction in terms. All social sciences, in so far as they deserve the name of science at all, cannot fail to reflect both the social *Standort* and the particular intellectual interest of the observer. A social science which strives for unattainable objectivity can at best collect the raw materials of science in the form of a mass of unrelated or but superficially and irrelevantly related facts. Social science is of necessity science from a certain point of view, and that point of view is determined by the over-all outlook of the scholar as well as by the particular interest with which the scholar approaches the segment of social reality which he intends to investigate.

Second, it follows that the quantity of facts collected is not necessarily proportionate to the quantity of truth discovered. In order to understand a particular area it is not necessary, even if it were possible, to know all the facts about it. Nor is it true that our knowledge of the world around us increases necessarily with the number of areas investigated and the number of facts known about those areas.

Third, regardless of whether the immediate purpose of area research is theoretical or practical, only a theoretical approach to area research can assure useful, practical results, which are not useful merely by accident. A non-theoretical approach to area research can do no more than elaborate upon the common-sense approach which the layman uses when he must solve a practical problem. An area study, to be useful not only for the practical problems raised by yesterday's news but for a whole series of practical problems to be expected in the future, must rest on theoretical foundations which are able to support a whole series of practical solutions by virtue of their theoretical nature.

Fourth, an area for research is not necessarily identical with a geographical, political, or cultural area. The definition of the area and of the problems to be investigated within the area is a function of the intellectual interest of the scholar. Theoretically, then, one can imagine as many definitions of areas and of area problems as there are scholars interested in that particular region. In practice, of course, the number of area definitions and problem selections is limited by the number of legitimate intellectual interests with which members of a certain culture will approach other areas at a particular time. Obviously, scholarly interest in the Soviet Union today is focused in a certain way by the general intellectual interests of our culture in which all potentially interested scholars partake.

Fifth, it follows from this observation that the interdisciplinary approach to area studies that is likely to proceed by way of integration and to result in cross-fertilization must be more than the addition of a number of different disciplines concerned with the same area and the same problems within that area. The unifying element in an interdisciplinary area study is not the common concern with an area or even the common concern with certain problems within that area. It is rather the identity of focus directed toward the same problems within the same area which gives unity to an interdisciplinary area study. In other words, representatives of different disciplines stand, as it were, on the same hill looking in the same direction at the same object and try to discern the same thing about this object, be it its nature, its movements, its influence upon other objects, or the influence to which it is subjected by other objects, and the like. These onlookers differ, however, in the kind of instruments they use in order to discern the common object of their intellectual curiosity. This is integrated area research.

Since the different scholars use different instruments on the same object, they are bound to see different qualities in that object. By communicating to each other what they have seen, the minds of all concerned correlate the results of the researches of the others with their own. This mutual communication is what is called "cross-fertilization."

Sixth, the different disciplines that are brought to bear upon an area problem are not equal with each other. If they were, true and full integration would be impossible. We have said that integrated research means that different disciplines want to know the same thing about the same object. But who determines what that same thing is going to be? Area research may center upon the economic structure of the Siamese village, and then it is economics which determines the common object of intellectual curiosity; and the other disciplines called in for co-operation, such as anthropology, geography, political science, must subordinate their own specific interests to the interests of economics. Or we are interested in the political structure of the Siamese village, and then it is political science which sets the theme and determines the outlook of the auxiliary sciences. In one word, interdisciplinary area research requires more "discipline" than disciplinary research; for it requires the subordination of the specific interests of certain disciplines to the dominant one. Integration requires a hierarchy of interests in which one interest has the function of integrating the others.

Seventh, underlying all area research must be the awareness that all the specific manifestations of a particular culture contain an element of universality, however undiscoverable or unprovable it may be in a particular instance. Area research, then, must take into account an element that transcends the limits of any particular area. More than that, it is this transcendent element which makes area research possible in the first place. For if we could not assume that, while investigating a foreign area, we should find not only things that are strange but also things that are familiar, we would not be able even to try to understand a foreign area and would face it uncomprehendingly.

The element of universality, transcending any particular area and common to all, may be called human nature. However different its specific manifestations at different times and places, it is the same everywhere and at all times. Without assuming its identity in time and space, we could see in other cultures, past or present, nothing more than either a mass of incomprehensible facts or else a distorted image of our own culture. Thus every historian and area specialist must assume implicitly the identity of human nature in time and space in order to be able to understand at all, however loudly he may deny its existence. It is at this point that we come face to face with what is perhaps the most serious shortcoming of contemporary area studies.

Contemporary area studies assume that the key to the understanding of a foreign area lies in the investigation of the specific phenomena that make up that area. If we want to understand China we must study China; if we want to understand France we must study France. Yet might it not be said that, in order to understand China or France or any other area, it is first necessary to understand mankind, of which all areas are but particular manifestations? If I know something about human nature as such, I know something about Chinese and Frenchmen, for I know something about all men. It is true that this something I know about all men is general and liable to lead me astray if I try to explain through it the concreteness of a particular historical situation. Yet without such a conception of human nature, made articulate in a philosophy of man and society, a foreign area can be no more than a mysterious oddity, attractive or repulsive as the case may be, and at best to be understood in terms of one's own culture.

That this is not mere idle speculation everyday experience shows. Why is it that I am able to understand the Homeric heroes or Chaucer's pilgrims without having mastered the area research of ancient Troy and medieval England? Why is it that I am able to comprehend the domestic and foreign policies of contemporary Russia without being an area specialist in the Russian field? Why is it that I have a general understanding of contemporary China while I am virtually ignorant about China as an area? Why is it that the members of the British foreign service have been traditionally trained in the humanities and more particularly in the classics and then sent in succession to the four corners of the earth, showing frequently superb understanding of the areas in which they worked? The answer to these questions has already been given: if you know something about man as such you know something about all men. You know at least the contours of human nature which, when superimposed upon a concrete situation, may get blurred here and there and which always lack specific content and color. It is for area studies to provide an empirical check upon their correctness and that specific content and color. This, then, is a plea not for giving up area studies as at present executed and for reviving an exclusive humanistic approach, but rather for the recognition of the limitations of both. The future of area studies seems to lie in a combination of both approaches, with the emphasis upon one or the other according to the qualifications and preferences of the group undertaking such research.

A word might be said in passing about the lessons to be learned from the traditional classical studies which frequently have been referred to as the prototype of the area studies of our day. This they are not; for what distinguishes traditional classical studies and contemporary area studies is exactly the philosophical orientation in the former and lack of such orientation in the latter. The rationale underlying classical studies was no practical purpose or curiosity for its own sake or a special research interest, but the conviction that in the civilization of ancient Greece and Rome the nature of man in all its manifestations could be detected in its purest form, to be emulated by the generations to come. The error of that approach was its cultural absolutism which took classical civilization to be the norm by which all other civilizations were to be judged. The truth of classical studies, largely ignored by contemporary area studies, is to be found in their conviction, accepted as self-evident, that the study of any civilization requires an underlying conception of the nature of man which gives direction and form to the research to be undertaken.

Since what is wrong with area studies also handicaps international relations as an academic discipline, the remedies in both cases must be, *mutatis mutandis*, the same. We have seen that international relations has concerned itself indiscriminately with everything that is "international," that is, that transcends the boundaries of a particular nation. To establish an academic discipline with the adjective "international" as its focus is obviously no more possible than to center one on the adjective "national." Such attempts, on the national or international level, will lead either to the restoration, by dint of their own logic, of the traditional academic disciplines and consequently to the frustration of interdisciplinary integration, or else to the drowning of all discipline in a chaotic mass of unrelated data which will at best receive from the ever changing whims of public opinion a semblance of order and direction.

The need for a principle of order and a focus, narrower than the mere reference to things international and more germane to the things we want to know when we study international relations, could not have been lost on university administrations which were responsible for the organization of research and teaching in the field of international relations. The idea of the core, composed of what is considered to be the more important academic disciplines bearing upon international relations, has resulted from the recognition of that need. Yet it was a step in the wrong direction. The idea of the core fails to distinguish between the need for multidisciplinary knowledge, without which international relations cannot be understood, and the requirement of a principle of order or focus for intellectual curiosity, without which no academic discipline can exist. The idea of the core accepts the former while rejecting the latter.

An expert in international relations must of course know something about international law, international organization, international politics, international economics, international geography, diplomatic history. If he knows nothing more than that he possesses a collection of fragmentary knowledge taken from different disciplines; if he is able to integrate these fragments of knowledge into a new discipline called "international relations," as has already been pointed out, he does so by virtue of the integrative powers of his mind, not because of the training he has received. International relations, like area studies, must have a focus, and it cannot be law, politics, economics, geography, and what not at the same time. Not all that is important to know about international relations can have the same value as the integrating principle and focus of an academic discipline. International relations as an academic discipline, no less than area studies, requires a hierarchy of intellectual interests, one of which is predominant, providing the principle of integration, while the others are subsidiary, supplying the knowledge necessary for the satisfaction of the predominant interest.

What is the predominant interest of international relations as an academic discipline? Two different answers must be given to that question. The first is identical with the one we gave when we raised the same question with regard to area studies. That is to say, the possible predominant interests are as numerous as are the legitimate objects of intellectual curiosity. It is, then, as legitimate to put economics in the center of international relations as it is to put law or geography there and to subordinate other disciplines to the predominant economic, legal, or geographical interests. In this view as many "sciences" of international relations are possible as there exist predominant interests which correspond to legitimate objects of intellectual curiosity.

This answer to our question opens up three possibilities for academic organization. First, it is possible to deal with international relations, thus conceived, in the different established departments which are selected according to the predominant interest of the scholar and student. International economics would then be dealt with in the department of economics, which would request such aid from other departments as it needed. Second, special academic organizations can be established with one predominant interest as their focus. Thus one can visualize a department or institute of international economics which would group subsidiary disciplines around international economics as its center. Finally, a flexible program can be established, particularly useful for undergraduate instruction, to allow students to select within a department or committee of international relations a number of different combinations, which, however, all center upon one discipline which a student must master. It may be noted in passing that this last arrangement has been put into practice by some of the leading area institutes and schools of international relations.

The other answer to the question of what the predominant interest of international relations must be assumes that among a number of legitimate interests there is in a particular period of history one which demands special attention. The educator must ask himself which among the many foci of international relations is most important for the student's interest to center upon, and the scholar must ask himself which among the many perspectives from which one can investigate international problems is most important from the theoretical and practical point of view. Today most institutions and students have turned to the study of international relations because of their interest in world politics. The primacy of politics over all other interests, in fact as well as in thought, in so far as the relations among nations and areas are concerned, needs only to be mentioned to be recognized. The recognition of this primacy of politics cannot but lead to the suggestion that, among the legitimate predominant interests upon which international relations as an academic discipline might be focused, international politics should take precedent over all others.

For the academic organization of the discipline of international relations this answer can mean two different things. It can mean the establishment of departments, committees, or schools which focus on international politics, subordinating other disciplines to it. Or it can mean that international relations is dealt with in this same way by that traditional academic discipline whose main subject matter is supposed to be the study of politics in all its manifestations, that is, the department of political science. The advisability of this solution will depend upon whether a department of political science actually puts the study of politics in the center of its endeavors or whether—as most of them do—it merely offers a disparate collection of courses whose common denominator is a vague and general relation to the activities of the state.

While it is the task of political education to communicate the truth about matters political, it is an illusion, to which professional educators are prone, to believe that the success of the educational enterprise depends primarily upon the quality and quantity of professional education. This is not necessarily so in any field of education, and it is not even typically so in the field of political education.

It is an obvious fact of experience that professional education is only one—and not necessarily the most important—among several factors that mold the mind and character of those to be educated. Family, society, the experiences of life itself are more persistent and authoritative teachers than the schools. Education, to be effective, must be organically attuned to the totality of educational influences to which the individual is subject.

This organic relationship between professional education and the totality of educational experience is strikingly revealed in the field of political education. The measure of success that education in world affairs has had in the United States in recent years is primarily due not to the quality and quantity of its professional manifestations, but to the experiences that the American people have undergone during and after the Second World War and to their interpretation by political leaders. What is being taught today in American colleges, say, about the balance of power, to be accepted almost as a matter of course, was taught, however sporadically, thirty and twenty years ago, only to be dismissed as absurd. It is not professional education that has made political understanding in this respect possible. Rather it is political experience that has made the truth plausible. Professional education has proved the validity of political experience through historic example and analytic demonstration. Without that experience, however, political education would have remained as ineffective as it was before, while without professional education political experience would have remained unconvincing and inarticulate. What has been said of the three stages through which all truth must pass applies with particular force to political truth. First, people dismiss it as impossible; next, people dismiss it as immoral; finally, people accept it as self-evident.

This achievement of political education is the task of political leadership. Only those whom the people have elected because they have confidence in them, or those in whose judgment the people otherwise confide, can make the truth of political experience explicit. For only they have the authority to gain acceptance for a political truth which is not self-evident from the outset. What they need is the political judgment to see the truth and the political courage to tell it. Thus the most effective political educators in America have been the great presidents, senators, and commentators.

For their authority there is no substitute, either in professional education or elsewhere. Nor is there elsewhere a real substitute for the other two requirements: political judgment and political courage. Professional education may supply them in rather rare instances. But without the authority of the political leader, the voice of professional education does not carry far.

25 *Freedom*

During the Civil War, which was a war for freedom in a truer sense than most of the wars which have been so called, Abraham Lincoln laid bare the essentials of the dilemma which has baffled the philosophic understanding of freedom and which has made it appear that there was always something left to be desired in its political realization. On April 18, 1864, Lincoln gave a brief and unpretentious address to the crowd assembled at the Sanitary Fair in Baltimore.

"The world has never had a good definition of the word liberty," he said,

and the American people, just now, are much in want of one. We all declare for liberty; but in using the same *word* we do not all mean the same *thing*. With some the word liberty may mean for each man to do as he pleases with himself, and the product of his labor; while with others the same word may mean for some men to do as they please with other men, and the product of other men's labor. Here are two, not only different, but incompatible things, called by the same name—liberty. And it follows that each of the things is, by the respective parties, called by two different and incompatible names—liberty and tyranny.

The shepherd drives the wolf from the sheep's throat, for which the sheep thanks the shepherd as a *liberator*, while the wolf denounces him for the same act as the destroyer of liberty, especially as the sheep was a black one. Plainly the sheep and the wolf are not agreed upon a definition of the word liberty; and precisely the same difference prevails today among us human creatures, even in the North, and all professing to love liberty. Hence we behold the processes by which thousands are daily passing from under the yoke of bondage, hailed by some as the advance of liberty, and bewailed by others as the destruction of all liberty.

Political freedom, then, has two different and incompatible meanings according to whether we think of the holder or the subject of political power. Freedom for the holder of political power signifies the opportunity to exercise political domination; freedom for the subject means the absence of such domination. Not only are these two conceptions of freedom mutually exclusive in logic, but they are also incapable of coexisting in fact within any particular sphere of action. One can only be realized at the expense of the other, and the more there is of the one the less there is bound to be of the other.

From the *American Political Science Review*, September, 1957.

The concept of freedom is contradictory as seen from the vantage point of the political master and his subject. It is also ambivalent in that most members of society are not simply one or the other, master or subject, but both at the same time. B is the master of C and also the subject of A, and C, in turn, is the master of D, and so on. Most men play a dual role with regard to political power, subjecting some to it and being subjected to it by others. When they claim freedom for themselves, what do they mean: their freedom to dominate others or their freedom from domination by others? Perhaps they mean one; perhaps they mean the other; perhaps they mean both. This ambivalence makes inevitably for continuous confusion, manifesting itself typically in ideologies which rationalize and justify the freedom to dominate in terms of the freedom from domination.

It follows that universal and absolute freedom is a contradiction in terms. In the political realm, the freedom of one is always paid for by the lack of freedom of somebody else. The political master can have his freedom only at the price of the freedom of those who are subject to him; the latter can be free only if the master is made to sacrifice his freedom as a master.

What applies to the freedom to exercise political power also reveals itself in the profession and application of the political truth which justifies and informs the exercise of political power. He who believes that he has a monopoly of truth in matters political is free to propound his "truth," which to him appears to be all the truth there is, and to act upon it only if the non-believers are not free to oppose their "truths" to his; for freedom for error to corrupt thought and action is incompatible with the freedom of *the* truth to prevail. On the other hand, the freedom of the many to compete in the market place for acceptance of their different truths requires the abrogation of the freedom of the one to impose his conception of truth upon all.

In any given society not everyone can be as free as everyone else. Every society must decide for itself who shall have what freedom. The kind of freedom a particular society is able to realize in a particular period of its history, then, depends upon the kind of political order under which it lives. The nature of that particular order, in turn, is determined by the fundamental values with which that society identifies itself and which it attempts to realize through the medium of politics. In short, the kind of liberty a society enjoys is determined by the kind of political justice it seeks. Liberty cannot be defined without justice, and it can only be realized by a particular political order informed by a particular sense of justice.

All attempts at realizing freedom have throughout history derived from one of two incompatible conceptions of justice: one, minoritarian; the other, equalitarian.

The minoritarian conception of justice assumes that only a minority, determined by birth, supernatural charisma, or qualifications of achievement, is capable of finding and understanding the truth about matters political and of acting successfully on it. The majority, not so endowed, is subject to the will of the minority, both for its own sake and for the sake of the whole commonwealth. From Plato and Aristotle to the modern justifications of aristocratic and totalitarian government, the denial of political freedom for the majority has derived from a conception of political justice which limits to a minority the ability and, hence, the right to enjoy political freedom.

This conception determines not only the over-all character of political society but also the specific nature of its institutions. It claims for these institutions the attribute of freedom, if not in good faith, at least in good logic. To what Lincoln experienced in the controversies over slavery we can add our experiences with totalitarian arguments.

Communist theory claims that the government monopoly of information and control over the mass media of communication means freedom of the press and the only freedom of the press there is, while what we call freedom of the press is but a sham. The absurdity of the argument does not lie in the claim itself but in the underlying assumption of a government monopoly of political truth, from which the claim follows with logical necessity. For since we have all the political truth there is, so the Communist argument runs, how can we allow freedom of expression to those who refuse to recognize the political truth and, hence, are by definition enemies of the truth, that is, criminals, saboteurs, or foreign agents? And what you in the West call freedom of the press is nothing but the license to sow confusion by propounding error as truth.

The decisive argument against the Communist idea of freedom

and against all political philosophies reserving political freedom to a minority, however defined, must come to terms with the philosophic assumption from which those political philosophies derive. That argument is two-pronged.

It opposes the monistic assumption of a monopoly of political truth vested in a minority with the pluralistic assumption that, while no member of society has a monopoly of political truth or can even be certain what action political truth requires in a given situation, all members of society as rational beings have access to a measure of political truth, however dimly seen. From this equalitarian political ontology and anthropology evolves an equalitarian conception of political justice which postulates equality of political rights and equal treatment of equal situations. Since no conception of political truth, or any political philosophy and program of action derived from it, is necessarily and demonstrably superior to any other, they must all have an equal chance to prevail, but none of them must be given an a priori chance to prevail once and for all. The mechanism through which this equal chance materializes is the periodical majority vote, which decides the issue temporarily either through popular elections or through the enactments of legislative assemblies.

Equalitarianism, then, attacks the minoritarian conception of political justice on the grounds that no minority can be politically so wise in comparison with the majority as to possess a monopoly of political wisdom. No minority can be trusted with absolute power on the assumption that it possesses absolute wisdom. When Cromwell appeals to the representatives of the Church of Scotland, "I beseech you, in the bowels of Christ, to think it possible you may be mistaken," he expresses in the religious sphere the equalitarian mood.

Yet equalitarianism not only refuses to accept the explicit minoritarian claim of infallibility but also rejects its implicit claim to incorruptibility. Here is the other prong of the equalitarian argument. The minoritarian claim to a monopoly of political freedom derives from the overt assumption of a monopoly of political wisdom and of necessity implies a monopoly of political goodness. For the minoritarian claim can be defended by the minority and accepted by the majority only on the assumption that the minority will not abuse its absolute power. The nature of man, as it reveals itself to introspection and through the evidence of history, militates against the correctness of that assumption. The inevitable corruptiveness of power is the political manifestation of the inevitability of sin. Equalitarianism attempts to limit the opportunities for the abuse of power by limiting the political freedom of the holders of power. Western constitutionalism is an elaborate device to subject the political freedom of the holders of political power to institutional limitations and legal controls.

The decisive safeguard, however, against the abuse of political power is the institution of periodical popular elections. The very fact that political power is subject to recall and can be taken for granted only for limited periods of time limits the duration of political power with mechanical sharpness. But it also limits the freedom with which political power can be used as long as it lasts. For since the holders of political power have a natural tendency to keep themselves in power by having themselves re-elected, they must use their political freedom in view of winning the ever impending elections. Thus the preferences of the electorate, real or fancied, are an ever present limitation on the freedom of the holders of political power to use that power as they would like to. The absolute ruler is free to govern as he sees fit, subject only to the limits of physical nature. The freedom of constitutional government is hemmed in not only by institutional devices and, in so far as it is democratic, by the mechanical limits of popular elections but also by the political dynamics of the democratic process. It is this contrast between the complete freedom of the absolute ruler to exercise the authority of government at his discretion and the limits within which constitutional government must operate which Theodore Roosevelt had in mind when he expressed the wish to be for twenty-four hours President, Congress, and Supreme Court at the same time.

The democratic processes, in order to be able to delimit the freedom of the rulers to govern, must themselves be free to bring the will of the majority to bear upon the personnel and policies of the government. The freedom of the governed to control and replace the rulers and the limitations upon the rulers' freedom to govern are the two sides of the same coin, the latter being a function of the former. Without that freedom of the governed, democracy loses its substance; for it no longer provides the people with the freedom of choosing rulers and, through them, policies. A democracy that loses that freedom can survive only as the periodical plebiscitarian approval of the personnel and the policies of the government. This is the totalitarian type of democracy.

One would misunderstand the nature of democracy and of totalitarianism as well as their relationship were one to suggest that totalitarian elections are necessarily and always a sham and that they never reflect the true will of the people. They may well reflect that will, as elections in Nazi Germany and Fascist Italy undoubtedly did, expressing a consensus between the popular will and the government. Here lies the decisive difference between traditional autocracy and modern totalitarianism. Autocracy imposes its will upon an indifferent or hostile people; totalitarianism aims at, and may succeed in, governing with the consent of the governed.

However, what sets totalitarianism apart from genuine democracy is the manner in which the government attains the consent of the governed. Totalitarianism creates that consent through the monopolistic manipulation of the mass media of communication; the consent of the people does not set limits for the government but is a function of its unlimited freedom. In a genuine democracy, on the other hand, the consent of the governed is the temporary result of the interplay of antagonistic forces, competing freely with each other for popular support. The government enters this contest essentially as an equal; whatever advantages it may have by virtue of prestige, influence, and information do not substantially affect the principle of free competition. Thus a genuinely democratic government can never be certain whether it will survive the next election to be replaced by another which, in turn, must subject its personnel and policies to the popular judgment in still another election to come.

Genuine democracy must forever guard against the temptation to transform itself into an imperfect type and then to degenerate into totalitarianism. While democracy requires that the will of the people limit the freedom of the government, it also requires that the freedom of the popular will be limited. A popular will not so limited becomes the tyranny of the majority which destroys the freedom of political competition and thus uses the powers of the government to prevent a new majority from forming and to intrench itself permanently in the seat of power. There is only a small step from the destruction of the freedom of competition, that is, imperfect democracy, to the destruction of competition itself, that is, totalitarianism.

The freedom of political competition essential to democracy can be impaired in two different ways. The people are being deprived of their freedom of choosing among alternative policies by choosing among different candidates for office if the different candidates for office are not identified with different policies but compete for power as an end in itself, not as a means for a particular policy. The people may still be able to choose in terms of the personal qualities of the candidates, such as competence and trustworthiness; their choice has no meaning for the substance of the policies to be pursued. The people, if they do not vote for the person of a candidate as such, will then vote out of habit or not at all, and in the measure in which this happens democratic elections will have lost their ability to protect the freedom of the people by limiting the freedom of action of the government.

The other—and more insidious—threat to freedom of political competition stems from the tendency of all majorities to act upon the assumption that they are more—at best—than temporary approximations to political truth, that is, the repositories of all the political truth there is. They tend to think and act, as long as they last as majorities, as though their will provided the ultimate standard of thought and action and as though there were no higher law to limit their freedom. The majority, as long as it lasts, tends to become the absolute master, the tyrant, of the body politic, stifling in that body the vital spirit of questioning and initiative and evoking instead the submissiveness of conformity. Yet since there is no higher standard for thought and action than the will of the majority, in theory at least each successive majority may produce a new tyrant with a political truth of its own. One political orthodoxy may be succeeded by another, calling forth a new conformity, and the very relativism which is the philosophic mainspring of the supremacy of the majority will produce not only the tyranny of the majority but also a succession of tyrannies, all justified by the will of the majority.

While this is possible in theory, it is, however, not likely to occur for any length of time in practice. For the majority, by making itself the supreme arbiter of matters political, must at least implicitly deny to the minority the right to make itself the majority of tomorrow. Since the majority of today tends to claim a monopoly of political truth, it must also tend to claim a monopoly of political power, freezing the existing distribution of power. In one word, the majority of today tends to transform itself into a permanent majority and, by the same token, to reduce the minority of today to a permanent one.

This development not only reduces the minority to a permanent one but also deprives it of its democratic reason to exist. That reason is its ability, equal in principle to that of the majority, to have access to political truth and act upon it; hence its claim to compete freely for becoming the majority tomorrow. The assumption that the majority has a monopoly of political truth destroys the minority's political function and gives the respect for its existence an anachronistic quality. Since its continuing existence implicitly challenges the majority's monopolistic claims, is a living reminder of alternative rulers and policies, and may, by virtue of these attributes, become a political nuisance to the majority, the minority cannot for long survive the destruction of its philosophic justification and political function. With its destruction, democracy itself comes to an end. The unlimited freedom, that is, the tyranny, of the rulers corresponds to the unlimited lack of freedom of the ruled.

Thus decadent democracy goes through three stages before it transforms itself into its opposite: totalitarian tyranny. It starts out by emptying itself of part of its substance: it destroys the freedom of choosing policies by choosing men. Then it substitutes for the spirit of free political competition, which derives from a pluralistic conception of political truth, the monistic assumption that only the majority possesses that truth. Then it subjects the minority to restrictions which put it at a decisive disadvantage in the competition for intellectual influence and political power, thus transforming the majority into a permanent one, existing side by side with a permanent minority. The process of degeneration is consummated with the majority becoming the sole legitimate political organization, which combines the claim to a monopoly of political truth with a monopoly of political power.

Against these tendencies toward self-destruction, inherent in the dynamics of democracy, the institutions and the spirit of liberalism stand guard. Liberalism has erected two kinds of safeguards: one in the realm of philosophic principle, the other in the sphere of political action.

Liberalism holds certain truths to be self-evident, which no majority has the right to abrogate and from which, in turn, the legitimacy of majority rule derives. These truths, however formulated in a particular historic epoch, can be subsumed under the proposition that the individual—his integrity, happiness, and self-development—is the ultimate point of reference for the political order and, as such, owes nothing to any secular order or human institution.

It is on this absolute and transcendent foundation that the philosophy of genuine democracy rests, and it is within this immutable framework that the processes of genuine democracy take place. The pluralism of these processes is subordinated to, and oriented toward, those absolute and transcendent truths. It is this subordination and orientation that distinguishes the pluralism of the genuine type of democracy from the relativism of its corrupted types. For in the latter the will of the majority is the ultimate point of reference of the political order and the ultimate test of what is politically true. Whatever group gains the support of the majority for its point of view gains thereby also the attributes of political truth, and the content of political truth changes with every change in the majority. Out of this relativism which makes political truth a function of political power develops, as we have seen, first the tyranny, and then the totalitarianism, of the majority, unlimited as it is by an absolute, transcendent conception of political truth. Thus the relativism of majority rule, denying the existence of absolute, transcendent truth independent of the majority will, tends toward the immanent absolutism of a tyrannical or totalitarian majority, while the pluralism of genuine democracy assumes as its corollary the existence of such truth limiting the will of the majority.

As a matter of philosophic principle, the political order is oriented toward the individual; the political order is the means to the individual's end. Yet as a matter of political fact, as we have seen, it is the very earmark of politics that men use other men as means to their ends. That this cannot be otherwise is one of the paradoxes of the politics of liberalism; for political reality disavows, and does so continuously and drastically, the postulates of liberal philosophy. Liberalism believes in the truth of man's freedom, but it finds man everywhere a slave. Thus it adds another paradox—more shocking than the first for being the result of liberalism's own efforts—by creating political institutions which limit the freedom of some in order to preserve the freedom of others. Constitutional guaranties of civil rights and their legislative and judicial implementation are the liberal defenses of freedom of political competition. While the will of the majority decides how these guaranties are to be implemented, the existence of the guaranties themselves is not subject to that will. Quite to the contrary, these guaranties set the conditions under which the will of the majority is to be formed and exercised. They establish the framework of democratic legitimacy for the rule of the majority.

Yet the very need for these safeguards limiting the freedom of the majority points up the dilemma that liberalism faces. If the majority could be trusted with its power, the liberal safeguards would be unnecessary. Since it cannot be so trusted, its freedom must be curtailed for the very sake of freedom. The dilemma which concerned Lincoln in the individual relations between the wolf and the lamb reappears in the collective relations between majority and minority. It manifests itself here typically in the concrete terms of the antinomy between individual rights and some collective good, such as general welfare, administrative efficiency, national security. The liberal concern for individual rights may stand in the way of the maximization of such a collective good, and the greater the need for the full realization of a collective good appears to be, the greater is the temptation to sacrifice individual rights for its sake. Is individual freedom more important than national security, without which there will be no freedom at all? What benefits does a man draw from the Bill of Rights if, in the absence of measures of general welfare, it guarantees him the right to sleep under bridges and sell apples in the street?

This dilemma lies outside the purview of liberal philosophy, which inclined to identify itself in the nineteenth century with the individualistic prong of the dilemma and shifted in the twentieth to the other, collectivist, one. Thus the philosophy of liberalism can provide no intellectual tools with which to master this dilemma. The decline, in our time, of liberalism as theory and practice is the result.

Liberalism conceived of the problem of freedom in terms of a simple juxtaposition between society and the state. It saw the sole threat to individual freedom in the state, conceived either as an aristocratic minority or a democratic majority. Liberal policy, then, had a twofold aim: to erect a wall between the government and the people, behind which the citizens would be secure, and to confine the government behind that wall in as narrow a space as possible. The smaller the sphere of the state, the larger the sphere of individual freedom was bound to be.

However, the aspirations for power, and the struggle for power resulting from them, could not be so neatly confined; for these aspirations are not the exclusive property of any group but common to all men, ruler and ruled, oligarchs and democrats. The autonomous forces of society, left to themselves, engendered new accumulations of power as dangerous to the freedom of the individual as the power of the government had ever been. And while liberalism had assumed that the weakness of the government assured the freedom of the individual, it now became obvious that it also assured the unhindered growth of private power, destructive of individual freedom. Against these concentrations of private power, which derived primarily from economic controls, the state was called back from the corner in which it had been confined to do battle. The state, which had just been relegated to the inconspicuous and relatively innocuous role of a night watchman by a society fearful of its power, was now restored to power as the protector of individual rights. Thus the modern state bears a Janus head: one face that of a monster lusting for power over the individual, the other with the benevolent mien of the individual's defender against his fellows' infringements of his freedom.

The struggle for freedom in the modern state has thus become a three-cornered fight, and the old dilemma reappears in a new and intricate configuration. A new feudalism of giant concentrations of economic power in the form of corporations and labor unions vies with the old tyranny of the state for limiting the freedom of the individual, subjecting ever new spheres of formerly free individual action to ever more stringent restrictions. That new feudalism calls into being the "new despotism" of the administrative state, which, for the sake of individual freedom, superimposes its restrictions upon those of the concentrations of economic power. From the latter's vantage point, this is but the old tyranny in modern garb. Yet the mass of individual citizens welcomes the administrative state as the champion of freedom.

It is the measure of the inadequacy of the simple juxtapositions of nineteenth-century liberal philosophy and the measure of the inner contradictions and ambivalences of freedom as it actually operates in the modern state that both sides have a point. The administrative state can become a new despot to some and a new liberator to others, as majority rule can be both the nearest approximation to freedom in a mass society and a many-headed and, hence, unassailable destroyer of freedom.

26 *The New Despotism and the New Feudalism*

This precarious state of freedom in the modern age is most obvious in the economic sphere. It is the result of two factors: the denial of freedom from within the economic sphere itself through the accumulation of uncontrolled power in the hands of economic organizations, such as corporations and labor unions, and the denial of freedom in consequence of the intervention of the state in the economic sphere, in good measure in order to restore its freedom threatened from within. Thus the economic sphere has lost whatever autonomy it has had in the past: it is subject to political control as it, in turn, tries to control political decisions. We are in the presence of the revival of a truly political economy, and the major economic problems are political in nature.

This interconnectedness of the political and economic spheres is not peculiar to our age. Even in the heyday of nineteenth-century liberalism, the strict separation of the two spheres was in the nature of a political ideal rather than the reflection of observable reality. The monetary, tax, and tariff policies of the government had then, as they have now, a direct bearing upon the economic life—and so had the outlawry of the association of working men as criminal conspiracy. Yet the ideal of strict separation served the political purpose of protecting the economic forces from political control without impeding their influence in the political sphere.

What is peculiar to our age is not the interconnectedness of politics and economics but its positive philosophic justification and its all-persuasiveness. The state is no longer looked upon solely as the umpire who sees to it that the rules of the game are observed and who intervenes actively only if, as in the case of the railroads, the rules of the game favor one player to excess and thereby threaten to disrupt the game itself. In our age, aside from still being the umpire, the state has also become the most powerful player, who, in order to make sure of the outcome, in good measure rewrites the rules of the game as he goes along. No longer does the government or soci-

Committee for Economic Development, *Problems of United States Economic Development*, 1958.

ety at large rely exclusively upon the mechanisms of the market to insure that the game keeps going. Both deem it the continuing duty of the government to see to it that it does.

In the United States, the state pursues three main purposes in the economic sphere: observance of the rules of the game, maintenance of economic stability, and national defense.

The rules of the game are oriented toward the pluralistic objectives of American society. Thus they seek to prevent any sector of the economy from gaining absolute power vis-à-vis other sectors of the economy, competitors, or the individuals as such, by controlling and limiting its power. Regulatory commissions, legislation controlling and limiting the strong and supporting the weak, tariff and monetary policies serve this purpose.

While the state started to assume responsibility for the rules of the game in the last decades of the nineteenth century, it made itself responsible for economic stability in the 1930's. Economic stability, in this context, signifies the mitigation, if not the elimination in certain sectors, of the business cycle. Its main positive characteristics, as conceived by the government of the United States, are stability of employment, stability of the value of the dollar, and stability of agricultural prices. A plethora of legislative and administrative devices serves this purpose.

Since the end of the Second World War, technological research and industrial production have become to an ever increasing extent the backbone of military defense. The regular annual expenditure by the government of close to forty billion dollars on national defense, its decrease or increase from year to year, its shift from one sector of the economy to another, all exert a sometimes drastic influence upon the economic life of the nation. They have made the government the most important single customer for the products of the national economy. In addition, many tax and monetary policies and price and wage policies are determined by considerations of national defense.

With the government thus exerting an enormous controlling, limiting, and stimulating influence upon the economic life, the ability to influence the economic decisions of the government becomes an indispensable element in the competition for economic advantage. Economic competition manifests itself inevitably in competition for political influence. This political influence is exerted through two channels: control of, and pressure upon, government personnel.

The most effective political influence is exerted by the direct control of government personnel. The economic organization which has its representatives elected to the legislature or appointed to the relevant administrative and executive positions exerts its political influence as far as the political influence of its representatives reaches. In so far as the representatives of these economic organizations cannot decide the issue by themselves, the competition for political influence and, through it, economic advantage will be fought out within the collective bodies of the government by the representatives of different economic interests. While this relationship of direct control is typical in Europe, it is by no means unknown in the United States. State legislatures have been controlled by mining companies, public utilities, and railroads, and many individual members of Congress represent specific economic interests. Independent administrative agencies have come under the sway of the economic forces which they were intended to control. The large-scale interchange of top personnel between business and the executive branch of the government cannot help but influence, however subtly and intangibly, decisions of the government relevant to the economic sphere.

However, in the United States the most important political influence is exerted through the influence of pressure groups. The decision of the government agent—legislator, independent administrator, member of the executive branch—is here not a foregone conclusion by virtue of the economic control to which he is subject. His decision is in doubt, for he is still open to divergent economic pressures. The competition for determining the decisions of the government takes place not among the government agents themselves but between the government agent, on the one hand, and several economic pressure groups, on the other. Only after this competition among several pressure groups has been settled one way or another will the government agents compete with each other, provided the issue is still in doubt.

The political struggle, ostensibly fought for victory in periodical elections by political parties, reveals itself in good measure as a contest of economic forces for the control of government action. In consequence, the decision of the government, and more particularly of legislatures, ostensibly rendered "on the merits of the case," tends to reflect the weight of economic influence and, at worst, to give political sanction to decisions taken elsewhere. Legislators and administrators tend to transform themselves into ambassadors of economic forces, defending and promoting the interests of their mandatories in dealing with each other on behalf of them. The result is a new feudalism which, like that of the Middle Ages, diminishes the authority of the civil government and threatens it with extinction by parceling out its several functions among economic organizations to be appropriated and used as private property. And just like the feudalism of the Middle Ages, these new concentrations of private power tend to command the primary loyalties of the individual citizens who owe them their livelihood and security. In the end, the constitutionally established government tends to become, in the words of Chief Justice Marshall, a "solemn mockery," glossing over the loss of political vitality with the performance of political rituals.

If giant concentrations of economic power, in the form of corporations and labor unions, were thus to become laws unto themselves, deciding with finality the matters vital to them and using the government only for the purpose of ratifying these decisions, they would not only have drained the lifeblood from the body politic but also have destroyed the vital energies of the economic system. For the vitality of the American economic system has resided in its ability to renew itself on new technological opportunities, unfettered by the interests identified with an obsolescent technology. Seen from the vantage point of the individual enterprise, this is what we call freedom of competition. This freedom of competition has been a function of the rules of the economic game, as formulated and enforced by the state.

Yet the new feudalism, if it is not controlled and restrained, must inevitably tend to abrogate these rules of the game in order to assure the survival of the economic giants which, in turn, tend to take over the functions of the state. The consummation of this development, possible but not inevitable, would be a state of affairs in which for those giants the rule of life would not be freedom of competition, which might jeopardize their survival, but freedom from competition in order to secure their survival. The dynamics of the capitalistic system, especially in the United States, continually destroying and creating as life itself, would then give way to a gigantic system of vested interests in which the established giants would use the state to make themselves secure from competitive displacement, only to die the slow death of attrition.

It is the measure of the quandary which modern society faces in this problem that the most obvious cure raises issues as grave as the disease. That cure is a state strong enough to hold its own against the concentrations of private power. In good measure, such a state already exists. It is the state whose importance for the economic life of the nation we have discussed above. In so far as this state is able to act as an independent political force, controlling, restraining, and redirecting economic activities, it is indeed the strong state, capable of keeping the concentrations of private power in check. Yet such a state, by being strong enough for this task, cannot fail to be also strong enough to control, restrain, and redirect the economic activities of everybody. In other words, as the liberal tradition correctly assumes, a strong government, whatever else it may be able to accomplish, threatens the liberties of the individual, especially in the economic sphere.

Thus modern society is faced with a real dilemma: a government which is too weak to threaten the freedom of the individual is also too weak to hold its own against the new feudalism; and a government which is strong enough to keep the new feudalism in check in order to protect the freedom of the many is also strong enough to destroy the freedom of all. What, then, must it be: the new feudalism of private power or the new despotism of the public power? The problem thus posed cannot be solved by any simple formula which endeavors to restore the juxtaposition of society and state from which the philosophy of nineteenth-century liberalism evolved. Rather, the solution of the problem must start from the terms in which it poses itself in the twentieth century.

A fruitful approach to this dilemma is suggested by the principles underlying the constitutional devices, institutional arrangements, and political dynamics of the American system of government by which *The Federalist* successfully tried to combine, in the simple relations between society as a whole and the state, a strong government with a pluralistic society. The same combination, in the complex conditions of the contemporary, three-cornered contest, must rest upon the same foundation of the intricate interplay of multiple systems of checks and balances. These systems, if they work perfectly, limit on all levels of social interaction, private and governmental, the freedom of all for the sake of everybody's freedom. They do so in two different respects, through their internal structure and through their relations with each other. The classic analysis of these two functions is provided by Number 51 of *The Federalist*. As concerns the function of the internal structure of a particular system:

This policy of supplying by opposite and rival interests, the defect of better motives, might be traced through the whole system of human affairs, private as well as public. We see it particularly displayed in all the subordinate distributions of power; where the constant aim is, to divide and arrange the several offices in such a manner, as that each may be a check on the other; that the private interest of every individual, may be a sentinel over the public rights.

And for the relations among different systems:

It is of great importance in a republic, not only to guard the society against the oppression of its rulers; but to guard one part of the society against the injustice of the other part. Different interests necessarily exist in different classes of citizens. If a majority be united by a common interest, the rights of the minority will be insecure. There are but two methods of providing against this evil: The one by creating a will in the community independent of the majority, that is, of the society itself; the other by comprehending in the society so many separate descriptions of citizens, as will render an unjust combination of a majority of the whole very improbable, if not impracticable. . . . The second method will be exemplified in the federal republic of the United States. Whilst all authority in it will be derived from, and dependent on the society, the society itself will be broken into so many parts, interests, and classes of citizens, that the rights of individuals, or of the minority, will be in little danger from interested combinations of the majority. In a free government, the security of civil rights must be the same as that for religious rights. It consists in the one case in the multiplicity of interests, and in the other, in the multiplicity of sects. The degree of security in both cases will depend on the number of interests and sects. . . .

In the end, the freedom—economic and political—of the individual in the modern state is not the result of one specific constitutional device or institutional arrangement, although such a device or arrangement may well make freedom more secure. Freedom rather reposes upon the social order as a whole, the distribution of concrete values to which society is committed. It is not enough for society to recognize the inalienable right of the lambs to life, liberty, and the pursuit of happiness and to have on the statute books provisions against the activities of wolves detrimental to the lambs. The freedom of both the wolves and the lambs will in the end depend upon the values which society attributes, not in the abstract but in the carving out of concrete spheres of action, to the freedom of the wolves and the lambs. What is their due? How far can they be allowed to go? Since neither, and especially not the wolves, can be allowed to go as far as they would like and would be able to go, society must intervene, deciding the value it wishes to put upon their respective capabilities and interests and assigning to each a sphere and mode of action. That intervention may take the form of an explicit decision settling the issue once and for all. More likely and more typically, it will result from the interplay of the totality of social forces, opposing, checking, supporting each other, as the case may be, in ever changing configurations, forming an intricate web of horizontal and vertical connections. It is upon that complex and shifting ground that freedom rests in the modern world.

27 *The Decline of Democratic Government*

Democratic government in the United States has declined by virtue of three basic misunderstandings: misunderstanding of the nature of politics, of the purposes of government in a revolutionary age, of the function of government in a democracy. These misunderstandings have corrupted our political judgment and perverted our actions with a subtle yet well-nigh irresistible logic.

Under the impact of nineteenth-century liberalism, Anglo-American society has been strongly influenced, and at times dominated, by a philosophy that denies politics a prominent and honorable place in the order of things. Politics as a conflict of interests decided through a struggle for power is here regarded as an ephemeral phenomenon, a kind of residue of either aristocratic or capitalistic society, for the time being to be pushed into a corner fenced off by constitutional safeguards and ultimately to be abolished altogether. The corollary to this conception of politics as a passing and inferior phase of social life is the erection of the private virtues as the sole standard by which the qualities of both private and public action and the qualifications of both private and public persons are to be judged. This philosophy necessarily destroys the tension between the private and the public sphere, between man per se and man as a citizen, which has been a perennial theme of Western political thought. For that philosophy, Aristotle's question of whether the virtue of a good man is identical with the virtue of a good citizen is meaningless, for here the virtue of a good man and of a good citizen are by definition identical.

This philosophy is translated into the folklore of American politics as the conviction that the main qualification for a political career is personal honesty. A politician may be wrongheaded in judgment, weak in decision, unsuccessful in action. "But don't you see how sincere he is," people will say. "He is at least an honest man." "He means well." The man in the street transfers the values he cherishes in his private life to the political stage and judges the actors by the

From the *New Republic*, December 16, 1957.

same standards he applies to himself and his fellows in their private spheres.

The values of the Eisenhower administration, both in verbal expression and in the character of its most prominent members, conform to these popular standards, and its virtually unshakable popularity owes much to this identity of political standards. The President, with characteristic frankness and consistency, has time and again measured his public actions by the yardstick of private values and expressed his conviction that since he did not find these public actions wanting, when tested by the values of private life, they had passed the political test as well. He summarized his philosophy in his news conference of August 8, 1957, in these terms: "I, as you know, never employ threats. I never try to hold up clubs of any kind, I just say, 'this is what I believe to be best for the United States,' and I try to convince people by the logic of my position. If that is wrong politically, well then I suppose you will just have to say I am wrong, but that is my method, and that is what I try to do." The public sphere appears here as a mere extension of private life, devoid of those conflicts of interests to be settled by contests of power, by employing threats and holding up clubs—methods which are traditionally associated with politics—and subject to the same rational rules of conduct which are supposed to make the private sphere orderly, peaceful, and harmonious.

When President Eisenhower was asked at his news conference of July 31, 1957, about the circumstances under which Mr. Gluck was appointed ambassador to Ceylon, he replied with indignation, ". . . in the first place, if anybody is ever recommended to me on the basis of any contribution he has ever made to any political party, that man will never be considered. I never heard it mentioned to me as a consideration, and I don't take it very kindly as suggesting I would be influenced by such things." Here again, the issue was seen in strictly private terms. The issue for the President hinged exclusively upon his personal knowledge of a campaign contribution, and since he had no such knowledge there was no issue. In this philosophy there is no room for the recognition of an objective conflict of interests to which the state of the conscience of any single individual may well be irrelevant.

It stands to reason that Mr. George Humphrey's philosophy of government is simply the application of the alleged principles of private business to the political sphere. And for Mr. Charles Wilson national defense was a problem of production and organization within the limits of sound finance as defined by Mr. Humphrey, completely divorced from any meaningful political context. Of the many of Mr. Wilson's statements showing a complete unawareness of this political context, none is perhaps more revealing than the one he made June 29, 1956, as a witness before the Senate Armed Services Subcommittee on Air Power:

> The Russian people, the ones that I have known through the years, have a great many qualities that Americans have. As a matter of fact, basically I think that the Russian people rather like Americans.
>
> It is too bad that we have got this conflict of ideology and that they have got a dictatorship on their hands. They wanted to get rid of the czar and they got something that is just as bad or worse, temporarily.
>
> It is very interesting. One of the troubles, they think of our type of free competitive society as the same thing they had under the czars, and of course it is not that thing at all. They have replaced in what you might call their point of hate.
>
> It is too bad they did away with the czars completely. If some of them were still left in one piece of Russia so they could hate the czars, they would not be hating our people so much.

A defense establishment which is intended to cope with an international situation thus conceived in terms of private emotions is likely to be different from one that seeks to defend the national interest in a world of conflicting interests and competing power.

Not only have the dominant members of the Eisenhower administration expressed themselves and acted in terms of a philosophy alien to politics, but many of them have also been selected in view of their excellence as private citizens, on the assumption that the qualities which go into the making of a good man and, more particularly, of a good businessman, go also into the making of a good statesman. Indeed, many selections have been excellent within the limits of the standards applied. Certainly, men like Eisenhower, Benson, Humphrey, and Wilson are superior in private excellence to many of their respective predecessors. But these excellent men have in all innocence done greater damage to the political life and the political interests of the nation than many of their less worthy predecessors; for they have brought to their public offices nothing but personal excellence, no understanding of political life, let alone ability to cope with the processes of politics.

The experience of this contrast between personal excellence and, more particularly, success in business and failure in politics is by no means limited to this administration nor even to this country. Look at the records of Baldwin and Chamberlain in Great Britain, of Cuno and Bruning in Germany! They were all good men, and how ruinous their governments were for their respective nations! In this country it is particularly illuminating to compare the virtually uniform political failure of the production geniuses with the spectacular political successes of the investment bankers. Why is it that the Knudsens and the Wilsons have failed and the Forrestals, the Lovetts, the Nitzes have succeeded? Because the excellence of the investment banker is, as it were, akin to that of the statesman while the excellence of the production genius is alien to it.

A good man who becomes an actor on the political scene without knowing anything about the rules of politics is like a good man who goes into business without knowing anything about it or who drives a car while being ignorant of driving. Yet while it is well recognized that society must protect itself against the latter, it feels no need for protection against the former. The virtuous political dilettante has for it even a well-nigh irresistible fascination. It is as though society were anxious to atone for the sacrifices of private virtue which the political sphere demands and to take out insurance against the moral risks of political action by identifying itself with political leaders who sacrifice the public good on the altar of their private virtue.

Society has learned to take the bad men in its stride and even to protect itself against those who know the rules of the political game only too well and use them to the detriment of society. Society will have to learn, if it wants to survive, that it needs protection also from the good men who are too good even to take note of the rules of the political game. And it must reconcile itself to the uncomfortable paradox that bad men who put their knowledge of those rules at the service of society are to be preferred to good men whose ignorance and moral selfishness put the very survival of society in jeopardy. In short, it must learn what Henry Taylor taught more than a century ago when he wrote in the *Statesman:* "It sometimes happens that he who would not hurt a fly will hurt a nation."

From the soil of this misunderstanding of what politics is all about two intellectual and political weeds have grown: utopian liberalism and utopian conservatism. This country has had its share of the former; it is now being taught the political lessons of the latter. Conservatism has become a modish word, which has been made to provide respectable cover for a multitude of intellectual and political sins. As the nihilists of the Left call themselves democratic, while disavowing with their very being the tenets of democracy, so the nihilists of the Right, who used in the twenties and thirties to proclaim their adherence to "true" democracy, now try to monopolize conservatism for themselves. Yet the iron test of the authenticity of a professed conservatism is its attitude to civil liberties, that is, restraints upon the powers of government on behalf of the individual. By this test, Hegel, at the beginning of the nineteenth century, could deny Haller the right to call himself conservative, and the German resistance to Naziism was as authentically conservative as McCarthyism, in spite of its claim, was not.

Authentic conservatism concerns either the philosophy and methods of politics or its purposes. The confusion between these two types is likely to do more damage to American politics in the long run than political nihilism, pretending to be conservative, has done. Conservatism of philosophy and method is indeed part and parcel of the American political tradition. *The Federalist* is its greatest literary monument, Alexander Hamilton is its greatest theoretician, John Quincy Adams and Abraham Lincoln are in different ways its greatest practitioners, and Woodrow Wilson is its greatest antithesis in theory and practice. That conservatism holds—as we saw the realist philosophy of international relations to hold—that the world, imperfect as it is from the rational point of view, is the result of forces inherent in human nature. To improve the world one must work with those forces, not against them. This being inherently a world of opposing interests and of conflict among them, moral principles can never be fully realized, but must at best be approximated through the ever temporary balancing of interests and the ever precarious settlement of conflicts. Conservatism, then, sees in a system of checks and balances a universal principle for all pluralist societies. It appeals to historic precedent rather than abstract principles and aims at the realization of the lesser evil rather than of the absolute good.

A good case can be made, it seems to me, in favor of the proposition that this conservatism of philosophy and method presents political reality as it ought to be presented and deals with it as it ought to be dealt with. I have argued that case more than a decade ago in *Scientific Man vs. Power Politics*, when, I might say in passing, it was not fashionable but most unwelcome to argue the conservative side of political philosophy and method.

On the other hand, the conservative view of the purposes of politics endows the status quo with a special dignity and seeks to maintain and improve it. This conservatism lives in the best of all possible worlds, and, if it can conceive of a different world at all, it finds that world not in the future but in the past, a golden age to be restored. That conservatism has its natural political environment in Europe; it has no place in the American tradition of politics. Europe, in contrast to America, has known classes, determined by heredity or otherwise sharply and permanently defined in composition and social status, which have had a stake in defending the present status quo or restoring an actual or fictitious status quo of the past. But for the defense or restoration of what status quo could the American conservative fight? For private power, state's rights, the abolition of the income tax, exclusive male suffrage, nullification, slavery, or perhaps the British monarchy? The absurdity of this rhetorical question illustrates the absurdity of the conservative position in terms of purposes within the context of American politics.

The great issues of American politics concern neither the preservation of the present nor the restoration of the past but the creation, without reference to either, of the future. American politics does not defend the past and present against the future but one kind of future against another kind of future. While in philosophy and method conservatism is the most potent single influence in American politics, the purposes of our politics from the very beginning were unique and revolutionary, not only in the narrow political sense, but also in the more general terms of being oblivious to tradition. They have so remained throughout, only temporarily disfigured by periods which were dominated by a conservatism of purpose and, hence, in the context of American politics spelled stagnation. In other words, the point of reference of American politics has never been the present, and only in a historically inconsequential way has it been the past.

In the past, the United States could afford such intermittent periods of stagnation; for the world around it, relatively speaking, stagnated too, and, more importantly, when the United States moved forward again it set the pace for the world and in many respects left it behind. Today it is the world that moves ahead and the United States which is being left behind. All around us the world is in violent transformation. The political revolution has destroyed the state system, which for half a millennium had provided the political girders for Western civilization, and has brought to the fore two superpowers threatening each other and the world with destruction. At the same time it has dissolved the old order of empire into the anarchy of scores of feeble sovereignties, whose uncontrolled frictions may well provide the sparks for the ultimate conflagration. A succession of technological revolutions has virtually eliminated the elements of time and space from this globe and, by adding to the numerical superiority of the so-called backward peoples the social and military potential of modern industry, challenges Western civilization from still another quarter. Finally, the moral revolution of totalitarianism denies the basic values upon which Western civilization has been built and, as bolshevism, attracts millions of people throughout the world to its militant support.

How have we reacted to this triple challenge? We have reacted by a conservatism of stagnation, which is not only oblivious of the revolutionary dynamism of our national tradition but also self-defeating as a weapon in the international contest in which the nation is engaged. We have projected the antirevolutionary and conservative image of our national task and destiny onto the international scene, seeing in the political, technological, and moral ferment of the world but the evil effects of the cunning obstinacy of the doomed leaders of bolshevism. Unwilling to adjust the comforting and flattering picture we have formed of our national life to the national realities, we proceeded to adjust the international realities to that picture. Thus we are looking at a world which appears in need of improvement, adjustment, and reform, but not of radical, unheard-of change. The world cries out for transformations commensurate in their revolutionary novelty with the revolutions that threaten it; it cries out for political imagination, audacity, and the risky experiment. What we are offering it is nothing but stagnation, masquerading in the garb of a utopian conservatism. Faced with the moral and virtually certain danger that soon a great number of nations will have atomic weapons, we continue the old game of disarmament negotiations, which is no longer good even for purposes of propaganda. Our policies in Europe and Asia are stagnant; we continue unwilling either to change the status quo of which we disapprove or to recognize it. Latin America has become our forgotten back yard which we think we can take for granted. Asia, the Middle East, and Africa are for us primarily opportunities for the conclusion of military alliances and the expenditure of money for ill-defined purposes.

In consequence of underestimating the revolutionary tradition of our society and the revolutionary nature of the world with which we must come to terms, we have made underestimation of the Soviet Union a national habit of mind. All the evidence of the Russian capabilities, from General Guillaume's "Soviet Arms and Soviet Power," published in 1949 by the *Infantry Journal,* to our own intelligence reports, made no impression upon the official mind; for if it had, we would have had to discard a whole philosophy which we are mistaking for our way of life.

This retreat into a stagnant conservatism has been accompanied by a retreat from government itself. This is not surprising, since the conservative commitment to holding the line, to keeping things as they are in domestic and foreign policy, required less of an expenditure of energy and of ideas than dynamic and imaginative policies do. That this atrophy of government, inevitably resulting from the atrophy of its purposes, has been acutely aggravated by the lapse of leadership at the top is too obvious to require elaboration; but it might be pointed out that that lapse of leadership was, in turn, made possible and perhaps even temporarily tolerable by that decline in purpose.

When we speak of the atrophy of government, we obviously do not refer to the quantity of institutions and their activities which go by the name of government; for there has been no decline of those. What we have in mind is a subtle quality which is vital to a democratic government: its quality as a teacher and leader. In its absence the government cannot govern in a truly democratic fashion, that is, with the freely given consent of the governed. Modern government—democratic or non-democratic—is not merely the formulation and execution of policies. It is also and necessarily the creation of public consent for the policies formulated and to be executed. In non-democratic societies this consent is created by the government's monopolistic manipulation of the mass media of communication. Democracies create it ideally through the free interplay of plural opinions and interests, out of which the consensus of the majority emerges.

From these different conceptions of consent two different attitudes toward secrecy and truth follow. A non-democratic government can afford to conceal and misrepresent because there are no autonomous social forces which could expose it to scrutiny and propose factual and political alternatives. Under certain conditions, it will even be compelled to conceal and misrepresent because it will have no other way to create consent for its policy. A democratic government, while having an obvious advantage in the contest of opinion, ideally at least cannot afford nor does it need to conceal and misrepresent. A responsible parliament and an alert public opinion force it to lay its cards on the table or at the very least check the government version of the truth against their own. And the assumption of democratic pluralism that neither the government nor anybody else has a monopoly of truth in matters political minimizes the temptation for the government to impose its version upon society by concealment and misrepresentation.

It is the measure of the decline of democratic government in the United States that the administration has—not on occasion but consistently—concealed from the people and its elected representatives information in both the most vital and the most trivial matters and misrepresented the truth known to it. While the administration was aware of the deterioration of American power in comparison with that of the Soviet Union, its most eminent spokesmen assured us time and again that our strength vis-à-vis the Soviet Union was unimpaired if not actually increased. What we were told officially was, at best, but a hint of the actual state of affairs. To speak of very trivial things in passing, the American people have not been allowed to learn what present the king of Saudi Arabia gave the President on his visit in January, 1957.

Secrecy and misrepresentation, not as occasional aberrations but as a system of government, are in our case intimately related to the atrophy of government of which we have spoken earlier. The administration, philosophically and politically committed to stagnation and, hence, unable to lead and educate, has put appearance in the place of substance. Thus it is not by accident that the techniques of advertising have so thoroughly replaced the processes of free discussion in the relations between government and people. Judged by the standards of advertising, the result has been gratifying. The administration has been popular, and the people have been happy. Yet judged by the standards of the American destiny and survival, the result has been disquieting in the extreme. We witness the beginning of a crisis of confidence in the administration, and we must beware lest it turn into a crisis of confidence in the democratic processes themselves.

Before men want to be governed well, they want to be governed. Before they choose between good and bad policies, they want some policies to choose from. Regardless of the course they want the ship of state to take, they want to be sure that a strong hand is at the helm. The great revolutions of the modern age from the French Revolution of 1789 through the two Russian revolutions of 1917 and the Fascist revolutions in Italy and Germany to the Chinese revolution of the forties—were carried forward by men who were dismayed, not only at being governed badly, but also and more importantly at not being governed enough. These revolutions owed their success to the determination and ability of their leaders to seize power, to hold it, and to use it to govern perhaps badly but firmly. The modern masses have risen in despair and fury not against some particular policy but against the weakness of government, reflected in spectacular failures.

Of the failures which are likely to be in store for us, we have had only a first and very partial glimpse. We are but at the beginning of our disillusions, frustrations, and tribulations. Faced with this crisis in its fortunes, as taxing as any it has experienced, the nation certainly stands in need of sound policies. What it needs more is a government that restores its sense of mission, that galvanizes its latent energies by giving them a purpose, that, in short, acts as the guardian of the nation's past and an earnest of its future. The nation has no such government now.

28 *The Difference between the Politician and the Statesman*

On September 30, 1961, the eminent French sociologist and columnist Raymond Aron addressed in *Le Figaro* an open letter to President Kennedy. This letter is both a moving and an important document. It is moving because it is written with sympathy and concern by a man who calls himself an "enthusiastic partisan" of the President. It is important because it raises one of the two great issues of government which will ruin the Kennedy administration and perhaps the country if the President does not meet them successfully.

Mr. Aron addresses himself to the President's method of deciding issues of foreign policy, taking as his point of departure the invasion of Cuba. The President had to choose between two incompatible courses of action suggested by his advisers: to stage an invasion of Cuba, with American military support if necessary, or not to intervene. In order to avoid the risks which either course of action, consistently pursued, would have entailed, the President tried to steer a middle course, intervening just a little bit but not enough to assure success. Confronted with a choice between black and white, he chose gray. "Yet in foreign policy," as Mr. Aron puts it, "the half-measure, the compromise ordinarily combines the disadvantages of the two possible policies."

Mr. Aron was, and perhaps still is, afraid that the President might repeat this error in his approach to the Berlin crisis. For here again, the President must choose between counsels recommending diametrically opposed courses of action: a negotiated settlement which is bound to weaken the American position in West Berlin and West Germany, and an intransigent position which, at the very least for the immediate future, increases the risks of war. As Mr. Aron sees it, the President has chosen, at least in theory, the "hard" line; yet in his style, method, and language he has committed himself also to

From *Commentary*, January, 1962.

"flexibility." In consequence, nobody can be sure whether Mr. Kennedy intends to play the role of Churchill or of Chamberlain. Nobody—the American people, our allies, probably Mr. Khrushchev himself—knows what our negotiating position is, assuming we have one.

Mr. Aron did not answer the question, What has been the matter with Kennedy? For the indecisiveness of the Cuban intervention and the apparent indecisiveness of Mr. Kennedy's approach to the Berlin crisis are but the manifestations of a deficiency which is deeply embedded in the President's experience and personality. To put it bluntly: the President does not know what the statesman's task is while he knows only too well the politician's, and thus he endeavors to accomplish the task of the statesman with the tools of the politician. Yet the virtues of the politician can easily become vices when they are brought to bear upon the statesman's task.

The decision of the statesman has three distinctive qualities. It is a commitment to action. It is a commitment to a particular action that precludes all other courses of action. It is a decision taken in the face of the unknown and the unknowable.

The politician can take words for deeds, and in so far as his words seek to influence people to vote for him or for his measures, his words actually are deeds. He can make promises without keeping them, and his promises may not even be expected to be kept. He can run on a platform every two or four years and take his stand on quite different ground in between. He can equivocate between different courses of action and bridge the chasm between incompatible positions by embracing them both. He can vote one way today and another way tomorrow, and if he can't make up his mind he can abstain from voting. He can try to reduce to a minimum the uncertainties of the future by preparing his action with proper attention to the facts, organization, and planning.

The statesman, especially in his dealings with other nations, can hardly ever afford to do any of these things. His rhetoric is verbalized action, an explanation of deeds done or a foretaste of deeds to come. What still moves us today in the recorded oratory of a Churchill or a Roosevelt is not so much the literary quality per se as the organic connection between the words and the deeds. Listening to those words, we remember the deeds, and we are moved.

The statesman must commit himself to a particular course of action to the exclusion of all others. He must cross the Rubicon or refrain from crossing it, but he cannot have it both ways. If he goes forward he takes certain risks, and if he stands still he takes other risks. There is no riskless middle ground. Nor can he, recoiling before the risks of one course of action, retrace his steps and try some other tack that promises risks different and fewer. He has crossed the Rubicon and cannot undo that crossing.

The statesman must cross the Rubicon not knowing how deep and turbulent the river is, or what he will find on the other side. He must commit himself to a particular course of action in ignorance of its consequences, and he must be capable of acting decisively in spite of that ignorance. He must be capable of staking the fate of the nation upon a hunch. He must face the impenetrable darkness of the future and still not flinch from walking into it, drawing the nation behind him. Rather than seeking unattainable knowledge, he must reconcile himself to ineluctable ignorance. His is the leading part in a tragedy, and he must act the part.

The extent to which the style of the Kennedy administration resembles the politician's rather than the statesman's is revealed not only by the policies it has pursued but more particularly by its mode of operation. Rhetoric has been divorced from action and has tended to be taken as a substitute for it. To give only one glaring example: in July, 1961, the President committed himself in a speech to a program of fallout shelters, without having a policy. Ever since, his aides have searched for a sensible policy which would not be too much at variance with the President's words.

Yet the President cannot help making decisions and the method by which he has reached them suffers from three defects. It is informal to the point of being haphazard. It tends to lose sight of the distinction between what is paramount and must be decided by the President and nobody else, and what is only important enough to be decided not by the President but by somebody else. It has the quality of indecisiveness because it vainly seeks a certainty that is beyond its reach.

The President has wisely discarded the committee system through which his predecessor governed, shielding him from direct contact with the issues in all their complexity. Yet he has unwisely replaced this system with another one that threatens to overwhelm him with an unmanageable variety of issues and opinions.

The President exposes himself deliberately to advice from a great variety of sources. These sources are generally individuals who talk to him at length in his office or over the phone. This system, or lack of it, has the virtue of making the President familiar with all shades of opinion. It has the double vice of making it either too easy or too difficult for the President to make up his mind.

The President may well be swayed by a particular counsel, especially when it is presented with that subjective self-assurance which some mistake for objective certainty, and with that facility for expression and brilliance of formulation which some mistake for depth. Impressed with these qualities of form, he may commit himself to the substance of the advice without being fully aware of the meaning of that commitment. It has been reported on good authority that the President was once presented with advice concerning a policy of capital importance. He approved of that policy orally and asked the individual concerned to instruct the head of the department within whose jurisdiction the policy fell to put it into operation. This was done. When the head of the department some weeks later informed the President of the progress made in the execution of that policy, the President questioned its wisdom, obviously unaware that he had approved it and ordered its execution.

This casualness of policy formation puts two obstacles in the way of the President's making up his mind. Counseling on the spur of the moment with all kinds of people on all kinds of issues, the President is overwhelmed with issues to be decided and advice to be weighed. In consequence, his mind can no longer perceive clearly the vital distinction between the paramount issues he alone must settle and the merely important ones which others may decide with or without his guidance. The President has lost sight of the natural relationship that exists between the gravity of the issue to be decided and the level of authority that decides it. Thus some paramount issues will remain unattended or will be ineffectually attended to by officials lacking sufficient authority, while the President will concern himself with secondary issues which could be more effectively disposed of by subordinate authorities.

Thus it has come about after many months of deliberations by a great many officials that if we have a policy with regard to Berlin, neither the American public nor the allies of the United States are aware of it. The *New York Times* could publish on October 21 a report from Washington under the headline "Allied Confusion Stalls Thompson. Envoy Unable To Get Clear Stand for Moscow Talks." The result is not only confusion but also the surrender of the determination of policy to some other nation whose interests may or may not coincide with those of the United States. Thus, again, the *Times* reported on October 26 as the official position of the United States government that "the United States could not get nearer to war than the West Germans wish to go, and could not get nearer to peace than they were willing to go." Many months of contingency planning did not prepare the administration for the possibility that the East Germans might effectively seal East Berlin off by erecting a wall. Hence the administration did not know what to do when the wall went up in August, and did nothing. The show of force through which the United States in October tried to maintain the status quo concerning the access of its military personnel to East Berlin ended in confused retreat.

The President must overcome the indecisiveness of his own mind. That mind seeks the predictability to which it is accustomed from domestic politics. There meticulous ascertainment of the facts, precise planning, and elaborate organization years in advance paid off in victory in the primaries, the nominating convention, and the elections. To be sure, a margin of uncertainty remained, but it was small compared with what one knew and had prepared and planned for.

The President searches for the same kind of certainty in his conduct of foreign policy. He tries to eliminate the darkness of ignorance and to probe the depth of uncertainty that even so astute a mind as his cannot penetrate by drawing upon the most luminous and knowledgeable minds he can find and by making use of all the information he can lay his hands on. Yet those dark spots on the landscape of foreign policy are impervious to the most brilliant intelligence, and factual knowledge cannot prevail against them. Thus the President's mind hestitates and his will falters when he seeks the answer to the riddle in more advice and additional information.

The frantic search for advice and information performs for the

President the same function the employment of astrologers and soothsayers did for the princes of old: to create the illusion of certainty where there can be no certainty. The more facile the President's advisers are with words and the more self-assured they are in their convictions, the more adept they are in encouraging the President in such futile search. They cannot give him what he needs more than anything else: the tragic sense of politics. In view of that need, he could do worse than add to the ranks of his advisers a philosopher who would remind him at regular intervals that there are more questions than answers and that the great decisions must be made in ignorance and without certitude. The President, who knows his history, will remember that the princes of old reserved a place among their advisers for a man who called their attention to the limits of their power, beyond which there is the realm of Providence and fate.

This particular issue of government stems from the President's personal approach to his task. He has created it; it has never before in American history appeared in this way and is not likely to appear so again. The other issue of government with which the President must come to terms is inherent in the American system. All Presidents have had to face it and live with it one way or another. It concerns the relationship between domestic politics and foreign policy.

The issue is posed by the incompatibility between the rational requirements of sound foreign policy and the emotional preferences of a democratically controlled public opinion. As Tocqueville put it with special reference to the United States:

Foreign politics demand scarcely any of those qualities which are peculiar to a democracy; they require, on the contrary, the perfect use of almost all those in which it is deficient. Democracy is favorable to the increase of the internal resources of a state; it diffuses wealth and comfort, promotes public spirit, and fortifies the respect for law in all classes of society: all these are advantages which have only an indirect influence over the relations which one people bears to another. But a democracy can only with great difficulty regulate the details of an important undertaking, persevere in a fixed design, and work out its execution in spite of serious obstacles. It cannot combine its measures with secrecy or await their consequences with patience. . . .

The propensity that induces democracies to obey impulse rather than prudence, and to abandon mature design for the gratification of momentary passion, was clearly seen in America on the breaking-out of the French Revolution.

Confronted with this dilemma between the requirements of good foreign policy and the preferences of public opinion, the President has the supreme task of reconciling the two. The dilemma is tragic because it can never be fully resolved. If the President pursues uncompromisingly the foreign policy he regards to be sound, as Woodrow Wilson did, he risks losing the support of opinion at home; if he accommodates himself to that opinion at the expense of what sound foreign policy requires, he risks jeopardizing the interests of the country. In order to be able to avoid these two extremes—the one fatal to his personal power, the other fatal to the power of the nation—the President must perform the two historic functions of his office: to be the educator of the people and the conciliator of seemingly irreconcilable positions. The President must impress upon the people the requirements of sound foreign policy by telling them the facts of political life and what they require of the nation, and then strike a compromise which leaves the essence of sound foreign policy intact while assuaging domestic opinion.

It is the measure of Mr. Kennedy's failure that he has performed neither task. Instead, substituting again the politician's concerns for the statesman's, he has tended to subordinate the requirements of sound foreign policy to the requirement of winning elections in 1962 and 1964. The President knows that our Far Eastern policy has so far failed to result in catastrophe, not because it is sound, but because of circumstances which are likely to change drastically to our disadvantage. The President knows that what we call our German policy has been for fifteen years a verbal commitment to the illusion of unification rather than a policy. But the great mass of the American people know nothing of this because the President has not dared to tell them. To return to the fallout shelters: not only did the President commit himself in words to a fallout shelter program before he had a policy, but he now has committed himself to a policy in order to be able to compete in 1962 and 1964 with Mr. Rockefeller who has developed such a policy for the state of New York.

Yet the President, with his sense and knowledge of history, and groping as he does for his proper place in the scheme of things, cannot but feel where his true mission lies.

It is for the President to reassert his historic role as both the initiator of policy and the awakener of public opinion. It is true that only a strong, wise, and shrewd President can marshal to the support of wise policies the strength and wisdom latent in that slumbering giant—American public opinion. Yet while it is true that great men have rarely been elected President of the United States, it is upon that greatness, which is the greatness of its people personified, that the United States, from Washington to Franklin D. Roosevelt, has had to rely in the conduct of its foreign affairs. It is upon that greatness that Western Civilization must rely for its survival.

These words I addressed in 1949 to Mr. Truman and in 1956 to Mr. Eisenhower. It is the measure of the chronic weakness of Presidential leadership that the same words must be addressed to Mr. Kennedy in 1962, at the beginning of his second year in office.

29   *The Perils of Empiricism*

American foreign policy has in the past suffered from one great defect: the belief that a great power could somehow escape the risks and liabilities of foreign policy. It could escape them, so it was believed, by isolating itself from the affairs of the world; if it abstained from pursuing active foreign policies vis-à-vis other nations, other nations would reciprocate. It could escape them by promoting a grand design, such as the League of Nations or the United Nations, which, in the words of Franklin D. Roosevelt, would make an end to "the system of unilateral action and exclusive alliances and spheres of influence and balances of power and all the other expedients which have been tried for centuries—and have failed." In other words, the United Nations was expected to put an end to foreign policy itself.

We have learned the lesson that a great nation cannot escape the risks and liabilities of foreign policy by an act of will, by choosing either to retreat from it or to soar above it. Yet we are now in the process of going to the other extreme of surrendering piecemeal to the facts of foreign policy, of allowing ourselves to be sucked in by them, of thinking and acting as though there were nothing else to foreign policy but this particular set of empirical facts, say, of Laos or of Cuba. The President has admonished us to "look at things as they are," and we are following his advice. We are doing so in the name of pragmatism or empiricism. Nowadays these terms are used in Washington with pride. They are used as though to be pragmatic and empirical when faced with a political problem were to be rational almost by definition. The idea which the pragmatists and empiricists want to convey is that they are not escapists or utopians, that they have no illusions about the facts as they are or any grand design to change them; they have the courage to look the facts in the face and the willingness and ability to deal with each issue on its own terms. There is more truth in their claim than merit.

Reprinted from *Commentary*, July 1962, by permission. © 1962 by the American Jewish Committee.

This new attitude toward foreign policy stems from an intellectual disposition which is deeply imbedded in the American folklore of social action. That disposition shuns elaborate philosophies and consistent theories. It bows to the facts which are supposed to "tell their own story" and "not to lie." It accepts only one test of the truth of a proposition: that it works. It expects the problems of the social world to yield to a series of piecemeal empirical attacks, unencumbered by preconceived notions and comprehensive planning. If a social problem proves obstinate, it must be made to yield to a new empirical attack, armed with more facts more thoroughly understood.

That theory of social action, however persuasive it may sound to our ears by virtue of apparently being supported by our domestic experience, is in truth without foundation. Facts have no social meaning in themselves. It is the significance we attribute to certain facts of our sensual experience, in terms of our hopes and fears, our memories, intentions, and expectations, that create them as social facts. The social world itself, then, is but an artifact of man's mind as the reflection of his thoughts and the creation of his actions.

Every social act and even our awareness of empirical data as social facts presuppose a theory of society, however unacknowledged, inchoate, and fragmentary. It is not given to us to choose between a social philosophy and the unconditional surrender to the facts as they are. Rather we must choose between a philosophy consistent within itself and founded on experience which can serve as a guide to understanding and as an instrument for successful action and an implicit and untested philosophy which is likely to blur understanding and mislead action. The Wilsonian grand design and the isolationist abstentionism missed the mark in their refusal, each in its own way, to take account of the concrete facts of the political situation. On the other hand, the empiricism of our day has been led astray by its absorption with the empirical facts of particular situations. It endeavors to manipulate the trees without concern for the shape of the forest.

Thus we deal with Laos on its own terms; we deal with Vietnam on its own terms; we deal with Taiwan on its own terms. And we deal with Communist China on its own terms. We want to neutralize Laos, even at the risk of partial or complete Communist domination. We want to win the civil war in Vietnam, even at the risk of a full military commitment on the part of the United States. We want to maintain the status quo in the Taiwan Strait, even at the risk of war with China. And we want to contain Chinese power within its present territorial limits by committing ourselves to the defense of military positions scattered around the periphery of the Chinese empire, regardless of the over-all distribution of military power between China and the rest of the world.

It stands to reason that all these issues are interconnected and that their connection is of a hierarchical nature. The paramount issue in the long run is, at the very least, the peripheral containment of China. Will it be possible, once China has become a first-rate military power and, more particularly, has acquired an arsenal of nuclear weapons, to contain her within the present territorial limits of her power by continuing to commit American military strength to the support of her neighbors? Or will it then be necessary to strike at the heart of Chinese power? If this should prove to be necessary, as I indeed think it will, if—in other words—our present policy of peripheral containment will either fail or involve us sooner or later in an all-out war with China, it is necessary to ask now, not five or ten years from now when circumstances may have given the answer and left us no choice, two fundamental questions. What is the place of the containment of China within the hierarchy of the objectives of our foreign policy, especially in view of our relations with the Soviet Union? And if we assign to the containment of China a very high priority, worth the risk of all-out war, must we wait to fight this inevitable war until China feels strong enough to wage it on terms favorable to herself, or ought we not to fight it under conditions most favorable to ourselves?

These are indeed unpleasant and, hence, unpopular questions, and since they became acute twelve years ago in consequence of the Korean War, no administration has seen fit to raise them in public. Nor has any administration come to terms with them in its secret councils, if the actions of successive administrations give any clue to the over-all conception which has guided our Asian policies. The conduct of the Korean War and the origin of the Laotian crisis are cases in point. The Chinese intervention in the Korean War, being the inevitable response to our advance to the Yalu, could take us by surprise only because it did not occur to us to consider our Korean policy as an integral part of our relations with China. Similarly, our decision to replace the neutralist government of Laos with a pro-Western one, initiated in 1960 against the advice of our ambassador and the CIA agents in Laos, was predicated upon the unrealistic assumption that such an attempt to change the status quo in favor of the West might not call forth from the Communist neighbors of Laos a counterattempt, more likely to succeed in view of the distribution of local power.

As our policies in southeast Asia and the Taiwan Strait must be seen in the context of our over-all relations with China, so our policies in the different nations of southeast Asia are organically interconnected. Since we are committed to the military defense of South Vietnam, a commitment the soundness of which we have questioned before in this magazine, we cannot reconcile ourselves at the same time to the communization at the very least of those parts of Laos adjacent to South Vietnam; for our Vietnamese policy, questionable on other grounds, is doomed to failure by our Laotian policy, which provides the Vietnamese guerillas with a supply and staging area beyond the borders of Vietnam. The Greek and Algerian civil wars have shown in different ways that guerillas who have the support of the indigenous population cannot be defeated as long as they can be supplied from, and retreat to, areas beyond the borders of their native country.

What ails our Asian policy is its fragmentation, its compartmentalization into localized policies, independent of each other and of an over-all conception which would assign them their proper place in the total scheme of things. That ailment, however, is not limited to our Asian policy. It impedes our policies elsewhere and cramps the very style of our foreign policy. Berlin and the relations with our allies are cases in point.

It is of course obvious that the issue of the Western presence in West Berlin can no more be dealt with as a local problem, isolated from the over-all relations between the United States and the Soviet Union, than the issue of Taiwan can be considered in isolation from the over-all relations between the United States and China. Khrushchev raised the issue of Berlin in order to compel the United States to settle on Soviet terms the issue which has been the main concern of Soviet foreign policy since the end of the Second World War and to which the very origin of the Cold War can be traced: American recognition of the Western boundaries of the Soviet empire.

With regard to this issue, the United States can pursue one of two alternative policies. It can continue its present policy of non-recognition of the territorial status quo in Central Europe as a matter of law while implicitly recognizing it as a matter of political and military fact unchangeable short of a victorious war. This policy becomes increasingly precarious in the measure that the independent military power of West Germany provides support for a revisionist policy. The other alternative is for the United States to embark upon a new policy of at least edging toward the reconciliation of its explicit policy of non-recognition with its implicit recognition of the territorial status quo in Central Europe.

Our Berlin policy, soundly conceived, is a symbolic manifestation of our over-all German policy and of our over-all relations with the Soviet Union. Yet unwilling to face the realities of the German problem, we have either endeavored to manipulate the modalities of our presence in West Berlin in isolation from the underlying issue, or we have refused to engage in serious negotiations altogether, committing ourselves to the defense of the status quo in Berlin without really intending thereby to put into question the territorial status quo in Central Europe. In consequence, the Berlin issue is at the moment of this writing as unresolved as it was when it was first raised by Khrushchev in November, 1958, and our position with regard to the territorial status quo in Central Europe remains as ambiguous as it was fifteen years ago.

This refusal to face the problem of Germany and this tendency to approach the Berlin issue as though it could be dealt with in isolation from the German problem are in good measure due to the virtual veto with which the government of West Germany has been able to paralyze our Germany policy and stalemate our relations with the Soviet Union. Our relations with West Germany are duplicated by our relations with many of our other allies, such as Taiwan, South Vietnam, Laos, Pakistan, and France. These allies either prevent us from pursuing the policies we would want to pursue, or else pursue policies of their own which run counter to our own interests and expressed preferences.

Chiang Kai-shek has put some of his best troops on the offshore islands, and we have been unable to persuade him to desist from that folly. President Diem of South Vietnam bears the major share of responsibility for the disintegration of his regime and the advances of communism, but we have been unable to make him change his policies. The policies which Pakistan has been pursuing toward its neighbors Afghanistan and India have been a continuous irritant to our relations with those nations, but we have been unable to do anything about them. The policies of France have only by coincidence any relation to our interests and preferences. The policies Great Britain and Canada are pursuing vis-à-vis China run counter to our own and reduce their effectiveness; and so do the policies which Canada and some of our European allies pursue toward Cuba. While in theory we intend to give economic aid only to nations which through political and economic reform have at least cleared the path toward economic development, in practice the threat of a recipient government to collapse or go Communist is generally sufficient for us to give without conditions.

We have tried to manipulate the acute manifestations of this endemic crisis of our alliances in two different ways: through ineffective persuasion or through enthusiastic surrender. We have made the subversion of our interests and the frustration of our policies by our allies tolerable by investing the interests and policies of our allies with a peculiar virtue. We have done so through the intermediary of our emotional commitment to certain rulers, such as Chiang Kai-shek, Diem, Ayub, and Franco. Some of our ambassadors have been emotionally committed to one or the other of these rulers to such a scandalous extent that, instead of representing the interests and policies of the United States abroad, they have become the advocates in Washington of the policies and interests of the governments to which they are accredited.

These are not isolated acts of misguided individuals, to be remedied by changes in personnel. We are here in the presence of a persistent pattern which points to a flaw in our conception of what an alliance is about, of the interconnectedness of different alliances, such as our alliances with France and Germany, and, more particularly, of the relationship which ought to exist between members of an alliance differing drastically in power. Again the remedy must be sought not in the manipulation of individual situations but in a revision of the modes of thought and action which we have brought to bear upon our alliances throughout the world. We could do worse than remember the warning of Washington's Farewell Address:

> So likewise, a passionate attachment of one Nation for another produces a variety of evils. Sympathy for the favorite Nation, facilitating the illusion of an imaginary common interest, in cases where no real common interest exists, and infusing into one the enmities of the other, betrays the former into a participation in the quarrels and wars of the latter, without adequate inducement or justification. . . . And it gives to ambitious, corrupted, or deluded citizens (who devote themselves to the favorite nation) facility to betray, or sacrifice the interests of their own country, without odium, sometimes even with popularity; gilding with the appearances of a virtuous sense of obligations, a commendable deference for public opinion, or a laudable zeal for public good, the base or foolish compliances of ambition, corruption, or infatuation.

Our foreign policy, then, has disintegrated into a series of disconnected operations whose extent is determined by the facts of a particular crisis situation, be it Vietnam, Laos, or Berlin. It must be said in passing that this disintegration of substantive foreign policy is paralleled and accentuated by the *modus operandi* of the administration, which tends—through what I have called elsewhere "the equalitarian diffusion of the advisory function"—to dissolve the powers of decision-making into a series of disconnected acts. Trying to escape the Scylla of utopianism and isolationism, we have come dangerously close to being swallowed by the Charybdis of empiricism. There is no middle ground; in order to escape this dilemma, we must—like Odysseus—sail ahead and leave it behind.

Historic experience indicates what our course must be. The statesmen who became masters of events and thus conscious creators of history—the Washingtons and the Lincolns, the Richelieus and the Bismarcks—had one quality in common: they combined a conscious general conception of foreign policy, of its direction and aim, with the ability to manipulate concrete circumstances in the light of that conception. In other words, Wilson had a point which Kennedy has missed, and vice versa. Without the grand design, informed by historic experience and seeking what is politically possible, foreign policy is blind; it moves without knowing where it is going. Without respect for facts and the ability to change them, foreign policy is lame; it cannot move in the direction the grand design has charted.

30 *International Relations*

In its broadest, literal meaning, this term denotes relations among the autonomous political units which today we call nations, or among individual members of such units. On the collective level, such relations can be political, military, economic, or cultural; they can comprise all kinds of individual relations involving members of different nations. Yet when we refer to international relations as a distinct object of human action and understanding, we have in mind only those collective or individual relations, transcending national boundaries, which affect the position of nations vis-à-vis each other. International relations in this sense are political relations; they comprise, aside from the foreign policy of nations, all collective and individual relations which impinge upon the political position of a nation vis-à-vis other nations. The term in this sense is a synonym for foreign relations, as used, for instance, in the name "senate foreign relations committee."

International relations are as old as political history itself and have shown throughout the ages constant patterns of relationships and policies, whether entered into by hereditary monarchs or elective governments, cities or nation-states, continental empires or tiny principalities, ecclesiastic or secular rulers. The consistency of patterns beneath the variety of historic manifestations makes both historic understanding and theoretical analysis of international relations possible. Thus we are able to understand the international relations of the Greek city-states that Thucydides describes, the international relations of the Indian states of the fourth century B.C. from which Kautilya derived his philosophy, the international relations of the ancient near east of which the Old Testament tells, as well as those of the more recent past. By detecting in the international relations of different cultures and historic periods identical responses to identical challenges, we are able to develop certain theoretical propositions about international relations that are true regardless of time and place.

From *Encyclopaedia Britannica*, 1961.

The dynamic force that molds international relations is to be found in the aspirations for power of autonomous political units. These aspirations crystallize into three basic patterns: to keep one's power, to increase one's power, to demonstrate one's power. From these patterns three basic types of policy ensue: the policy of the status quo, the policy of imperialism, and the policy of prestige. The clash of these policies—A trying to maintain the status quo, B trying to change it at the expense of A—leads to an unending struggle for power which characterizes all international relations. This struggle for power can be fought by two different means: diplomacy and military force. It leads of necessity to the balance of power through which nation A, either alone or in conjunction with other nations similarly threatened, tries to maintain itself against B. When A and B pursue their goals in conjunction with other nations, they embark upon a policy of alliances. When nations carry on the struggle for power by military means, they engage in an armaments race or war. When they try to justify and rationalize their positions in the power struggle by reference to universal values, typically of a moral nature, they develop political ideologies. Continuous peaceful contacts among them lead to the development of an institutionalized diplomacy.

Throughout the better part of history, several systems of international relations have existed side by side with little or no contact among them. Until the discovery of America, the American system or systems of international relations led a completely separate existence. The Chinese and Indian systems had only intermittent contacts with others.

Three different patterns of international relations can be distinguished according to the distribution of power within them: multiple, bipolar, and imperial systems. The multiple system is distinguished by a number of units of approximately equal strength which combine and oppose each other in ever changing alignments. Its main characteristics are flexibility, uncertainty as to the relative strength and future policies of its members, and the propensity for limited, inconclusive wars. The European state system, from the end of the Thirty Years' War in 1648 to the beginning of the First World War in 1914, with the exception of the period of the Napoleonic Wars, conformed to this pattern.

The bipolar system is characterized by the predominance of two major powers of approximately equal strength, around which the other members are grouped in different degrees of closeness. This system is rigid and stable as long as the approximately equal distribution of power between its two predominant members persists. Any marked shift in that distribution threatens the system with destruction. The structure of international relations that emerged from the Second World War exemplifies this pattern.

The imperial system consists of one predominant nation with a number of subordinate members clustered around it. The stability of such a system is great, and conflicts within it tend to be marginal. Its existence can be threatened by the disintegration of the predominant member, the rise of a number of subordinate members to a position from which they can challenge the predominant one, or by a challenge from outside the system. The system of international relations dominated by the Roman empire is the classic example of this pattern.

International relations have undergone in modern times four drastic changes: the formerly separate systems of international relations have merged into one world-wide system; the predominance of the European system has disappeared; the possibility and actuality of total war have come to dominate the international scene; the feasibility of universal destruction with nuclear weapons has radically altered the function of force as a means to the ends of foreign policy. While the first three changes do not affect the dynamics and structure of international relations as we have known them since the beginning of history, the last constitutes a veritable revolution, the only one in recorded history, in the structure of international relations.

The expansion of the European state system into the other continents by means of colonial empires, starting early in the sixteenth century, broke down the barriers which had separated the different systems of international relations. They were all brought into contact with, and into some form of dependence upon, the European state system, and through it they came into contact with each other. The two world wars of the twentieth century, in which most nations of the world participated, point in their very name to the transformation of a number of separate systems of international relations into one world-wide system. That process of political unification was greatly advanced and expanded to the individual sphere through the development of the technology of transportation and communications. This development started with the great voyages at the end of the fifteenth century and culminated in the drastic reduction of geographic distances for transportation and the virtual obliteration of the limits of time and space for communications.

The last phase of this transformation of international relations into a world-wide system, covering roughly the period from the end of the First World War to the aftermath of the Second, coincides with a radical change in the distribution of power within the system. From the beginning of the sixteenth century to the First World War the European system provided the dynamics and the preponderant power for this transformation; now two nations, either completely or predominantly non-European—the United States and the Soviet Union—have taken its place. This decline of Europe as the political center of the world may be said to have started with the Monroe Doctrine of 1823, declaring the mutual political independence of Europe and the Western Hemisphere. This declaration foreshadowed the fragmentation of the European empires which was virtually consummated after the Second World War in the colonial revolutions sweeping Africa and Asia. Most of the colonial possessions of European nations, one after the other, have gained their national independence, and many of them have either withdrawn their political support from the European nations or joined their enemies. The outstanding examples of these two different forms of political emancipation are India and China.

The decline of Europe resulting from the colonial revolutions coincided with the rise to predominance of formerly backward nations such as Russia and China. The technological unification of the world gave these nations the tools to transform their superior potential in geography, population, and natural resources into the actuality of national power.

The decisive factors in the decline of Europe as the political center of the world were the two world wars of the twentieth century. At the same time that they weakened the main European nations in their human and material resources, these conflicts brought non-European nations to the fore—the United States and Japan in consequence of the First World War, the United States and the Soviet Union in consequence of the Second World War. These two world wars differed not only in their consequences but also in their intrinsic character from other wars fought in the Western world in modern times. Most of the latter were limited wars in that only a fraction of the total human and material resources of the belligerents was committed to them. Only a fraction of the total population was morally identified with these wars and suffered from them, and each war was waged only for limited objectives. The two world wars, and those for which the most powerful nations have continued to prepare, were total in all these four respects. The actuality and threat of total war have been, indeed, the most important distinctive characteristics of international relations in the mid twentieth century. They have been due to an unprecedented accumulation of destructive power in the hands of the most powerful nations and to the incentive to use that power for national purposes. The accumulation of power has resulted from drastic changes in the distribution of political and technological power in the world; the incentive has been presented by the closing of the colonial frontier and the ascendancy of a universalistic nationalism.

Throughout the modern period, with the exception of the wars of religion of the sixteenth and seventeenth centuries and of the Napoleonic Wars, wars were limited in every respect. Power was so widely dispersed among a great number of sovereign states that no single state or possible combination of states was strong enough to gain more than limited objectives against its adversaries. The drastic reduction in the number of sovereign states and the resulting concentration of power in the hands of a few nations of the first rank, which occurred between the end of the Thirty Years' War and the end of the Second World War, created one precondition for total war. The treaty of Westphalia of 1648, for instance, reduced the number of sovereign states of which the German empire was composed from 900 to 355. The diet of Regensburg of 1803 eliminated 200 more. When the German confederation was founded in 1815, only 36 sovereign states were left to join it. The unification of Italy in 1861 and that of Germany in 1871 eliminated 31 additional sovereign states.

At the end of the Napoleonic Wars in 1815, only five nations of the first rank were left—Austria, France, Great Britain, Russia, and

Prussia. In the 1860's Italy and the United States joined them, followed toward the end of the century by Japan. At the beginning of the First World War in 1914, eight nations were of the first rank, with Germany having replaced Prussia. After the First World War the trend toward reduction of the number of sovereign states was reversed; their number almost doubled because the Ottoman, Austro-Hungarian, British, and French empires were broken up. Yet the trend toward concentration of more and more power in the hands of fewer and fewer states continued. At the end of the Second World War the number of nations of the first rank was reduced to two: the United States and the Soviet Union.

It is not by accident that the two most powerful nations capable of threatening each other with total war are also most advanced technologically and industrially. The mechanization of warfare in terms of weapons, supplies, transportation, and communications requires, in case of actual hostilities, the virtually total commitment of the industrial productivity of the nation. This total commitment has been made possible by the enormous increase in economic productivity brought about by a series of technological and industrial revolutions starting in the eighteenth century. By contrast, in earlier periods of history, economic productivity was so low that after it had barely provided for the needs of the population, little was left for military purposes. Thus premodern technology could support only limited war, while modern industry is productive enough to allow the commitment of the lion's share of its products for military purposes.

One incentive for the great nations to use this enormous productive power for the purposes of mutual destruction was provided by a change in international relations which can be called the disappearance of the colonial frontier. The generally limited character of the means and ends of foreign policy from the end of the middle ages to the First World War was in good measure due to the opportunity for the great European nations to seek satisfaction for their aspirations for power not in all-out contests with each other but through competitive expansion into Africa, the Americas, and the part of Asia bordering on the eastern oceans. Colonial competition and conflict during that period provided outlets through which the European nations could compete for power without endangering their existence. But by the beginning of the twentieth century the colonial frontier was, for all practical purposes, closed. Virtually all politically weak or empty spaces around the globe had been transformed into colonies or spheres of influence by one or another of the European nations. From then on, as the two world wars showed, the great European powers, deprived of the colonial safety valve, fought each other not for limited advantage but for total stakes, and they could do so with the instruments of total war.

These stakes have become total, not only in that total war threatens the belligerents with total destruction, but also in that the issue over which nations compete and fight has become total. That issue is no longer a limited military or territorial advantage but the universal triumph or defeat of a particular philosophy and way of life, which is supposed to be incarnate in a particular nation. While traditionally the international relations of the Western world have been carried on within the framework of common moral principles and a common way of life, which imposed effective limitations upon the struggle for power, international relations in the mid-twentieth century have been dominated by the conflict between democracy and communism, each putting forth a universal message of salvation, each trying—with different intensity—to extend its dominion to all mankind, and each identified with one of the two great powers left in the world. Thus international relations have come to be characterized not only by the traditional threat and use of military force on behalf of the aspirations of individual nations but also by a struggle for the minds of men. The proponents of the two antagonistic philosophies and ways of life, using the instruments of propaganda, foreign aid and foreign trade, have endeavored to gain the allegiance of uncommitted nations. By the same token, the traditional methods of diplomacy have been in eclipse. Nations can negotiate and bargain about their interests and conclude compromises concerning them, but they feel that they cannot yield an inch where their philosophies and ways of life are at stake.

While similar situations have existed before, temporarily and on a limited scale, especially in periods of religious conflicts and wars, international relations after the First and Second World Wars have been marked by a change in structure unprecedented in recorded history. Throughout history, there has existed a rational relationship between the threat and use of military force and the ends of foreign policy. It was rational for a nation to ask itself whether it could achieve its ends vis-à-vis another nation by peaceful means or whether it had to resort to military force to achieve them, for the risks involved in the resort to military force were generally not out of proportion to the ends sought. Great ends justified great risks, since the risks were generally not so great as to obviate the ends. Yet all-out nuclear war, likely to destroy all belligerents and thus to eliminate the very distinction between victor and vanquished, is a completely irrational undertaking. No possible end can justify it; it is an instrument of mass murder and mass suicide.

International relations, then, are faced with two interconnected dilemmas upon the solution of which depends the survival of Western civilization and perhaps of mankind itself. The first dilemma consists in the contrast between the technological unification of the world and the parochial moral commitments and political institutions of the age. Moral commitments and political institutions, dating from an age which modern technology has left behind, have not kept pace with technological achievements and, hence, are incapable of controlling their destructive potentialities. The second dilemma consists in the contrast between the need of nations to support their interests by resort to violence and the irrationality of resort to nuclear arms. If a nation cannot resort to nuclear weapons without risking its own destruction, how can it support its interests in a world of sovereign nations which is ruled by violence as the last resort?

These two dilemmas put into question the very survival of the existing system of international relations. The first dilemma suggests a higher principle of international organization, transcending the nation-state, in the form either of a universal organization, such as the United Nations, which would minimize threats to international peace, or of regional organizations, such as the European communities or a projected Atlantic union, which would eliminate local threats to peace and facilitate the rational use of regional resources. The second dilemma suggests the abolition of international relations itself through the merger of all national sovereignties into one world state which would have a monopoly of the most destructive instruments of violence. Both kinds of solutions are supported by the awareness of the unity of mankind underlying the inevitable fragmentation of international relations. However inarticulate and submerged, this awareness has never completely disappeared even in the heyday of nationalism, and it has been sharpened by the threat of nuclear destruction facing all mankind. These solutions are also supported by the longing to give that unity a viable political form, a longing which has time and again endeavored through theoretical schemes and practical measures to transform international relations into a supranational political order. This longing, in times past mainly a spiritual or humanitarian impulse, in the nuclear age has been greatly strengthened by the desire, innate in all men, for self-preservation.

31 *Alliances*

Alliances are a necessary function of the balance of power operating within a multiple state system. Nations A and B, competing with each other, have three choices in maintaining and improving their relative power positions. They can increase their own power, they can add to their own power the power of other nations, or they can withhold the power of other nations from the adversary. When they make the first choice, they embark upon an armaments race. When they choose the second and third alternatives, they pursue a policy of alliances.

Whether or not a nation shall pursue a policy of alliances is, then, not a matter of principle but of expediency. A nation will shun alliances if it believes that it is strong enough to hold its own unaided or that the burden of the commitments resulting from the alliance is likely to outweigh the advantages to be expected. It is for one or the other or both of these reasons that, throughout the better part of their history, Great Britain and the United States have refrained from entering into peacetime alliances with other nations.

Yet Great Britain and the United States have also refrained from concluding an alliance with each other even though, from the proclamation of the Monroe Doctrine in 1823 to the attack on Pearl Harbor in 1941, they have acted, at least in relation to the other European nations, as if they were allied. Their relationship during that period provides another instance of a situation in which nations dispense with an alliance. It occurs when their interests so obviously call for concerted policies and actions that an explicit formulation of these interests, policies, and actions in the form of a treaty of alliance appears to be redundant.

Both Great Britain and the United States have had with regard to the continent of Europe one interest in common: the preservation of the European balance of power. Thus when Great Britain went to war in 1914 and 1939 in order to protect the European balance of

From *Confluence*, Winter, 1958.

power, the United States first supported Great Britain with a conspicuous lack of that impartiality befitting a neutral and then joined her on the battlefield. Had the United States been tied to Great Britain by a formal treaty of alliance in 1914 and 1939, it might have declared war earlier, but its general policies and concrete actions would not have been materially different than they actually were.

Not every community of interests calling for common policies and actions also calls for legal codification in an explicit alliance. On the other hand, an alliance requires a community of interests for its foundation. Under what conditions, then, does an existing community of interests require the explicit formulation of an alliance? What is it that an alliance adds to the existing community of interests?

An alliance adds precision, especially in the form of limitation, to an existing community of interests and to the general policies and concrete measures serving them.[1] The interests nations have in common are not typically so precise and limited as to geographic region, objectives, and appropriate policies as has been the American and British interest in the preservation of the European balance of power. Nor are they so incapable of precision and limitation as concerns the prospective common enemy, for while a typical alliance is directed against a specific nation or group of nations, the enemy of the Anglo-American community of interests could in the nature of things not be specified beforehand. As Jefferson shifted his sympathies back and forth between Napoleon and Great Britain according to who seemed to threaten the balance of power at the time, so during the century following the Napoleonic Wars Great Britain and the United States had to decide in the light of circumstances ever liable to change who posed at the moment the greatest threat. This blanket character of the enemy, determined not individually but by the function he performs, brings to mind a similar characteristic of collective security, which is directed against the abstractly designed aggressor, whoever he may be.

The typical interests which unite two nations against a third are both more definite as concerns the determination of the enemy and

---

[1] Glancing through the treaties of alliance of the seventeenth and eighteenth centuries, one is struck by the meticulous precision with which obligations to furnish troops, equipment, logistic support, food, money, and the like were defined.

less precise as concerns the objectives to be sought and the policies to be pursued. In the last decades of the nineteenth century, France was opposed to Germany and Russia was opposed to Austria, while Austria was allied with Germany against France and Russia. How could the interests of France and Russia be brought to a common denominator, determining policy and guiding action? How could, in other words, the *casus foederis* be defined so that both friend and foe would know what to expect in certain contingencies affecting their respective interests? It was for the treaty of alliances of 1894 to perform these functions. Had the objectives and policies of the Franco-Russian alliance of 1894 been as clear as are the objectives and policies of Anglo-American co-operation in Europe, no alliance treaty would have been necessary. Had the enemy been as indeterminate, no alliance treaty would have been feasible.

Not every community of interests calling for co-operation between two or more nations, then, requires that the terms of this co-operation be specified through the legal stipulations of a treaty of alliance. It is only when the common interests are inchoate in terms of policy and action that a treaty of alliance is required to make them explicit and operative. These interests, as well as the alliances expressing them and the policies serving them, can be distinguished in five different ways: according to their intrinsic nature and relationship, the distribution of benefits and power, their coverage in relation to the total interests of the nations concerned, their coverage in terms of time, and their effectiveness in terms of common policies and actions. In consequence, we can distinguish alliances serving identical, complementary, and ideological interests and policies. We can further distinguish mutual and one-sided, general and limited, temporary and permanent, operative and inoperative alliances.[2]

The Anglo-American alliance with regard to Europe provides the classic example of an alliance serving identical interests. The alliance between the United States and Pakistan is one of many contemporary instances of an alliance serving complementary interests. For the United States it serves the primary purpose of expanding the scope of the policy of containment; for Pakistan it serves primarily

[2] Sanskrit has sixteen words for different types of alliances.

the purpose of increasing her political, military, and economic potential vis-à-vis her neighbors.

The pure type of an ideological alliance is presented by the Treaty of the Holy Alliance of 1815 and the Atlantic Charter of 1941. Both documents laid down general moral principles to which the signatories pledged their adherence and general objectives whose realization they pledged themselves to seek. Much more typical is the addition of ideological commitments to material ones in one and the same treaty of alliance.[3] Thus the Three Emperors' League of 1873 provided for military assistance among Austria, Germany, and Russia in case of attack on any of the three and at the same time emphasized the solidarity of the three monarchies against republican subversion. In our times, the ideological commitment against Communist subversion, inserted in treaties of alliance, performs a similar function. The ideological factor also manifests itself in the official interpretation of an alliance, in terms of an ideological solidarity transcending the limitations of material interests. The conception of the Anglo-American alliance, common before the British invasion of Egypt in 1956, as all-inclusive and world-embracing, based upon common culture, political institutions, and ideals, is a case in point.

As concerns the political effect of this ideological factor upon an alliance, three possibilities must be distinguished. A purely ideological alliance, unrelated to material interests, cannot but be stillborn; it is unable to determine policies or guide actions, and misleads by giving the appearance of political solidarity where there is none. The ideological factor, when it is superimposed upon an actual community of interests, can lend strength to the alliance by marshaling moral convictions and emotional preferences to its support. It can also weaken it by obscuring the nature and limits of the common interests which the alliance was supposed to make precise and by raising expectations, bound to be disappointed, concerning the extent of concerted policies and actions. For both these last possibilities, the Anglo-American alliance can again serve as an example.

Ideally, the distribution of benefits within an alliance should be one of complete mutuality. This ideal is most likely to be approxi-

---

[3] It ought to be pointed out that both the Holy Alliance and the Atlantic Charter actually supplement material commitments contained in separate legal instruments.

mated in an alliance concluded among equals in power and serving identical interests; here the equal resources of all, responding to equal incentives, serve one single interest. The other extreme in the distribution of benefits is one-sidedness, in which one party receives the lion's share of benefits while the other bears the main bulk of burdens. In so far as the object of such an alliance is the preservation of the territorial and political integrity of the receiving party, such an alliance is indistinguishable from a treaty of guarantee. Complementary interests lend themselves most easily to this kind of disproportion since they are by definition different in substance and their comparative assessment is likely to be distorted by subjective interpretation.

The distribution of benefits and determination of policies is thus likely to reflect the distribution of power within an alliance. It is for this reason that Machiavelli warned weak nations against making alliances with strong ones except by necessity.[4] However, this correlation between benefits, policies, and power is by no means inevitable. A weak nation may well possess an asset which is of such great value for its strong ally as to be irreplaceable. Here the unique benefit the former is able to grant or withhold may give it a status within the alliance completely out of keeping with the actual distribution of material power. The relationships between the United States and Iceland with regard to bases and between Great Britain and Iraq with regard to oil can serve as examples.

The misinterpretation of the Anglo-American alliance, mentioned before, is also a case in point for the confusion between limited and general alliances. In the age of total war, wartime alliances tend to be general in that they comprise the total interests of the contracting parties both with regard to the waging of the war and the peace settlement. On the other hand, peacetime alliances tend to be limited to a fraction of the total interests and objectives of the signatories. A nation will conclude a multitude of alliances with different nations which may overlap and contradict each other on specific points.

A typical alliance attempts to transform a small fraction of the total interests of the contracting parties into common policies and measures. Some of these interests are irrelevant to the purposes of

[4] *The Prince*, chap. xxi.

the alliance, others support them, others diverge from them, and others still are incompatible with them. Whether and for how long an alliance will remain operative depends upon the strength of the interests underlying it as over against the strength of the other interests of the nations concerned. The value and the chances of an alliance, however limited in scope, must be considered within the context of the over-all policies within which it is expected to operate.

General alliances are usually of temporary duration and most prevalent in wartime. The overriding common interest in winning the war and securing through the peace settlement the interests for which the war was waged is bound to yield, once victory is won and the peace treaties are signed, to the traditionally separate and frequently incompatible interests of the individual nations. On the other hand, there exists a correlation between the permanency of an alliance and the limited character of the interests it serves, for only such a specific, limited interest is likely to last long enough to provide the foundation for a durable alliance. The alliance between Great Britain and Portugal, concluded in 1703, has survived the centuries because Portugal's interest in the protection of her ports by the British fleet and the British interest in the control of the Atlantic approaches to Portugal have endured. Yet it can be stated as a general historical observation that while alliance treaties have frequently assumed permanent validity by being concluded "in perpetuity" or for periods of ten or twenty years, they could not have been more durable than the generally precarious and fleeting configurations of common interests which they were intended to serve.

The dependence of alliances upon the underlying community of interests also accounts for the distinction between operative and inoperative alliances. For an alliance to be operative, its members must agree not only on general objectives but on policies and measures as well. Many alliances have remained scraps of paper because no such agreement was forthcoming, and it was not forthcoming because the community of interests did not extend beyond general objectives to concrete policies and measures. The Franco-Russian alliances of 1935 and 1944 and the Anglo-Russian alliance of 1942 are cases in point.

The examination of contemporary alliances in the light of these categories will be divided under three headings: the Atlantic alliance, the Western alliances outside Europe, the Communist alliances.

The vital interest of the United States in the protection of the nations of Western Europe against Russian domination is identical with the interest of these nations in preserving their national independence. Yet this foundation of the Atlantic alliance has undergone a change both subtle and drastic. The Atlantic alliance is beset by a crisis which the events of November, 1956, made obvious but did not create.

Seen from the perspective of the nations of Western Europe, three factors sustained the Atlantic alliance in the decade following the Second World War: the atomic monopoly of the United States, the economic weakness of the nations of Western Europe, and the intransigence of Stalinist policies. The conjunction of these factors confronted the nations of Western Europe with the choice between suicide and the acceptance of the political, economic, and military support of the United States. In other words, the Atlantic alliance was for the nations of Western Europe a prerequisite for national survival.

This connection between national survival and the Atlantic alliance is no longer as close nor as obvious as it used to be. The atomic monopoly of the United States provided the nations of Western Europe with absolute protection against Russian conquest. With the Soviet Union having become an atomic power equal, if not superior, to the United States, the Atlantic alliance is no longer solely a protection for the nations of Western Europe, but has also become a liability. The atomic stalemate threatens not only the two superpowers but also their allies with total destruction. Paradoxical as it may seem, the drastically increased threat of Soviet power has drastically weakened the Western alliance. The Soviet Union has not been slow to point out, and the man in the street in Western Europe has not been slow to understand, that if there is a chance for the nations of Western Europe to survive in an atomic war, it may lie in not being too closely identified, or perhaps not being identified at all, with the United States. Thus a latent neutralism has had a slowly corrosive influence upon the Atlantic alliance. The rise of this neutralism in Western Europe as a popular mass movement is not primarily the result of Communist propaganda, or of faintness of heart, but of the new objective conditions under which the nations of Western Europe must live in the age of the atomic stalemate.

Secondly, the economic recovery of the nations of Western Europe has greatly diminished their dependence upon the United States. The Coal and Steel Community, Euratom, the Common Market, and the development of East-West trade are likely to decrease it still more. Thus while the nations of Western Europe are still in need of American economic aid, that aid is no longer a question of life and death, as it was ten years ago. Today they have, or at least have evidence that they soon will have, an alternative. They can stand on their own feet again and look beyond the wall of containment for new outlets for their energies and products.

These factors affect West Germany's attitude toward the Atlantic alliance with particular intensity. Their effect is strengthened by the political issue which has the widest, and is likely to have an ever deepening, emotional appeal: unification. The Western alliance has been presented to West Germany, both by American and German official spokesmen, as the instrument through which unification would be achieved. While this view was from the outset open to serious doubts, the historic experience of its failure has led to a crisis of confidence which is likely to deepen as time goes on. The Atlantic alliance, far from being supported as the instrument of unification, is ever more loudly and widely blamed as the main obstacle to it.

The Soviet Union has been eager to use these new political, military, and economic conditions under which the nations of Western Europe live for the purpose of weakening and ultimately destroying the Atlantic alliance. What has been called the "new look" of Soviet foreign policy is essentially a new flexibility which has taken the place of the monotony of the Stalinist threats. In the face of these threats, no nation which wanted to survive as a nation had any choice; thus Stalin was really the architect of the Atlantic alliance. The new Soviet foreign policy alternately threatens and tempts, as the occasion seems to require, but always seeks to hold before the eyes of Western Europe an acceptable or even preferable alternative to the Atlantic alliance. In consequence, the Atlantic alliance has lost much of its urgency and vitality. Great Britain and France, for instance, no longer feel that they have to subordinate their separate national interests to the common defense against the Soviet Union; and they have begun, in different degrees, to pursue those interests regardless, and sometimes at the expense, of the common interests of the alliance. They have also begun to vent openly their resentment at their lack of great-power status and to allow their policies to be influenced by it. The rise of Germany to a position of political, military, and economic eminence cannot but add to the opportunities of the new Soviet foreign policy.

As viewed from the vantage point of the United States, the Atlantic alliance is also in the process of undergoing a subtle change, which in the end is bound to be drastic. For the United States, the Atlantic alliance is the political and military implementation of its perennial interest in the maintenance of the European balance of power. However, the military implementation of this interest is likely to change under the impact of a new technology of warfare. As long as the main deterrent to Russian aggression remains the atomic bomb delivered by plane, the military strategy of the United States requires military installations in Western Europe; and the nations of Western Europe have a corresponding interest in providing them. To the extent that the intercontinental guided missile will replace airplanes as a means of delivering atomic attack, the interest in American military installations in Western Europe will diminish on both sides of the Atlantic. This interest will decrease still further when some of the nations of Western Europe have atomic installations of their own. When this day comes, the Atlantic alliance will take on a new complexion, probably losing some of its specific military aspects and tending to revert to an implicit community of interests like that which tied the United States to Great Britain from 1823 to 1941.

However, the interests of the United States and the nations of Western Europe are not limited to that continent. Those of the United States and Great Britain are world-wide, and France is engaged in Africa. And whatever the community interests within the Atlantic alliance in Europe, these interests do not necessarily coincide elsewhere. The coincidence or divergence of these non-European interests has had a strengthening or debilitating, as the case might be, effect upon the Atlantic alliance itself; and the vital interest of all members of the alliance has, in turn, limited their freedom of action outside Europe.

The United States in particular, in dealing with the colonial revolutions which are directed primarily against Great Britain and France, has been continuously confronted with a painful and inherently insoluble dilemma. The horns of that dilemma are the interest of the United States in the continuing strength of Great Britain and France as her principal allies and the American interest in preventing the colonial revolutions from falling under the sway of communism. If the United States underwrites the colonial position of Great Britain or France, as it did in Indochina, it may strengthen its principal European allies, but will impair its standing with the anticolonial peoples of Asia and Africa. If the United States sides unreservedly with the Afro-Asian bloc, as it did in the United Nations on the occasion of the Suez Canal crisis of autumn, 1956, it weakens Great Britain and France and, in consequence, the Atlantic alliance. Faced with this dilemma, which can only be solved at the price of impairing the vital interests of the United States in one or the other respect, the United States has inevitably been reduced to straddling the fence by halfheartedly supporting one side on one occasion and the other side on another, or else keeping hands off altogether. Algeria and Cyprus exemplify at present the dilemma and its evasion. In such situations, then, the Atlantic alliance does not operate at all, for there are no common interests which could support its operation.

That such divergencies of interest and policy have not imposed greater stresses upon the Atlantic alliance and have left it essentially unimpaired testifies to its inherent strength. But that strength cannot be taken for granted. The common interests underlying the Atlantic alliance have thus far prevailed over the divergent ones only because of the conviction of the members of the alliance that they have a greater stake in their common than in their divergent interests. But in recent years the latter have grown stronger, and the former weaker. If this trend should continue unchecked, it would indeed put in jeopardy the very survival of the Atlantic alliance.

Common interests are the rock on which all alliances are built. Yet upon this rock all kinds of structures may be erected, some solid and spacious, others crumbling and confining. In other words, there are good and bad alliances: some work smoothly and are enthusiastically supported, others are cumbersome and are grudgingly accepted as a lesser evil. While the existence of the alliance depends upon a community of interests, the quality of the alliance is determined by the manner in which common interests are translated into concrete policies and day-by-day measures. It is in this latter respect that there is cause for concern about the Atlantic alliance. Here, too, the crisis of November, 1956, has made obvious defects which antedate that crisis. Three such defects have continuously and to an ever increasing degree impaired the operation of the Atlantic alliance: its organizational structure; the policies, domestic and international, of its leading members; and the prestige enjoyed by some of its leading statesmen.

The common interest of the members of the Atlantic alliance in the military protection of their independence has found its organizational expression in the North Atlantic Treaty Organization. The strategic conception which underlies NATO is the assumption that the European members of the Atlantic alliance are able to defend themselves through a co-operative effort against a military attack by the Soviet Union. But NATO has never developed a convincing philosophy of purpose. All members of NATO are agreed upon one objective: to defend their independence without having to fight for it. But how is this purpose to be achieved? Is primary reliance to be placed upon atomic retaliation with the local forces of NATO performing the function of the "plate glass" or "trip wire," or is a prospective aggressor to be deterred by the inherent military strength of local forces? The members of NATO have not seen eye to eye on this fundamental question, and NATO itself in its official proclamations and policies has not seemed to be of one mind either. More particularly, the declared purposes of NATO have been consistently at variance with the measures requested of its members for implementation of these purposes; and the measures requested, in turn, have been invariably at variance with the measures actually taken. Furthermore, declared purposes, requested measures, and the measures actually taken have been subjected to a number of drastic and confusing changes which cannot be explained exclusively by the revolutionary transformation which military technology is in the process of undergoing.

This confusion in policy, itself conducive to political disunity and friction in day-by-day operations, has been magnified by the elaborate organizational superstructure which is intended to put the policies of NATO into practice. This superstructure, which encompasses a plethora of committees charged with co-ordinating a variety of political, military, and economic policies of the member states, must make for friction and inefficiency even under the best of circumstances. It magnifies defects because it is much too ambitious in purpose and elaborate in operation for the agreed purpose of NATO. In the absence of agreement on philosophy and basic policy, an elaborate organizational superstructure can be a source of weakness rather than of strength.

Since an alliance, in its day-by-day operations, rests in good measure upon mutual confidence, the character and ability of its leading statesmen and the policies they pursue become of critical concern. In both respects, the Atlantic alliance has shown itself deficient. There can be no doubt that the prestige of the United States as leader of the Atlantic alliance has drastically declined. Rightly or wrongly, the United States is no longer looked upon by its allies, as it was during the period immediately following the Second World War, as the leader whose strength and resolution can be relied upon to keep the Atlantic alliance on an even course. Three factors are in the main responsible for this crisis of confidence.

In foreign policy it is sometime useful to keep the enemy guessing. But to keep allies guessing is bound to erode the foundations of confidence upon which an alliance must rest. The allies of the United States have noted discrepancies between the policy pronouncements of our leaders and the actual policies pursued, which appear to them to have evolved into a consistent pattern of unreliability.

This slow accumulation of loss of confidence reached a critical stage in the Suez Canal crisis, for here unreliability in policy appeared to be joined by indifference, if not hostility, to the vital interests of America's principal allies. For the vital interests of the United States and her allies to coincide in Europe and diverge elsewhere is one thing; but for the vital interests of her principal allies elsewhere to be actively opposed by the United States is quite another. To the former, the allies of the United States could reconcile themselves with relative equanimity; the latter could not help but raise for them the crucial question as to whether the Atlantic alliance was worth so high a price. That they answered the question in the affirmative testifies to the vitality of the alliance. Their resentment was kindled by the demonstration of their inability to pursue active foreign policies of their own without the support and against the opposition of one or the other of the superpowers. Thus, under the dramatic impact of the experience which saw the interests and power of our allies destroyed in a region vital to themselves, with the approval and active participation of the United States, the Atlantic alliance has tended to transform itself for them from an association of like-minded nations into a burden grudgingly borne.

As far as long-range policies are concerned, the relations among nations must be conceived in terms of interests. As concerns their day-by-day relations, we must also think in terms of personalities. We say that the United States and Great Britain have agreed on a certain policy, but tend to forget that Great Britain and the United States are abstractions and that in actuality the President and Secretary of State of the United States and the Prime Minister and Secretary for Foreign Affairs of Great Britain, speaking in the name of their respective nations, have agreed with each other. The smooth and effective operation of an alliance, then, depends in good measure upon the maintenance of trust and respect among its principal statesmen. There is no gainsaying the fact that the absence of such relations has become a great handicap in the day-by-day operations of the Atlantic alliance. Regardless of the objective merits of the case, there can be no doubt that the leaders of our European allies no longer have the same confidence in the judgment and the authority of the President of the United States they had in times past, and that they dislike and mistrust the Secretary of State with varying degrees of intensity but with virtual unanimity. These reactions have increased the strains under which the Atlantic alliance operates at present.

Our reactions, similarly negative, cannot help but add to the strain. The instability of French governments, the collapse of the Eden cabinet, the seeming futility of British and French policies in Cyprus and Algeria, the failure of their intervention in Egypt, all have produced some doubt regarding both the power of our principal allies and the wisdom of their leadership.

The traditional political rhetoric on both sides of the Atlantic has tended to gloss over all these stresses and strains and has made it appear as though the Atlantic alliance were something broader and smoother and also something more diffuse than it actually is. It is indeed built upon a rock of common interests, but the rock is of limited dimensions and its surfaces are sometimes rough. In spite of the great damage which the crisis of November, 1956, has done to the Atlantic alliance, it has been useful in circumscribing more closely its limits and demonstrating for all to see its still considerable strength.

While the Atlantic alliance reposes upon the firm foundation of identical interests, no such general and reassuring statement can be made about the Western alliances outside Europe. Considering Asia and the Middle East, it can be said that of the American alliances only those with Formosa, South Korea, South Vietnam, and Japan are based upon identical interests. These nations, with the exception of Japan, owe their very existence as nations to the interests and power of the United States. Yet only their complete dependence upon the United States has prevented some, if not all, of these nations from pursuing policies at variance with those of the United States. Thus the stability of these alliances rests both upon identical interests and extreme discrepancy of power.

Our alliance with Japan, like that with Germany, was, during the first decade following the Second World War, likewise based upon the dual foundation of identical interests and overwhelming American power. Yet neither foundation can be any longer taken for granted. Three factors have combined to restore Japan's freedom of choice. First, Japan has again become the strongest power in Asia, leaving even China a considerable distance behind. If the wartime memories of Japan's imperialism were not still alive in the rest of Asia, Japan would be the favorite candidate for taking over the economic and political leadership of Asia. Second, the atomic stalemate has had the same psychological effect on Japan as on Western Europe; the American alliance has become for Japan a mixed blessing, if not a liability. Finally, to the degree that the aggressiveness of Stalinist and Chinese Korean War policies is replaced by a new flexibility which stresses the complementary character of Russian, Chinese, and Japanese interests, Japan may find a practical alternative to its identification with the United States.

The other Asian alliances, of which SEATO and the Baghdad Pact provide the outstanding examples, are of an entirely different type. They have three characteristics in common: complementary interests tending toward transformation into incompatible ones, a radically unequal distribution of benefits, and an ideological emphasis.

These alliances, on the face of them, were conceived in terms of common action on behalf of common interests. However, in view of the remoteness of the apparent *casus foederis*, that is, Communist attack upon a member, and of the virtual impossibility in case of such an attack for most members to act in common, commitment to common action has receded into the background and been distilled into an anti-Communist ideological commitment. Of the Asian members, this commitment requires nothing more than membership in the alliance; it requires no common objective, policy, or action—beyond anticommunism at home and abroad. Yet of the Western members, especially the United States, it requires specific policies and actions on behalf of the Asian members.

The Asian members are interested in these alliances primarily because of the economic, military, and political support they receive from the United States. Many of them consider their membership in the alliance to constitute a special claim upon the American treasury, American weapons, and American political support for their special national aspirations. However valuable the United States judges this membership to be, in terms of actual policies and measures it bears a unilateral burden. The United States is under continuous pressure to act as an ally, while the Asian allies, once they have signed the treaty of alliance, preserve virtually complete freedom of action. Their foreign policies, for instance, vis-à-vis China, could hardly be more different if they were not members of the alliance. In order to show the irrelevance of the alliance in terms of common objectives, policies, and actions, the prime minister of one Asian nation has gone so far as to equate his country's membership in SEATO with membership in the United Nations.

In so far as the West wants the maximum number of Asian allies and the Asian allies want the maximum amount of Western support, the interests of the two parties can be said to complement each other.

This compatibility is bound to disintegrate whenever a latent conflict of interests between two allies or an ally and another nation becomes acute. The conflicts between Pakistan and India over Kashmir, between Great Britain and Greece, and Turkey and Greece, over Cyprus, and between Iraq and Israel are cases in point. It is only because these alliances limit a commitment to common action to the very unlikely event of Communist aggression that they have survived such incompatibilities. The United States, in particular, is frequently forced into the uncomfortable position of having either to straddle the fence, as between Great Britain and Greece, or else to sacrifice its interests to its alliance, as between India and Pakistan.

Thus, by virtue of its alliance, the United States increases the armed strength of Pakistan and thereby forces India to increase its expenditures for armaments from thirty million pounds in 1955 to ninety million pounds in 1957. This diversion of scarce funds from economic development to armaments threatens India with economic and political disaster, which the United States has a vital interest in staving off through financial aid. In consequence, the United States engages, as it were, in an armaments race with itself by proxy, its left hand supporting Pakistan by virtue of the alliance, its right hand aiding India by virtue of its vital interests.

As for the alliance among the nations of the Western Hemisphere, appearances are deceptive. As long as the supremacy of the United States within the Western Hemisphere provided unchallengeable protection for the independence of the American nations, these alliances could indeed be taken for granted. For the United States, these alliances provided complete safety since, in view of its unchallengeable supremacy within the hemisphere and of the protection of two oceans, its security could be endangered only by a non-American nation acting in concert with an American one. For the other American nations, these alliances provided complete security from great-power domination since the United States would use its superior power only for the protection and not for the subversion of their national independence.

This identity of interests and the ability of the United States to implement it have provided the rationale and lifeblood of the American state system from the proclamation of the Monroe Doctrine to this day. The intercontinental guided missile confronts this system with a challenge never before experienced, for the supremacy of the United States within the Western Hemisphere, as unchallengeable as ever from within, is of no avail as protection against these novel weapons of tomorrow. The United States can no more protect its American allies against these weapons than it can protect itself. The American allies will come to view the alliance with the United States with the same misgivings with which the European allies and Japan view it already. They may no longer regard their interests as identical with those of the United States and may conclude that safety lies not in closeness to, but rather in distance from, the United States. While these considerations are admittedly speculative from the vantage point of 1957, they may well reflect the actuality of 1960.

The Communist alliances present three different types, which must be sharply distinguished: the alliances of the Soviet Union and China, on the one hand, with North Korea and North Vietnam, on the other; the alliances between the Soviet Union and the nations of Eastern Europe; the alliances of the Soviet Union, on the one hand, with China, Egypt, Syria, and probably Yemen, on the other.

The position of North Korea and North Vietnam within the Communist alliances is identical—in the particulars which interest us here—with the position of South Korea and South Vietnam within their alliances with the United States. There is complete identity of interests and extreme disparity of power.

The alliances between the Soviet Union and the nations of Eastern Europe, codified in the Warsaw Pact of 1955, are in a class by themselves. They are not true alliances in that they do not transform a pre-existing community of interests into legal obligations. It is their distinctive quality that a community of interests is irrelevant for their existence and operation and that they are founded on nothing but unchallengeable superiority of power. Power is here not superimposed upon common interests but becomes a substitute for them. Such so-called treaties of alliance are in truth in the nature of treaties establishing a modern version of protectorates, and the nations subjected to them are correctly called satellites rather than allies.

The nature of this relationship has not been affected, although it might well be in the future, by the development of a community of interests between the Soviet Union and certain satellites, such as Poland and Czechoslovakia, resulting from the emergence of Ger-

many as the predominant power in Europe. Poland and Czechoslovakia, situated as they are between two nations of superior strength,
have had to seek protection either from one neighbor against the
other or from Western Europe against both. Their present relationship to the Soviet Union provides this protection. Given a change in
both Russian and German policies, this protective function might
well form the basis for a future genuine alliance.

While this development is purely speculative, the relations between the Soviet Union and the satellites have in recent years undergone an actual transformation similar to that which has affected
the Atlantic alliance, and for similar reasons. The emergence of an
atomic stalemate between the United States and the Soviet Union
has loosened the ties of the satellite relationship. The threat of mutual atomic destruction has stimulated both the desire for self-preservation in the form of neutralism and the aspirations for national independence which had lain dormant under the yoke of the Red Army.

These latent tendencies were brought to the fore by the "new
look" in Russian policy following the death of Stalin. In response to
it, the spirit of national independence started to push against the lid
of Russian oppression, and the Russian proconsuls yielded to the
pressure. They rehabilitated most of the national leaders who had
tried to combine communism and at least a measure of national independence and relaxed the authoritarian controls over the economic
and intellectual life of the satellite. Yet popular reaction went beyond domestic reforms to a striving for national independence, that
is, the end of the satellite relationship itself. At this point, the Soviet
Union called a halt, reasserting the paramountcy of its interests by
the supremacy of its power.

The exact nature of the community of interests between the
Soviet Union and China is a matter for speculation. Russian and
Chinese interests appear to be identical in so far as their common
objective is the strengthening and expansion of the Communist and
the weakening and retraction of the anti-Communist camps. They
appear to be complementary in so far as the alliance serves the Chinese interest in economic and military development and the Russian
interest in keeping the United States militarily engaged and politically handicapped in the Far East.

The alliances between the Soviet Union and the Middle Eastern nations clearly serve complementary interests. The Middle Eastern nations allied with the Soviet Union are enabled by the military support they receive to pursue actively their specific interests, all with regard to Israel, some with regard to Jordan, Saudi Arabia, Turkey, and the remaining British possessions and spheres of influence. The Soviet Union, on the other hand, has no stake in these specific interests except in so far as their active pursuit serves to maintain a state of tension which keeps the Western nations engaged and handicapped in still another region and threatens them with economic stress.

Considering the over-all picture of the alliances as it emerges from the foregoing analysis, one is impressed by the similarity of the changes which have occurred in the structure of the European alliances on both sides of the Iron Curtain. The seemingly irreversible trend toward a two-bloc system which marked the immediate postwar era has been arrested, if not reversed. The uncommitted nations not only want to remain uncommitted but also have, with a few exceptions, shown the ability to do so. On the other hand, many of the European nations which are committed as allies of one or the other of the superpowers would like to join the ranks of the uncommitted nations but have, with the exception of Yugoslavia, been unable to do so. They have at best been able to move to the outer confines of the blocs to which they belong. In consequence, the two-bloc system is in the process of loosening but not of breaking up.

The satellites may become even more unwilling and unreliable partners of the Soviet Union than they are already. Short of outside intervention, which is unlikely, they cannot move out of the Soviet orbit as long as Russian interest—backed by Russian power—requires their submission. And the interest of Russia in the domination of Eastern Europe has been perennial, despite drastic changes in the personnel, philosophy, and structure of government. The weakening of that interest cannot be foreseen short of a revolution in military technology which would make the control of outlying territory irrelevant.

The fate that may be in store for the Atlantic alliance is similarly not its formal dissolution but rather its slow erosion to the point of becoming inoperative. The common fear of communism, either as a subversive force from within or an aggresive one from without, and the common dedication to the values of Western civilization are likely to remain stronger than the disruptive tendencies of divergent and incompatible interests and thus keep the common framework of the Atlantic alliance intact. The demonstrated inability of even Great Britain and France to pursue positive foreign policies against the opposition of the United States adds to this outward stability of the Atlantic alliance. The real danger lies in this common framework becoming an empty shell, drained of its vitality. History abounds with legal compacts, constitutional devices, and institutional forms which have, sometimes—as in the case of the Holy Roman Empire—for centuries, survived as ritualistic observances, or in the words of Chief Justice Marshall, "a solemn mockery," without any longer being capable of directing the interests of men into the channels of common policies and actions.

The danger with which the German situation threatens the Atlantic alliance is, however, far more serious. The tension between the German commitment to the Atlantic alliance and the national goal of unification, which can be achieved only on Russian terms, inevitably raises in German minds the question of whether that commitment and this objective are truly compatible and whether the former must not be sacrificed in order to achieve the latter. This conclusion can be prevented from being translated into actual policy only by the intransigence of Russian and the wisdom of American policies. The danger of German defection from the Atlantic alliance, then, raises in specific terms the general issue of the merits of our alliance policy and of our response to the structural changes which the alliances have undergone in recent times.

Our alliance policy partakes of the doctrinaire, legalistic, and mechanical character of much of American foreign policy. These perennial vices reappear in it in a new form. Instead of recognizing that alliances can be useful, harmful, or superfluous depending on the circumstances and therefore discriminating among them in view of the interests to be served and the policies to be pursued, we have followed what might be called the collector's approach to alliances: the more nations to sign a legal document declaring their support for our policies, the better. While once we were, on principle, against all "entangling alliances," now we are, again on principle, in favor of all alliances.

This emphasis upon the quantity of alliances and, more particularly, upon their military advantages—actual or illusory—has tended to jeopardize our political interests. Frequently our allies have turned our interest in the alliance per se to their political advantage, without any corresponding political advantage accruing to us or, at worst, at the expense of our political interests. In consequence, the weak members of the alliance, knowing what they want to get out of it, have tended to convert the alliance into an instrument of their policies, with the United States paying the political and economic cost.

This tendency to see intrinsic merit in any alliance has been most pronounced in Asia. SEATO, originating in an indiscriminate invitation by the United States to join, is the classic example. Its membership was determined not by the United States in view of its interests but by the other members in view of theirs. Nor has the issue of the mutuality of benefits and liabilities been correlated to our over-all Asian interests, which—except for Formosa, South Korea, and South Vietnam—are political rather than military.

SEATO is for the United States a useless alliance from the military point of view and a harmful one politically and economically in that it alienates the broad masses of Asians. NATO, on the other hand, especially in view of its elaborate organizational superstructure, may well prove to be a superfluous alliance—a view held by a minority within and outside the government when NATO was created in 1949. It may well be asked again—as it was then—whether the obvious identity of interests between the United States and the nations of Western Europe could not have been adequately served by a unilateral guarantee on the part of the United States, fashioned after the model of the Monroe Doctrine. While the very existence of NATO has made this question obviously academic, the rationale underlying it could still be put into practice by dismantling what is useless and harmful in NATO and strengthening what is useful, essential, and lasting.

These speculations culminate in the observation that the problem of alliances must be considered in the context of the over-all character of world politics. If the task facing a nation is primarily military, not to be mastered by its isolated strength alone, a policy of alliances is the answer; and this answer is still the correct one in Europe and in certain exposed regions of Asia. In so far as the task is political, requiring a variety of means to be applied with subtlety, discrimination, and imagination, a policy of alliances will be useless, if not harmful; and this is indeed the situation which confronts the United States in most of the world today where the issue is political allegiance and not military defense. A policy of alliances, in its doctrinaire insistence upon joining the club, in its legalistic concern with signatures and stipulations, in its mechanical counting of heads, serves as but a substitute for political creativeness, the lack of which it may temporarily conceal. What it can neither conceal nor stave off is the failure which attends upon wrong policies as punishment follows the crime.

32 *Diplomacy*

The traditional methods of diplomacy have been under continuous attack since the First World War and have to a considerable extent been discarded in practice since the end of the Second World War. Three main arguments have been directed against them. First, they have been held responsible for the political catastrophes which have befallen mankind in the last four decades or so; methods that appear to have been so unsuccessful must be replaced by better ones. Second, traditional diplomacy has been held to run counter to the principles of democracy, and from the assumption that democracy makes for peace—and autocracy, for war —it has been concluded that diplomacy must be "open," that is, exposed to public scrutiny in all its processes. Finally, the traditional diplomatic practices with their seemingly useless and wasteful formalities, horse-trading, and compromises have seemed to violate moral principles with which democratic nations have felt themselves identified; in other words, the age-old conflict between political realism and idealism has been transferred to the sphere of diplomacy.

These arguments against traditional diplomacy arise from the basic philosophic position, prevalent in our time, that political practices are the result of subjective preferences, to be changed at will. In truth, however, the traditional methods of diplomacy have not been invented by stupid and evil or, for that matter, wise and good men —even though they have certainly been used and abused by such men—but have grown ineluctably from the objective nature of things political. In their essence, they are the reflections of that objective nature, to be disregarded only at the risk of political failure. Whenever two autonomous social entities, anxious to maintain their autonomy, engage in political relations with each other, they cannot but resort to what we call the traditional methods of diplomacy. And it does not matter in this respect whether these diplomatic relations are carried on between two members of a family, two businessmen, two baseball clubs, two political parties, or two sovereign nations. On all levels of such relations, secrecy of negotiation—to

From *The State of the Social Sciences,* edited by Leonard D. White, 1956.

mention only the most prominent and controversial aspect—is not an arbitrary procedural device to be used or dispensed with at will but grows from the objective nature of negotiations. No negotiations of any kind—be they for the contraction of a marriage, the sale of a piece of property, a deal for baseball players, or an international treaty—can be carried out in public without defeating their very purpose: the transformation of conflicting or inchoate interests into a common purpose of the contracting parties.

The specific arguments against the traditional methods of diplomacy are as untenable as is the basic philosophic position from which they stem. If it is true that the traditional practices of diplomacy constitute the method by which the business of foreign policy must be transacted, the failure of a particular foreign policy or of a whole era to bring peace and order to the world cannot be attributed to these practices per se but, at worst, to their incorrect use. This logical deduction is borne out by the experiences of recent history. For the disorganization of international society since the First World War has indeed been concomitant with the neglect, misunderstanding, and abuse of the traditional practices of diplomacy. While it would be far-fetched to suggest that the decline of diplomacy is responsible for the catastrophes that have befallen the world in recent times, it cannot be doubted that that decline has contributed to international disorder, being itself an outgrowth of a deep-seated disorder in the intellectual sphere.

Both the arguments—that democracy means peace and that diplomacy is immoral and therefore undemocratic—have grown from an intellectual attitude hostile to the very idea of foreign policy as an independent sphere of thought and action. They assume that the kind of foreign policy a nation pursues is determined by the kind of domestic institutions it possesses and the kind of political philosophy to which it adheres. All of recorded history militates against that assumption. The national interest of great powers and, in good measure, the methods by which it is to be secured are impervious to ideological or institutional changes. As far back as April 30, 1823, George Canning warned that "the general acquisition of free institutions is not necessarily a security for general peace." Our experience of total wars, waged by democracies for democratic tenets, gives substance to that warning.

The argument that diplomacy is particularly immoral and, hence, incompatible with democratic government similarly assumes that one can escape from the moral dilemmas of foreign policy by forswearing foreign policy itself. At the bottom of this argument there is a dual illusion: the illusion of the moral superiority of domestic politics over foreign policy and the illusion of the possibility of escaping foreign policy altogether. Both philosophic analysis and historic experience show that the moral problems that foreign policy raises are but a peculiar—and particularly drastic—manifestation of the moral problem of politics as such. Taking a wider view, one can even say that the moral problem of politics is but a peculiar instance of the moral problem which man encounters whenever he acts with reference to his fellow men. What distinguishes in this respect foreign policy from domestic politics and from the human situation in general is not the substance of the problem, which is identical on all levels of human interaction, but the social conditions under which the problem arises on the international plane.

There is, then, no way to escape the moral problem of politics, domestic or international; we can only endeavor to smooth down its sharp edges and to mitigate its practical consequences by changing not its substance but the social environment within which it is bound to arise in one form or another. It is not by accident that those who have tried to do more have taken a negative attitude toward foreign policy; for in the traditional methods of diplomacy they could not help seeing the outward manifestations of the political risks and moral liabilities of foreign policy itself. Opposition to the traditional methods of diplomacy is everywhere intimately connected with either an isolationist or universalistic attitude toward international relations. Both consider the traditional methods of diplomacy at best superfluous and at worst pernicious, for they so regard foreign policy itself. In the isolationist view, a country can afford to dispense with an active foreign policy and, hence, with diplomacy. In the universalistic view, foreign policy, carried on through diplomatic methods by sovereign nations, belongs to a dying age and is a stumbling block to the establishment of a more peaceful and orderly organization of the world.

This thought reveals itself in the recent attempts to set up the procedures of the United Nations as an alternative to the traditional methods of diplomacy. Here again, we are in the presence of the assumption that nations have a choice between the traditional methods of diplomacy and some other way of dealing with each other, a way that somehow leads to freedom from the risks and liabilities of foreign policy. In truth, of course, the procedures of the United Nations, as they have emerged in the practice of the organization, do not differ in substance from the traditional practices of diplomacy. What distinguishes the former from the latter is nothing but the social setting and the legal requirements which influence the way in which the traditional business of diplomacy is carried on within the agencies of the United Nations. The United Nations and traditional diplomacy are not mutually exclusive alternatives between which nations must choose. Rather, they supplement each other, serving identical purposes and partaking of the same qualities and characteristics. The secretary-general of the United Nations, in his *Annual Report on the Work of the Organization for July 1, 1954 through June 15, 1955*, has called attention to this relationship in these words:

We have only begun to make use of the real possibilities of the United Nations as the most representative instrument for the relaxation of tensions, for the lessening of distrust and misunderstanding, and for the discovery and delineation of new areas of common ground and interest. . . . Conference diplomacy may usefully be supplemented by more quiet diplomacy within the United Nations, whether directly between representatives of Member Governments or in contacts between the Secretary-General and Member Governments. The obligations of the Charter, the environment of institutions dedicated to seeking out the common ground among the national interests of Member States, the wide representation from all continents and cultures, the presence of the Secretariat established as a principal organ of the United Nations for the purpose of upholding and serving the international interest—all these can provide help not to be found elsewhere, if they are rightly applied and used.

Within the framework of the Charter there are many possibilities, as yet largely unexplored, for variation of practices. . . . It is my hope that solid progress can be made in the coming years in developing new forms of contact, new methods of deliberation and new techniques of reconciliation. With only slight adjustments, discussions of major issues of a kind that have occurred outside the United Nations could often be fitted into its framework, thus at the same time adding to the strength of the world organization and drawing strength from it.

With these considerations we are entering into the positive task of ascertaining the functions of traditional diplomacy and its permanent value. A nation, existing as it does as an equal among other nations, can deal with the outside world in one of three different ways. It can deny the importance of the other nations for itself and its own importance for them and retreat into the impotence of isolation. Or it can deny the equality of the other nations and try to impose its own will upon them by force of arms. In either case, at least in its pure, extreme realization, a nation can afford to dispense with diplomacy. Or a nation can want to pursue its interests in active contact and on the basis of equality with other nations, assuming the universality of that desire. In that case it cannot do without the constant redefinition and adjustment of its interests for the purpose of accommodating the interests of other nations.

Conflict of interests—actual, seeming, or potential—is the overriding fact of international society, as it is one of the overriding facts of all societies, even those most highly integrated and centralized. Diplomacy in all its diverse historic and social manifestations is the technique of accommodating such conflicting interests. That technique proceeds in two stages: the ascertainment of the facts of conflict and the formulation of the terms of settlement.

Nation A pursues certain interests and so does nation B, and the interests of A and B are on the face of them in conflict. Both nations want to settle this conflict peacefully. How can they go about it? They have to define their respective interests and ascertain the point of conflict. That investigation may lead them to one of three possible conclusions.

If what A wants and finds vital to itself B cannot cede without endangering its vital interests or its very existence, because of the intrinsic importance of the territory, frontier, port, or air base at issue, diplomatic accommodation is impossible. When Francis I of France was asked why he always made war against Charles V of Austria, he is reported to have answered: "Because we both want the same thing: Italy." As long as both kings wanted Italy badly enough, they could either go to war over it or else leave the issue unsettled, hoping for future developments to deflect the energies of both sides toward less contentious objectives. Often in history nations have indeed avoided war over their vital interests by allowing time to take the sting out of their conflicts. Yet in such cases it is to the restraint of warlike passions and the renunciation of quick and radical solutions rather than to the practices of diplomacy that the credit for the preservation of peace must go.

Nation A may again pursue an objective vital to itself which nation B could cede only at the price of a vital interest of its own. Yet, in contrast to the type of conflict just discussed, the importance of the objective to both sides is here not intrinsic to the objective itself but rather the result of a peculiar configuration of interests which are subject to manipulation. For instance, the Soviet Union has a vital interest in preventing a united Germany from joining the Western alliance, and the United States has a similarly vital interest in preventing such a Germany from being absorbed by the Soviet bloc. Taken by themselves, these positions are obviously incompatible and, as the history of East-West negotiations has thus far shown, not subject to diplomatic accommodation. Yet one can well imagine, without committing one's self to its practical feasibility in the immediate future, an over-all European or world-wide settlement of which a German settlement would form an organic part, satisfactory to the interests of both sides which could not be reconciled to the unification of Germany considered in isolation. In situations such as this, it is the task of diplomacy to redefine the seemingly incompatible, vital interests of the nations concerned in order to make them compatible.

This task of diplomacy is, as it were, strategic in nature and truly creative, not often attempted and rarely successful. It yields in practical importance to that function with which diplomacy is typically associated in the popular mind: the function of bargaining issuing in a compromise. In conflicts to which this function applies, nation A seeks an objective which nation B either is willing to grant only in part or refuses to grant at all without compensation. Conflicts of this kind concern non-vital interests of which nations are willing to dispose by way of negotiations. The technique of diplomacy consists here in ascertaining the interests of both sides and in allocating the objective at issue in view of these interests and of the power available for their support.

The same diplomatic technique serves not only the peaceful settlement of conflicts among nations but also the delineation and codification of common interests. In this respect it performs its classic function for the negotiation of treaties serving a common purpose of the contracting parties. Called upon to settle a conflict between two nations, diplomacy must create out of the conflicting interests a community of interests, a compromise, which cannot satisfy all parties completely but with which no party will be completely dissatisfied. When the representatives of two nations meet to negotiate a treaty, say, of commerce or alliance, they must discover and make precise an already existing community of interests. This community of interests, before it is crystallized in legal stipulations, is amorphous and inchoate, obscured and distorted by seeming and real conflicts. It is the task of diplomacy to define the area of that pre-existing community of interests and to express it in terms sufficiently precise to serve as a reliable foundation for future action. It need only be mentioned in passing that this function of diplomacy is identical with that of contractual negotiations on all levels of social interaction.

It must be obvious from what has been said thus far that the traditional methods of diplomacy are of vital importance to a nation that seeks to pursue its interests successfully and peaceably. A nation that is unwilling or unable to use diplomacy for that end is of necessity compelled either to forsake its interests or to pursue them by war. As pointed out before, nations have always had a choice among three alternatives: diplomacy, war, renunciation. Which one of these alternatives a nation chose in a concrete situation was a matter of rational calculation; none of them was excluded a priori on rational grounds.

Modern technology, especially in the form of all-out atomic war, has destroyed this rational equality among diplomacy, war, and renunciation and has greatly enhanced the importance of diplomacy. In view of that technology, there is no longer safety in renunciation or in victory in war. From the beginning of history to the Second World War the risks inherent in these three choices were commensurate with the advantages to be expected. Nations would miscalculate and suffer unexpected losses; but it was never rationally foreordained that they could not win. War, in particular, was a rational means to a rational end; victory would justify the risks and losses incurred, and the consequences of defeat were not from the outset out of all proportion to the gains to be expected from victory.

The possibility of all-out atomic war has destroyed these rational relationships. When universal destruction is the result of victory and defeat alike, war itself is no longer a matter of rational choice but becomes an instrument of suicidal despair. The pursuit of a nation's interests short of all-out atomic war, then, becomes a matter of self-preservation. Even on the assumption—at present a moot one—that limited wars can and will still be safely waged, the risk of such a limited war developing into an all-out atomic one will always be present. Hence, the imperative of the avoidance of all-out atomic war gives, at the very least, unprecedented urgency to the pursuit of a nation's interests by peaceful means. Such peaceful pursuit, as we know, spells diplomacy. Neither diplomacy nor all-out atomic war is today one among several rational choices available to a nation. As all-out atomic war is tantamount to suicide, so successful diplomacy provides the only certain chance for survival. A nation which under present conditions is either unwilling or unable to take full advantage of the traditional methods of diplomacy condemns itself either to the slow death of attrition or the sudden death of atomic destruction.

The vital importance that the traditional methods of diplomacy receive from the possibility of all-out atomic war is underlined by the more specific political developments which may well mark the end of the first postwar decade as the beginning of a new era in international relations. The first decade following the Second World War was characterized on the international scene by three basic political phenomena: the bipolarity of international politics, the tendency of this bipolar political system to transform itself into a two-bloc system, and the policy of containment. These three basic facts combined in minimizing the traditional methods of diplomacy, both as a matter of fact and in terms of the objective opportunities available.

During that decade, effective power for purposes of foreign policy was concentrated in Washington and Moscow, and these two power poles tended to attract like magnets most of the other centers of power. Whatever they might have preferred had they been free to choose, Great Britain and France, Poland and China had to lean upon one or the other of the superpowers for political, military, and economic support. Such countries could not have remained neutral, let alone have changed sides, in the East-West conflict, short of a domestic revolution of radical dimensions. In such a situation, rigid in its alignments and inflexible in either side's conception of the interests involved, the main task of both sides is not to make and receive concessions but, at the very least, to hold the line and, at the very best, to advance it unilaterally. Since the balance of power made the latter alternative unfeasible short of a general war, both sides were of necessity reduced to a policy of containment which for all practical purposes forsook advancement at the expense of the other side while at the same time preventing the other side from advancing.

Such a situation of "cold war" offered little opportunity for the use of diplomatic methods either within the two power blocs or between them. The inner coherence of the two blocs resulted primarily from the ineluctable necessity which made their members seek shelter under the roof of one or the other of the superpowers. During that period, the discrepancy of strength between the two superpowers, on the one hand, and their respective allies, on the other, was so obviously extreme and the consequences for those who would dare step out of line so obviously dire that there was very little need for diplomacy to crystallize so obvious a community of interests.

The relations between the two blocs were no less clearly defined by the objective situation. The essence of the policy of containment was military rather than political. It consisted in the main in the warning, supported by actual preparedness, that a step taken by the other side beyond the line of military demarcation of 1945 would of necessity lead to a general war.

The services diplomacy was able to perform for this policy of containment were hardly different from those diplomacy has traditionally performed for the conduct of real war. It could announce the conditions for the settlement of the Cold War and use such and similar announcements for purposes of psychological warfare. The very modalities of the Cold War, then, inevitably transformed diplomacy into a mere auxiliary of a war waged against the enemy, not for the purpose of accommodating conflicting interests, but for the triumph, however verbal, of one nation over the other. Thus it is not by accident that during the first decade following the Second World War the traditional methods of diplomacy virtually ceased to operate in the relations between East and West and that the moves carried on under the labels and with the personnel of diplomacy at the many East-West conferences and within the United Nations served purposes not only far removed from but often diametrically opposed to those of traditional diplomacy.

This period of postwar history has come to a close. It is being replaced by an era marked by greater flexibility within the two power blocs—a tendency toward the loosening of their inner coherence if not toward their dissolution—and, consequently, by greater flexibility in the relationship between the two power blocs as well. To meet the problems of this new era the methods of the Cold War are inadequate. As the conditions of the Cold War led necessarily to the disuse and misuse of the practices of diplomacy, so the new era of international relations with equal necessity calls for the restoration of these practices.

Four facts are in the main responsible for this change in international relations: the decrease in the dependence of the powers of second rank upon the superpowers; the impending rise of Germany and Japan to great-power status; the impending dispersion of atomic power among a multitude of nations, some of which, by virtue of their possession of atomic power, will gain or regain the status of great powers; finally, the spread and sharpening of the colonial revolutions in Asia, Africa, and Latin America.

Viewed from the vantage point of the United States, each of these new facts requires the vigorous application of the traditional practices of diplomacy. Since neither the American atomic monopoly nor extreme dependence upon American support can any longer be relied upon to secure the coherence of the Western alliance, the United States must again resort to the time-honored diplomatic method of fashioning a legally and politically viable community of interests out of the one that exists objectively in an inchoate and ill-defined form. Germany and Japan, no longer the object of the victor's dispositions, must be persuaded by the same methods to see in association with the West the best chance for pursuing their interests. It is hardly necessary to emphasize that a similar approach to the colonial revolutions has been long overdue.

Thus the situation that confronts the United States at the moment of this writing poses the perennial problem of diplomacy with renewed urgency. The objections to the use of diplomacy are without merit. Its indispensability for a successful and peaceful foreign policy grows from the very nature of things political. The possibility of all-out atomic war has made its successful use the condition of survival. The new era of international relations has made its restoration of vital concern for the foreign policy of the United States.

33 *The Economics of Foreign Policy*

Foreign policy makes use of the total power of the nation for the defense and promotion of the national interest vis-à-vis other nations. Nine factors go into the making of national power: geography, natural resources, national morale, industrial capacity, military preparedness, population, national character, quality of diplomacy, and the quality of government in general. Of these, three come under the heading of the economic factor: natural resources, industrial capacity, and the quality of government. It is the government that co-ordinates the foreign policy pursued with the available economic resources and that brings the different claims upon these resources into balance with each other.

A nation that is self-sufficient in food has a great advantage over a nation that must import foodstuffs or starve. Thus, the power of Great Britain—and her chances of survival in times of war—has always depended on the Royal Navy's ability to keep open the sea lanes. On the other hand, nations enjoying self-sufficiency in food, such as the United States and the Soviet Union, need not divert their national energies from their primary objectives in order to assure their food supply. They have thus been able to pursue much more forceful and single-minded foreign policies.

What holds true of food is also true of those natural resources which are important for industrial production and, more particularly, for the waging of war. With the increasing mechanization of warfare, national power has become more and more dependent upon the control of raw materials in peace and war. "One drop of oil," said Clemenceau during the First World War, "is worth one drop of our soldiers' blood." It is not by accident that the two most powerful nations today, the United States and the Soviet Union, are most nearly self-sufficient in the raw materials of modern industrial production and that they control at least the access and the sources of those raw materials which they do not themselves possess.

From *Challenge, The Magazine of Economic Affairs*, February, 1959, published by Institute of Economic Affairs, New York University.

Yet while control of raw materials is an element of national power, it is but a potential source of strength if it is not transformed into industrial capacity. The technology of modern war has made industrial capacity, especially in the field of heavy industry, an indispensable element of national power. Thus the competition among nations for power transforms itself largely into competition for the production of a greater number of more effective implements of war. The quality and productive capacity of the industrial plant, the know-how of the working man, the skill of the engineer, the inventive genius of the scientist, the managerial organization—all these are factors on which the industrial capacity of a nation and, hence, its power in international affairs depend. Thus the great powers are bound to be identical with the leading industrial nations. The spectacular rise of the Soviet Union as a world power, and the aspirations of China to equal and then surpass both the United States and the Soviet Union—these are developments in which industrial capacity plays an indispensable role. It does not follow, however, that economic strength in terms of natural resources and industrial capacity is tantamount to national power. Economic strength is, as it were, the indispensable raw material out of which government must construct the edifice of national power. In order to achieve this, government must perform two different operations. First, it must bring its foreign policy into balance with its economic resources. Second, it must bring the different claims upon these resources into balance with each other.

The economic resources of all nations are limited, and consequently, the means and ends of the foreign policy of all nations are limited by the amount of the available resources. A nation must estimate how far it is able to go in its relations with other nations in view of the available economic resources, and it must choose the ends and means of its foreign policy in the light of that estimate. Its task is completed only when it has distributed wisely the sum total of its economic resources among the different ends and means of its foreign policy. How much ought to be devoted to the armed forces in relation to the foreign aid commitment? How much ought to be allocated to the instruments of atomic war in proportion to conventional weapons? And how should we divide our resources between foreign economic and foreign military aid? What kind of military establishment is the national economy able to support in view of the demands the civilian population makes upon it? How many guns can the economic system provide for the nation, and how many guns and how much butter can it provide for other nations in view of the amount of butter the nation wants and needs for itself?

The United States must make these decisions against the background of a triple challenge: the military challenge of the Soviet bloc, the economic challenge of the Soviet bloc, and the challenge which is presented by the widening gap between the highly developed industrial nations of the West and the underdeveloped masses of Asia, Africa, and Latin America.

The Soviet Union has been explicit in its resolution to prove Marx and Lenin correct in their prophecy that capitalism is doomed. While Marx and Lenin believed that disaster would result from a series of world wars fought primarily among the capitalistic nations themselves, Khrushchev has declared that capitalism will fall because of its inferiority in economic organization and productivity. As he put it to the noted newspaper columnist and author, Walter Lippmann, America enjoys "the last years of its greatness." The Soviet Union is destined to surpass the United States in economic productivity and well-being; and by demonstrating its economic superiority over the United States, it will set an example which the underdeveloped masses of the earth will want to emulate. They will choose the Soviet rather than the American way of life. Furthermore, this economic superiority will enable the Soviet Union to wage full-scale economic war against the United States by taking away its foreign markets and integrating the underdeveloped areas of the world into its economic and political system. Thus, without firing a shot, the Soviet Union will triumph over the United States.

How has the United States responded? Its diplomacy has emphasized the military threat and the military response. Thus it has concentrated throughout the world upon strengthening the existing alliances and concluding as many new ones as possible. Foreign aid, too, has been primarily of a military nature. Only a small fraction of the resources earmarked for foreign aid has been used for economic and technical assistance. Our foreign trade policy has followed the traditional pattern: maximize exports and protect the domestic producer against foreign competition. The subordination of our foreign trade policy to the broader purposes of our political foreign policy, in terms of the challenge of the Soviet Union and of the underdeveloped nations, has been in the nature of sporadic and minor deviations from the traditional pattern. This response has been deficient both in its conception and in the specific policies pursued. The challenge with which the Soviet Union threatens the United States is total, both as to the goal to be attained and the means being employed. The Soviet Union marshals its total economic resources in order to bring about the downfall of the United States. The American response has been for the greater part misdirected and for the remainder halfhearted and piecemeal.

Our diplomacy has been misdirected in its emphasis upon local military arrangements, especially outside Europe, as ends in themselves. The ability of the United States to deter Soviet aggression through its own retaliatory power is indeed the essential minimum requirement of American foreign policy. Yet the concentration upon maintaining and developing local military forces has been useless and even self-defeating in so far as the Soviet challenge has been economic. It has done the United States no good to develop the military forces of, say, an Asian nation which lies outside the effective range of Soviet military power but which is vulnerable to Soviet economic penetration. This misdirected military approach to what is essentially a political and economic problem also tends to distort the distribution of political and economic forces in an irrational manner; it damages the interests of the United States in that it creates political and economic tensions to be exploited by the Soviet Union.

If our military approach is defective, our foreign aid policies suffer from different but no less serious weaknesses. We have not developed a coherent foreign aid policy, subordinating the concrete measures taken in the field of foreign aid to the objectives of both our over-all and local political policies and co-ordinating them with the measures taken in other fields. What is the over-all purpose of our foreign aid? To keep our allies on our side and acquire new ones? To protect uncommitted nations from communism? Or to satisfy the so-called revolution of rising expectations, which is supposed to sweep Asia, Africa, and Latin America? Is it true that all the nations which ask us for aid need it and can use it? To what extent is foreign aid really in the nature of a bribe to foreign governments? And to what extent does it perform the politically useful function of the traditional subsidies that were common in the eighteenth century, especially in British foreign policy? To what extent does it have the function of a stimulus to genuine economic development? A rational foreign aid policy requires empirical answers to these and similar questions. It is the measure of the irrationality of our foreign aid policy that the answers have largely been derived from unexamined popular assumptions of doubtful validity. We have preferred to allocate foreign aid by impulse rather than base it upon a carefully thought-out philosophy which has stood the test of experience.

Our policy of foreign trade shows in still another way the obsolescence of our foreign economic policy. Ideally, foreign trade is carried on by private enterprises for the purpose of private gain. Actually, however, governments have time and again endeavored to use foreign trade as an instrument of national policy. So-called dollar diplomacy is a case in point. It is not true, even though it is widely believed, that private enterprise used the government to further private foreign commercial ventures. Quite to the contrary, the government used private enterprise abroad for the purposes of United States foreign policy. Today, the need for such use has become overwhelming in view of the Communist challenge. Yet the government, shackled by ancient shibboleths and sectional domestic interests, has not dared to develop a policy which would make foreign trade a potent instrument of American foreign policy.

Our foreign economic policy in all its manifestations is deficient in two major and related respects. First, it is in good measure divorced both in conception and execution from the purposes and operations of our foreign political policy. We still regard foreign economic policy, as we did military policy, as a self-sufficient technical entity following its own course according to its own laws, quite independent of extraneous political considerations. Second, hardly anything in our foreign economic policy reflects the total character of the challenge with which the Communist world and the underdeveloped masses confront us. We are not unaware of the existence of that challenge, but we act upon it as though it could be successfully met through a relatively minor effort, with our domestic economic business being carried on as usual. Yet the truth of the matter is that the Soviet bloc subordinates its economic life completely to the purposes of its foreign policy. Are we rich and powerful enough to withstand this total effort, let alone to win out in competition with it, by making only minor and haphazard efforts in response to it? The answer implicit in our foreign economic policy is in the affirmative. Yet it is virtually certain that this is not the right answer.

A sound foreign economic policy must use economic resources as a weapon with which the political interests of the United States are to be defended in competition with the Soviet bloc. In terms of organization, this means that the weapon must be in the hands of the political leaders to be used for political purposes, not in the hands of the economic experts to be used for narrow technical ends. In terms of substance, this means two things. It means that we must apply a political standard both to the purposes and the methods of our foreign aid, and that we must spend more for foreign aid where our political purposes seem to require it and less or nothing where our political goals can be served otherwise. And it means first of all that everywhere and, more particularly, in the field of foreign trade, the public interest in the survival and the safety of the United States must take precedence over private gain.

It would be an illusion to believe that these general principles can be applied to the concrete issues of our foreign economic policy without drastic changes in our domestic economic system or that these changes will not narrow the freedom of private choice. These changes will not be the result of ideological preference, nor can ideological preference be allowed to stand in their way. Faced with an all-out economic challenge to our very existence, we shall have to sacrifice much that is important and much that in the past appeared to us even essential. We must do it for the sake of something that is more important than any other consideration: the survival of the nation itself.

34   *Prospect for a New Foreign Policy*

Exactly eight years ago, I sat down to write an article explaining why great things could be expected from Messrs. Eisenhower and Dulles in the conduct of American foreign policy. On paper, the estimate was reasonable. The President-elect enjoyed enough prestige to marshal popular support for any foreign policy he might have chosen, from unilateral disarmament to preventive war. The new Secretary of State was uniquely prepared, and appeared to be eminently qualified, for the position: Dulles' *War or Peace*, published in 1950, was as sound a statement of the principles of American foreign policy as could then be found. Yet before I was able to finish the article, certain depressing indications of what the new foreign policy was likely to be had already appeared. The article was never finished, and the history of the last eight years has shown how mistaken my original estimate was.

These sobering reminiscences provide an appropriate background for evaluating the prospects of American foreign policy under the new administration. On paper, again, Rusk, Bowles, Stevenson, and Harriman each looks at least as good as Dulles ever did, and Mr. Kennedy's *The Strategy of Peace* is as sound a statement of the requirements of American foreign policy for the sixties as was Mr. Dulles' book for the fifties. The foreign policy of the United States has probably never been entrusted to so high-powered a team, every member of which is qualified, in his own particular way, to be secretary of state. Nevertheless, while personal excellence in those who make and carry it out is indispensable for a sound foreign policy, it does not assure a successful one. The new men must work within old circumstances, domestic and international, and the circumstances will put their excellence to the test. Regardless of their convictions and intentions, they are the prisoners of the past—of established institutions, policies, and habits of mind. They may at best be able to gain a little freedom of movement by loosening some

From *Commentary*, February, 1961.

chains, but they cannot break down walls. Whatever they may have hopefully counseled or planned or worked for when they were not in office, once they assume office, they are in prison, and their ability to do what they would like to do depends only in part upon themselves.

Eisenhower and Herter have left to Kennedy and Rusk a heritage much inferior to that bequeathed by Truman and Acheson to the Eisenhower administration. At the beginning of 1953, the foreign policy of the United States was still a going concern. Brilliantly conceived in the spring of 1947 to counter the threat of Stalin's imperialism, it was still serviceable five years later, even though its weaknesses had by then become clear. Those weaknesses were in part owing to inherent misconceptions, such as the nature of the military role of NATO and the German contribution supposedly indispensable to it; and in part they stemmed from such new circumstances as the changes in the balance of world military power and the awakening of Asia. (The persistence of the issues of our foreign policy is indicated, I think, by the chapter headings in a book of mine published in 1951: one reads "The Precarious State of the Atlantic Alliance"; another, "The Struggle for Asia as a Struggle for the Minds of Men.")

It was the great failing of Dulles that he subordinated the requirements of a sound foreign policy to the demands of domestic politics; in consequence, he was compelled to accentuate the weaknesses of the foreign policy he had inherited while at the same time resisting its adaptation to new conditions. When Dulles assumed office, he resolved that what had happened to Mr. Acheson would not happen to him. Mr. Acheson, the architect of a sound and successful foreign policy, found himself deserted by public opinion, and, more particularly, by congressional opinion, and hence was handicapped in the conduct of his policy. Dulles made it his first order of business to secure for his person and policies the support of the Congress and of public opinion at large; in this endeavor, he was eminently successful. But as a result something happened to him that had never happened to Mr. Acheson: he became the prisoner of a public opinion—in good measure created by his own words and deeds—which limited his freedom of action to a foreign policy conceived in the image of a world-wide Maginot line around the Russo-Chinese empire, manned by invincible American military might and its steadfast allies. However popular that policy was, it proved unsuccessful outside Europe. A military policy which vacillates between the implausible threat of "massive retaliation," on the one hand, and ineffectual response, on the other, is incapable in the long run of containing the military expansion of communism. And so far as the acute threat of Communist political expansion through "competitive coexistence" is concerned, the policy yields not only an irrelevant response but actual ammunition for the enemy. Meanwhile, with the United States embarked upon an essentially futile, and even self-defeating, foreign policy, the world situation has changed in at least four important respects.

The Soviet Union, of course, now ranks with the United States as an atomic power. And if the present trend continues, an indefinite number of nations will have acquired atomic weapons within the next decade. Second, the countries of Western Europe and Japan, having recovered their economic strength, are now in the process of building up their military and political strength as well. China, above all, is likely to become a first-rate power: it need only add to its enormous population and territory the achievements of modern technology. Third, the emancipation of the colonial and semicolonial peoples of the world has entered its last stage in Africa and has begun in Latin America. Finally, both the Soviet Union and (to a lesser extent at the moment) China have embarked upon a new expansionist foreign policy; it is no longer based so much upon a combination of the infallibility of Marxist prophesies and open military pressure as upon the achievements, actual and potential, of the Communist system.

The task of the new administration, if it hopes for success in coping with the changed world situation, lies in rethinking and refashioning American foreign policy in five major areas: the relations with our allies, the relations with the uncommitted nations, the relation between domestic politics and foreign policy, the relations with the Communist bloc, and, finally, the supranational control of atomic power.

The several alliances of which the United States is a member owe their existence to two different factors: the need in which our European allies, as well as our former enemies, found themselves after the Second World War to have American economic, military, and political support; and the United States objective of containing by military means the Soviet Union and Communist China in the Middle East and Asia. In recent years, the foundations for the first type of alliance have changed radically; whereas the foundations for the second type were weak from the very outset. The economic recovery of the nations of Western Europe and the former enemies has made them less dependent upon American support than they once were. As a consequence, they have at times been able to pursue their own narrower interests regardless of—indeed, to the detriment of—the common interests of the alliance. The Kennedy administration must find a new foundation for these alliances, one which reflects more faithfully the present underlying community of interests of the major nations of the non-Communist world. These alliances were primarily conceived in military terms. They must now be given an economic, political, and cultural content as well. The transformation of the Cold War into what is now called "competitive coexistence" has revealed the essential unsoundness of the policy of military containment as extended to Asia and the Middle East. For the conflict between East and West has taken on more and more the aspects of a struggle for the minds of men, especially in the uncommitted nations of Asia, Africa, and Latin America—a struggle to be fought with the weapons of prestige, subversion, political pressure, foreign aid, and foreign trade. Military alliances—in any contest for men's minds—are likely to be at best of minor importance and at worst a political handicap.

If the United States is to wage this struggle for the minds of men with any chance of success, the Kennedy administration must devise a new grand strategy. Two fundamental reforms are called for: the integration of all the factors involved in the struggle for the single purpose of maintaining and expanding the influence of the non-Communist world, and the adaptation of these various factors to the local conditions prevailing in any one country. In particular, the Kennedy administration must develop, and act upon, a coherent philosophy of foreign aid and foreign trade.

The uncommitted nations confront the Kennedy administration also with a problem in political organization. Many of the new nations owe their existence to mere accidents of colonial history and are therefore not likely to become viable political, economic, and military units within the boundaries they now occupy. This being the case, they present a standing invitation for a new imperialism to establish a new order where the old colonial order has disappeared; alternatively, they are threatened with anarchy, into which the rest of the world might well be sucked. This enormously complex problem will test the political creativity and determination of the new administration.

It is obvious that the domestic policies pursued by the United States, especially in the field of race relations, are bound to have a direct influence upon our ability to wage the struggle for the minds of men with any chance of success. The new administration needs to be fully aware of this influence in its conduct of domestic policies. Where it cannot entirely control these policies, it must at least give moral support to the positions which conform most closely to the best traditions of America. Throughout the better part of American history, our foreign policy drew strength and its attractiveness to other nations from the character of our domestic politics. The American experiment in government and social organization was intended from the very outset—and was received by other nations as being so intended—not only for America but for the world. It was meant as a model for other nations to emulate. The new administration has the duty to restore that meaning.

The ultimate outcome of these new policies, which we must look to the Kennedy administration to undertake, will depend upon the kind of relations which are established with the Communist bloc; for, if in the course of the successful pursuit of these policies, our relations with the U.S.S.R. and Communist China should further deteriorate, our very success might in the end turn out to be self-defeating in so far as it would bring closer the probability of a third world war fought with atomic weapons. Thus the Kennedy administration must achieve the supreme task of statesmanship of successfully waging the competitive struggle with the Communist bloc without at the same time increasing the risk of war. The first precondition for minimizing that risk is the stabilization of the present territorial frontiers between the Western world and the Communist bloc. The second precondition is the maintenance and, if need be, the restoration of the Western atomic deterrent. The risk of war will diminish only in the measure that the points of conflict which might ignite a war can be reduced, at the same time that deterrence against the starting of a war is strengthened.

Finally, even if the Kennedy administration should be successful in the pursuit of all these policies, the United States and the world will still be confronted with a mortal danger: the spread of atomic weapons to an indefinite number of nations. This danger we can cope with only in co-operation with the other great nations of the world. The prospect of such a spread is bound to become a reality unless the present trend is reversed; if the trend continues, it is likely to cause unprecedented anarchy which will finally be beyond the control of the big powers. To bring nuclear weapons under supranational control is indeed the overriding task of the age. History is likely to judge the Kennedy administration by its approach to this task and its success in accomplishing it.

Nevertheless, even if the new administration were to devise sound policies for the five areas I have mentioned, their success would in good measure depend upon factors, such as the policies of other nations, over which the government of the United States has no control. It would also depend upon the ability of the American government to put the policies, once decided upon, into actual operation. This problem is peculiar to the United States, stemming from our constitutional arrangements and political system. The problem arises in four different areas of policy formation: in the relations between the President and the Secretary of State; between the Secretary and the Department of State; between the President and Secretary of State, on the one hand, and other executive departments, on the other; and, finally, between the President and Secretary of State, on the one hand, and Congress and public opinion at large, on the other.

The President is ultimately responsible for the conduct of American foreign policy, and the Secretary of State is supposed to be his main aide in the discharge of that responsibility. In reality, the relations between the President and the Secretary of State have conformed to this constitutional intent only when the President was in effect his own Secretary of State and used the titular head of the State Department as a mere instrument, as in the Roosevelt-Stettinius relations; or if the President and Secretary were continuously of one mind, as in the case of Truman and Acheson. Otherwise, the President has either bypassed the Secretary of State, as Roosevelt did with Hull, or given him a free hand, normally ratifying his decisions, as Eisenhower did with Dulles. When both the President and the Secretary of State have had their strong and different convictions about foreign policy, conflict has more often than not been the result. Within the State Department, the chance of conflict is always present, and conflict has frequently materialized when the Secretary's subordinates have had strong policy preferences of their own. The relations between Hull and Sumner Welles and the independent and contradictory policies pursued in the thirties by Ambassador Kennedy in London and Ambassador Dodd in Berlin come to mind. That problem is superimposed upon the ever present task of fashioning a bureaucracy, set in its ways, into a pliable instrument of a new policy.

The new Secretary of State faces a slow-moving, if not recalcitrant, department. He and the President must also impose their new foreign policy upon other departments of the executive branch which may be committed to a different policy. The official Far Eastern policy of the United States, for example—for all practical purposes, the policy of two Chinas—not only is being obstructed by the government of Taiwan but has also been opposed in practice by certain groups within the State and Defense Departments. The official policy of the United States concerning the cessation of atomic tests has been openly challenged in word and deed by the Atomic Energy Commission. The new administration, which must soon make crucial decisions on this latter problem, minimizes its chances for successful negotiations—slim as they are in view of the objective nature of the issue and Russian attitudes—if it is unable to commit its own agencies to a common position.

Finally, it is obvious that the government of the United States can only go as far in its conduct of foreign policy as Congress and public opinion at large permit. The task of combining sound foreign policies with popular support is always difficult, and the temptation to sacrifice the former to the latter is always great and at times has proved irresistible. The foreign policies upon which the new administration must embark are not only new in that they differ from those which have been pursued up till now. They are also startling in that they run counter to cherished popular preconceptions. The international developments of the last eight years have transformed these preconceptions into illusions; neither the words nor the deeds of our government took cognizance of those developments. The new administration, in order to marshal public opinion behind its new foreign policies, must first of all restore a sense of reality to the American people.

The demands which these tasks make upon the courage, wisdom, and ability of the Kennedy administration are superhuman, in view of which the prospects for a wholly successful American foreign policy are of necessity less bright than is suggested by the contrast between the personal and intellectual qualities of the new team and those of its predecessor. Whoever expects spectacular changes is likely to be disappointed. We others will be grateful to the Kennedy administration if it can give American foreign policy a new spirit and awareness and a consistent movement in the right direction.

35 *The China Policy of the United States*

In order to understand the policy of the United States toward China it is necessary to go back to the Chinese civil war. It is at this point that the confusion over the real issue obscured the thinking and frustrated the policies of the United States. When it became obvious that the Nationalist regime was unable to cope with the revolutionary situation even if supported by American arms and advice, only two courses, which General Wedemeyer's report of 1947 clearly envisaged, were logically open to American policy. One was military intervention on such a scale as to be sufficient not only to crush the Communist armies but also to keep discontent permanently in check. Military intervention of this kind would have entailed military and political commitments of incalculable magnitude. This course of action was rejected by the framers of the United States' foreign policy on the advice of, among others, the then Secretary of State, George Marshall. The other course of action was predicated on the assumption that the triumph of the Communist revolution in China was inevitable. It would then have been incumbent upon American policy to reconcile itself to the inevitable—as policy, being the art of the possible, frequently must—and to exploit whatever potentialities there were for the promotion of American interests; for while Chinese communism is the ideological ally of Moscow, its rise to power owes little to Russia, nor will it need to rely on Russian support to maintain itself in power.

This fundamental difference between Chinese communism and the Communist regimes of Eastern Europe, which would not have come to power nor could have stayed in power without Russian support, allows the Communist government of China a freedom of action in international affairs which the Communist governments of Eastern Europe almost completely lack. Consequently, the Communist government of China can, if it chooses, pursue a course in foreign policy which is determined not by the interests of the Soviet

From the *China Quarterly*, May, 1962.

Union expressed in orders from Moscow but by the traditional interests of China. These interests may or may not coincide with the interests of the Soviet Union, and Chinese and Russian policies may or may not be parallel.

It must be remembered that the traditional objectives of Russia in the Far East have more often than not been at odds with the traditional objectives of China. Furthermore, and more importantly, the Soviet Union cannot look with equanimity on the economic and military development of Communist China; for if Communist China should add to its enormous superiority in manpower the achievements of modern technology under the firm political direction of the Chinese Communist party, it would then become of necessity the most powerful nation on earth, overshadowing by far the Soviet Union. The rulers of the Kremlin, considering the opposition they face at home and their uncertain relations with the satellites of Eastern Europe, must also fear—and probably already have reason to fear—the influence which China can exert in the struggle for power within the ruling group of the Soviet Union and in the struggle for a certain measure of independence which the satellite nations are waging against Moscow. Whether there will be further coincidence or divergence of Russian and Chinese interests and policies will depend in good measure upon the policies of the non-Communist nations.

There was the chance for the United States to pursue a policy which, although difficult to explain to the general public and necessarily devoid of spectacular short-run successes, offered the only chance, granted the inevitability of the Communist domination of China, to further the traditional American interest of maintaining the balance of power in Asia. The United States chose neither of the two courses open to it, or rather, it chose both of them, pursuing them sometimes simultaneously, sometimes alternately, but always half-heartedly and without consistency. During the civil war the United States intervened on the side of the Nationalists but limited its commitments in matériel and men so strictly as to preclude any chance of success. Simultaneously, the United States tried to bring about a coalition between the Nationalists and Communists which, if it had succeeded, would, of necessity, have led to the absorption of the former by the latter.

General Marshall's attempt in 1946 to end the civil war by forming a coalition government of Communists and Nationalists partook of the same underestimation of Nationalist weakness which underlay all of 'American policy in the immediate postwar years and compounded it by misunderstanding the character of Chinese communism. It was grounded in two false assumptions. One was that the Chinese Communists were really agrarian reformers at heart using Marxist slogans without believing them. The other was a misplaced faith in the Nationalist regime as an efficient and reliable machine of government. Actually it had become impossible at that stage to do business with Chiang Kai-shek with any expectation of future efficient and honest performance, and it was to misunderstand completely the nature of communism, as it manifests itself in China and elsewhere, to disregard its necessary aspirations for total power as a means to realize the truth of Marxism.

After the end of the civil war, the United States continued this essentially contradictory and indecisive policy. Under the impact of the Chinese intervention in the Korean War and influenced by domestic politics, the United States drifted into a policy of counterrevolution per se. That is to say, the United States has refused to recognize the Communist regime as the legitimate government of China and has denied its right to represent China in the United Nations. On the other hand, the United States has continued to recognize the Chiang Kai-shek regime of Formosa as the only authentic voice of all China. The United States has given it political, economic, moral, and military support, assuring its very existence through the commitment of the armed forces of the United States. The United States has countenanced small-scale operations of the Chiang Kai-shek forces against the Chinese mainland and has given its active military support to the Nationalist defense of the offshore islands.

The result of this policy has been inconclusive in terms of the very assumptions upon which that policy is based; for while that policy has strengthened the Nationalist forces on Formosa, that policy being the very precondition for their survival, it has done virtually nothing to weaken the Communist domination of the Chinese mainland. Thus, on the one hand, the United States refuses to recognize that the Chinese Communists are here to stay, and on the other hand, it has done nothing to dislodge that regime by counter-revolutionary measures. The United States has done nothing effective because there is nothing it can do short of an all-out war against China which it fears will degenerate into an all-out world war destroying the United States and its enemies. This policy has had one positive result: it has kept Formosa out of the hands of the Communists. It has had two major negative results: it has isolated the United States completely from its allies, and it has lost the United States the support of public opinion throughout the world. The Chinese Communists have not been slow to exploit the difficult position in which the United States finds itself today by virtue of its own policy.

While the United States has tried to extricate itself from the impasse of its Far Eastern policy, the Chinese Communists have refused to lend a helping hand. From their point of view it is much more advantageous to let the United States remain entangled in a web of self-created contradictions, unable to advance or retreat, than to co-operate with the United States in the search for a compromise settlement. The Chinese Communists are aware of the difficult American position, and they also know that time is on their side, for the balance of military power is bound to tilt more and more toward the Chinese side. Communist China will become an independent military factor in world politics, and the world-wide opposition to American policy toward China will grow stronger as America's military position grows weaker. Thus, paradoxically enough, the main issue is today no longer whether or not the United States wants to recognize Communist China. The issue is, rather, whether Communist China wants to be recognized by the United States, and obviously it does not want to be recognized if it has to pay the price of recognizing the status quo in the Formosa Strait.

What is the rationale of the Far Eastern policy of the United States which has led to such unfortunate results? That policy is based upon two fundamental assumptions: first, the use of force as an instrument of national policy cannot be countenanced anywhere in the world; and second, the policy of containment can be successfully applied to the Far East. The first assumption derives from the fear that the use of violence, however limited, may leap by stages to the use of nuclear weapons and to the destruction of civilization itself. A policy derived from this assumption, however, requires the existence of a status quo which is reasonably acceptable to all concerned and therefore does not offer an incentive for change by violent means. This condition does not prevail at present in the Far East. The other assumption holds that the threat that confronts the United States around the world is primarily military in nature and therefore must be countered primarily by military means. The policy of military containment, eminently successful in Europe where it originated, must then be applied around the world. The correctness of this assumption is subject to very serious doubt. What threatens the United States in Asia is not primarily military aggression but political aggression and, more particularly, a slow and insidious shift of the allegiance of hundreds of millions of people to Russian and Chinese communism. To try to stem this tide by military means is likely not only to be useless but also to be self-defeating. Furthermore, even if the threat emanating from Communist China were primarily of a military nature, the United States' military policy in the Far East would be inadequate.

The balance of military power between Communist China and the United States is quite different from that between the United States and the Soviet Union in Europe. The Soviet Union has thus far been deterred by the retaliatory nuclear power of the United States; but can China, in its particular position and with its particular tactics, be so deterred? In terms of conventional war, a strong China is as superior to southeast Asia as the United States is to Central America. Southeast Asia has been the traditional sphere of influence of a strong China. In order to deny that region to China, peripheral military measures will not suffice. Whoever wants to contain a strong China must strike at the center of that power. The United States has never been willing, and for good reasons, to contemplate such a strike. Thus the United States has been caught in a contradiction between what it wants to achieve and the measures it is willing and able to apply in order to achieve it. Only a radical revision of the very assumptions upon which its China policy is based will extricate it from that contradiction.

The chances that the government of the United States will take the initiative in revising its China policy are virtually nil. A considerable number of high officials are aware of the facts of life in the Far East, yet quite a number, especially in the military establishment, are not. Furthermore, and most importantly, public opinion has been conditioned for more than a decade to support a negative policy toward China, unaware of the risks, expecting at worst an indefinite continuation of the status quo and at best some kind of miracle which will make the Chinese Communists go away. The present policy could only be reversed through the President's initiative, requiring a combination of political insight and courage that has not been forthcoming in the past and cannot be expected in the foreseeable future.

More likely than not, then, the China policy of the United States will be changed not by a deliberate act of statesmanship, but under the impact of irresistible pressures from without. One of these pressures is likely to emanate from the United Nations; the other, from the growing military power of China. The United States cannot but yield to the former; the latter will confront it with the painful alternative of retreat or war. Wise policy would anticipate these alternatives and try to avoid them by creating conditions opening up different and more favorable alternatives. It would explore the degree of the Chinese Communists' present weakness and, if it should appear promising, exploit it politically, militarily, and economically. On the other hand, it would assess the likelihood of future Chinese strength and would, before it became acute, prepare positions designed to withstand it with a minimum of risk. To do nothing and wait for something to happen and then react by improvisation is the very opposite of rational policy; it is tantamount to its abdication. It sacrifices reason and interest upon the altar of a domestic political peace which in the nature of things is bound to be precarious and temporary.

Index

Academic life, corruption in, 35ff.
Acheson, Dean, 24, 130, 148, 179, 293, 408, 413
Achilles, 96, 210
Adams, Charles Kendall, on political science, 241ff.
Adams, John, on power, 11f.
Adams, John Quincy, 336
Adenauer, Konrad, 139, 148
Administrative state, 323f.
Afghanistan, 105f., 164, 172, 356
Africa, 105, 339, 377, 399, 403f., 409f.
Afro-Asian bloc, 98, 339
Alexander the Great, 94, 110
Algeria, 354, 377, 400
Alliances, 161, 178f.; ideological, 371; as policy, 339, 354ff., 368ff., 387ff., 408f., 418; types of, 370. *See also* individual nations
America, limits of power of, 101. *See* United States
American Civil War, 8
American political thought, escapism of, 10ff., 212ff.
Appeasement, 25
Aquinas, Thomas, 45
Arab nations, 165. *See also* individual nations
Area studies, 299ff.
Aristocracy, political philosophy of, 315
Aristophanes, 191
Aristotle, 44, 251, 253f., 267, 269, 287, 293, 315, 332
Aron, Raymond, 343
Art, 190, 198f.; modern, compared with modern political science, 255, 267f.
Asia, 104f., 155ff., 339, 353f., 377, 380ff., 399, 403f., 408, 410

Atlantic alliance, 129, 135ff., 374ff., 386ff., 399
Atlantic community. *See* Atlantic alliance
Atlantic union, 366
Atomic power. *See* Nuclear power; Nuclear war; Nuclear weapons
Atomic war. *See* Nuclear power; Nuclear war
Augustine, 269
Autocracy, 318; political philosophy of, 94
Ayub Khan, Mohammed, 356

Baghdad Pact, 163, 165, 382
Balance of power, 22, 96ff., 108ff., 134f., 140, 142, 146, 151, 174, 206ff., 213f., 360, 368f., 376, 398
Baldwin, Stanley, 227
Barker, Sir Ernest, 256
Barnard, Frederick August, on political science, 199
Beard, Charles A., on national interest, 219f.
Benson, Ezra Taft, 334
Bentham, Jeremy, 30
Berlin issue, 101, 126ff., 202, 291, 343ff., 347, 354f., 357
Bill of Rights, 322
Bipartisanship in foreign policy, 50f., 219
Bipolarity of world politics, 99, 361, 364, 397
Bismarck, Otto von, 14, 28, 77, 277, 282, 357
Blackett, P.M.S., 285n.
Blake, William, 95
Bluntschli, J. K., 252
Bodin, Jean, 267

Radford, Admiral Arthur W., 158, 181, 185
Ranke, Leopold von, 277, 285
Realism, political, 13, 204ff., 217, 225ff., 336, 390
Reason, 198
Reason of state, 14, 205
Relativism in political science, 266f., 319, 321
Religion, 190, 196, 198
Religious Wars, 100
Resources: balance among, 111f.; balance of, with objectives, 110, 115
Reston, James, 119
Revolution: moral, 100f.; political, 97ff.; technological, 112. *See also* individual continents and nations
Revolutions: colonial, 362, 377, 409; popular, 197; of twentieth century, 338f., 341
Rhetoric, political, 344f.
Richard III, 192
Richelieu, Cardinal, 14, 134, 357
Ridgeway, General Matthew B., 181
Robson, W. A., 269
Rockefeller, Nelson, 349
Roe, Thomas, 94
Roman Empire, 361
Roosevelt, Franklin D., 31, 288, 344, 350, 351, 412f.
Roosevelt, Theodore, 317
Rousseau, Jean-Jacques, 3, 252f., 282
Rusk, Dean, 407f.

St. Pierre, Abbé de, 277, 282
Salisbury, Lord, on national interest, 217, 236
Satellites, Soviet, 384ff., 415f. *See also* individual nations
Saudi Arabia, 386
Science, psychological origin of, 190
Scientism, 3ff., 286
SEATO, 163, 165f., 382, 388
Seeley, Sir John Robert, 284
Semantics, general, 260
Shakespeare, William, 192

Singapore, 155, 177
Social philosophy, 352
Social sciences, 4f., 240, 246, 248, 304
Social world, created by man, 352
"Socialism in one country," 122
Sociology, development of, 246f., 250
Socrates, 46f., 191
Soral, Georges, 255
Soviet Union, 96f., 100f., 123ff., 353, 362, 384ff., 395, 401ff., 409; erroneous evaluation of power of, 27f.; foreign policy of, 7, 14, 232ff.; and after World War II, 122; and China, 385, 416; and Europe, 374ff., 386; and France, 142; and Germany, 135f., 142f., 149ff.; and imperialism, 32, 119, 124, 155; and the Middle East, 165, 385f.; pacifism in, 125ff.; policy of prestige, 124, 126; technological achievements of, 117ff., 123f.; traditional foreign policy of, 122; and uncommitted nations, 117f., 124, 156ff., 174; underestimation of, 339; and world revolution, 121f., 124. *See also* Communism
Spain, 149
Spheres of influence, in Europe, 146
Stalin, Joseph, 24, 31, 94f., 121ff., 141f., 146ff., 277, 375, 381, 408
State, Department of, 413
Statesmanship, 30f., 55, 116, 179, 277f., 335, 343ff., 357f.
State system, destruction of, 97f.
Status quo, defense of, 168; policy of, 337, 339, 355, 411, 419
Stebbing, L. Susan, 236n.
Stein, Gertrude, 251
Stettinius, Edward R., 412
Stevenson, Adlai, 407
Stimson doctrine, 173, 286
Strategy, as distinct from tactics, 103
Suez Canal crisis, 53f., 56, 377, 379ff.
Suicide, 197
Sukarno, President, 129
Sully, Duc de, 282
Summit meeting, 128f.
Switzerland, federalism in, 210
Syria, 384